SCOTLAND, EUROPE
and the
AMERICAN REVOLUTION

'Scottish Universities'...

edited by

Owen Dudley Edwards
&
George Shepperson

St. Martin's

New York

Scotland, Europe and The American Revolution originally
appeared as a series of essays forming Nos. 35 and 36 of the
magazine **New Edinburgh Review**, published by Edinburgh
University Student Publications. Gratitude is due to the
Scottish Arts Council, the Court of the University of
Edinburgh, and the Scottish Universities American
Bicentennial Consultative Committee for financial assistance
in the production of this publication.

Printed in Great Britain
Library of Congress Catalog Card Number: 74-48756
ISBN: 0-312-70402-x
First published in the United States of America in 1977

contents

Editors   Owen Dudley Edwards
                     George Shepperson

Design/Production   John Forsyth
                               Andrew Brown
                               Susanna Goodden
                               William Turnbull

Cover design   James Hutchinson

Typesetting   Bill Spence

Administration   Bill Campbell
                            Margaret Roxton
                            Moira Smith

EDITORIAL

"Scotland, Europe and the American Revolution" is the product of the Scottish Universities' American Bicentennial Conference which took place at the Pollock Halls of Residence, Edinburgh University, 25-28 June 1976. It embraces the major papers read at that conference, and also includes expansions of the arguments of several participants in the six-panel sessions. Some exceptions to this general principle may be noted. The initial meeting at which Scottish academic recognition of the bicentennial was raised took place on 25 March 1975 at the University of Dundee, and that occasion was inaugurated with a paper on "American Studies in Scotland: Past, Present and Future", by Professor Shepperson. It seemed appropriate to include the text of this, with minor revisions, in the present volume.

Among the constructive results of the conference was the activity and effects of the panel on archives. In the case of this panel, because of the implications of its work for the future, it seemed desirable to have a document prepared summarising its proceedings, and this Mr Michael Smethurst, the chairman, has nobly done. The achievement of Mr Smethurst and his associates, Mr Richard Dell, Dr John Imrie, Dr Edward Papenfuse and Mr Michael Moss, must be recognised in its full co-operative form, and to their work at the conference must be added the assistance given the organisers by Dr Imrie and his staff in the Scottish Record Office, specifically with reference to their Bicentennial exhibition, as well as by the Director and staff of the National Library of Scotland, especially Dr T. I. Rae.

Of the major papers delivered at the conference, that by Dr Andrew Hook received publication elsewhere and he has therefore most generously given us another contribution whose re-examination of the themes at the vortex of the Scottish-American connection in the Revolutionary era will be warmly welcomed. Each of the major papers was followed by a formal comment prior to floor discussion, but in the case of one of these, that on Professor Robin Winks's paper by Professor Peter Marshall, its originality of content necessitated the exceptional step of our seeking its publication. The editors are conscious of the unusual nature of this step, and in saluting Professor Marshall's achievement wish in no way to detract from the outstanding work done by the other seven formal discussants at the conference.

In like manner, our invitation .to the first session's chairman, Lord Cameron, to introduce the present volume, recalls the splendid inauguration which he gave to our proceedings, and symbolises a Scottish identity, given his place as one of the foremost jurists in Scotland's unique legal system, but it does not detract from the accomplishments of the chairmen who presided over subsequent sessions. And,' while many panellists chose not to submit texts for publication — an option at all times open to them — it must be understood that, while not represented here, they were fully taxed at the time and paid in generous measure. But two texts which we had hoped to include are unhappily not here. The conference deeply valued the panel contributions from Dr Jeffrey Nelson of Harvard, on the Loyalists, and from Ms Maire Cruise O'Brien, poet and linguistician, on the Gaelic world during the Revolution. Illness in Dr Nelson's case, and family bereavement in Ms Cruise O'Brien's, have robbed us of essays we would have been deeply honoured to present.

The Scottish Universities' American Bicentennial Conference was, as its name implies, funded by generous grants from the eight universities of Scotland: Aberdeen, Dundee, Edinburgh, Glasgow, Heriot-Watt, St Andrews, Stirling and Strathclyde, just as all eight made major contributions in terms of academic talent on the programme. Our thanks is extended to each of these institutions, but must also go to our other kind sponsors, of whose generosity we are likewise most appreciative: the United States-United Kingdom Educational Commission, the United States Information Service, the Government of Canada, the Committee for the Celebration of the American Bicentennial in Scotland, Cameron Iron Works Ltd., and the Cummins Engine Co. Ltd.

The conference was enabled to take shape as a result of the operations of the Scottish Universities American Bicentennial Consultative Committee, which met under the chairmanship of Professor W. R. Brock, of Glasgow: its other members were Dr Hook and Dr William Forsyth, of Aberdeen; Dr David Swinfen, of Dundee; Professor Shepperson, of Edinburgh; Mr W. R. Angell, of Heriot-Watt; Professor Bruce Proudfoot, of St Andrews; Professor David Waddell, of Stirling; and Professor John Butt, of Strathclyde. In recording their thanks to them, the editors, who were local chairman and secretary of the conference, wish also to express their gratitude to the local committee at Edinburgh, notably to Dr Rhodri Jeffreys-Jones, convener of the North American Studies Programme at Edinburgh, and to Mr Glyn Harrison, graduate student in that Programme.

Finally, the editors wish to record their sense of privilege and pleasure that these proceedings are appearing as a double issue of the **New Edinburgh Review** and to indicate their very great gratitude to the Edinburgh University Student Publications Board, its chairman, publications manager, staff and volunteers, as well as to its former publications manager, Mr John Forsyth. We also thank the Board's **New Edinburgh Review** subcommittee and on behalf of the journal we express our gratitude to the Scottish Arts Council and the Court of the University of Edinburgh for grants in aid of the publication of this and other issues.

INTRODUCTION

LORD CAMERON

It was singularly appropriate that the Scottish Universities should organise and conduct a conference at the time and on the topic of the American Bicentennial and to put in the forefront of discussion the relationship of the American Revolution and the British Empire. To many minds the most notable constitutional aspect of the "American Revolution" lay in the fact that it was so lacking in revolutionary constitutional elements. The constitutional structure adopted bore, and bears, many signs that the "revolutionaries" took the crown from the head of King George III and placed it, symbolically, on the brow of George Washington. The Congress reproduced in considerable measure the structure and powers of the late 18th century English Parliament. Indeed, the spark that triggered off the political explosion conveniently named the "Revolution" was no more than a re-assertion of the century-old cry of the English Commons - "no taxation without representation" - with its silent corollary that at the end of the day this meant no taxation without the consent of those who are represented.

The phrase "American Revolution" when analysed in the context of reality concealed rather than proclaimed its truth, or did it? That it was not regarded as a cataclysmic shaking of the foundations of society was demonstrated by the attitude of King George himself once the war had been determined and diplomatic relations initiated between Britain and the new Republic. That the Revolution and the constitutional settlement provided the impulse and the means

for the preservation and development of "parliamentary-democratic" institutions within a growing and increasingly powerful society cannot admit of doubt and therefore its influence world-wide and not least upon the constitutional developments within the British Empire. It may well be that the geographical accident of the insular position of England on the other hand helped to generate a xenophobic attitude of mind towards people who were separated by oceanic distances and whose development of independent attitudes began to qualify them as potential "foreigners" - comparable be it said to Scots, Irish and Welsh - "lesser breeds without the law".

One inevitable consequence of the Revolution was to change radically the direction of development of the British Maritime Empire, and not in a manner immediately obvious to politicians or economists with their eyes still turned towards the Caribbean and the wealth to be drawn from or created in the much contested West Indies. The centre of gravity, if the phrase will serve, by the logic of events shifted to the East. India, and not America, became "the brightest jewel in the British Crown". The safeguarding of the sea routes to the East and the maintenance of communication became of prime strategic, therefore political importance, and maritime strategy dictated the need, and frequently the siting, of those "staging points" essential to the support and protection of the naval forces necessary to secure these vital strategic objectives. With the loss of India, and the growth of the independent Commonwealth of Australia, the raison d'etre of much of the structure of this strategic maritime chain (with the other expansions and developments logically consequent thereon) disappeared. That this would have occurred irrespective of the American Revolution in the light of the decline of Britain's economic strength may well be so, but equally the secession of the former American colonies made such a dismantling of an essentially maritime empire almost inevitable in the light of historical developments of the 19th and 20th centuries. Without the Revolution the course of British imperial history would almost of necessity take a radically different turn. What would have been the consequences of the industrial development and expansion of those colonies given self-government? Would the centre of gravity of the empire have moved West to a continental base? Would expansion to the East and the Pacific have proceeded at all? Or would an inevitable and final break between the ''Britain-in-America'' and ''Britain-in-Europe'' have occurred at some point in the 19th or almost certainly the 20th century?

Such speculations may be regarded as fanciful, but in considering the actual impact and influence of the American Revolution upon the British Empire, it may be relevant to consider the issue upon which the War of Independence was fought. From whatever angle, or by whatever name, the American Revolution is viewed or described, its influence on the fortune and future of the British Empire was critical and conclusive, constitutionally, strategically and politically, far greater than that of the Empire upon the growth and direction of the Great Republic.

In this celebration and consideration of the American Bicentenary it was both just and courteous to pay tribute to the constitutional heads and representatives of both the United States and Britain. The presidency of the United States was carved in the image of the English monarchy as viewed in the eyes of 18th century Englishmen looking at St James's across the distance of the dividing Atlantic. But the monarchy was to be elective and its powers set down and confined within the limits of a written constitution. But in so doing the founding fathers ensured that these great powers should remain and that the Chief Executive of the Republic should not be transformed into the living symbol of the sovereignty of the State. With the growth of the power and of the influence and responsibility of the Republic demands on capacity and character of the President in office have expanded in like degree. In the inscribed roll elected Presidents has it not been matter for remark and for gratitude that there have been so many who have shown themselves in times of tension, trial and crisis equal to the demands on their courage, wisdom and foresight? Few in the Western World can or should forget how within the span of one man's active life, on two memorable occasions when the fate of Western Europe and of its civilisation was in the balance, the genorisity and wisdom of the democracy of the West led by men of outstanding character preserved it for future generations. These men, great in that they rose to meet and fulfil the demands of history, were the elected chosen of a democracy founded and nurtured on the parliamentary traditions of this United Kingdom. Such an office of awful responsibility and of power can only be filled by men who in the last resort have the instictive respect for the principles and foundations of democratic government as they were devised and developed here and transplanted and enshrined in the Constitution of the United States. It was the first and one of the greatest of all the Presidents who in his farewell message to his fellow Americans wrote this: ''The unity of Government which constitutes you one people is also now dear to you. . . . This Government the offspring of your own choice, uninfluenced and unawed, adopted upon full investigation and mature deliberation, completely free in its principles in the distribution of its powers, uniting security with energy and containing within itself a provision for its own amendment, has a just claim to your confidence and your support. Respect for its authority, compliance with its laws, acquiescence in its measures, are duties enjoined by the fundamental maxims of true liberty . . . the constitution which at any time exists till changed by an explicit act of the whole people is sacredly obligatory upon all. The very idea of the power and right of the people to establish government presupposes the duty of every individual to obey the established government''. In these words are set out the vital principle of ordered government in a free society and Washington's phrases still, fortunately, find an answering echo in the democracy of the United States today, the heirs and benefeciaries of this most unrevolutionary of Revolutions.

This conference, well organised and comprehensive in scope as it was, can fairly be said to have been worthy of the occasion which caused it to be.

THE AMERICAN REVOLUTION AND THE BRITISH EMPIRE
An American Reflection

ROBIN W WINKS

To write on the theme of "The American Revolution and the British Empire", is to set out to boil the curate's egg of the cliché. For there are many scholars, and two especially who know far more than I about the subject, two scholars who have written the best we have on the tangled question of the "effect of the loss of the American colonies upon British Policy" - this precisely the title of William R. Brock's superb essay, in The Historical Association's "Aids for Teachers Series" as but a modest summary. The other scholar, Charles Ritcheson, has given us a major book, **Aftermath of Revolution**, the subtitle of which (**British Policy toward the United States, 1783-1795**) reveals that he has taken up one of the strands of British reassessment after the Revolution and followed it to Jay's Treaty. Professor Brock's essay has more recently been reprinted, the patina acquired since 1957 glowing nicely in Esmond Wright's collection of readings on the **Causes and Consequences of the American Revolution** (New York, 1976), while Professor Ritcheson twice wrote more briefly on the theme, once in the **South Atlantic Quarterly**, and a quarter century ago in **Parliamentary Affairs**. To retred this ground makes little sense.

But wait. Buried within this brief bibliographical recitation is a thought: Is it not interesting that, in the two hundred years since the Revolution began, in the one hundred years since the Johns Hopkins honoured the first heavily-footnoted doctoral dissertation history, in the twenty to twenty-five years since Messrs. Brock and Ritcheson first published their work no

scholar has written a full length study of the influence of the Revolution on British policy, imperial, foreign, and domestic? Given the piling of dissertation upon dissertation, in Britain, Canada, and the United States, why (one wonders) have there not been dozens of monographs on a subject so obviously ready-made for the historian's mode of questioning, of pursuing priorities in cause and effect relationships? When Charles Ritcheson chose, also in 1969, to edit a book of readings on **The American Revolution: The Anglo-American Relation, 1763-1794**, the only interpretive essays he could incorporate which seemed relevant to the post-war changes in British policy were a selection from Vincent Harlow's **Founding of the Second British Empire**, and his own essay from the **South Atlantic Quarterly.**

And now we celebrate the two hundredth anniversary of the moment when Americans have, by their Scripture, decided when they began. Surely this moment should have led to that outpouring of new books on the meaning of the Revolution. After all, the Centennial of the American Civil War produced a new journal, three Pulitzer Prizes, and over a thousand new books, some of them good. Yet an examination of the American, Canadian, and English historical associations' current lists of doctoral dissertations in progress and completed history, from 1972 to the present, shows studies on John Adams and the American press, biographies of Isaac Bronson, William Paterson, Robert Troup, Jedidiah Morse, Samuel Chase, William Rotch,

William S. Johnson, and David Jones, but no study of the effects of the American Revolution on the British Empire.

These people must know what they are at. Clearly the subject is either too complex, too boring, or too insignificant to warrant further effort. The field should be left to Messrs. Harlow, Brock and Ritcheson; to the many Canadians who pursue the Quebec Act; to those of all nationalties who write about the Durham Report; and to those who specialise in the founding of the colonies that became Australia. In short, either there was no major effect wrought by the revolution on British policy (and Harlow suggests this at times), or the effect was so fragmented as to require examination within the individual constituencies of the members of the Commonwealth.

Yet, there is objective evidence, after all, that ultimately the American Revolution meant some difference - indeed, a profound difference - for the British Empire. Drive southwest from York on the A64 to the A1, then turn briefly south to the road for Aberford. In the village turn right on a road post for Berwick, and take the first turning on the left, into the grounds on the Parlington Estate. This is private property but no one is likely to object to well-behaved visitors. Follow the lane a mile, and there you will confront the Parlington Arch, still in excellent condition, the only triumphal arch erected in Britain to celebration of the victory by the American colonies in the Revolution. Designed by John Carr at the behest of Sir Thomas Gascoigne, a Rockingham Whig who favoured making peace with the colonies, and who at Wentworth Woodhouse often said so, the arch bears the inscription, "Liberty in N. America Triumphant MDCCLXXXIII". Alternatively, strike north from York, to Pickering, in which the parish church contains brasses commemorating Walter Hines Page and the Anglo-American alliance of World War I, and thence drive along Thornton Dale through Forestry Commission land and by a narrow lane posted for Beck Hole. Here one sees, arising ahead and to the right, the moonscape globules of the Anglo-American Distant Early Warning Station. Can anyone seeing these two artifacts upon the Yorkshire landscape really doubt that the American Revolution did have effect on the British Empire?

This effect comes in at least four ways. Let us look briefly at each of the ways.

In rhetoric, as we all surely know, the American Revolution came to mean much for the world and ultimately for many parts of the new British Empire. The ideas of the revolutionaries were quoted, the slogans were shouted, the arguments were used time and again. Perhaps fewer times and agains than Americans have taken credit for throughout their history, but used nonetheless. Americans saw themselves as the precursors of freedom for the oppressed of the world. They would "extend the area of freedom", would "make the world safe for democracy", would provide minute men against communism, would force monarchy from the New World. That I recite these slogans without reference to chronology is deliberate, for Americans have little sense that their revolution was truly different from others, or that the freedoms for which they fought in the eighteenth century were eighteenth century freedoms, or that their assumption that they were a revolutionary nation was not shared by others, especially in the last quarter century. As we all know, it was to the challenge of the United States that Winston Churchill referred when he declared that he would not preside over the dissolution of the British Empire.

During this Bicentennial year of 1976, Americans have faced a flood of commentary on how their revolution established or reflected a world ideal. Yet if Americans have exaggerated the impact of their revolution, surely they are correct in thinking it no small thing. As children of the Enlightenment, certain that mankind was one, subject to the same natural laws and entitled to the same rights, the founding fathers were convinced that theirs would be a city set upon a hill. When Patrick Henry declared that America had "lighted the candle to all the world", when John Adams asserted that the Revolution was being fought "for future millions", when Tom Paine opined that "the Birthday of a new world is at hand", they were giving evidence of their persuasion that the revolution would influence not only the entirety of the Empire but the whole of mankind.

We are all familiar with this rhetoric. We all know that, as one remembers the racial compromises and the social restrictions in America as the fact that the "whole of mankind" was often interpreted to mean what today we call Western man, some of the high sounding phrases are hollow. We also know that John Adams went on to declare that the Revolution would "spread Liberty and Enlightenment everywhere in the world", and that this and many other statements like it would become the basis for American expansionism and imperialism. With a chill, we can recognise the risks as well as the honour in Thomas Jefferson's declaration of worldwide intent: "We feel", he said, "that we are acting under obligations not confined to the limits of our own society. It is impossible not to be sensible that we are acting for all mankind". Here are the kernals of Lend Lease and the Marshall Plan (which Churchill called "the most unsordid act in history"), of the Fulbright scholarships (called by Arnold Toynbee "an act of love") by which many of us first came to study each other; here too are the kernels of the need for the Spot Resolution and of the escalation of the War in Vietnam.

Since we celebrate the Bicentennial of the American Revolution this year, let us pause for a moment to state an obvious home truth or two about the problem of the world's views of that Revolution. The words I quote above echo with heroism and optimism in the history texts in which they were embedded in the 1930s and 1940s - for I draw them from David S. Muzzey's best-selling text for American high school students. When Benjamin Rush said that he was "acting for the benefit of the whole world", when Benjamin Franklin declared that "Our Cause is the Cause of all Mankind", they were rightly hailed as idealists. Yet today precisely the same words, if employed by a nation of such power, frighten the very liberals of Europe who once joined the echoes. The American who would quote the words of the Revolution, of the Declaration of Independence or the Preamble to the Constitution of the United States, is playing a no win, zero sum game: the very ambivalence of his position is too well known today. Stephen Spender finds in the Anglo-American relationship a love-hate symbiosis. Henry Fairlie tells us that European liberals hate America because it disappointed them, not becoming that which they wished it to be for them, land of the beau sauvage, a country that had avoided the Leviathan. Here is the basic American dilemma, then: by becoming what it **is**, that is, objectively, America, it failed to become that which others wanted it to be. Had it become what they wished it to be, it would not have become culturally independent, for it would have been but a projection of the desires of others, rather than a creation of its own desires. America must be what Americans wish it to be. If it belongs to the world, then it may not be criticised for thinking that it acts for "the benefit of the whole world". If it is to be of its own making, of its own design, then it is not to be criticised for isolationism, that sin with which the world charges Americans when they do not march to the tunes of another nation's historiography, a charge not made when America is told to mind its own business when the rhythm of the march changes.

If these words seem testy, let me put them two different ways. First, the Bicentennial message for the occasion, to which I will not refer again. However much some may have come in recent years to feel that they regret the rise of the United States out of the American Revolution, can they - and here I put the question counter-factually - believe that the world would be a freer place had there been no United States these two hundred years? I think not. And this is one answer to the question. What was the influence of the American Revolution? If Latin American independence movements sprang more directly from the French Revolution, it was the American Revolution with its promise of optimism, democracy, and material progress that continued to inspire Latin American revolutionaries. When Rhodesia resorted to its Unilateral Declaration of Independence, it was the rhetoric of the American declaration that was used. Just as Ceylon hurled back the rhetoric of English 19th century liberals during the days of agitation for independence, so did the North Vietnamese use the language of the American Declaration. During his recent tour through Africa, the American Secretary of State, Henry Kissinger, gave four major policy addresses, in Lusaka, Monrovia, Dakar and Nairobi. In each he asserted that the United States was a prime mover of decolonisation; in each he used the rhetoric of the American Revolution, and twice consciously quoted the language of the British Empire against itself, promising that the United States sought no paramountcy in Africa. He compared the Lusaka Manifesto directly to the American Declaration of Independence, professing to find in these words:

By this Manifesto we wish to make clear, beyond all shadow of doubt, our acceptance of the belief that all men are equal, and have equal rights to human dignity and respect, regardless of color, race, religion or sex. We believe that all men have the right and the duty to participate, as equal members of the society, in their own Government

close similarity to these words:

We hold these Truths to be self-evident, that all Men are created equal, that they are endowed by their Creator with certain unalienable Rights, that among these are Life, Liberty and the Pursuit of Happiness - That to secure these Rights, Governments are instituted among Men, deriving their just Powers from the Consent of the Governed . . .

Asserting that the United States did not and would not recognise the Rhodesian minority regime, making it clear that the use of any alleged parallels in the Rhodesian imperial situation to the American colonial-imperial situation two centuries before was unhistorical, and insisting that the United States was committed to the United Nations Security Council resolutions of 1966 and 1968, Secretary Kissinger - by specific citation, by rhetorical device, by phrase and rhythm, and by constant inference - invoked the Declaration of Independence. Where that Declaration was required by "a decent respect to the opinions of mankind", American policy now arose from "principles (that) have impelled" the playing of "a vigorous and possibly decisive role in promoting the process of decolonisation". In sum, as Kissinger walked and talked in Africa in April and May, as this man born in Europe who speaks for America in the heavy accents of the Hessians sought to rekindle the century of the American dream, he was seeking to be Tom Paine once again, the Tom Paine who saw America big with blessings: "Her cause was good. Her principles just and liberal. Her temper serene and firm. Her conduct regulated by the nicest steps, and everything about her wore the mark of honour".

Let me be clear on my point. Americans continue to use the rhetoric of their revolution. They are convinced that it was a revolution without parallel. They above all see it as truly their revolution, not one made for them elsewhere. They believe its principles even yet to be powerful. They believe that those principles inevitably will cross international boundaries. Some are prepared to be called imperialists for that. Some are prepared to see parallels with the British Empire as they come to hear the same epithets hurled at them. Most feel that their revolution has not been completed, that the national goals stated so explicitly in the Declaration have not yet been achieved. Most feel that it is still for them to achieve these goals, and not for others external to America to redefine the national goals. They are convinced that the American Revolution had a massive impact upon the world, the British Empire, and most recently Africa. It matters little whether one thinks Kissinger is posturing, that the Revolution had little influence; it is of little significance that Vincent Harlow may demonstrate that the Revolution brought few changes to British policy; for the fact remains that in understanding the past, above all we must understand what a people believe to be true. That historians might pile note upon note, dagger upon asterisk, showing that the Revolution had little influence, is not to the point. If an entire nation believes that it had massive influence, then it did have such influence - in the lives of those of the nation that believe.

The Americans, we all know, use their history to their own advantage (what people do not?). When Richard B. Morris writes **The Emerging Nations and the American Revolution,** he is asking whether the American Revolution was a model for emerging nations. He finds that it is, on several grounds. The American Revolution "determined the ritual observed by most later revolutions". In its use of sustained guerrilla operations, it bears comparison to recent wars of national liberation. The Revolution was a mass movement, to be compared with the peasant unrest on which emerging nations have capitalised. "Crises of legitimacy" confront all post-revolutionary societies similarly (here Morris is drawing on Seymour Martin Lipset). In its diplomacy, and especially in its post-independence disposition toward nonalignment, Revolutionary America was like emerging nations in Asia and Africa. The Revolution was both moral and evangelical, as were the movements of leaders like Nkrumah and Sukarno. America also fixed the character of "much of modern nationalism" so that the emerging nations must sleep in the American bed willynilly. Again it does not matter whether these sweeping, and very loose, comparisons are legitimate; what matters is that a distinguished historian thinks them so. "Success has a hundred fathers and failure is an orphan". By definition, as a mathematical given, the Revolution is seen to be a success, if one can show that the Belgian constitution of 1830, or the Dutch, the Danes and the Japanese have copied parts of the American constitution. Even by demonstrating that the British North America Act of 1867, which distributed the balance of powers almost oppositely to the manner in the American constitution, was shaped by a John A. Macdonald who had read and annotated the **Federalist Papers,** American historians have demonstrated the all permeating presence of the American Revolution. One is bound to think of that title meant for other purposes, that he we are studying "the influence of influence".

Let me circle back to my other meaning, that of Americans sensing that they must define for themselves what it is that they wish to be, even if those goals betray what foreign observers may have wished for them, and let me draw a parallel between the problems of decolonisation in the British Empire, and the European disappointment that the United States failed to develop the revolutionary tradition along lines for which they, the European observers, hoped.

To decolonise formal holdings within a modern empire, and most particularly the British, usually entailed one of three processes.* If the imperial masters believed firmly in the doctrine of preparation, with its notions of trusteeship or stewardship, then they usually assumed a series of measurable, clearly defined steps through which a colonial society would pass until it was deemed ready for independence. This readiness was to be judged in part by the coloniser and in part by the colonised, though seldom in equal measure between them. Since the doctrine of preparation implied clear stages of progress toward the stated goal of resuming those rights held only temporarily in trusteeship by an imperial power, the process itself tacitly accepted the eighteenth century assumption that rights were unalienable, even though they might for a time be placed in trust. The assumption followed that the imperial power was largely responsible for judging where in the scale of readiness the colony stood. Since the imperial power defined the stages through which a colony must pass, and in large measure was the only effective judge of where amidst those states the colony stood at any given moment, the imperial nation controlled the process to the end. After all, it and not the colony had designed the ladder to freedom, had defined each rung upon it, and could tell the colonial - by invoking emergency powers, or suspending a constitution, a charter, or a house of assembly here and there - how soon he might contemplate taking the next step. If the colonial seemed unclear as to the lesson he had learned, he might be asked to go through one or more of the steps again. As Tom Mboya was to remark, "Efficiency is the last refuge of the imperialist". To be sure, this is an idealised and simplified statement for a very complex process, but it is near enough for the parallel I wish to suggest.

This first, gradualist, form of decolonisation carried with it a strong assumption that the appropriate means by which progress toward the top rung on the ladder was best measured lay in the political sphere, ordinarily (in the British Empire) through progressive transfer to the colony of the Westminster model of Parliament. One result of this assumption is that those who held to the doctrine of preparation saw decolonisation first in political terms and only then in economic, social, or intellectual ones. That there was a catch to the process was clear enough in Africa and Asia: rioting or corruption (the latter as defined by the West) on the part of the indigenous society would be taken as evidence that the process had been carried out too quickly, justifying slowing or stopping the process entirely.

Colonial populations, or at least their élites, saw the two ironies inherent in this situation soon enough. The first was that many former colonies became independent, whether as the Old Dominions or later as the so-called "emerging nations" of Professor Morris's analysis - that is, received back their full rights after the period of trusteeship - only by accepting independence upon imperial terms. At the very moment of birth the new nation was, in the eyes of many

* This and the two following paragraphs are drawn from my article, "On Decolonisation and Informal Empire", **American Historical Review,** LXXXI (June, 1976), 540-556.

subgroups within it, fatally compromised; its form of government was not autochthonous, its independence being a gift from above rather than an assertion of a collective will (a common phrase for nationalism) from below, the new nation's very nature Europeanised. For where independence came by devolution rather than by revolution, the nation's definitions of self, its nationalism, was of a nature often quite different from other nationalisms. The second of the ironies followed from the first, from the necessity on the part of the colonial leadership to accept formal decolonisation according to a theory designed for the colony from outside. Zenobia, in Boris Vian's play **The Empire Builders,** asked the question, "if there's no staircase any longer, after we've moved up once again", where are we to go? What is one to do when the ladder of success no longer exists, having been carted away along with other now extraneous carpentry by the master craftsmen as they departed? In fine, nationalist leaders of a colony found that they had one set of goals as they worked toward independence, and that these had to be exhausted almost overnight for another set of goals as those leaders became (assuming that they succeeded in doing so) the inheritors of power. Developmental goals differed from custodial goals, and accordingly so did the tactics for economic or further political disengagement.

By saying all of this, which will readily be recognised as a pastiche from Ronald Robinson, Jack Gallagher, Eric Stokes, and D. A. Low, I have three relevant points in mind. First, while it may be true that the American Revolution had little immediate, or sweeping, effect on official thinking in Britain about the problems of empire, it is no coincidence that this would be a rare instance in British imperial history of successful decolonisation by armed revolution, and that after being burned the British clearly saw to it that they held to an evolutionary scheme for future decolonisations, even to the point of creating their own Opposition in Sierra Leone (I am here begging certain issues that arise in relation to Ireland, Kenya, Aden and Rhodesia, of course). Second, both the victor and the defeated in the American Revolution embraced all the more ardently the ideas of the eighteenth century, of unalienable rights, trusteeship, and the need to speak plainly to a candid world, for the United States became, as it still is today, essentially an eighteenth century nation, its Congressional and Presidential systems the product of the thought of that age, while ultimately the **post hoc,** vulgarised, never-quite-official but nonetheless widely believed British justification for empire in the late 19th and early 20th centuries was simply a version of the same eighteenth century thought. Third, without an act of revolution, the nationalist movement in many countries was effectively compromised - a lesson surely learned between 1776 and 1783 - for to play the game of evolutionary independence, to accept the judgment of others on the process itself, was to subtly deny independence itself. Long after political independence had been achieved, Indians, Nigerians, and Jamaicans were still looked upon

as being in some form of tutelage to Britain (or, more precisely, to England), however much one might speak of the members of the Commonwealth being equal in status.

When I spoke earlier of the disappointment many friends of America felt that the United States did not develop as they wished the States to do, I was also speaking of the continuation of this assumption of cultural tutelage in the European-American relationship. Europeans had their goals for America, defined their own rungs within a notional ladder of their own creation, and passed judgment on America's lack of readiness for full adulthood. In this sense they set themselves in judgment upon another's progress, attempting to compromise the political independence won in the Revolution by substituting economic or cultural definitions of independence. When nationalistic Americans then reacted chauvinistically to this intellectual shell game, the alleged friends of America declared that Americans would once again have to prove their worth to be a member of the world community of nations. This game has continued to the present time, and is in fact a compliment to assumptions about basic American probity, in that demands for proof of worth are made more frequently and more urgently for the United States than for half the regimes in that "world community of nations". In short, much of the mind-set (if one may use so ugly a set of stilts) that supported the ideas behind the British Empire also applied to the United States after independence. Again the game was one of no-win, for to the extent that American mores actually evolved away from English definitions of justice, from the heritage of the common law, or from the English language, and thus the more the United States began to assert independence that was cultural rather than purely political, the more the United States was seen to be abandoning the high standards for which the States presumably had fought in the first instance. In this sense, the anti-George III historiography within Britain would have its vengeance on the Bancroft historiography of the United States. And because the ties between the United States and Britain nonetheless remained close, neither party to the ties could agree upon a definition of genuine independence. It is a Mexican proverb, but no less applicable for that, which says that to divorce one's wife is simple; to divorce one's mistress impossible.

However, enough of this Bicentennial rhetoric. Some will feel I have done little more than restate the cliché about the United States fighting three times for its independence, and others will find the parallel to formal empires of the 19th and 20th centuries tenuous at best. I am less concerned here with whether these views are either fresh or correct, however, than with the principle already asserted: given that they represent a widely held American view of the relationship with Britain, they help account for much of the continued hostility found in the United States to the idea of the British Empire.

But if Americans had their "vital lies" (as Hans Kohn phrased it) by which they ordered their thoughts about their nation's relationships to the British Empire, or to the Irish Question, or to Britain's role in the New World after the Monroe Doctrine, so too did the American Revolution set in train a number of "vital lies" basic to Canadian assumptions of identity. I do not mean here the obvious subjects for inquiry, such as the role of the Loyalists, or Canadian fear for American annexation, or even John A. Macdonald's use of the American Constitution and the **Federalist Papers** as a tool for negative leadership. Rather, I mean Canada's particular view of its special position in the British Empire. Here again I am concerned with what a people believe to be true rather than with the realities of, say, the Durham Report or the functioning of the double-mandated system of representation in post-B.N.A. Quebec. Just as Wilbur Howell traced the internal logic of Jefferson's draft of the Declaration of Independence convincingly back to William Duncan, professor of natural philosophy at Marischal College in Aberdeen, and his work **Elements of Logick** so too many one trace in Canada the impress of a series of negative reactions of revolutionary thought.

As we all know, Canada saw itself as the First Dominion, as in truth it was, and Canadian leaders were responsible for the very word Dominion itself, choosing it despite preference for the word Kingdom in order not to give offense to the rambunctious republicanism of the United States. As we also know, Canadians saw themselves sold time and again "on the block of Anglo-American harmony", so that one cannot understand Anglo-American history without including Canadian history. As Canadians often assert, their was also the first Dominion in another sense,, in that by choosing the evolutionary path toward independence, and by treading that path first, Canadians set the majority of the precedents by which other dependencies of Britian climbed the ladder to nationhood. Thus one cannot understand the history of Nigeria, it is asserted, unless one understands Canadian history, for the rungs on the Nigerian ladder were defined less by British administrators than by Canadian initiatives and circumstances. And as historians in the United States sometimes assert - those few who are aware of Canada at all - one must see much of Canadian political and social, and above all economic, development as a series of reactions to impulses flowing from the United States, so that one cannot understand Canadian history without understanding American history. (The reverse case is seldom maintained). The First Dominion, as the first evolutionary state within the Empire, thereby insinuates itself into a variety of other historiographies.

If I have stated the above propositions at all negatively, or derisively, it is not my intention to do so. Rather, my negative comments are reserved solely to those who insist that history is best organised, whether in books or in university curriculae, in terms of national identities. Surely it is a triumph of Whiggish history that we should group our historical data under such headings as "The History of France", "The History of Germany", "The History of the United States", or "The History of Canada". Not only does this encourage our less alert students to assume that the rise of the nation state is what history is all about, but it leads even the professional scholar to conclude that the nation state is the best receptacle for historical facts. Yet given that nearly all of us adhere to this conventional wisdom, let me recite the received Canadian view, admitting that if one accepts the premise of national history, then the view seems essentially a correct one to me.

Britain had learned at least this lesson from the Revolution: that one may maintain power without making a show of it; that friendly partings lead to greater power than unfriendly ones; that one may maintain power without appearing to do so; that the roots of power are often in the intangibles. As Britain came to believe that colonies were a liability which were bound by the ripe fruit school of horticultural diplomacy to fall away in time, and which could not indefinitely be retained by coercion, Britain realised that the time and place of the breaking must be dictated by her policies and needs, if she were not to lose the remaining valid reasons for empire, i.e., prestige and balance of power. Thus, as Nicholas Mansergh points out, Britain readily used force (even a Whig government did so) in Canada when, in the 1830s, the conflict between Upper and Lower Canada threatened to become a struggle between two fragment societies. The result was that a struggle originally focussed on the old question of control of revenue broadened into a struggle about definitions of rungs on a not-yet-defined ladder. The notion of "responsible self-government" began to take on genuine functional meanings, and Durham's Report, however racist, short-sighted, or parochial it may in fact have been, provided a rationale after the fact for a policy that already was being put into practice. Thus was set in train an evolutionary independence that was at once a series of countervailing moves against pressures from the United States, a long-range rebuke to those who earlier had felt that revolution was essential to regain those unalienable rights, and a set of points to be set forth later, with historical hindsight, as the precedents for imperial devolution. The First Dominion achieved its identity not in a traditional nationalism but in showing that the American Revolution need not have happened.

If David Muzzey's textbook demonstrated to generations of American high school students how the American Revolution had to be fought three times, any number of Canadian textbooks demonstrated how well the evolutionary lesson had been won, thus providing yet one other source for Canadian pride in establishing a clear distinctiveness from the United States. Consider Jack T. Saywell and John C. Ricker's representative, and excellent, little high school book, **How are we Governed?** with its list of 22 precedents on the evolutionary scale which were due to Canadian initiative or which arose from Canadian circumstance. (This left only four precedents in the usual textbook list to be granted to other nations: Ireland, Burma, India and South

Africa each possessed one). Everyone knows well the litany: in 1846, the Governor in Canada was instructed to introduce responsible government. In 1849 Lord Elgin's signing of the Rebellion Losses Bill confirmed such government. In 1858 Alexander Galt's tariff established "Canada's independence in economic affairs" - from Britain, one takes this to mean, since Canada appears united today in the conviction that such independence is yet to be established from another imperial power. In 1867, with Confederation, came "the beginning of a nation". In 1871, imperial troops were withdrawn so that the Canadian militia had to go it alone (this begs some questions about when a precedent is a precedent, and the withdrawal of the legions from New Zealand). In 1880, Canada took the lead in appointing their own diplomatic representation to Britain, to be sure a High Commissioner and not an Ambassador. Between 1887 and 1911 Canada led in asking for and mounting the mounting the imperial and colonial conferences. In 1904 a Canadian commander was appointed for the Canadian militia, and in 1909 the Dominion created its own Department of External Affairs.

I do not continue, for others cast the worry beads as well as I. There is the bead for the Imperial War Cabinet, and the bead for the Chanak crisis, and the bead for the Halibut Treaty, and the bead for Canada's independent declaration of war in 1939 against Germany. Each was used in past to demonstrate to a crouching United States that Canadians were an independent people, in part to move forward with the resumption of unalienable rights, in part because the countervailing scenario of the British Empire required such steps. I do not mean to suggest anything so grotesque as that the decolonisation of Canada was one grand exercise to spite the American colonies over their successful revolution - after all, Nova Scotia had been part of the original fourteen - but I do mean to suggest that if one again puts a question counterfactually: could one contemplate this scenario had there been no American Revolution? The answer must be in the negative.

Before leaving the Canadians, let me return to one of the less well polished of the beads. Not enough, surely, has been made of Alexander Galt's tariff of 1858. Perhaps Galt disappears into the more generalised Canadian historiography, for on the whole Canada appears to have been the product of organisation men - of those who worked for the Hudson's Bay Company, and the fisheries, and the railway companies, and in the Wheat Pool - and has lacked for the individualised shootouts at the OK corral. But Galt engaged in such a shootout, and it is worth reminding ourselves that there is more than one way to frame a declaration of independence. Galt's tariff of 1859 was the first framed in Canada with the express purpose of developing home industry. It nerved New Brunswick and New South Wales, which soon after raised their own tariffs. It produced an outcry from the Sheffield cutlery interests, and it produced a reprimand from the Colonial Secretary, the Duke of Newcastle. Galt's reply to Newcastle is a brilliant play upon all the unresolved fears and issues of the years since 1783, issues which (as Harlow pointed out) the British never really confronted directly. Consider the crescendo within Galt's warning: "The Government of Canada cannot in any manner waive or diminish the right of the people of Canada to decide for themselves both as to the mode and the extent to which taxation shall be imposed. ... even if it should unfortunately happen to meet the disapproval of the Imperial Ministry. Her Majesty cannot be advised to disallow such acts, unless her advisers are prepared to assume the administration of the affairs of the Colony irrespective of the views of its inhabitants". Thereupon American history impinged again, the Civil War broke out, and neither Whitehall nor Downing Street replied to Galt's declaration. From Galt to John A. Macdonald's National Policy of 1878 was but another evolutionary step.

Of course, this is but a fragment of Canadian history, and many other forces were at work than a memory of the American Revolution. Canada is entitled to the autonomy of its own historiography. Yet to call this summary of Canadian history merely a fragment is rather like Freud's reference to his study as "a fragment of a fragment", or Melville's statement that **Moby Dick** was "but a draft of a draft". For the Canadian sense of self surely is expressed in that set of precedents summarised so well by Saywell and Ricker. In any event, as Daniel Yankelovich and Ruth Clark demonstrate in **The New Morality,** a significant shift in behaviour need not be the product of a parallel shift in attitudes.

What, then, were the attitudes as revealed by British policy makers in the years immediately following the revolution? So far we have dealt upon the periphery, upon the impact of the Revolution upon post-independence American attitudes, and upon the Canadians. Let us return briefly to the centre, to look again at the consequences of the Revolution for British imperial thought in the years immediately following the Revolution. And let us now bring the Prince of Denmark onto the stage, for how can any one have ignored Ireland for so long?

The American Revolution was crucial to Ireland. One need not go so far as Shane Leslie, who in 1917 wrote that "American independence had as great an effect on Ireland as the Russian revolution has had on the modern world at large", to show how significant the Revolution was to this part of the British Empire. L. Perry Curtis, Jr., has credited the Revolution with beginning "the slow, often painful process, accelerated by the French Revolution, of educating Irishmen about their right as well as obligation to seek redress for the social, economic, and political injustices in their midst". In this he is echoing several historians of Ireland, Maurice O'Connell and R. B. McDowell in particular. The Revolution gave Irishmen an example of the success of violence, provided a set of well-stated ideals, and forced upon the British government a willingness to make concessions. Further, the United States thereafter became a refuge for the Irish, a centre of agitation for continued resistance to Britain, and (unhappily so) even today a source of revenue for the extremists of guerrilla warfare. Just as the majority of school teachers in Massachusetts prior to the Revolution were Irish, so were the majority of police in cities like Boston in the following century. Between 1831 and 1870, nearly two and a half million Irish came to the United States, or put differently, during this time America received 85 per cent of all Irish who left their island.

Where one remarked earlier upon the paucity of studies of the effect of the American Revolution on British imperial policy, one must remark here upon the richness of the materials when one turns to Ireland. Although the proportions given to Eighteenth Century Irish history by W. E. H. Lecky - one volume to the years before 1760, three to the years after - have been condemned, and attributed to his political prejudices, an imperial historian is still inclined to find these the right proportions, for however imbalanced this may have made the smooth chronology of Irish historiography, it correctly reflects the preoccupations of those who deal with Ireland as one of the two major stories (sometimes called "exceptions" by those who would wish to avoid them, the other being India) in British imperial history. A glance at Herbert Butterfield's recent essay on the eighteenth century in T. W. Moody's volume on **Irish Historiography** quickly reveals the depth of involvement in the questions adjudicated by arms, within the Revolution, for the Irish people. R. R. Palmer has attested to this connection in his **Age of the Democratic Revolution,** and more fundamentally, so too has Owen Dudley Edwards in his perceptive piece on "The American Image of Ireland" in the 1970 volume of **Perspectives in American History** from the Charles Warren Centre at Harvard University.

There are other points on the globe to which I should direct attention, of course. There are also other questions which, when asked in the context of the American Revolution, might well take on different answers than those customarily given. William Brock enumerated several of these. There is the question of British naval power, viewed in the light of the loss at Yorktown, and while this has been much written of, much remains to be done. There is the question of the Loyalists, their settlement in the British North American Provinces, and the ideology that arose from amongst them, which Esmond Wright and others have well in hand. There is the rise of the so-called "Gibralter complex", or the added post-Revolutionary emphasis on strategic values in imperial planning, of which Richard Glover and others have written; and of which Bermuda became the experimental base. There is the rethinking that followed the Revolution which focussed on Britain's "splendid isolation", a theme much examined by Michael Roberts and many others, and perhaps best summed up in Henry Taylor's classic work on the art of personal advancement, **The Statesman,** written in 1836 and meant to be taken as a guide to success for states as well as for individuals, in which he advised that, "Ambition being almost the vocation of a statesman, he must be expected to marry ambitiously. One who would thrive by seeking favours from the great should never trouble them for small ones". Britain was ready to apply such advice to the world at large. Long since, Britain had come to accept a domino theory of its own; originally George III feared in 1779 that if America succeeded, the West Indies, then Canada, then Ireland would follow. Now the dominoes were either independent states or those who would expect to move toward independence.

Nor were these the most pressing questions. Far more immediate was the problem of the West Indies, the problem of Ireland, the problem of commercial policy, and the problem of how best to develop relations with the new United States. Even the last was essentially an imperial question, for many in Britain hoped to and some expected to woo the new Republic back into the Empire. For years to come, the British government would worry about the risks in "the American disease" crossing the Atlantic, that ocean not only providing the "free security" of which C. Vann Woodward would later write in American history but a cordon sanitaire against infection in the British Isles.

And here above all I scarcely need dwell upon that most obvious of coincidences that, upon examination was no coincidence at all. Adam Smith's **Wealth of Nations** also appeared in 1776, and it is well to remember his scepticism about the American colonies:

The rulers of Great Britain have, for more than a century past, amused the people with the imagination that they possessed a great empire on the west side of the Atlantic. This empire, however, has hitherto existed in imagination only. It has hitherto been, not an empire, but the project of an empire; not a gold mine, but the project of a gold mine; a project which has cost, and which continues to cost, and which, if pursued in the same ways as it has been hitherto, is likely to cost, immense expense, without likely to bring profit. . . . If the project cannot be completed, it ought to be given up.

If Britain was incapable of running an empire effectively, Smith argued, then she should "endeavour to accommodate her future views and designs to the real mediocrity of her circumstances". The Revolution made this message immediate rather than distant. What had looked like the exercise of arbitrary power to the Americans was revealed to be, in fact, a lack of power in British leadership. Vacillation on tax and on land policy was weakness but was read as arbitrariness. By the end of the Revolution, the British would be certain that thereafter these two issues must be handled more firmly, and with greater clarity, in the remaining empire, and in the new empire developing in the Pacific simultaneously with the loss of a major portion of the old. If the British felt in their hearts that they were not tyrants, or even potentially tyrants, this did not offset the simple fact that they could find no adequate way to convey their conviction to the colonists. In future, they decided, they would not waffle. In short, the American Revolution contributed importantly to changing British attitudes toward empire.

Thus we are having our cake and eating it too. Two schools of thought have begun to merge. One, best exemplified by Richard Morris, held that the Revolution had a fundamental impact on Britain and on the nature of constitution making around the world. The other, most closely associated with Vincent Harlow, suggested that the impact of the Revolution was not of fundamental significance in understanding British colonial policy. The two schools were, in fact, emphasising different things: the one attitudes, the other policy. Both were right within the narrow frameworks from which they reasoned.

Now we have a statement which brings the two strands of thought together, with a thrust toward the "little influence" school of thought. John Manning Ward, of the University of Sydney, has produced a convincing study of **Colonial Self-Government: The British Experience, 1759-1856** (Toronto, 1976). Turning away from the briefly fashionable tendency to look to Ottawa, Canberra, Accra, and New Dehli as the centres of the Empire, Ward one again focusses attention on the true centre. In doing so he reminds us that the pragmatic British almost always generated theoretical explanations for what they were doing well after they had begun to do it. Thus to see the Durham Report as a well calculated step in an orderly process toward responsible government is to ignore the reality that only later was the Report cited as a kind of decoloniser's gospel, as with Oldham, Leys, Delamere, Cameron, and others in East Africa, when the report was cited in support of white settler dominance over Indians, or of indigenous African emergence at the expense of Indian settlers. Responsible government was worked out by trial and error and thus could not be exported, since no one agreed upon what it meant. Accepting Ged Martin's conclusions, if not the manner of stating them, John Ward argues that "The eloquence of the Durham Report and the long term coincidence between its recommendations and the subsequent course of imperial history formerly persuaded historians that successive ministers had gratefully acted upon his enlightened counsel." Rather, an attenuated subordination might make true independence lose its attraction. Ward suggests that, in fact, Britain came to realise that it could exort the idea of responsible government only when such was practised at home, in the sense that British governments must command a majority in the House of Commons. (Thus, incidentally, Ward makes imperial history central to British domestic history). There must be equity among the subjects of the Queen. This at least, the British had learned as a result of the series of events that arose from the American Revolution.

I now return to the United States. As I have suggested, one effect of the American Revolution was to lead Americans to believe that they were revolutionaries. Another, corollary result, was to lead them to fight shy of the word "imperialism" or of the notion of "empire" to describe themselves. After all, they had been the victims of imperialism and could not, it followed, be imperialists themselves. Of course this is nonsense, but the conviction bit deeply into American thought, so that our textbooks and our orators invariably refer to "American expansionism" (even in the Philippines or Cuba) and never to "American imperialism". Some years ago when C. Vann Woodward edited a series of American Forum radio talks on the comparative approach to American history, talks subsequently published as a collection of essays, he asked me to speak on American imperialism. The Voice of America opposed such a talk on the ground that no such animal existed. In 1975 a colleague from Puerto Rico testified to a Congressional committee on the approaching American assumption of sovereignty in the former Japanese trust territories in the Pacific, and in the course of testimony referred to "American imperialism", to be greeted by howls of outrage from a highly liberal Congressman (and supporter of the American Civil Liberties Union) who insisted that such a word could never be applied to the American experience. This last year, when I received a Guggenheim Fellowship to devote the coming year to a study of the "the nature of American imperialism", everyone assumed that I was making a political statement in my choice of words.

I did not feel that I was doing so, and I hope the day may come when a word that ought to be used for dispassionate analytical purposes, but which **has** been totally and destructively politicised, might be returned to the general vocabulary. To me "imperialism" need not carry automatic pejorative connotations. That the word does so is, in part, a legacy of the Revolution, in part a collapse in the face of its persistent acquisition and frequent misuse by the political left. One result of an American inability to think in terms of having had an imperial experience of their own is that the scholarship on that which we have called "American expansionism", while voluminous, is surprisingly thin in comparative insights or in theoretical content.

This is not to say that there are not numerous books on the idea of an American empire, ranging from the still excellent study of **Manifest Destiny** by Albert Weinberg through the descriptive volumes of Foster Rhea Dulles, the "New Left" work of William Appleman Williams, the anti-revisionist work of several more recent scholars, the careful studies of the impact of the American business community on the shaping of foreign policy, to such fine volumes as Marilyn B. Young's **Rhetoric of Empire.** My point, rather, is that all of these works by American historians on American imperialism strike me as having been written in intellectual vacuum. They suffer from the parochialism that is so common to much American history, from the notion of American "exceptionalism". This means that virtually all of the books, however good they may be from any of a variety of other perspectives, seem to have been written without any knowledge of the formidable body of theoretical literature developed in the last twenty years by British (and German and French) scholars. Not one of these books draws upon the collaborator model used so well by John Gallagher and Ronald Robinson as long ago as 1953; not one sees that Thomas Paine was essentially the anti-collaborator in the "white settler collaborator" model developed most recently by Robinson. Not one shows any awareness of the exceptional work done by D. A. Low, especially in **Lion Rampant,** on the problems of colonial governance. Not one appears to be aware of Eric Stokes's insights into the problems of disengagement from colonies, insights that have much to tell us about Cuba, Vietnam and now Puerto Rico. No writer on the organic acts by which American territories became states has remarked on the similarity of the stages developed by the British for the devolution of power. No scholar has shown how the referendum concerning indedpendence or statehood for Puerto Rico was a direct reflection of the Newfoundland referendum after World War II by which that independent nation joined Canada. In short, writers on America seem not to have read the British literature, much less reflected on the British experience.

Here then, and at home, is one telling modern influence of the American Revolution. The post-Revolutionary development of an American sacred scripture in the Declaration of Independence and the Constitution of the United States; the conviction that the United States was unique; the aversion to the use of terminology that would diminish the assumption of uniqueness - such traits in the nation's thought have led American historiography on the subject of empire, on the very subject central to the Revolution itself, to exist in an exceptionalist vacuum. As one result of the American Revolution, the British Empire became irrelevant to the received opinions of a unique American historiography. American historiography took the road less travelled by. And that has made all the difference.

THE AMERICAN REVOLUTION AND THE BRITISH EMPIRE
An English Comment

PETER MARSHALL

Sixty years ago, with memories of a New World, soon to be dulled by concern for the structure of eighteenth century English politics, still fresh in mind, Lewis Namier observed with repugnance how "historical memories, which in their tragical greatness are a sacred inheritance of the Anglo-Saxon race" had been allowed to gain a general circulation. In consequence, any direct descendant seeking to reclaim his heritage must needs confront "the Legend of the Revolution, ossified, dried, cut up, distributed in the form of saintly relics among many shrines ..."(1) Professor Winks's paper underlines the fruitlessness of Namier's protest and indicates how much further, in the years since he made it, the reverberations of the initial Declaration have continued to be heard. This deplorable link with the wider world was nowhere more evident than in the influences exerted on the development of the late eighteenth and nineteenth century British Empire, creating a system that could claim to originate as clearly as did the United States from the events of the Revolution.

This, at least, might seem the view of John Adams. In 1775 his third Novanglus letter declared that "the term **British Empire** is not the language of the Common Law, but the language of newspapers and political pamphlets". "I say we are not a part of the British Empire; because the British government is not an empire". That term could only be understood in a wholly deleterious and hence inapplicable fashion. "An empire if a despotism, and an emperor a despot, bound by no law or limitation but his own will; it is a stretch of

tyranny beyond absolute monarchy".(2) Yet Adams, if justified by precedent, was contradicted by contemporary usage. His distrust of George III can hardly have been lessened by the language of the speech from the throne at the opening of the new 1774 Parliament: "You may depend on my firm and steadfast resolution to withstand any attempt to weaken or impair the supreme authority of this legislature over all the dominions of my crown; the maintenance of which I consider as essential to the dignity, the safety, and the welfare of the British Empire".(3)

Confusion, not clarification, would seem the natural background of revolutions: it is not unreasonable to suggest that the disruption of the First British Empire was as much a consequence of uncertainty as to its nature as of certainty as to colonial grievances.(4) Conflict in the understanding of key terms was the inevitable accompaniment of more dramatic and violent disputes. Political, military, and economic issues should not, however, be allowed to assume undue prominence over constitutional, legal, and social aspects of the Revolution, matters to which contemporaries attached great importance but which historians have, for long stretches of time, chosen to ignore. The nature of Empire, as illuminated by these facets, may be seen to have given rise, both in the short and in the long term, to problems and reactions which remain inadequately delineated or explored.

In the years prior to 1776 the imperial predicament was expressed in a variety of forms: legal and constitutional difficulties will not be adequately understood until biographies of Mansfield, Thurlow and Wedderburn interpret ministerial actions while accounts of Adair, Dunning and Glynn improve our understanding of Opposition attitudes. The course of the conflict was not solely determined by material interests; the degree to which the cumulative xenophobia of the English created a situation incompatible with harmonious relationships between different nations demands consideration. There was nothing exceptional about the English disapproval of Americans seen as children whose disobedience could only be countered by firmness and discipline. This was a relatively mild judgment when compared with views of the Irish, who were regarded, if Protestant, as dangerously Whig, and if Catholic, as potentially treasonable - those who could, like Burke, be traced to both beliefs being held to combine both failings; the Scots, thanks to their Jacobite heritage, were feared as actually treasonable, and through Bute, Mansfield, and a swarm of lesser adventurers, on the point of securing complete sway over both Crown and Ministry; East Indian Nabobs and West Indian planters occasioned violent reactions to undue displays of wealth and position; resistance to the Jew Bill of 1753 had demonstrated the ease with which popular feelings could be aroused; all European nations were, it seems hardly necessary to add, considered beneath contempt. By the outbreak of the Revolution Englishmen did not confine their resentment to rebellious Americans: they possessed a loathing for the peoples of the world, with the possible exception of Corsicans.

The American revolt might then be regarded as exceptional in its success rather than in its justifications. It might also be seen as denying to other parts of the Empire any immediate opportunity to fullow suit: separation had provoked the construction of a new imperial system designed to eliminate the conflict between local and central powers which had shaped the course of disruption. With the loss to the Empire of the most effective colonial assemblies the seat of authority shifted decisively away from local liberties towards central government, and a process was set in motion that found expression in a sequence of constitutional events - the spread of crown colony government, the steady encroachment upon the powers or the East India Company, the Canada Act of 1791, and the ending of the Irish Parliament. The freedom secured by the United States had been gained at the price of confirming the subordination of the remaining and subsequently acquired parts of the Empire.

But did this mark the end of American influence on Imperial affairs? Far from it: the Empire that emerged after 1783 was, as a unified structure, fatally flawed by the existence of the United States. No matter how impressively maps of the world became coloured red in the course of the nineteenth century, economics and emigration told another, more downright, tale. Imperial expansion proved, all too often, a second-best alternative, both for capital and labour: politically, the growth of the United States commanded a radical enthusiasm unmatched by countervailing imperial sentiments. The connections - and the contrasts - between the Old and the New Worlds were as evident in the nineteenth as they had been in the previous century, and the superiority of the appeal of the United States was sufficiently constant to ensure that the new Empire, whatever its apparent grandeur, would be steadily undermined as a political, constitutional, economic and social entity.

Professor Winks has indicated some of the ways in which this process may be glimpsed to be taking place but a full survey would represent task likely to exhaust even his energies. He has, however, made clear one vital and central feature of the relationship between the creation of the United States and the existence of the British Empire: no matter how profound the differences that distinguished the two systems, an understanding of either depends on a knowledge of both. Pleas of uniqueness are but demands for ignorance. Let us hope that, in the future, historians can turn deaf ears to such labour-saving and decitful appeals. It will not be Professor Winks's fault if their acceptance continues.

REFERENCES

1. L. B. Namier, **Skyscrapers and Other Essays** (London, 1931), p. 16.
2. Richard Koebner, **Empire** (New York, 1965), pp. 212-213.
3. **Ibid,** p. 215.
4. Peter Marshall, "The British Empire and the American Revolution", **Huntington Library Quarterly** XXVII (1964), 135-45. "The First and Second British Empires: A Question of Demarcation", **History** XLIX (1964), 13-23.

DUMAS, THE FIRST AMERICAN DIPLOMAT

J W SCHULTE NORDHOLT

Perhaps it is a fashionable thing to do to introduce the subject of this paper not as a hero but as an anti-hero. By an anti-hero I mean a man who lacks all that is characteristic for a hero — a man, who has two left hands, as the Dutch expression goes, who has always bad luck, who almost seems to attract it. The anti-hero is popular today, discovered by authors and historians; the little man, the common man. He merits our compassion.

There is much in Mr Dumas, the man I am introducing to you, to which this anti-hero hidden typology could be applied, but the paradox is that he is at the same time the protagonist of my story and not just playing a passive role. In many ways he may seem a pathetic figure, but he is also a man who is for several years in the centre of diplomatic activity in The Hague, a man whose merits, as Wharton rightly remarks, have never been fully appreciated by his employers, the Continental Congress. They used him for long years, and perhaps they never had a more faithful servant, yet they never fully acknowledged him.

He was in many respects their first representative in Europe, and that is why I have given this paper the challenging subtitle: the first American diplomat. But actually he was neither an American nor a diplomat, only, as Jefferson formulated it, "a person who is charged with American affairs".(1) He himself used the word agent, had it even written on his front door: "Agent der Verenigde Staten", and appealed to that distinction all his life: the first agent of the United States **ad omnes populos.** (2)

If he was underrated in his own time, I believe he still is and that is why I have taken this opportunity to let you make his acquaintance. As yet, not much has been written about him; there is a short survey of the data of his life, which are known (3), there is an interesting but rather outdated and not very accurate book by the French historian Francis P. Renaut, vol. 5 of a never-completed series of **Les Provinces-Unies et la Guerre d'Amérique**, called **La Propaganda Insurgente: C. W. F. Dumas** (Paris 1925), and finally there is an amiable article by Joseph C. Morice in the **Duquesne Review**, in which the sources have not been used. (4) Yet all the sources are there. Dumas kept a very extensive correspondence with many of the leaders of the American Revolution, and of all his letters he kept a draft in his Letterbook, which is in the archives in The Hague. This is a real treasure, containing e.g. 90 letters to John Adams, 98 to Thomas Jefferson, 108 to Benjamin Franklin etc., etc. Of course this wealth of information has not remained undiscovered; in the current editions of the Papers of Jefferson, Franklin and others the letters of Dumas are printed in their chronological place.

His relations are now beginning to be understood in their real value and proportions. Yet the man himself is still hideen mostly in the shadows. One has to plough through the enormous pile of papers in the Dutch archives to really get to know him and that is exactly what I have done in the last year in a seminar with a group of my students. We have bent ourselves over hundreds of letters in his handwriting and concluded that it is rather clear and legible as long as he is certain of himself, but that it becomes a chaos of scratched-out words and lines and others written in between, of blots and smudges, when he becomes nervous. The man is completely present in his writings with all his ups and downs, his aspirations and disillusions. And there is no other way to know him, opinions about him are scarce. One has to go to the sources.

To state the simple facts: Charles Wilhelm Frédéric Dumas was born on February 15, 1721, at Ansbach in Germany, from a French Huguenot family. We know nothing about his formal education, only that he became a teacher and scholar who made a living, like so many intellectuals of those days by tutoring children of rich families, and in between dedicated himself to the publication of books, mostly translations and annotated editions of such famous books as Vattel's treatise on international law. After a stay in Switzerland, Dumas came to Holland, where he settled in The Hague around 1750. It was there that he married a widow, Loder, who had two sons from a former marriage. Together they had a daughter called Anna Jacoba, born in 1766.

His first contact with America was probably his acquaintance with Benjamin Franklin, whom he must have met when Franklin visited Holland in 1766. This at least may be deduced from a letter which Franklin wrote to him in 1768 advising him not to execute the plan which he evidently had conceived of migrating to Florida. "If you cannot remain contented with your situation in Holland", Franklin wrote, "my advice to you would be to purchase a plantation ready formed in one of the old settled provinces, New York, New Jersey or Pennsylvania". (5) Nothing came of it but the Pennsylvania Sage did not forget his friend. They exchanged some more letters and when in 1775 the Revolution began and the Americans were looking for reliable contacts in the old world, Franklin, then a member of the Committee of Secret Correspondence, wrote to Dumas to ask him whether he would be willing to become a correspondent of the committee. (6)

Dumas replied with great enthusiasm: "I am deeply penetrated by the honour done me, and the confidence reposed in me by the committee. . . . I shall die content if the remainder of my life can be devoted to the service of so glorious and just a cause". (7) So it happened, Dumas dedicated himself to his new task with an unequalled fervour, 20 long years, till his death in 1796. This, he felt, was the fulfilment of everything he had ever hoped, yet it would be an exaggeration to say that from now on he lived content. On the contrary, there were, to use a metaphor that he liked to use himself, many thorns on the roses, and when he died in 1796, he was completely exhausted.

Perhaps he had always had a weak constitution, or perhaps his was an interesting case for a psychologist. In his letters to his doctor, James Jay, and others, we read about his many ailments, his illness of the veins — Benjamin Franklin comforts him: "Honey is a good thing for obstruction in the veins" (8) — his nervous breakdowns —

again Franklin gives a paternal stroke: "Your last letter had a melancholy turn. Do you take sufficient bodily exercise? Walking is an excellent thing for those whose employment is chiefly sedentary". (9) Dumas is the type of an active man who is at the same time too sensitive for the hard world in which he moves, and hence easily hiding himself and preferring to act in secret. He is the little man who loves to make friends among the great but trembles when he encounters them and winces at their slightest frown. The man who braces himself at the wrong moments and ends by expressing excessive regrets. Indeed the anti-hero at one moment finding a marvellous metaphor for his whole situation: "I am like an owl in the daylight". (10) A hard-boiled and unpleasant man like Arthur Lee gives a severer judgment: Dumas is "entirely his (Bej. Franklin's) creature and an old woman". (11)

Benjamin Franklin is indeed for Dumas the embodiment of everything exalted and great. Already in 1774 he sends him Latin verses and when, in 1776, Franklin comes to Europe he incorporates his adored friend in an ode of Horace. (12)

Navisque tibi creditum debes Franklinum
finibus Gallicis reddas incolumem
praecor, et serves animae dimidium meae.

Ship that hold our Franklin in trust
may you deposit him safely on the shores of France,
as I pray, and preserve the man who is half my very soul.

Send Franklin to Holland, he begs his friend Carmichael, he will be received like a god: "Here is a Baucis to cocker him up, a Philemon to follow him like a shadow". (13) And to the doctor himself again: "Come and you will be moved to tears by a Republican people ready to welcome you. My tears flow already while I am writing this". (14) And "I am dying to see you, like the Jews the Messiah". (15)

Should we say that the nervous sensitivity of Dumas is typical for the late 18th century sentimental romanticism, not yet developed into the full flower of romantic feeling, still bourgeois-orientated, still optimistic, but already unnerved by vague aspirations and easily moved to tears? There is — and that again might be called a typical romantic aspect — much in Dumas of the child who loves the adventure, who with boyish eagerness develops his own cypher-code and who adopts significant pseudonyms to play his deeply mysterious role as secret agent. In reality there is not much secrecy kept. All too soon his enemies - as he loves to call them — know his whereabouts and actions, but the role to be played is, at least in the beginning, very exciting. So he uses the name St John, precursor of the Messiah, or the name **Concordia**, from the motto of the coat of arms of the Dutch Republic: **Concordia res parvae crescunt.** (16)

But Dumas is a romantic who is true to his dreams. He is indeed willing to give everything up. "I have no higher reward than to serve you, it makes me happier than to serve a King". (17) The pity is that he actually does not receive a much higher reward. It is only too true what Bemis remarks: that Dumas was a friend "to whom the United States owe a debt of gratitude never adequately recognised". (18) Congress was willing to pay him a small salary, more a kind of reimbursement for his expenses, and his letters are full of complaints about his financial situation and appeals for help. His enemies are indeed active. Probably through the pressure of Sir Joseph Yorke, the English Ambassador — "who wants to destroy me" (19) — he loses his job as tutor after a long period of unbearable banterings. "I live in a hell governed by a fury, but the **vultus inpotentis tyranni** can never shake my fixed mind". (20)

He may truly say: I have no ambition, no greed. (21) But he has to live, to care for his wife and daughter, as he argues again and again. Yet he never hesitates to give himself completely to his great task. All kinds of plans he sets up, he proposes to start a factory for the trade of American tobacco and rice, he gives information to the American agents at Paris about English ships which leave the Dutch ports, he reports to Congress on the passage of the Hessian troops through Holland, he keeps a close contact with the Dutch press, especially with Jean Luzac, the editor of the **Gazette de Leide**, one of the most important newspapers of the time. He is always busy.

But of course he cannot do everything by himself alone. From the beginning Dumas seeks the co-operation of the French Embassy at The Hague. He understands that the American cause in Europe can only be promoted with French support and that any attack on the traditional Dutch-English politics of alliance has to have the assistance of France. Only gradually he begins to discover that French and American interests are not running parallel and that discovery will bring him into the greatest difficulties.

As soon as he has received his commission as American agent he seeks contact with the French charge d'affairs, the Abbé Desnoyers, and in January 1777 he warmly welcomes the new French Ambassador, the Duc de Vauguyon. With his customary confidence he emphasises the great possibilities for the future, if the young King of France and the young nation of the West will work together. He defends the French position of neutrality in the conflict. France can, to use a modern term, become the arsenal of democracy. But already in 1777 he confides in secret to a good friend like William Carmichael that France would be wise if it sided openly with the American rebels. All Europe would follow. (22)

The French from their side are only too willing to respond to Dumas' overtures. Vauguyon himself is impressed by the talents and zeal of the agent and decides to use him as a source of information. Dumas' correspondence with the American plenipotentiaries at Paris is sent through the French diplomatic channels. So they help and control him at the same time, stimulate him to make all possible contact, yet check him when he does not follow their directions. In the first years Dumas is their faithful follower, he is overcome with joy when in the spring of 1778 the French American treaty is concluded, and with deep gratitude he reports how the French substitute De Bérenger (Vauguyon is in Paris at the moment) presses his hands and exclaims: "Nous sommes frères". With much glee he records an anecdote about a reception at the British Embassy just after the conclusion of the treaty. Yorke is enraged. "You violate my daughter", he snaps at De Bérenger. But the Frenchman responds: "She is emancipated, to give her what she asks for is not to violate her". The young girl who tells Dumas the story asks him what he would have answered. With French "esprit" he replies: "Les Français font volontiers ce qui plaît aux dames". (23)

What Dumas sees as his first and most important task is to influence and possibly change the public opinion in Holland. The country is, as we have already remarked, traditionally allied with England, but there is, since the 17th century, a popular mood of anti-English feeling. If we may believe the rather credulous Dumas, the great majority of the Dutch people, especially the young, sympathise with America, and good news from the revolutionary war is discussed with joy in all the coffee houses. All the papers rejoice in the capitulation of Saratoga and one of them, the **Oprechte Haarlemmer Courant**, even brings out a special edition. (24) But in general, as Dumas begins to understand, the Dutch are not so easily moved to enthusiasm, they are, as he writes, like their peat, not lightly enflamed. But when they burn, they burn for a long time. (25)

But the deeper problem in Holland is that the nation has lost most of its vigour, that it is no longer the energetic power of the 17th century, but a country in decline. There has lately been much discussion about the economic and other aspects of this deterioration of the Dutch Republic, whether it really was as serious as common opinion wants to have it. Be that as it may, there is in any case in the time itself, a cloud of witnesses for the case. John Adams is one of them, Dumas another. Time and again he describes the Dutch malady: Holland is too rich (26), it is weak and without real power, its fleet is dilapidated (27), it is a sick state (28). Yet its wealth is still enormous and should be tapped. "Faisons le dégorger en Amérique". (29) It is my task to resist the English party in Holland, "to hinder the English to draw this republic into their quarrel, which by her immense wealth and public credit would have had very bad consequences". (30)

Dumas flatters himself that at least in this negative way he performs a great joy by preventing the Dutch Republic from siding with England. He is, to say the least, exaggerating his own role in the game. There may be in Holland some enthusiasts who out of genuine sympathy support the American cause, there is a great majority who are hardly interested at all, and those who are the policy-makers of the country, especially the great bankers and merchants of Amsterdam, are not guided by ideals or principles but by commercial interests alone. Their one great fear is that they will miss the opportunity to open a supposedly enormous profitable trade with America once the shackles of English mercantilism have been broken. The French-American treaty of February 1778 is an alluring example of what may be possible, but what if the English and their American colonies decide to make peace? The Amsterdam merchants react nervously to every rumour of reconciliation between the British Government and the rebels, and when in 1778 there is actually sent an English delegation to America they proceed to action.

What would be more reasonable than that Dumas played a chief role in that action? Since the summer of 1777 he has become acquainted with the most powerful man in the Amsterdam Government, the Pensionary Eugène François van Berckel, and together they devise plans to make a good deal with America. They have to be careful, since the government in The Hague, strongly influenced by the pro-British Stadholder and his clique is still adamantly opposed to any rapprochement with the Americans. In the spring of 1778 Dumas still believes that the Dutch will not hesitate to follow the French example, but he soon finds that the resistance to a French-orientated policy is too strong and that moreover the French themselves are not too eager to draw the Dutch in their alliance. A neutral Holland is in the conception of Vergennes of more use to France than an ally. It must have been a great disillusion to Dumas who in his credulous imagination had already seen himself as the central figure in a new breakthrough in Dutch policy. I will "frapper le grand coup"; "if I cannot take the place by storm, I will yet compel them to capitulate". (31)

There is as yet no chance of an official recognition of America. But the regents of Amsterdam cannot let their chances go by without doing anything. In July Van Berckel asks Dumas to give him all possible information and Dumas answers him that there is a good chance of an English-American reconciliation, which will mean that England will receive all the advantages- of the American trade. So the Amsterdammers decide to act for themselves. But now the unheard-of, the unbelievable happens. Happens to Dumas! Poor little Dumas! In the deepest secrecy a representative of the Amsterdam Burgomasters, the banker Jean de Neufville, meets the American agent William Lee, in Aix-la-Chapelle, and together they draw up the draft for a treaty of commerce between the Dutch Republic and the United States, and Dumas is completely left out of the whole business! All he gets to know is that an Amsterdam merchant is in Germany to discuss a loan with Lee, and he warns van Berckel that it is not Arthur Lee they are dealing with — as they presume in their hurry — but his brother, William. Van Berckel promises him not to do anything without him, but the real contents of the deal at Aix remain hidden from him and his eyes will only be opened completely when in 1780 the whole business is revealed through the capture of Henry Laurens by the English.

Does he suspect something? Already early in 1779 he expresses his fear that somebody tries to move him aside, to supplant him, a cruel thing after all he did for the American cause. (32) And later in the same year when the semi-official negotiations about a treaty are carried on, he begins to surmise that Lee has cheated him, that there was more to the dealing at Aix-la-Chapelle than just a loan. It is curious to notice how Dumas puts all the blame on Lee, who "unknown to me . . . concerted with M. de Neufville. It is with the most painful concern I mention to your excellency this attempt of Mr William Lee to undermine me in this manner". (33) Van Berckel is exonerated; this "good gentleman" was under the impression that Lee "was one of the Commissioners at Paris". And with de Neufville Dumas even strikes up a friendship in 1779. When in October 1780 Laurens is caught Dumas can write to Franklin how foolish the whole enterprise has been, "une démarche aussi prématurée . . . de ces têtes un peu trop chaudes". Lee "wanted to rob me of the honour and fruits of all that I had done". (34)

From one problem Dumas stumbles into another. In the fall of 1779 John Paul Jones arrived at the roads of Texel and overnight became a hero of the Dutch public. Dumas, excited by such an opportunity, helped him as much as he could and arranged all supplies, significantly through the house of Jean de Neufville! Jones, the gallant sailor, visited Amsterdam and The Hague and fell in love with Dumas' 13-year-old daughter. The girl, nourri dans le serail, dedicated him an ode, and the Commodore replied with his own poem. So far, so good, it was all quite harmless and idyllic. But the presence of John Paul Jones had other less pleasant aspects. The Dutch Government, under pressure from the British Ambassador, ordered him to leave as soon as possible, and the only way to get around their threat of violence was to hoist the French flag. Only with the greatest power of persuasion was Jones prevailed upon to accept this in his eyes humiliating condition. When the French Ambassador also proposed that he accept, as protection, a French letter-of-marque as captain of privateers, Jones flatly refused. In this whole conflict, more extensively discussed in Morison's fine biography of the American hero-sailor, Dumas took part with Jones and this became the first cause of his rupture with De Vauguyon. (35)

Other reasons could be added, but may it suffice to point out the deepest cause of this for Dumas very damaging conflict. As long as the French and American interests seem to run parallel, his position is not too difficult, but when the divergence between the two becomes more and more evident, Dumas gets into trouble. His real loyalty was to America not to France, and the domineering attitude of the Duc towards him had long since caused his resentment, as is very clear from the letters he wrote to his American principals. On December 30, 1779, he writes about "certain false friends, highly incensed against me for not having found me as blind and complaisant to their particular treacherous views as they had expected I would be". And John Paul Jones receives as his advice not to trust De Vauguyon. "He betrays you. Go back to the purity of the new world. You are too good for the corruption of the old''. (36)

But to quarrel with an ambassador, a duke moreover, is in the deferential 18th century society no small thing for a little man like Dumas. When one of his letters about Vauguyon is intercepted and handed over to that gentleman the results are nearly disastrous. There is no more pathetic document in all his letters than the one he writes to his French protector to ask his forgiveness, after Benjamin Franklin has strongly advised him to do so. In the draft of it, almost every word has been crossed out, every sentence rewritten. "Je vous aime, Monsieur le Duc. I am completely wrong. I ask your pardon. I ask it again and I shall remain asking it till it is granted me. May your Excellency forget the one moment in which I displeased him for a thousand in which I have pleased him so much''. (37) Poor Dumas! Two weeks later he regrets his prostration: "ma lache lettre. I was out of my mind for fear of what would happen to my family''. (38)

Benjamin Franklin fatherly admonishes him: "Permit me to tell you frankly what I formally hinted to you, that I apprehend you suffer yourself too easily to be led into personal prejudices by interested people, who would engross all our confidence to themselves. . . . There does not appear to me the least probability in your supposition that (Vauguyon) is an enemy to America''. (39)

For a long time the relations between Dumas and the "Grand Facteur" remain bad, and it never really is completely restored. Officially the rupture is healed when in 1780 John Adams appears on the stage of the Dutch Republic. Dumas introduces him to Vauguyon, who himself must have been informed by Vergennes not to give too much trust to this new American representative of a new style in diplomacy soon to be characterised as militia-diplomacy. For Dumas there now begins a new phase in his agency. He has to be content to play only the second role, to adjust himself to the strong leadership of John Adams. But so he is relieved from much responsibility.

His greatest care in this time is for his own position. He wants to safeguard himself against a repetition of the things that have happened. If the Americans would guarantee him a permanent position in their diplomatic service he would be content and safe. But there exactly lies the problem. In the first hours of their rebellion they have clutched at every straw. Dumas was their first choice, but can they keep him, a foreigner, in their corps? To circumvent this barrier Dumas, at the end of 1780, takes the oath of allegiance to the United States of America upon the holy Evangelists and Almighty God, in the hand of John Adams and James Searle. (40) In his own as always exaggerated opinion he is now a citizen of the United States, and makes this the basis of his claim for a permanent appointment.

In long letters he enumerates all his merits for his adopted country, everything he has suffered for it: "I must perish for want, grief and mortification if I am not soon supported by a more generous provision'' (41); "My enemies are after me. I am abused, shunned publicly as an infected and dangerous person''. (42). Especially his financial troubles worry him, and in February 1782 he decides to give up the house he lives in at The Hague because he can no longer afford the cost. He sends his wife and daughter to a little farmhouse out in the country and rents a room for himself in the city. "The separation is very difficult for it deprives us of the sweetness of living together''. (43)

But the darkest hour is before the dawn, even for an accident-prone person like Dumas. Just in this same time, in the spring of 1782, everything turns for the best for the American cause in the Netherlands. In April the long-awaited official recognition by the States-General is finally obtained and audacious John Adams has already anticipated the glorious event by buying an official residence for his country at The Hague. Dumas closes the bargain in February and what would be more proper than that he himself should become the first secretary of the new legation and his wife the caretaker of the house? He proposes this to Livingston in a letter on April 4, and John Adams gives him support: "He is a man of letters and of good character; but he is not rich and his allowance is too small at present for him to live with decency. . . . I think it is in the interest and duty of America to send him a commission as secretary to this legation, and chargé d'affaires, with a salary of five hundred a year sterling, while a minister is here, and at the rate of a thousand a year while there is none''. (44)

But although Dumas and his wife moved into the Hotel des Etats-Unis and so escape from an involuntary divorce, the American Government hesitates to acknowledge their claim. After all, Dumas is not an American citizen. What a tragedy for a man who wanted to be nothing else than an American that pure formalism defeats his most ardent wish. All these misfortunes together begin to wear him out. He is already over 60 years old and he literally collapses on the first day of January 1783. When paying his several respects around the city he is struck by a severe attack from his old ailment, his veins, and falls down at the feet of (could it be more symbolic?) the French chargé d'affaires, De Bérenger. (45)

The old fears have him in their grip: "I will be forgotten like Joseph by succeeding kings, perhaps turned out by some new Minister coming here, with a less scruple as in the savage countries they eat a fellow creature or elsewhere a chicken, and then mocked and laughed at like a damned fool''. (46)

There is in Dumas something of the romantic soul, described in the same time by Goethe:

Himmelhoch jauchzend
zum Tode betrübt.

He is not so completely forgotten as he has us believe in his jeremiads. One of the men who unexpectedly warmly recommends him is the French Minister Vergennes, who in 1786, writes to the American Ambassador at Paris, Thomas Jefferson, to request the title of Resident and a

D

salary of 4,000 dollars for Dumas. (47) Three months earlier Congress has already bestowed a fixed salary of 1,300 dollars on her agent in Holland, with retrospective effect to April 19, 1775, and on July 24, 1787, it is officially resolved that Dumas be permitted to occupy and reside in the house of the United States at The Hague. (48) Moreover, a French stipend of 1,500 lires is given him in 1786. (49) So it looks that now, finally, he is coming into his own and can look forward to a carefree old age.

Répos ailleurs! For this year 1787 had an ugly surprise in store for the patriotic faithful. Just at the moment when Dumas, to use the words of Vergennes, began to enjoy much consideration in Holland, the scales were turned upside down. At the request of Princess Wilhelmina, wife of the weak Stadholder William V, troops were sent by her brother, the King of Prussia, to quell the turmoil and trouble which had been growing since several years and had almost plunged the Dutch Republic into a civil war. The Orangist party now, for the time being, shouted victory, and the Patriots — the "Kezen" as they were nicknamed — became the victims of a true reign of terror. Many of them fled to France, others were hunted down in the streets, imprisoned, their houses plundered, their property destroyed. Dumas was in real danger and could only save his life by seeking refuge in the French Embassy. That at least is what he reports to Thomas Jefferson, now the American Ambassador in Paris, describing the horrors he had been exposed to. He had been threatened by a mob "écumante de rage", called names like "Kees" and "Yankee" (an early example of the Yankee-go-home sentiment), and with the greatest difficulty he and his wife and daughter had been able to escape. Sentries were now posted before the American Hotel to protect it from plunder. (50)

Jefferson immediately protested to the Dutch and Prussian ambassadors at Paris, with the result that protection was given to Dumas. But his position had completely changed. No longer did he have any standing or influence with the new conservative government at The Hague. What was worse, the States-General even required from the American Government that he be no longer employed, not, as they argued, because he was an American agent, but because he was the friend of France and a partisan of the Patriots. (51) Adams advised Congress to dismiss Dumas or to ask the States-General what exactly their objections to him were. But Jay, at this time Secretary of Foreign Affairs, refused both propositions. It would, he wrote, be improper to dismiss any of the public servants of the United States on the complaint of a foreign power, but on the other hand, neither could it be asked from the Dutch Government to express its objections to Dumas, since he was not officially a servant of America. All that rested was to beg for magnanimity towards the poor agent. That seemed to be the end of the case but in the following year Dumas was again annoyed by the Dutch authorities. He was summoned to appear before a Government commission and ordered to remove from the American Hotel his name and title, written on the door — "Dumas, Agent der Verenigde Staten van Amerika" — and even the coat-of-arms of the United States. "Obéissez", the chairman of the committee snarled at him, but Dumas, for all his lack of heroism, refused to execute at least the second requirement, explaining that he could not take down what the American plenipotentiary himself had ordered to be displayed.

Yet Dumas, with all his troubles and cares, remained his true self, always active, full of plans, zeal and self-pity. He kept sending his stream of letters to America, he published important American documents like the Northwest Ordinance and the Constitution in the Dutch papers, he proposed to Jefferson a plan to go to Brussels to conclude a treaty of amity and commerce with the authorities there. And he continued to complain about his bad health, his unstable position, his fear of being removed or even forgotten. Jefferson, like Franklin in earlier days, had to ask him to calm down and with almost the same words: "My dear sir, tranquillise yourself and your family upon this subject". (52)

With all his infirmities, Dumas lived on to see another revolution, coming to Holland from the outside like the other one. This time, in January 1795, it was the French revolutionary armies which crossed the frozen rivers and held their victorious entry in the Dutch cities. They brought liberty, equality and fraternity and in their trail the Patriotic refugees of eight years earlier. Again the tables were turned, the Stadholder and his family sought shelter at the court of their royal relations in England, and the Patriots began to try to realise their old dream of a more or less democratic government. So the Batavian Republic was born. Dumas happily reported to the American Secretary of State: "Providence has confounded the despotism of the odious oligarchy by the strongest frost opening a highway for the French revolutionaries". (53) Rightly he might be content, his dreams seemed to become true and he received complete personal satisfaction for all the insults and damage done to him under the Ancien Régime. "Satis vixi, vindicata existimatione". (54) And to John Adams he exulted: "Thanks to the King of the Ages (the only one that I adore and love) . . . I am now the Makarios of the Gospel (St. Matthew 5, 11)". (55)

A happy ending to a tragic story. Now he could, like Simeon, depart in peace. The next year, 1796, he died. After life's fitful fever he sleeps well.

For a long time it looked as if he were completely forgotten. The gift of his letterbook and other papers to the Dutch archives has caused some renewed interest. But it is still difficult to evaluate the significance of our hero or anti-hero or whatever he may have been. After reading the very extensive correspondence which he carried on with so many important leaders I venture to come to some modest conclusions. It must be admitted that Dumas did not play the great and significant role that he anticipated when he started his American adventure in 1775 when, to use his own words, "with an exalted soul I threw myself into the flames of the burning house of the virtuous people, dearly beloved by me, which I saw struggle for liberty". (56) His significance was that he made the first contacts between Holland and the representatives of France and of the American colonists. It was through him that the city of Amsterdam became involved in the negotiations with America, and all the more tragic it was that others reaped the fruits of his labour. It was his enthusiasm that kept up the contacts between the American plenipotentiaries in Paris and the Dutch officials and sympathisers. Through his many connections with Dutch scholars, editors and politicians he was able to prepare the way for John Adams. There is indeed no better characterisation of Dumas than the one which he gave himself, St John, a prophet, yea more than a prophet, a messenger before the face of the future, preparing a way in the wilderness of Dutch politics and emotions.

That is the tone in which we must talk about Dumas, we must see him as a typical example of the American enthusiasts, so common in the late eighteenth century. They were found all over Europe, especially in France where they have been well described in the excellent book of D. Echeverria, **Mirage in the West** (Princeton, N.J., 1957). In the Netherlands there certainly was not an interest in America comparable to that in France (but let us not forget that the Abbé de Pauw was a native of Amsterdam), and there were only a few of these exalted admirers of America. Dumas, the foreigner in Holland, is perhaps the finest specimen of the type. Reading his letters one is again and again impressed by the richness of his imagination, the beauty of his particular "Mirage in the West".

Already in his earliest letters to Benjamin Franklin he expresses his highest admiration for the American revolution. This struggle is the material for a great historian like Tacitus. Virtues in battle with vices! The dawn of a total revolution in the whole world! Seven or eight new states called Providence to bring back the glorious age of ancient Greece! (57) Classicist examples abound in Dumas' writings. The Americans are like the Romans in their austerity, like the Greeks in their wisdom. Their Congress may be called, like Cineas called the Roman Senate, an assembly of kings. (58) How true as in the case of Dumas the well known remark of Huizinga that the late 18th century classicism is nothing but an aspect of the Romantic movement. Even the religious overtones, so typical for the romantic mind, are there. "Here in The Hague

there is a little church of five members (his own family) which distinguishes itself not by its orthodoxy but by its sentiment, simplicity and innocence, and which says its daily prayers for America". (59)

A corresponding aspect of this romanticism is its adoration of unspoiled nature. "Bring me to Jersey or New York to chase our enemies. Then we go to your estate in Maryland where, crowned with oak leaves, we will dance with the nymphs of the Canton around the big tree which twelve men cannot embrace". (60)

In other letters he is a bit more precise. What is it that we expect from America: a new constitution, a new legislation. (61) America will be the example for the rest of the world: your cause is the cause of nature, of all mankind. (62) Though these quotations express his early enthusiasm for the American cause, he remains true to them in the times of disillusion and distress. It is completely wrong to state, as Renaut does in his book, that in later years Dumas loses his fervour. (63) Still in 1794 he writes to John Adams: "I believe firmly that Providence in the end will turn all the troubles of our moral world into good, just like she turns to the best the volcanoes and earthquakes of the physical world. Waiting, witnessing the happiness of the Americans, I pray that God may bless them more and more with representative democracy". (64) And almost a year later, stirred by the spreading of the French revolution over Europe and Holland in particular, he expresses his hope "for a constitution in Europe, when all the fatal prejudices have been wiped away, which during so many centuries have been sucked in with the mothermilk, like hereditary monarchy, passive obedience to the governments, vestiges of feudal institutions, ecclesiastical hierarchy, mercenary armies, unjust wars". And he proposes to let his old friend, van der Kemp, now an emigre in up-state New York, write such a constitution. (65)

His whole creed is summarised succinctly in his own Dumasian version of the old dictum of Tertullian: "Americanus sum ne quidquam Americani a me alienum puto. Patior cumi illis ita ut olim gavisurus cum iisdem" (66) : I am an American and I deem nothing American strange to me. Now I suffer with them so that once I may rejoice with them. To that faith he remains true till the very end. In one of his last letters he confesses: "My principles are still and always will be the same, they will follow me into another life". (67)

REFERENCES

1 **The Papers of Thomas Jefferson,** ed. Julian P. Boyd, 19 vols. Princeton, N.J., 1950-), vol. 12, p. 199.
2 A.R.A., Staten-Generaal, Lias America, 7462 IV.
3 **Verslagen omtrent 's Rijks Oude Archieven,** XLI, 1918, vol. I, p. 481-484.
4 Joseph R. Morice, "The Contributions of Charles W. F. Dumas to the Cause of American Independence, 1775-1783", **Duquesne Review,** 1961, VII. I, p. 17-28.
5 **The Papers of Benjamin Franklin,** ed. L. Labaree, W. Wilcox e.a., 19 vols. New Haven, 1959-), vol. 15, p. 179.
6 F. Wharton, ed., **The Revolutionary Diplomatic Correspondence of the United States,** 6 vols. Washington, 1889), vol. II, p. 64.
7 ib. II, p. 85-89.
8 ib. IV, p. 12.
9 ib. IV, p. 240.
10 A.R.A., Brievenboek Dumas, Aug. 11, 1780.
11 **The Deane Papers, 1774-1790.** Collections of the New York Historical Society for the years 1886-1890, 5 vols. (New York, 1887-1891), vol. III, p. 462-65.
12 Brievenboek, Dec. 18, 1776 (henceforth Br.).
13 Br. March 21, 1776.
14 Br. Oct. 1778.
15 Br. Jan. 15, 1779.
16 Br. March 18, 1777.
17 Br. May 1, 1777.
18 S. F. Bemis, **The Diplomacy of the American Revolution** (Bloomington, Ind 1957), p.125-126.
19 Br. Feb. 22, 1777.
20 Br. Aug. 22, Sept. 23, Nov. 18, 1777.
21 Br. Dec. 24, 1777.
22 Br. May 6, 1777.

23 Br. March 24, 1778.
24 Br. Dec. 12, 1777.
25 Br. Feb. 10, 1778.
26 Br. May 5, 1777.
27 Br. Aug. 14, 1777.
28 Br. Aug. 4, 1777.
29 Br. May 5, 1777.
30 Wharton, o.c.,   III, p. 566.
31 Br. March 27, April 27-28, 1778.
32 Br. Jan. 7, 1779.
33 Br. March 21, 1780.
34 Br. Oct. 23, Oct. 25, 1780.
35 S. E. Morison, **John Paul Jones: a Sailor's Biography** (Boston, 1959), p. 251 ff.
36 Br. Feb. 18, 1780.
37 Br. March 24, 1780.
38 Br. April 7, 1780.
39 Wharton, o.c., IV, p. 625-626.
40 Dumas Papers, Manuscript Division, Library of Congress, Dec. 16, 1780.
41 Br. Dec. 16-19, 1780.
42 Br. May 16, 1781.
43 Br. Feb. 5, 1782.
44 **The Works of John Adams,** ed. Ch. F. Adams, 10 vols. (Boston 1850-56) vol. VII, p. 589.

45 Br. March 13, 1783.
46 Br. Feb. 4 1783.
47 **The Papers of Thomas Jefferson,** vol. 9, p. 180-81.
48 A. R. A., Staten - General, Lias Amerika, 7462 IV.
49 ib., Arch. Brantsen.
50 **Jefferson Papers,** 12, p. 168-69.
51 ib., p. 292.
52 ib., p. 695-96.
53 Br. April 12, 1795.
54 Br. Aug. 9, 1795.
55 Br. Oct. 11, 1795.
56 Br. Feb. 21, 1781.
57 Dumas to Franklin, American Philos. Society, Philadelphia.June 30, 1775.
58 Br.Aug. 19, 1778, Jan. 9, 1779, June 14, 1777.
59 Br. March 11, 1777.
60 Br. March 21, 1777
61 Br. Aug. 4, 1776.
62 Br. May 17, 1775.
63 Renaut, o.c., p. 212: ''Dumas se desinteresse de plus en plus de la politique americaine''.
64 Br. Nov. 30, 1794.
65 Br. Aug. 1, 1795.
66 **Adams Works,** vol. VII, p. 323.
67 Br. Oct. 31, 1795.

SUNRISE IN THE WEST
American Independence and Europe

V G KIERNAN

In 1764, when the American troubles were about to begin, the bicentenary of Shakespeare's birth was being commemorated with great eclat at Stratford, the first big affair of the kind to take place in this country. Hindus of old, who measured time in millions of aeons, would not have dreamed of noticing the passage of a couple of centuries. Rome built firmly in a less shadowy world, but built for ever, and had a patriotic festival to be celebrated every five hundred years: we owe more to it for Horace's 'Carmen Saeculare' than we are likely to owe for any literary effusion of 1976. Rome's empire was still expanding then, Britain's has disappeared; its felicitations this year would have been awkward if it were still ruling India. In 1876 it was only 19 years since the quelling of the Indian Mutiny. On July 4 that year **The Times** fulminated an editorial which opened on a note of pitying contempt for the vulgar tastelessness to be expected in the day's rejoicings across the water. 'let us escape from the painful attempt to realise the series of pomps', it went on. Some perfunctory compliments followed. 'The nation has not been so prosperous as it might have been', but economic growth is not lacking. Unluckily nearly everything else **is** lacking: 'the United States have as yet done so little for the world beyond increasing the affluence of the means of animal existence...'. No speedy improvement could be looked for from the novice. 'Perchance', **The Times** concluded, 'a hundred years hence it will yet be only at the dawn'.

This was its second editorial of the day: the first was reserved for a weightier topic, the latest twist of the Eastern Question. Russia and Turkey were drifting towards one of their wars. Between 1768 and 1774 they fought an earlier one, ending with the treaty of Kuchuk Kainardji which in a strain nearly as high-flown and highminded as America's Declaration of Independence recognised that of Crimean Tartary, under its legitimate sovereigns of the lineage of Ghenjiz Khan, as a buffer between the two antagonists. (1) (One of these, Catherine the Great, annexed it ten years later.) Europe's centre of gravity had been shifting towards the east, and another symptom of this was the first partition of Poland in 1772. There was some talk in Britain of an understanding with France on behalf of the Poles; (2) if there was any possibility of it the gathering clouds beyond the Atlantic must have helped to blot it out.

For a while the war of American Independence, with France entering in 1778 and Spain in 1779, brought the limelight back from east to west, but even then there were other things going on, among them the war of the Bavarian Succession in 1778-79 between Prussia and Austria. Far more important than any such royal scufflings, the Declaration of Independence was closely preceded and followed by two other rebellions, on opposite sides of the world, which had nothing to do with it. In 1773 the Pugachev revolt, greatest of all risings of the enserfed Russian peasantry, broke out; in 1780 a widespread insurrection of the Peruvian Indians, led by a descendant of the Incas, Tupac Amaru. Between them they were prophetic of two major forces of the future, social revolt and racial revolt.

The humbling of a swellheaded John Bull in the American war was a matter of general satisfaction to Europe. There was no goodwill for him even at St Petersburg, the capital likeliest to show distaste for rebels of every kind everywhere. Karl Marx was to dwell with gloomy relish on 'the anxious, impatient haste' with which Britain pressed for a Russian alliance, as revealed in the papers of James Harris, then envoy to Russia. (3) Catherine's condition for assistance against the Americans, Harris learned, would be British support against the Turks. It was too high a price, and instead of coming to the rescue she headed in 1780 the unfriendly Armed Neutrality. Meanwhile her government was considering a scheme to take advantage of the British predicament by diverting the trade of India to an overland route to Russia, and Suvorov, the great captain, was employed to reconnoitre the ground for an invasion of Persia. (4) Literate Russians had access to a good deal of information about the American colonies, and were allowed to take a benevolent interest in them. (5) Their struggle could arouse far more ardent feeling in an individual like Radishchev, destined to be the first martyr of Russian liberalism. He wrote shortly after the war an ode to Liberty, that favourite topic of poets for a hundred years, glowing with sparks from the American anvil. A more sedate wellwisher was the Princess Dashkov who became an admirer of Franklin during a sojourn at Paris and then went to Edinburgh — to Holyrood Palace — to keep an eye on her young hopeful at the university, where he graduated in 1779. When Franklin got her elected to membership of the Philosophical Society of Philadelphia she was vastly honoured, and displayed his letter with much pride to the empress.' (6)

Catherine and her friend, Voltaire, found nothing to write to each other about America, though she was jocular about the 'Marquis de Pugatschev's' coming execution. (7) For them as for most Europeans overseas politics had meaning chiefly as affecting their own continent. Voltaire does not seem to have taken amiss the hope expressed by another correspondent, the Landgrave of Hesse, who was selling soldiers to Britain, that with the help of his 12,000 Hessians the rebels would soon be subdued. (8) Many Germans of the educated minority, Schiller among them, took the nefarious traffic very much amiss; their self-respect was insulted, and this indignation was one of the first taproots of modern German national consciousness (9) — the other being, as Goethe tells us in his autobiography, admiration for the victories of Frederick the Great. (10) Something of immense consequence to Europe was thus nourished by events in North America, intrinsically quite alien to it. Frederick himself was a typical central European in his lack of interest in them; his acolyte Hitler was to miscalculate 20th century America more hazardously. Kant, on the other hand, was impressed by the American revolution, as he was later by the French. Half a century after the Declaration, Goethe congratulated himself on having lived through an epoch 'when the greatest events that agitated the world occurred', and instanced 'the separation of America from England' along with the Seven Years War and the French Revolution. (11) Hesse's sale of troops to George III can be seen as the starting-point of another long strand of history: the Landgrave's financial expert was Meyer Rothschild, who founded his fortunes and his dynasty on it.

Only ten years before entering the American war, France bought Corsica from the Genoese, and proceeded to crush the movement for independence which had come close to success. Its leader, General Paoli, now lived in London on a British pension and could scarcely express the regard he must be supposed to have felt for General Washington; but his fellow-countryman, Bonaparte, in his youthful days as a patriot, romantically bewailed the fate of his native land and thrilled to the thought of Washington delivering his people from a tyranny as brutal as the Genoese. (12) A decade later, as First Consul, he had Washington's statue placed in the gallery of the Tuileries, in a very mixed company including, impartially, Brutus and Caesar. Another patriot, Kosciusko, crossed the seas in 1777 to join the rebels, sword in hand, but he was wafted thither by an affair of the heart, not by politics, though doubtless his years in the colonies did something to raise his mind to higher things.

A second pursuer of tempestuous loves, Alfieri, published in the same year, 1777, his **De Tirannide**, that private declaration of war against all despots. Some part of its inspiration may be credited to winds of change from beyond the Atlantic; though it might not be easy to trace this either in the tract itself or in his memoirs, which reveal a Byronic poet hurrying about Europe and England in chase, at one moment, of an English countess. In the same year also Beaumarchais wrote **The Marriage of Figaro.** He had been in America and though his purpose was only to make a fortune by selling arms to the rebels, a breath of their free air as well as business mortifications must have found vent in Figaro's outburst in Act 3 against idle aristocrats whose privileged status gave them everything without any exertion. 'Vous vous êtes donnés la peine de naître, et rien de plus. . .'. If we are indebted to America for this tirade, we are far more deeply indebted to it for Mozart's **Figaro**, which came out in 1786.

To the average European the colonies meant chiefly tobacco; the intelligentsia was often more intrigued by the Red Indians than by their enemies, the settlers, because the former could be regarded as living illustrations of the state of nature. 'In the beginning all the world was America', Locke had written (today he might be tempted to write 'In the end all the world is America'), and much theorising went on, in France and Scotland especially, about successive stages of economic history; theorising which led in the direction of the Marxian sequence of modes of production. (13) The other side of the ocean was very far off, in any case, even from Britain. That devourer of gossip, Horace Walpole, grew impatient, as he told the Countess of Upper Ossory in 1777 at the sluggish arrival of news: 'People should never go to war above ten miles off, as the Grecian states used to do. Then one might have a **Gazette** every morning at breakfast. I hope Bengal will not rebel in my time . . .'. (14)

Still, some in Britain and a few abroad got to know Americans living there, or making visits, as traders, students, tourists. More and more travel books were coming out, some better informed than others, though it is probable that there was a long time-lag, and the colonies as they existed in European minds were things largely of the past. They were in fact being transformed rapidly during the 18th century by commercial and financial growth, and the manipulation of local politics that went with it; besides the simple, comfortable farmer or shopkeeper there was now the **nouveau riche** driving through Philadelphia in a carriage and six, with Negro flunkeys in attendance. Those who drank success to the rebels must often have been drinking to an America of earlier days. Not all who drank either success or confusion can have realised that, as Crèvecoeur said, only a few provinces were ethnically English, all the rest 'a mixture of English, Scotch, Irish, French, Dutch, Germans and Swedes'. (15) Englishmen aware of this might be less willing to listen to colonial grievances; foreigners who recognised it, Germans for instance, might be more willing to sympathise with them.

'Without doubt the American war was popular in England', wrote Thackeray, just as the Inquisition was popular in Spain. (16) It is of interest to find that a contemporary historian, Gibbon, saw British policy as dictated by veering public opinion, rather than by ambitions of ministers or merchants. At first an irritated pride, a 'national clamour' for action which the government had to obey; then anti-war feeling growing out of the never-ending struggle and its reverses; 'the representatives of the people followed, at a slow distance, the changes of their opinion', and ministers had to give way, or be pulled down. (17) Dr Johnson thought his anti-American diatribe of 1775, **Taxation No Tyranny** — commissioned and revised by the government — did not provoke much controversy; Boswell, who privately considered it a 'rhapsody' of nonsense, thought it **did**. 'Five or six shots of small arms in every newspaper, and repeated cannonading in pamphlets . . . '. (18)

'They have tried to infect the people of England with the contagion of disloyalty', was one Johnsonian charge: no one ever questioned the right of authority to tax for public purposes 'till it became disputed by those zealots of anarchy'. (19) At home also 'no taxation without representation' was the cry, and some colonials in England had been connected with radical circles, like the brothers Arthur and William Lee, admirers of Wilkes who wanted his party to be identified with imperial along with domestic reform. (20) Social as well as political protest and disorder were to be feared. England's social system, Franklin had commented, degraded 'multitudes below the Savage State that a few may be rais'd above it'. (21)

To counteract the menace, Johnson — no imperialist when he wrote his tract on the Falkland Islands in 1771 — was appealing to pride of empire, as conservatives were to continue to do war in and war out. How far ordinary Britons had come by that time to identify themselves with their empire is debatable, but Demos in the big towns was vain enough of the navy which had won it, and drum-beating during these years must have done much to deepen the jingoism of the streets. We were being warned, Johnson wrote disdainfully, of the Americans' indomitable love of liberty and their formidable numbers — 'they multiply with the fecundity of their own rattle-snakes' — but from Englishmen such talk would only rebound. 'Men accustomed to think themselves masters do not love to be threatened'. (22) Franco-Spanish intervention reinforced this attitude by expanding the war into another contest with Britain's old colonial rivals. Cowper was one of many whose pro-American inclination ended when the rebels joined hands with the enemies of the motherland. (23)

In Galt's **Annals of the Parish** a country district in western Scotland may be seen reacting to the war. Its mood follows the same curve as Gibbon observed in England, from excitement and pugnacity to the day when 'all gave themselves up to joy' at the signing of the peace treaty. Its worthy minister shakes his head over promising young men seduced into joining the army and its 'wild and wicked profligates', and takes occasion to preach 'an affecting discourse about the horrors of war' which is spoiled by the behaviour of two giddy young women. (24) Only three decades had passed since fighting was taking place on Scottish soil, and many Scots must have shared the distress of a lady who wrote to a friend in January 1778, after news of a bloody battle where Washington was said to have been wounded and caputured: 'I have seen so many tears and horrors already from the accursed war, I am sure it is sent for a scourge'. (25)

One Scot who could proclaim: 'I am an American in my Principles', was David Hume, Franklin's host in Edinburgh in 1771. (26) News of the Declaration reached Edinburgh a few days before his death on August 25, despondent over 'the numberless calamities that are awaiting us'. (27) In his **History** he had defended the Revolution of 1688, and it may be wondered how many of his readers were prepared by it to defend the American revolution. (Johnson did not read it, (28) though he read the History of Birmingham.) For semi-accidental reasons most Scots were regarded in America as hostile; and whatever antipathy there was would not be allayed by economic hardships caused by the interruption of trade or by the depredations of the Scots-born former slave-trader and future mercenary in Russian service, Paul Jones. Reading Fenimore Cooper's novel about him, Walter Scott remembered Paul Jones in 1779 — Scott was then eight — 'advancing above the island of Inchkeith with three small vessels to lay Leith under contribution'. (29)

Up to 1776 it appeared to Boswell, as he wrote regretfully to the **London Chronicle** in January under his pseudonym 'Borax', that the prevalent mood of Scotland was one of indifference. (30) He himself had done little thinking about America until a year earlier. 'It is a subject vast in its present extent and future consequences', he wrote to Johnson on January 27, 1775, and he suspected that ministers might have been too hard on the Bostonians. 'Well do you know that I have no kindness for that race. But nations, or bodies of men, should, as well as individuals, have a fair trial, and not be condemned on character alone . . .'. Evidently the Bostonian character did not stand high. 'Corsica Boswell' might be expected to applaud a struggle for independence beyond the Atlantic as well as in the Mediterranean, and his compatriots might have been expected, on national as well as religious grounds, to share such a sentiment. In 1976 Scotland is seeking independence for itself, with the encouragement of American Scots; but it drew up its own declaration of independence at Arbroath in 1320, nearly two centuries before Columbus. Moreover, in 1776 it was not very long since it had been deprived of its self-government by England, and resentment at this still smouldered among the common people — some of whom may possibly have thought more about the American war than their betters guessed or than history has recorded.

The upper classes had accepted the merger with England, and were making the most of its opportunities, especially in the colonial sphere. Writing to Lord Monboddo in 1781, Allan Ramsay, fashionable painter and son of the poet, was perturbed by a mounting insecurity of life and property, and he attributed both this and the American difficulties to the weakness of the executive. Britain's wealth and territories were now so huge that only a strong government could safeguard them; a 'free empire' was a mere will-o-the-wisp; a choice must be made between factious insubordination, masquerading as liberty, and all Britain's possessions overseas, whose loss would spell the end of its national existence. (31) So devotees of empire were often to reason. On their side radicals were quite aware that they as well as the rebels were to be dragooned if things prospered for George III, and they followed the march of events as anxiously as their descendants followed the war in Vietnam. Their reflections emerge clearly from the diary of Silas Neville, a young English adherent of the parliamentary reform movement, studying medicine at Edinburgh as Americans had often done. On June 7, 1776, he 'heard very bad news from America which made me exceedingly low and uneasy. . . . If the Government succeeds in making slaves of America, Lord have mercy upon us here at home'. (32) It was exactly what the Parliamentary party in England felt in 1638 when Charles I was setting out to subdue the Scots.

At the close of the long-drawn Revolt of the Netherlands, of which some Dutchmen were being reminded, Spain signed only a truce, hoping still for reconquest. After the peace of 1783 few diehards can have gone on hoping to bring the colonies back under the yoke, though Robespierre in a speech of November 17, 1793, was to accuse the British government of plotting a fresh blow at them. (33) But the ruling class was left in a mood of mingled apprehension and vindictiveness at the thought of the 'American **Reps**' - 'A fashionable abbreviation in the higher circles for Republicans', Coleridge tells us, in line with 'Mob'. This rancour was of a sort to instigate reactionary policies both at home and abroad. Pitt had opposed the war, but when he came into office at the end of 1783 he took over (in accordance with the conventions of the constitution) the philosophy of the other party. Parliamentary reform became anathema, a spirited foreign policy took its place. Escape was sought from bafflement and isolation in the Triple Alliance of May 1788 with Holland and Prussia, much as the Boer War was followed by the Entente with France.

Significantly, this arose out of British support for Prussian armed intervention in Holland in favour of the house of Orange. The Orange faction had been anti-American; the Stadholderate, endeavouring for two centuries to turn itself into a monarchy, was more unstable and vulnerable than any established thrones. It still had its traditional backing from the masses, and its familiar opponents, the financial and civic elite. A new force, the 'Patriot' movement, both republican and progressive, but lacking any distinct programme, took shape very much round the agitation in favour of the Americans. (35) Here as in Germany the New World supplied a substitute for a missing link in European politics. Britain and Prussia were setting a precedent of intervention in the party strife of another country, the crime for which before long they would be so ready to blame the French revolutionaries. Something like an anti-Jacobin drive on behalf of Legitimacy was being launched before the Jacobin Club's birth. Going to war with France in 1793, hounding radicals at home, Tory England can be seen fighting its American battles over again.

In 1775 the French foreign minister Vergennes was hesitant about giving any succour to the colonists, for fear that their mutiny might spread, not to Europe as Johnson feared, but to Frenchmen in overseas settlements. (36) His misgiving was not confined to France, and from now on it would haunt all countries with bodies of settlers in their colonies, and often seem graver than any rish of native revolt. Cape Boers, grumblers at the rule of the Netherlands East India Company, took an interest in the American happenings; (37) in 1795 they would throw off the Company's control, while remaining nominally loyal to Holland. But at the time of the Declaration most of the colonies liable to catch the plague lay in the New World. In the 18th century they enjoyed as a rule a fair measure of autonomy, under local oligarchies of landowners and slave-owners. Madrid suffered some twinges of doubt as the war went on. It was a long time since, in the 1540s, any of its settlers had actually tried to break away. That was when the Crown tried to interfere in order to protect the Indians of Peru from their conquerors; it soon had to relinquish the attempt. In the later 18th century it was seeking to tighten its hold, and there were disturbances in protest against taxes and enactments in 1763 and 1767, with rumours of seditious stirrings. (38) Here was some dry tinder for Yankee sparks to fall on. It was while serving, as a number of South Americans did, with the Spanish in North America, that Francisco Miranda first conceived the idea of independence for white Spanish America; three years later, by his account, a plot was hatched at New York, with British collusion.

Fomenting colonial revolt was a game two could play at, and a couple of years earlier there had been a prospect of a Franco-Spanish invasion of Ireland. This, rather than any two-edged fighting in north America, was the strategy preferred by Spain; (39) it fitted into a tradition going back to Philip II. Ireland was very much a settler-colony, with Protestants in the role of Creole or Boer, Catholic peasantry in that of Amerindian or Kaffir. Like their congeners elsewhere, the Protestants were chafing at restrictions on their desire to rule the roost. Hence they were disposed to be loudly sympathetic to the American rebels, and there was a spate of pamphleteering, still more of toast-drinking by convivial societies like the 'Free Citizens' of Dublin. Memories of James II mingled with dark suspicions that the Irish papist troops who were being recruited would be brought back, after cutting the throats of the colonists, to do likewise with Protestant throats. Catholics automatically took the opposite line, and instead of being eager to welcome their French and Spanish co-religionists were loyally looking to King George as their protector. Protestants were determined to protect themselves, and organising volunteers. (40) All this ferment - political, theological, alcoholic - fed the excitements which were to convulse Ireland in the next quarter-century.

Britain inherited other colonial anxieties from the war. One individual sensitive to them was Nelson, who learned his trade in this war, much of the time in the Americas: this by itself might be counted among the ramifying consequences of the American rebellion for European history. In 1784 he was posted to the West Indies, where he made himself unpopular by strict enforcement of the Navigation Act against Yankee shipping long accustomed to a lucrative share in the Trade. It must be kept out, he wrote, for fear of political infection. 'The residents of these Islands are Americans by connection and by interest, and are inimical to Great Britain. They are as great rebels as ever were in America, had they the power to show it'. (41) At St Kitts he refused an official invitation because - it was St Patrick's day - Irish colours were flying all over the town. (42) A temper fostered by these experiences revealed itself a dozen years later when Nelson was implicated in a massacre of some other rebels, the Jacobins of Naples. British alarms extended to the East Indies as well as the west. In the early 19th century the government maintained a ban on emigration to India, whom James Mill thought so indispensable to progress - 'trembling, forsooth', he wrote indignantly, 'lest Englishmen, if allowed to settle in India, should detest and cast off its yoke!' (43)

Perhaps the fear was not quite so chimerical as he assumed. In any case no chances were to be taken: India was too valuable now. While Britain was trying to suppress tax-objectors in America, the East India Company was carrying out punitive expeditions against proprietors and peasants of the Carnatic who objected to paying land-tax to it. (44) Britain's involvement in war with France gave Hyder Ali of neighbouring Mysore fresh spirit for his running duel with the Company, which until his defeat by Sir Eyre Coote at Porto Novo in 1781 was hard pressed. Luckily for it the French were so busy in the west that they neglected a rosy opportunity to turn the tables in the east, and their first few reinforcements did not arrive until early in 1782; but 'strong fears were excited that the ruin of the English interests, in that part of the world, was at hand'. (45) Had it come, on top of the impending loss of America, Britain's empire would have been crippled indeed. Instead, in India it was ballooning, and providing compensation. Busily enlarging it by fair means or foul, the first governor-general, Warren Hastings, must have been buoyed up by confidence that additions of territory would be welcomed in London. His successors carried on the work. In 1799 an Anglo-Indian army despatched by an Anglo-Irish governor-general, with his brother, not yet Duke of Wellington, among its commanders, stormed the Mysore capital, Seringapatam, and put an end to its independence. A year later disaffected Ireland was deprived of its parliament and its autonomy.

Loss of America was quickly followed in 1784 by an India Act which brought the Company's political business under government direction. In 1786 the Cornwallis of the Yorktown surrender five years before was appointed governor-general. It is permissible to conjecture that his Permanent Settlement of Bengal, the worst turn that any British administrator ever did to India, owed something to memories of rebels in America; it consisted in the creation of a class of big landowners, who would owe everything to British power and form a bulwark between it and the peasantry. He intended, as he explained in his despatch of August 2, 1789, to strengthen the upper classes generally, so that 'a regular gradation of ranks may be supported, which is no where more necessary than in this country for preserving order in civil society'. In other words he wanted to ensure that there would be even more Loyalists in Bengal than there had been just in America. He had known on August 2 that the Parisians had just knocked down their Bastille, he would have wanted it all the more. From Calcutta he proceeded in 1798 to Ireland, once more to deal with rebellion, this time triumphantly. In the next century upper-class Ireland was reconciled to English rule very much, like Scotland, earlier, by getting a share of imperial loaves and fishes; the Wellesley brothers had shown the way. Ordinary Britons were to be reconciled to upper-class rule by the flattering illusion of a share in the imperial power and possession.

It may be tempting, though more speculative, to wonder whether America had some bearing also on the Industrial Revolution. As we may learn from Adam Smith, it had been taken very generally for granted that American profits were vital to the British economy. It would be ruinous to go on trying to recover the colonies by force, Cowper wrote in 1781, but either way the outlook was desperate, 'for I consider the loss of America as the ruin of England'. (46) This loss profoundly disturbed men's notions of economics, as well as the prestige of the landed and mercantile oligarchy. A search for wealth to be produced at home by new methods, as well as for plunder to be got by very old methods from Asia, might follow logically. Arthur Young called on the country to seek prosperity within its own limits, instead of wasting energy on attempts to wrest blood-stained gold from East or West Indies. (47) It was of course the fruits of the soil that he had in view, but the argument was equally valid for manufacturers. Industrial Revolution may then have been, consciously or not, an alternative to empire-building. Glasgow set one example when, with its Virginia tobacco trade disrupted by the war, it surmounted the crisis by turning to other foreign markets and by developing cotton textiles. (48) With a rich monopoly gone, British production must take itself more competitive. At any rate, the Industrial Revolution was getting under way immediately after the Declaration of Independence; if this was simple coincidence, it was a remarkable one.

Europe in general was more interested in American events from the point of view of economic prospects than of political ideals. Dutch businessmen, though reluctant to give the rebels loans until sure that they were going win, indulged in brilliant hopes of future dealings with a free American market. (49) Emigration to the United States was swelling, and among the classes it attracted were skilled craftsmen; so many of these were quitting England by the 1790s that the government tried to check the flow. (50) Here may have been another incentive to adoption of machines, as substitutes for men. With Highlanders too flocking across the Atlantic, a loss 'universally lamented', according to the Earl of Selkirk, was that of a 'valuable supply of soldiers'. (51) Politically on the other hand America was already beginning to serve a a safety-valve for Europe's surplus hands and restless spirits, thus doing much to relieve the very ferment its emergence as a free nation did much to stir up.

Washington himself was a beacon of material as well as moral progress. In the early days of the French Revolution he was unanimously elected to the Royal Society of Agriculture, because Arthur Young, who was in Paris, assured it that 'the general was an excellent farmer, and had corresponded with me on the subject'. (52) On the ground Washington and his royal namesake Farmer George stood cheek by jowl. Even Franklin can scarcely have made a deeper impression on Europe than an American of the rival camp, the Loyalist officer Benjamin Thompson who sailed to London in 1776 on the fall of Boston, entered government service and carried out experiments with gunpowder and other utilities, - went to Bavaria and blossomed into Count Rumford and War minister, invented all sorts of things, and concocted a wonderful soup, cheap but nourishing, for paupers, soldiers and convicts. (53) His more pacific achievements earned him, among many other rewards, a sonnet from Coleridge honouring him as one of those who have alleviated the human lot. Europe was being introduced to Yankee ingenuity.

It has been said that by 1789 Europe at large was ready for an explosion. Some regions were already in a state of revolt, France in turmoil. The question arises of how much American independence had done to bring the continent into this condition, and in particular to hasten the French Revolution, through which its influence was taken up and magnified and presented to Europe on European terms. Answers to this question are more visible on the material or economic level than on that of ideology. Except for lucky profiteers, the long-drawn American war brought heavy losses and difficulties, and was followed by a period of dislocation instead of effervescence. France's growing textile industry suffered from the cutting off of supplies of cotton. So did that of Catalonia; Spanish trade with the colonies was damaged, and the government was embarrassed by the cessation of its imperial tribute. Cabarrus's expedient had to be adopted, the issue of **vales reales,** 'royal bonds' which circulated as paper money like the French **assignats** in the 1970s, and swiftly depreciated, though a national bank was set up to bolster them; for many years to come they were a millstone round the ailing government's neck. Tension and protest still found expression in Spain more in regional than in class relations and a recent study of Navarre in that period makes plain how much friction was caused by demands for extra taxes and conscripts for the war. (54)

There was not yet in retarded Spain a situation where a ministry's flounderings could arouse national criticism and desire for constitutional change. France was much more advanced, and therefore more inflammable. By humbling the old enemy England, the Court counted on reviving its halo, and it made the most of its airy success. A set of tapestries produced at Beauvais in 1786 improved on the well-worn theme of the Four Continents by depicting a French Minerva presiding in Europe over the recognition of the United States, in America triumphing over a vanquished Britain attended by cringing leopards. (55) This was all very well, but victory brought no tangible gains, and its costs were heavy. How far they were responsible for the government's slide into bankruptcy is debatable. 'Une guerre dispendieuse, mais honorable', was the prime reason alleged by Louis in his opening address to the States- General on May 5, 1789; its costs had swelled the tax burden, and made its inequality more irksome. This may have been overstatement; it might well be felt that a glorious war was a better excuse to put forward than court pensions and extravagances. But ministers not good at book-keeping might easily believe what they said; so would many others, and any such conviction takes on the force of truth. In this sense the American breakaway was responsible in a very definite degree for the French Revolution coming when it did.

When the colonists started quarrelling with George III they were far from being the only standard-bearers of progress in sight. Europe considered itself to be making excellent headway, under the guidance of monarchy enlightened by philosophy. In 1772 a royalist coup d'etat in Sweden put Gustavus III firmly in power. 1774-76, at the outset of Louis XVI's reign, were the years of the reforming Turgot ministry. In 1776 the progressive Conde de Florida Blanca was appointed chief minister to Charles III of Spain, and Joseph II made his first move to introduce religious freedom into the Hapsburg empire, a more daring innovation than anything announced in the Declaration. In Paris a young Frenchman was planning a prize declamation in praise of Louis XIII; a year before he had been chosen to recite in Latin welcome to the king and queen when they visited the Lycée Louis-le-Grand. He was now eighteen; he was Robespierre; before long he would be an Enlightened Despot himself, if of a novel minting.

But in the years after 1776 monarchy as the torch of progress was burning dimmer, hopes of genuine reform imposed by fiat were faltering. In Portugal in 1776 Pombal was pulled down at last by his conservative foes; Turgot was given no second chance. Frederick was aging before his death in 1786, Catherine's reformism was proving a sham; while Joseph made things harder for himself by reckless foreign policies, and was being challenged by resistance in Bohemia, Hungary, the Austrian Netherlands, when he died in 1790. As against this depressing record America's could stand out as one of success; and to a Europe more and more acutely aware of need for change, it might well seem to point a more practical path. John Adams had some right to exult at the end of the war in the thought of his country having given a pattern, of self-liberation for Europe to emulate, (56) much as Pitt was to do after Trafalgar.

There was no falling off of curiosity about the new nation after its establishment. In France a flood of writings contrasted it, less or more accurately, with the state of things at home. What Johnson had called 'the delirious dream of republican fanaticism' (57) was coming true. More Europeans lived it is true under republican institutions than Americans, in the Netherlands, Switzerland, Venice and Genoa, the Free Cities of the Empire. But none of these were flourishing: they had all come to look obsolete and futile by comparison with monarchy. America was giving the republican ideal a new lease of life. More still, most meaningful of all it may be, it had transformed theory into fact by taking up arms, challenging legitimate authority by force. Most of its ideas came from Europe, but it was a long time since any Europeans except ignorant peasants had been prepared to fight for any rights. In a century riddled with wars over dynastic successions - Spanish, Polish, Austrian, Bavarian - a 'War of American Independence' was a portent in itself. Subsequent Irish movements, for instance, show the American precedent lending justification to resort to physical force. (58) They like many elsewhere shared its national character: even where this was absent, America might be said to have demonstrated, in advance of Karl Marx, in the face of all doctrines of peaceful painless change, that grand alterations can be brought about only by revolution.

Not many of Lafayette's fellow-officers who fought in America, nearly all of them nobles, went there to fight for liberty and fraternity, if it was not in something like the spirit of Marie Antoinette playing at shepherdess. It may be recalled that in 1782 while the war was still going on France carried out an intervention in Geneva, along with Berne and Sardinia, to restore aristocratic power in the city-republic, exactly as Prussia and Britain were to do in Holland six years later. Still, some of the more intelligent French officers brought ideas back with them, if mostly of liberty for their own class, and other Frenchmen envied American felicity. Here again myth could acquire the force of fact: it came to be believed that, as Gentz wrote in 1800, Frence's revolution was 'for the greatest part brought on by the part she had taken in that of America'. (59) Honorary citizenship was bestowed on Washington, and before long he was incorporated into the cult of Theophilanthropy, with its veneration of benefactors of the human race from Socrates onward. In his speech of November 17, 1793, Robespierre assured the Assembly that beleaguered France could reckon on three friends in the world - her neighbour Switzerland, her old ally Turkey, her late ally the United States.

Of how the French Revolution reawoke memories of the American, but absorbed them into its own louder tumult, in Britain above all, an epitome may be found in the word 'revolutionary', first heard in 1774 but only in vogue after 1794 as an echo of the new French word **Révolutionnaire**.(60) Hitherto impressions bequeathed by the American conflict, if we look at their record in English poetry, then approaching its richest harvest but one, seem suriously meagre or muffled. This is notably the case with Burns, seventeen in 1776 and passionately devoted to the legend of Wallace. Washington supplied a fresh symbol of patriotism, but one that stirred him far less. He once designed 'an irregular ode for General Washington's birthday', but got no further with it than a fragment on Liberty, all about Wallace and the degeneracy of modern Scotland, and in Burns' stilted English style. His poem 'The American War', at the other extreme, is in broad Scots, but in humorous rustical vein, a chronicle of events without any heroics, largely by way of satire on London politicians. This was all that Burns the radical poet had to say about America; Burns the letter-writer had even less; and the Burns who was driven by penury to think of emigrating, about 1786, fixed on Jamaica, not New England, as his haven. (61)

Of the poets of the first Romantic generation in England, Crabbe was reaching early manhood during the American conflict, but was absorbed in his own painful gropings for a place in the world. Wordsworth was born in 1770, Coleridge in 1772, Southey in 1774. Their boyhood lay under the shadow of war, and the firm anti-militarism they all grew up with must be traced to this, though it was the French Revolutionary wars that brought them to expression. Wordsworth's 'Guilt and Sorrow' belongs to the first years of those wars; it was in 1798 that young Hazlitt walked ten miles through winter mud to hear Coleridge preach a sermon on the miseries of war. (62) This theme, rather than any lure of American institutions, seems to have come first with them; and it is noteworthy that when Southey and Coleridge laid plans for settling in America they - like many later Utopians - meant to enclose themselves in a Pantisocratic community of their own, collectivist as well as egalitarian, not to join in the Yankee race for enrichment.

There is little or nothing about America in Coleridge's verse, even where it might be looked for in the longer political poems of the 1790s, a time when tributes in verse or song to both 1776 and 1789 were part of the staple of radical agitation. Blake, two years senior to Burns and already rhyming when the colonial leaders were writing their Declaration may have taken a more positive view of America as a new society. (63) But his long 'prophetic' poem or rhapsody, **America**, was not written until 1793, the year when Britain went to war with France. Evidently it now appeared to him that the American revolution ought to have dazzled men more than it did; he explained its failure to do so in poetic fiction by saying that its light was impeded by one of the supernatural beings of his poem from reaching Europe fully until 1789 (lines 216-8).

It reached Blake himself much refracted, or so to speak with a strong shift of the spectrum towards the red. His poem was an outcry against all domination of man over man -
'For Empire is no more, and now the Lion and Wolf shall cease.
Early on Washington warns his fellow-patriots that Albion is bent on chaining
'Brothers and sons of america till our faces pale and yellow,
Heads deprest, voices weak, eyes downcast, hands work-bruis'd,
Feet bleeding on the sultry sands, and the furrows of the whip
Descend to generations that in future times forget'
This pathetic picture fitted Washington and his well-to-do friends much less well than it fitted the bondsmen too many of them owned; in Blake's mind these seem to blend with the miserable wage-slaves who were industrial England's new progeny. His fantasy is one of many illustrations of how America and then France, like Russia or China later, could be a potent symbol for emotion or aspiration far away, more than a reality. For the American leaders as personages Blake cared little. Americans, he foresaw with regret, 'will consider Washington as their god', just as 'the French now adore Bonaparte ... I have the happiness of seeing the Divine countenance in such men as Cowper and Milton more distinctly than in any prince or hero'. (64) As one of his first biographers was to say, Blake viewed the American revolution as a sublime chaos only expressible as the wrestling of 'vast mythic beings', amid which 'the merely human agents show small and remote, perplexed and busied in an ant-like way.' (65) And his dithyrambic conception of history and its immense impersonal forces may have been a truer one than any hero-worshippers or many academic historians have subscribed to.

On the other flank of Europe, in benighted Russia, Radishchev who had watched the American rebellion with so much ardour was brought fully to political life only by the French Revolution. This set him writing his **Journey from St Petersburg to Moscow,** where he printed his poem on Liberty, lauded the British and American freedom of the press, and, more daring still, maintained that serf-labour in Russia was as evil as slave labour in the New World. Catherine might have seen no harm in Franklin and his Philosophical Society, but she was old now, and vociferous against French doings. In their alarm over these doings, Russian conservatives could see, as many progressives everywhere did, American events stirring again; memories of Pugachev, even of Cromwell, jostled with them. (66) Radishchev was exiled to Siberia; he was lucky to get off with his life.

But while for reactionaries the American revolution might in retrospect derive a sinister hue from the French, to more moderate conservatives or cautious liberals it could appear, by contrast with Jacobin extremism, praiseworthily sober and moderate. In Poland, where the last years of independence set men look abroad for lessons, (67) the American model came into fashion with the right wing, the feudal landowners, as against the Jacobin-tinged ideas of the urban middle class. Kosciusko returned home in 1786, and strove to save his country from the two final partitions in 1792 and 1794. He wanted concessions to the peasantry, but instead had to allow the gentry to make use of him for suppressing urban radicalism. They were no more prepared to free their serfs and enlist them in the cause than Virginians had been to free their slaves. Warsaw was then easily captured by the Russian Army. So was Kosciusko; when released he made his home not in America, but in France. Similarly American federalism could be extolled now by conservatives in the northern or southern Netherlands, or in the Swiss cantons, defending old regional autonomies as strongholds of privilege against the centralising, levelling momentum of the new democracy.

Friedrich von Gentz, converted liberal and budding ideologue of European reaction, published his comparison between the American and French revolutions at Berlin in 1800. He had little but praise for the first, nothing but blame for the second. He could thus make some show of consistency with former principles, like Burke lauding the principles of 1688 at the expense of those of 1789. It was a pity, he acknowledged, that the Declaration and the States constitutions contained that loose talk of natural right, too likely to breed notions of popular sovereignty. But the American revolution was a defensive one, forced on its makers by English heavy-handedness, whereas the French was offensive, unprovoked, unnecessary. (68) This was music to the ear of the young John Quincy Adams who came to Berlin in 1801 as envoy, and made haste to translate the work and get it published at Philadelphia. Gentz had rescued the American revolution, he proclaimed, from 'the disgraceful imputation' of being of the same stripe as the French, a misconception nowhere more widespread than in the United States. (69)

Its spread there might well be alarming to pillars of the establishment like himself. By getting a great part of its fighting done for it by foreign allies, the American rebellion had managed to remain only half-revolutionary. It was not compelled to mobilise its own people, even its white people, fully, as France was in 1793; that would have forced on it a social programme, something more solid than high sounding phrases. There was danger now of humbler Americans falling under the French spell and taking such phrases too literally; and it was a useful precaution to persuade them that 1789 was completely at variance with 1776, a travesty of Republican purity. Gentz and Adams - son of the John Adams who had boasted of his country setting an example to the world - were already pointing the way from the revolutionary America of 1776 towards the ultra conservative America of days to come. In 1955 the translation was republished at Chicago, with an introduction smelling of Cold War, to convince good citizens that once again 'the prescriptive wisdom of American politics confronts the levelling frenzy of ideology and the ferocity of the enraptured Jacobin'. (70)

During 1803-13 Adams was minister at St Petersburg, where in the more liberal or pseudo-liberal climate of Alexander I's reign he was made welcome. He often took walks with the tsar, who one day, shortly after annexing Finland smilingly enquired about the annexation of West Florida. (71) Alexander invited constitutional suggestions from Jefferson as well as Bentham, in the spirit of his grandmother cultivating Voltaire- his more soberly modernising minister Speransky took little notice of the United States politically, though he took note of financial experiences there since independence. (72) American political ideas had a rebirth, though a still birth, in the minds of the Decembrist conspirators of 1825, men some of whom were really progressive, but who represented an upper class, not unlike the Polish gentry, desirous of replacing autocracy with oligarchy. They abounded in Greek and Roman images of liberty, as recostumed by French revolutionaries, but they were ready to think of a republic on American lines as a suitable régime for Russia. (73)

At the time of their plot and failure a longer struggle was being waged in Greece, more akin to the American precedent in being the breaking free of a colony, through not a settler colony, from an empire. It too caught some of its fire from America.Greek immigrants first reached Florida in 1767, (74) and the Greece of the islanders and sea traders was not unaware of events at Lexington or Saratoga. Some American as well as European volunteers took part in the Greek war of independence. (75) as others were to do long afterwards in the Spanish civil war. Turkey retorted by bringing in an Egyptian army against the Greeks, much as Britain brought its Hessians into America or as America was to bring its Koreans into Vietnam. Free Greece took over from the United States and other lands the liberal maxims inscribed in its constitution, if scarcely perceptible anywhere else in the national life.

While this was going on Britain had its tit for tat with Spain and its continental friends by conniving at the liberation of Spanish America, that is to say of the Creole oligarchy. Since Tupac's rising the Indian masses had been subjugated anew; in a war of independence the risk for the dominant class might be of the poor whites getting out of hand. Their betters could find reassurance in the success of the United States in surmounting the same risk before them, and keeping rebellion firmly under the management of 'land-owners, slave-owners, prosperous merchants', so that property and the social order were never in jeopardy. (76) With a social structure far more undemocratic than New England's, Spanish America started its new life crippled by the narrowness of its political basis, which it has still not got away from. All the same, its revolt perturbed European conservatism far more than North America's had done, because in between the spectre of Jacobinism had come to haunt it, and these were the days of the Holy Alliance. Catherine cold shouldered George III, her grandson wanted a European crusade on behalf of Ferdinand VII. In Spain itself the Patriotic Societies which sprang up with the revolution of 1820 had American as well as British and French ancestry. (77) One at Barcelona brought out a rambling manifesto where 'immortal Washington' somehow figured along with Sulla and Christina of Sweden. (78)

Revolutionary inspiration from the fountain of 1776 dwindled away, though by the fact of its existence the United States - when not too closely inspected - continued to hearten men like the Democrats starting their uphill task in Spain, or the Chartists in Britain. Indistinctly but emotively, there was a better land beyond the sea:
'Friends of Freedom, swell the strain
That peals across the 'Atlantic main',
wrote a Chartist poet. (79) Chartists indeed who believed in 'physical force' must have looked back at times to the stormy birth of the Republic for warrant. Preachers of peaceful patience, Cobbett had written in 1816 on the demand for parliamentary reform, forgot that neither Magna Carta nor the Bill of Rights, nor American independence were 'won by the fireside . . . These were all achieved by **action**, and amidst hustle and noise'. (80)

On the whole if European applause for the French Revolution was followed by speedy, often excessive, disappointment, a similar though obscurer train of disillusion overtook its precursor. It too left a literary record, marked by sundry cross-currents. Among British poets of the second Romantic generation Thomas Campbell took the most favourable view. Born in 1777 son of a merchant who had traded in America, he displayed far more interest in it than his fellow-Scot Burns. His long poem **Gertrude of Wyoming** came out in 1809, amid the Napoleonic bloodshed, and depicted the cause of American independence as a righteous one, unhappily condemned to make its way through fratricidal strife—
'Sad was the year, by proud oppression driven,

When Transatlantic Liberty arose'. (81)

Shelley may have come by much of his regard for America through close association in his early political life with Ireland. In his Irish pamphlet of 1812 he linked 1776 and 1789 in terms of what was becoming an accepted myth: after France had bowed under despotism for ages 'her soldiers learned to fight for freedom on the plains of America'. (82) In his speech at the Dublin meeting on February 28, 1812, he pointed to the United States as the exemplar of religious freedom, (83) meaning presumably that this was something for Ireland, above all, to copy. That year Britain and America were drifting into their second war, and Shelley was typical of progressive opinion in lamenting it; now that liberty had long been snuffed out in France and lingered only feebly in Britain, its survival in America was all the more precious. Walter Scott on the contrary was indignant when the war ended, at a wasted opportunity to teach the Americans a salutory lesson. 'It was our business to have given them a fearful memento that the babe unborn should have remembered . . .'. (84) A few years later, in the preface to **The Revolt of Islam** (1818), Shelley called up the glorious memory of the French Revolution, but was silent about the American; though in introducing **The Revolt of Hellas** in 1821 he did refer to young Americans in Greece, well-wishers of the national cause. How often Shelley 'looked for vindication and immortality' for how own works to the free citizens of the Republic, as Ernest Jones the Chartist was to assert, (85) might be hard to guess.

A far gloomier view was taken by Wordsworth, in a long episode in Book III of **The Excursion,** a poem finished at the end of 1811 when its author had grown piously respectable. His hermit, the sole dramatically impressive character, fled across the Atlantic from a Europe blighted by the collapse of the soaring hopes of 1789. Very quickly the exile met with fresh embitterment in 'this unknit Republic', where

'a motley spectacle
Appeared, of high pretensions - unreproved
But by the obstreperous voice of higher still;
Big passions strutting on a petty stage'—

and retreated into 'the unviolated woods', only to discover that the noble savage was

'A creature squalid, vengeful, and impure'.; - and so back across the waves to Lakeland, as the final refuge. He had a flesh-and-blood successor in the Austrian lyric poet Lenau, who turned his back on his country to escape from the police despotism of Metternich, but was soon disgusted afresh, wrote indignantly about the banishment of the Red Indian from his haunts, returned home, and found a final refuge in madness. (86)

A less romantic emigrant was Keats' brother George, driven forth by an empty purse, not drawn by any magnetic expectations. John was worried about his prospects: 'be careful of those Americans', he wrote to him in 1819. It might be prudent to come back as soon as he could save £500. 'Those Americans will, I am afraid, still fleece you'. (87) The sonnet to Kosciusko has no mention of the hero's transatlantic exploits; it is besides one of Keats' poorest.

Some writers' motives for falling foul of the Republic were not of the most elevated. Moore was snobbishly querulous about the decline from Washington, who 'threw all the graces and courtesies of aristocratic ceremony round his republican court', to a vulgarly democratical Jefferson. (88) 'Moore abused America', Byron recorded in a letter to Murray of August 12, 1819, and joked about his friend's present financial plight as a nemesis he had invited. 'It seems his Claimants are **American** merchants?' Byron sent his Don Juan travelling all round Europe, but not beyond; and when he himself thought of shaking the dust of Europe off his feet, it was to Venezuela that he turned his eyes. 'The Anglo-Americans are a little too coarse for me, and their climate too cold'. (89) In the southern hemisphere it would be easier, he might have added, to continue the **grand seigneur** life he was enjoying in Italy. His half-dozen poetical allusions to Washington are, it is true, uniformly laudatory, if a trifle stilted. In **The Age of Bronze,** especially, Washington as the selfless liberator of his country is placed in honourable contrast with Napoleon, led astray by ambition. This was written in 1823, the year before Byron departed to Greece, where he must have seen himself playing a similar if smaller role. His much-admired Goethe took an intelligent interest in the United States; at nearly eighty he predicted a Panama Canal built by American energy, and credited the new country, somewhat prematurely, with a ripening culture. (90) He may be placed among those liberal-minded Europeans who could never digest the French Revolution, but for whom the American was comfortably distant and well-regulated.

It struck an American student in Britain some years ago that the only thing the inhabitants all knew of American independence was the Boston Tea-party. Whether or not this says more for their love of tea than of history, it must be confessed that they belong to a very insular continent, which has been singularly impervious to nearly all currents of influence from outside; nearly as impermeable as old China, or 20th-century America. Here is one main reason why the names and images of the American revolution entered so little, and so sluggishly, into European, even British, consciousness. Schoolboys in modern England as well as Scotland have heard far more about William Wallace, remote and half-legendary as he is, than about George Washington, and they were taught to admire Scotland's national struggle long before they were authorised to admire America's.

True, it happened long long ago, and Scotland had long since returned to the fold, and Wallace could be no excuse for mutineers in India or Africa. Apart from this, Britain was a country grown-up and tenaciously itself, less prone than giddier ones to sudden enthusiasms for anything outside; or, if many Englishmen did feel enthusiastic in 1789, they felt for a close neighbour, the same France they at most times detested and now thought they saw transformed. When that bitter anti-aristocrat Hazlitt wanted an

34

emblem of plebeian talent unfettered, equality enthroned, it was not to Washington or Jefferson that he instinctively turned. Rendering thanks for his deliverance from the poisoned grip of legitimacy, or conservatism, he added in tones of religious solemnity: 'He who did this for me, and for the rest of the world, and who alone could do it, was Bonaparte'. (91) There was something wrong-headed, it must be allowed, in the doggedness with which he—like Heine—kept his Gallic allegiance to the bitter end. Approving mention of the United States can be found scattered through his writings. But when he looked back to the war of independence it was less to commend the rebels than to censure the arbitrary misrule through which England lost America, and by which 'we still keep Ireland in a state of vassalage'. (92)

Europe might be hard of hearing, but it was not merely wrong-headed. In terms of significant new ideas and achievements, north as well as south America was little more than a provincial back water. (93) Worse, the egg it was hatched out of, bourgeois puritanism, was always a hybrid of vaulting virtue and grovelling greed; and in the bare New World acquisitiveness has been more blatant than in the Old World with its wardrobe of masks and disguises. It was not by any slow process of their own that the United States were evolving towards capitalism and imperialism, but by force of habits and ambitions imbibed from Europe. Washington's coat of arms, as the tourist gazes at it in the window of Selby Abbey, with the stars and stripes it bequeathed to the flag, might be said to epitomise all that bad inheritance, at odds with aspirations of democracy. In 1784 the first American ship, 'Empress of China', reached Canton, where others, privateers, during the war, were soon taking a hand in the opium trade. (94) In short the fledgling was picking up predatory ways from its parent, far more than the elder learning better ways from the younger. In the heat of the revolutions of 1848 when Engels was denouncing the perennial willingness of his countrymen to serve as tools of tyranny, his mind went back to the Germans who fought for George III, rather than to the colonists who resisted them. (95) It was only a few months, whether Engels recalled this or not, since the end of the war against Mexico and the seizure of half a million square miles.

In prison in 1850 Ernest Jones cheered himself by composing a poem to 'The New World': he thought of the uprising and congratulated the Americans and their 'new Atlantis' on having cast off the shackles which were now crippling England. (96) In an article written the following year, his mind on an unlovely present instead of a gilded past, he dwelt on the condition of the United States as sad proof that 'Republican Institutions are no safeguard against social slavery'. Democracy there now faced long, painful toil to 'undo the mischief of but seventy or eighty years of centralising wealth and growing monopoly'. (97) Carlyle in 1850 was critical of America, much like The Times penman of 1876, for having nothing to offer except cotton and dollars. Its constitutional ideas of 1776 were very well, but they all came from England. 'What great human soul, what great thought, what great noble

thing . . . has yet been produced there? None.' (98) He as well as Hazlitt could discern a Hero of sorts in Napoleon, and he unearthed another in Paraguay; Washington as a candidate for Hero-worship did not occur to him.

Over and above everything else there was, to blot out any rejuvenating message of the American revolt, the obstinate survival of slavery. Here the Republic was not only not better than its fathers, but worse: the Mansfield judgment virtually ended slavery on English soil four years before the Declaration of Independence. One who hailed it was Johnson, and in his broadside of 1775 he enquired ironically 'how is it that we hear the loudest yelps for liberty among the drivers of negroes?' He referred to a proposal from such quarter to tame the rebels by freeing and arming and endowing their slaves. (99) It would have been a curious anticipation of Austria's tactics in 1846 of turning Galician peasants loose against disaffected Polish landowners. But though Britain might make use of Red Indian tomakawks, it could not, with its rich Caribbean slave plantations, enlist black allies. Well wishers of the rebels who took their 'self-evident' principles at face value must have assumed that once the country was free, slavery would soon die out. Instead, British critics of post-war America could take pleasure in underlining the discrepancy between principle and practice. (100) With all his admiration, Radishchev was repelled by its treatment of both Negroes and Indians. Kirk White's 'Ode to Liberty', in the first years of the 19th century, paid no compliments to the United States, and much of it was a threnody on African servitude. Some Chartist verses addressed to the poets of America in 1844 extolled their past good work, but asked why slavery now left them mute. (101)

Johnson and Blake were at one in expecting the colonial rising to have a catastrophic effect on the thrones and dominations of the old world. In a passage excised by his ministerial patrons, as too frightening we may suppose - it must have been designed as a warning to Europe to keep out of the quarrel - Johnson wrote that within a century and a quarter the American population might well outnumber the European; and 'When the Whigs of America are thus multiplied, let the princes of the earth tremble in their palaces'. (102) At the close of his **America** (lines 219-21) Blake wrote in the same conviction—

'Stiff shudderings shook the heav'nly thrones! France, Spain and Italy In terror view'd the bands of Albion and the ancient Guardians Fainting upon the elements, smitten with their own plagues'.

Neither of these Englishmen of opposite genius could have dreamed that at the end of two centuries the princes of the earth, the high and mighty of all the continents, would be America's grateful clients and obedient humble servants.

REFERENCES

1. Text in M. S. Anderson, **The Great Powers and the Near East 1774-1923** (London, 1970) pp. 9 ff.
2. D. B. Horn **British Public Opinion and the First Partition of Poland** (Edinburgh, 1945), p. 64, etc.
3. Marx, **The Eastern Question** (ed. E. M. and E. Aveling, London, 1897), pp. 606-7.
4. K. Osipov, **Alexander Suvorov** (trans. E. Bone, London, n.d.), p. 60.
5. See N. N. Bolkhovitinov, 'The American Revolution and the Russian Empire', in **The Impact of the American Revolution Abroad** (Library of Congress symposium, Washington. 1976).
6. **The Memoirs of Princess Dashkov** (trans. K. Fitzlyon, London, 1958), pp. 149, 232.
7. Catherine to Voltaire, 9 Jan. 1975, in **Documents of Catherine the Great,** ed. W. F. Reddaway (Cambridge, 1931), p. 205.
8. **Ib.,** pp. 321-2.
9. See G. P. Gooch, **Germany and the French Revolution** (London, 1920), pp. 36-7; H. Kohn, **The Idea of Nationalism** (New York, 1945), pp. 378 ff.
10. Goethe, **Poetry and Truth** (trans. M: S. Smith, London, 1913), Vol. 1, pp. 248-9.
11. **Conversations of Goethe with Eckermann** (trans. J. Oxenford, London, 1930), p. 43 (1824).
12. See J. M. Thompson, **Letters of Napoleon** (Oxford, 1934), pp. 6-9.
13. See R. L. Meek, **Social Science and the Ignoble Savage** (Cambridge, 1976).
14. Letter of 8 Oct. 1777.
15. **Letters from an American Farmer** (London, 1782), cited by H. S. Commager, **America in Perspective** (New York, 1948), p. 27.
16. **The Four Georges** (London edn, 1909), p. 94.
17. **Autobiography** (London edn, 1907), p. 197.
18. **The Life of Samuel Johnson** (London edn, 1926), Vol. 2, pp. 111, 125.
19. **The Political Writings of Dr Johnson** (ed. J. P. Hardy, London, 1968), pp. 121, 100.
20. W. L. Sachse, **The Colonial American in Britain** (Madison, 1956), p. 186.
21. **Ib.,** p. 205.
22. **Loc.cit.,** p. 102.
23. Letter to Rev. John Newton, 26 Jan. 1783.
24. See chaps. xv-xxiv. The novel came out in 1821.
25. Mrs Alison Rutherford, **Letters and Memoir of her own life** (ed. T. Craig-Brown, Edinburgh, 1900), p. 130.
26. E. C. Mossner, **The Life of David Hume** (London, 1954), pp. 553-4.
27. Hume, **The History of Britain** (abridged by W. Kilcup, Chicago, 1975), p. 158n.
28. **The Life of Samuel Johnson,** Vol. 2, p. 53 (1773).
29. Letter to Maria Edgeworth, 24 Feb. 1824.
30. **Boswell: the Ominous Years 1774-1776** (ed. C. Ryskamp and F. A. Pottle, London, 1963), p. 221.
31. W. Knight, **Lord Monboddo and some of his Contemporaries** (London, 1900), pp. 179-81.
32. **The Diary of Silas Neville 1767-1788** (ed. B. Cozens-Hardy, London, 1950), p. 245.
33. J. M. Thompson, **Robespierre** (Oxford, 1939), p. 425.
34. Coleridge's note to his satirical poem in letter form, 'Talleyrand to Lord Granville', 1800.
35. J. W. Schulte Nordholt, 'The Impact of the American Revolution on the Dutch Revolution', in **The Impact . . .,** pp. 50-1.
36. J. B. Perkins, **France in the American Revolution** (London, 1911), p. 49.
37. R. R. Palmer, 'The Impact of the American Revolution Abroad', in **The Impact . . .,** P. 10. On the discontents of the Cape Dutch see C. B. Boxer, **The Dutch Seaborne Empire 1600-1800,** chap. 9.
38. M. Rodriguez, 'The Impact of the American Revolution on the Spanish and Portuguese speaking World', in **The Impact . . .,** p. 103.
39. Perkins, **op.cit.,** pp. 57-8.
40. See R. B. McDowell, **Irish Public Opinion 1750-1800** (London, 1944), pp. 40 ff.; O. D. Edwards, 'The Impact of the American Revolution on Ireland', in **The Impact . . .**
41. O. Warner, **A Portrait of Nelson** (Harmondsworth edn, 1963), pp. 57-8.
42. **Ib.,** p. 60.
43. **The History of British India** (abridged by W. Thomas, Chicago, 1975), p. 548.
44. See G. J. Bryant, **The East India Company and its Army 1600-1778** (unpublished thesis, London Univ., 1975), pp. 203-4.
45. Mill, **op.cit.,** p. 425.
46. Letter to J. Hill, 9 Dec. 1781.
47. **Annals of Agriculture,** 1790; see the anthology **Writing and Action,** ed. M. Palmer (London, 1938), p. 141.
48. See T. C. Smout, **A History of the Scottish People 1560-1830** (London, 1938), p. 141.
49. Nordholt, **loc.cit.,** p. 49.
50. J. H. Plumb, 'The Impact of the American Revolution on Great Britain', in **The Impact . . .,** p. 75.
51. Lord Selkirk, **Observations on the Present State of the Highlands of Scotland** (London, 1805), p. 60. Too many, he thought, assumed that all Britain's possessions in the Americas were destined to be swallowed up by the United States (p. 159).
52. Arthur Young's diary, 18 June 1789, in **Travels in France and Italy** (London edn, 1915), p. 137.
53. See S. C. Brown, **Count Rumford, physicist extraordinary** (London, 1964).
54. R. Rodriguez Garraza, **Tensions de Navarra con la administraction central (1776-1808)** (Palplona, 1974), pp. 79-81.
55. These tapestries were formerly in Osterley House, London; see its guidebook (London, 1972), pp. 20-1.
56. Letter of 16 May 1783; see Nordholt, **loc.cit.,** p. 41.
57. **Political Writings,** p. 112.
58. Edwards, **loc.cit.,** pp. 146-7.
59. Friedrich Gentz. **The French and American Revolutions Compared** (trans. John Quincy Adams; Chicago edn, 1955), p. 5.
60. **Oxford Dictionary of English Etymology,** ed. C. T. Onions.
61. See D. Daiches, **Robert Burns** (London, 1952), pp. 94-5.
62. Hazlitt, 'My First Acquaintance with Poets', in **Winterslow** (1839).
63. Cf. G. R. Sabri-Tabrizi, **The 'Heaven' and 'Hell' of William Blake** (London, 1973), p. 208.
64. Letter of 24 May 1804, in H. Adams, **Blake and Yeats: the Contrary Vision** (Ithaca, 1954,), p. 83.
65. A. Gilchrist, **Life of William Blake** (1863: London edn, 1942), p. 93.
66. D. M. Lang, **The First Russian Radical: Alexander Radishchev, 1749-1802** (London, 1959), pp. 128-9.
67. R. R. Palmer, **loc.cit.,** p. 9.
68. Gentz, **op.cot.,** pp. 63, 47.
69. Preface to his translation of Gentz, p. 3.
70. R. Kirk, Intro. to 1955 edn of Gentz, p. xi.
71. D. Brewster, **East-West Passage. A Study in Literary Relationships** (London, 1954), p. 81.
72. See M. Raeff, **Michael Speransky** (Hague, 1957), pp. 86, 88, etc.
73. Bolkhovitinov, **loc.cit.,** pp. 91-3.
74. C. M. Woodhouse, **The Greek War of Independence** (London, 1952), p. 39.
75. **Ib.,** p. 89.
76. J. H. Parry, **The Spanish Seaborne Empire** (London, 1966), p. 341. Cf. J. Ellis, **Armies in Revolution** (London, 1973), p. 71: 'the American "Revolution" was no sense a social revolution . . . All the efforts of the American leadership were devoted to ensuring that . . . (social) unrest was kept firmly in check'.
77. See A. Gil Novales, **Las Sociedades Patrioticas (1820-1823)** (Madrid, 1975), pp. 5, 444, 450, etc.
78. **Ib.,** p. 255. This is the solitary allusion to Washington in all the copious material cited.
79. Benjamin Stott, 'Song for the Millions', in Y. V. Kovaleva, **Anthology of Chartist Literature** (Moscow, 1956), p. 108.
80. Article from **Political Register,** Nov. 1816, in M. Palmer, **op.cit.,** p. 229.
81. Part III, stanza vi.
82. K. N. Cameron, **The Young Shelley. Genesis of a Radical** (London, 1951), p. 151.
83. **Ib.,** p. 147.
84. Letter to J. B. S. Morritt, 19 Jan. 1815.
85. J. Saville, **Ernst Jones: Chartist** (London, 1952), p. 136.
86. See J. G. Legge, **Rhyme and Revolution in Germany** (Lpndon, 1918), pp. 129-131.
87. Letters to B. Bailey, 28 May 1818, and George Keats, 22 Sept. 1919.

88. Journal, 7 Sept. 1818.
89. Letters to John Cam, 3 Oct. 1819, and John Murray, 29 Oct. 1819.
90. **Conversations of Goethe,** pp. 173-4 (1827) and 39 (1824).
91. **Collected Works** (London, 1902), Vol. 3, p. 34.
92. **Ib.,** Vol. 13, p. 26.
93. Cf. Kohn, **op.cit.,** p. 291: 'for a very long time to come, culturally and politically, the young nation remained on the outskirts of the civilised world'.
94. L. Dermigny, **La Chine et l'Occident . . . 1719-1833** (Paris, 1966), pp. 1131-3.

95. Article of 3 July 1848, in Marx and Engels, **Articles from the Neue Rheinische Zeitung 1818-49** (Moscow, 1972), p. 60.
96. See Saville, **op.cit.,** p. 133.
97. **Ib.,** pp. 145-6.
98. 'The Present Time' (1850).
99. **Political Writings,** pp. 132, 130.
100. D. J. Macleod, **Slavery, Race and the American Revolution** (Cambridge, 1974), p. 27.
101. 'W.B.', in Kovaleva, **op.cit.,** pp. 63-4.
102. See Boswell, **Life,** Vol. 2, pp. 112-3.

THE RIGHTS OF MAN
From John Locke to
Tom Paine

H T DICKINSON

During the century from the appearance of Locke's **Two Treatises of Government** (1690) to the publication of the two parts of Paine's **Rights of Man** (1791-92) the extent to which political theorists and propagandists were prepared to concede political rights to their fellowmen depended on whether their primary concern was to preserve order or to secure liberty. Those who were most anxious to safeguard their own privileged position in an ordered, hierarchical society were alarmed at the prospect of anarchy which they were convinced would ensue if political rights were given to the lower orders. Those who most feared tyranny and arbitrary government maintained that liberty could only be preserved if it were recognised that all men possessed certain inalienable rights. In their desire to defend or to attack an existing political order in which only a minority enjoyed full rights of citizenship both the authoritarians and the libertarians were clearly motivated by self-interest, but they endeavoured to support their claims with moral, rational and empirical arguments. The theorists of order stressed God's ordinance, the evidence of Scripture, the essential sinfulness of human nature, the evident differences between men and the historical experience of regimes which collapsed into anarchy when too much power was conceded to or seized by the lower orders. The advocates of greater liberty emphasised the harmonious state of nature, the social contract, the immemorial rights of man, the natural equality and essential goodness of man, and the success of those regimes which governed with the consent of the people. In other words, these two extremes were marked by either a pessimistic or an optimistic view of human nature and human experience. Between these two poles there was a wide middle ground where men stressed the need for order while being prepared to confer limited rights on all men or more extensive rights on a small minority. When actual political rights harmonised, at least to a reasonable extent, with the reality of social and economic power, then a measure of political consensus and constitutional stability was attained. This was certainly the case in Britain during the middle decades of the eighteenth century. When this balance was not achieved, as in the late seventeenth and late eighteenth centuries, then revolution or the threat of revolution polarized political opinion between the authoritarian defenders of order and the libertarian advocates of the inalienable rights of man.

I

When John Locke wrote his **Two Treatises** to defend man's natural rights to life, liberty and property, he had to challenge a prevailing theory of order which refused to grant subjects any rights at all. After the restoration of Charles II most men of property had reacted sharply to what they regarded as the horrifying combination of military tyranny and mob rule that had distinguished the 1640s and 1650s. From the republican experiments of Cromwell and the radical concepts of Levellers and Diggers they turned with undisguised relief to the theory of the divine right of kings. The restored Church of England preached the doctrines of non-resistance and passive obedience with greater fervour than ever before. On each anniversary of Charles I's execution both Houses of Parliament invited eminent Anglican divines to preach and then publish sermons on the sinfulness of rebellion and the horrors of anarchy. Most of these clergymen chose as their text Romans xiii, in which St Paul commanded every soul to be subject to the powers that be.

The posthumous publication of Sir Robert Filmer's **Patriarcha**, in 1680, was the high water mark of a flood of political literature defending the absolute authority of the king. Filmer maintained that God had ordained absolute monarchy as the only legitimate form of government. In his view the kings of England enjoyed absolute, arbitrary sovereign authority. Subjects could on no account forcibly resist the commands of their king. The liberties of the subject, even the rights of Parliament, were not inviolable, but could only be enjoyed at the discretion of the king. The royal prerogative was so extensive that it was superior to both statute and common law and it could revoke any right or privilege previously granted to any subject. The king therefore had absolute power whereas subjects were denied any real political rights whatsoever. While Filmer's case rested heavily on Scripture and on his interpretation of natural law, Robert Brady buttressed the theory of absolutism with evidence derived from his historical researches into England's past. Brady claimed that the Norman Conquest had stripped the Anglo-Saxons of all their rights and had given William I the powers of an absolute king. Parliament did not appear on the political scene until the reign of Henry III and then only as the result of royal grace and favour. Thereafter it was summoned and dissolved at the king's pleasure. (1)

This authoritarian political theory was regarded by its supporters as the only means to prevent anarchy and mob rule. Absolute sovereignty had to be placed in the hands of one man in order to avoid constant political disputes. This astonishing surrender of rights and liberties by men of substance can only be explained by their fear of the 'mob'. Men of property had witnessed the collapse of the established hierarchical order in the 1640s and 1650s. Many of them were convinced that subjects must be denied any claim to inalienable political rights because these only encouraged rebellion. To prevent the rabble trying once more to turn the world upside down they preferred to place their own privileges at the mercy of an absolute king. Tyranny seemed less of a threat than anarchy. They believed that the king would not in fact so misuse his absolute authority as to threaten the privileges and property of his most important and useful subjects. The lower orders, on the other hand, were a rabble incapable of responsible political action. They were ignorant, lazy, licentious and easily led by ill-designing men. Democracy was equated with mob rule. As Filmer put it: "There is no tyranny to be compared to the tyranny of a multitude." (2)

Although the theory of the divine right of kings survived the shock of the Glorious Revolution it collapsed after the failure of the 1715 rebellion. (3) Meanwhile, a more liberal political theory had been built up by John Locke, Algernon Sidney, James Tyrrell and other Whig propagandists. Although this political theory was to be considerably and increasingly modified by more conservative Whigs during the Hanoverian period, in its original version it posed a considerable challenge to the authoritarian views of Filmer and Brady. It offered a more optimistic assessment of human nature, it laid claim to inalienable rights based on reason, natural law or the ancient liberties of Englishmen, and it advanced the cause of liberty in a number of significant ways. In the first place, the Whig theorists rejected the absolute power of the king and the exclusive privileges of the Church of England. In doing so they condemned the doctrines of divine right, indefeasible hereditary succession and non-resistance and they advocated the toleration of other Protestant sects. Second, they developed a concept of government by consent to replace the theory of a divinely ordained, absolute and arbitrary monarch. This Whig theory still rested on a religious and moral view of politics, though appeals were made both to reason and history. Working on the assumption that all men were naturally equal in the eyes of God, it was claimed that in the state of nature, where the natural law prevailed, all men had a right to their life, liberty and property. Unfortunately, in the state of nature the individual could not always protect his rights against those with greater strength or cunning. Civil government had therefore been established to preserve all men's natural rights to their life, liberty and property. In creating civil government men contracted to establish an authority which had the right and power to judge disputes between one man and another. By means of an explicit contract or at the very least by tacit consent the members of the community resigned to the civil government their individual rights to act as judge in their own disputes, but they did not surrender all their rights. The contract established a civil government which was in the nature of a trust. Men accepted the authority of the government in return for the protection of their natural, inalienable rights to life, liberty and property. Whenever a government sought to infringe these rights, by punishing criminals or raising taxes for example, then it must first secure the consent of the community. This could most readily be obtained through a political system in which the government or executive authority shared its legislative function with some kind of representative assembly. Should the government betray the trust placed in it by acting in a tyrannical or arbitrary fashion, then subjects were free to resist in defence of their natural rights. The members of the community were absolved from their duty to obey and recovered their individual right to protect life, liberty and property. They could resist those in authority in order to restore the terms of the contract or to set up a new civil government following the dissolution of the old.

The Whig contract theory of the late seventeenth century clearly marked a significant advance in the cause of individual liberty. Whereas the doctrine of the divine right of kings denied subjects any political rights, the Whig theorists and propagandists claimed four important rights. These were: (1) the natural right to life, liberty and property; (2) participation in the creation of civil government by means of a contract of some kind; (3) the right of subjects to give their consent to decisions which affected their life, liberty and property; (4) the right to resist an illegitimate exercise of power by those entrusted with authority. Put simply like this, these rights suggest that the Whigs favoured popular sovereignty and a democratic form of government. This was in fact far from being the case. None of the Whig theorists of the late seventeenth century, not even those who prided themselves on being Real Whigs or Commonwealthmen, pushed their interpretation of these rights to their logical, radical conclusion. Instead, they hedged each of them about with qualifications which meant that these political rights were granted in full to only a small minority of subjects. A careful scrutiny of Whig propaganda betrays the essentially aristocratic concept of the political rights to which they laid claim.

The Whigs conceded all men a natural, inalienable right to their life, liberty and property, but there can be no doubt that they were most concerned to protect private property. The rights to life and liberty were simply civil liberties and not positive rights to exercise political power. These liberties included freedom of conscience, the right to subsistence and to the fruits of one's labour, and the recognition that a man's personal freedom could only be infringed after due process of law. The right of men to protect their property, however, was so important that it was necessary to grant men of property a share of political power. We do not have to accept C. B. Macpherson's claim that John Locke was anxious to defend unrestrained capitalism in order to agree with him that Locke was concerned above all else to protect men of property from the depredations of an absolute, arbitrary monarch. (4) Locke deliberately sought to justify the ownership of property as a natural right and to maintain that property was divided unequally in the state of nature, long before the creation of civil society. Indeed, he went out of his way to stress repeatedly that the chief reason for men creating civil government was to enjoy their property in peace and safety. (5)

While the Whigs stressed the importance of the contract which created civil government, they did not claim that every individual gave his express consent to this compact. They not only ignored the claims of all women and all children, but much of the adule male population too. Even in the state of nature they denied all but the minority who owned property the full enjoyment of natural rights. They believed in a natural social order which was patriarchal and hierarchical. Locke, for example, recognised that all men are, at birth and by nature, equally capable of liberty and reason, but he stressed that individual men did in fact develop differently. Some men fulfilled their capacity for reason, but the majority of men failed to develop into fully rational creatures. Consequently, the latter were not capable of enjoying full liberty or of acquiring adequate amounts of property. Only a minority of men owned sufficient property to be economically independent and to enjoy the leisure necessary to exercise their rational capacities. While all men might be allowed to give their tacit consent to the decisions of civil government, only this minority of rational property owners could be actively engaged in framing the political compact which created civil government. Thus, Locke's theory initially appears "democratic", but it is eventually so qualified that it can only be termed "aristocratic". (6)

Other Whig theorists were even more explicit than Locke. Algernon Sidney claimed that "they who place the power in a multitude, understand a multitude composed of freemen, who think it for their convenience to join together, and to establish such laws and rules as they oblige themselves to observe". James Tyrrell warned his readers from the outset: "I desire always to be understood, that when I make use of the word people, I do not mean the vulgar or mixt multitude, but in the state of nature the whole body of free-men and women, especially the fathers and masters of families; . . ." By the term "free men" the Whigs always meant men who owned sufficient property to be economically independent. As one Real Whig claimed:

It is owned, that all governments are made by man, and ought to be made by those men who are owners of the territory over which the government extends. It must likewise be confessed, that the FREEHOLDERS of England are owners of the English territory, and therefore have a natural right to erect what government they please. (7)

When they discussed who should have the right to a share of political power in any government actually established, the Whig theorists limited this claim to the propertied minority. Algernon Sidney explicitly denied that he wished to set up a democratic form of government. Although he argued in favour of an elected legislative assembly, Sidney restricted the franchise to freeholders in the counties and to merchants and master craftsmen in the towns. John Locke argued that once civil government had been established then only the legislature had the right to give express consent to the actions of the executive. The members of the community surrendered their individual right to voice their consent to this sovereign legislature and could not recover their right unless the executive or the legislature betrayed their trust. Although he recognised that every man **might** have a vote in electing the representative legislature, he did not grant all men the right to claim a vote. He was quite content to accept as legitimate a political system in which the franchise was restricted to the propertied minority. (8)

No Whig propagandist had any qualms about accepting a propertied franchise. Daniel Defoe regarded the vast majority of the inhabitants of England as living in the country merely at the discretion of the freeholders. The masses were not citizens, but merely the servants of the minority who enjoyed full political rights. Robert Molesworth maintained that only men of substantial landed property should be allowed to sit in Parliament. If merchants, bankers and other monied men wished to do so, they should purchase an estate as a pledge to the electors that they would not flee the country with their wealth in the event of a serious emergency. Even when the more radical Whigs campaigned for a measure of parliamentary reform in the late seventeenth century they did not advocate an extension of the franchise. They despised the poor as ignorant and disorderly, and as entirely lacking in the ability to resist bribery or to judge who was the best candidate in a parliamentary election. It was therefore advisable to restrict the franchise, perhaps to owners of property worth 40 pounds not 40 shillings p.a. Thus, even to radical Whigs, the poor still meant the licentious mob who could never be trusted with active political rights. Indeed, it was essential to keep the lower orders in their place. (9)

It is quite clear then that for all Whigs, however radical, civil society was divided into masters and servants, the rulers and the ruled. Some Whigs were prepared to recognise merchants, traders and master craftsmen as men of property, but they certainly regarded the owners of freehold land as the most important citizens. Even for the more radical Whigs the ideal political system was a republic of freeholders who armed themselves to protect their property and to preserve their liberties. They praised the republic of Rome and the ancient Gothic constitution of Anglo-Saxon England for embodying these political virtues. Almost all the radical Whigs were admirers of James Harrington and, like him, they claimed that the distribution of political power must harmonise with the actual distribution of property in every society. "Thus it appears that land is the true centre of power, and that the balance of dominion changes with the balance of property." (10)

The one right which Locke appears to have given to all men was the right to resist a government which abused its trust. Yet, even in this case, he was careful to suggest that it was a right which could only be used in an absolute emergency to oppose manifest acts of tyranny. He did not allow subjects to claim a right to resist merely in order to protect their individual interests and he certainly did not concede them the right to choose a better form of government simply because they had grown dissatisfied with the existing government. Other Whig theorists were not prepared to go as far as Locke in legitimising revolution. They claimed that the right of resistance was restricted to the responsible men of property. This was certainly Benjamin Hoadly's position, while James Tyrrell declared:

I do by no means allow the rabble or mob of any nation to take up arms against a civil government, but only the whole community of the people of all degrees and orders, commanded by the nobility and gentry thereof. (11)

II

When examined in their social context the political theories of the first Whig propagandists emerge as aristocratic rather than as democratic. Only men of property were regarded as having a legitimate claim to the positive political rights which made them full citizens of the state. All men were entitled to enjoy the benefits of living under the rule of law, but only the property-owning minority was to be concerned in the making and the administering of that law. Whig ideology was designed to refute the claims of an absolute king, but it had no intention of appealing to the sovereignty of the people. In the immediate circumstances of the late seventeenth century the enemy was Stuart absolutism, but the Whig theorists did not forget the potential threat of anarchy. Their desire for an ordered, hierarchical society was as great as Filmer's, but they differed sharply on how this desirable end could be attained. Their objective was a limited monarchy in which men of property gave their consent to the decisions of the legislature by being represented in Parliament. Under the Hanoverians the establishment Whigs steadily retreated even from the moderate position built up by Locke, Sidney, Tyrrell and others.

This conservative modification of the Whig position was partly the consequence of actual political changes, but it owed even more to a continuous ideological retreat from the more liberal implications inherent in the political theory of Locke and his allies. Once established in power the Whigs made certain that the crown would never regain absolute authority, but they were quite prepared to preserve and even to extend royal patronage so long as this could be used for their own benefit. They were determined that the lower orders, the vast majority of the population, would be denied any positive political rights which would enable them to influence the decision-making process. Active political power was granted to a narrow oligarchy of great landowners, rich merchants and financiers, and a sprinkling of professional men. The propertied franchise was retained, the electorate in some constituencies was reduced by decisions taken by the House of Commons, and the frequency of contested elections steadily declined. Only men of property were in a position to make the law, administer the law and enforce the law.

This aristocratic form of government was provided with an intellectual defence by a host of Whig propagandists. These writers resolutely defended the rights of Parliament against the claims of the electorate and against the interests of the masses. Subjects were informed that they had no right to challenge the authority of king, lords and commons. Conservative Whig ideology now enshrined the doctrine of parliamentary sovereignty and totally rejected the concept of popular sovereignty. (12) To maintain the delicate balance of king, lords and commons, and to avoid the dangers of an unstable democracy, it was regarded as essential that the monarch and the nobility should be represented in the House of Commons by a host of placemen, pensioners and clients. (13) The voters were expressly denied the same degree of influence over their own representatives. The establishment Whigs stressed the independence of M.P.s once they were elected. They were to be left to debate and vote in secret and the electors were to have no right to impose their opinions upon their own representatives. If once the right to instruct M.P.s how to vote in Parliament were conceded to the electorate, then the balance of the constitution would be destroyed. Pure democracy, that most unstable of political systems, would replace the present admirable mixture of monarchy, aristocracy and democracy. The opinions of the ignorant, licentious mob would then prevail. (14)

The conservative Whig ideology which came to prevail among the ruling elite of the eighteenth century was not confined to a defence of oligarchical government and an aristocratic constitution. The more liberal theories of Locke were increasingly criticised by propagandists who regarded themselves as orthodox Whigs. The natural rights to life, liberty and property were still endorsed, though the emphasis was increasingly on the right to protect the unequal distribution of property. (15) Both the contract theory and the right of resistance, however, were condemned as dangerous threats to all established order. (16) At first Locke's name was quoted with approval even while his supposed admirers retreated from the moderate position he had built up. By the later eighteenth century Locke's **Second Treatise** was indicted as a major threat to the established order because it seemed to be encouraging radicals to demand the reform of the existing constitution. (17) The right of resistance was now condemned as open invitation to the mob to revolt against their masters. The principle of an equal right to liberty in the state of nature and the notion of government created by a contract were regarded as the first firm step towards anarchy. On the basis of these claims radicals were now demanding the vote for all men and might soon campaign for equal property rights. If the radical demands were generally accepted, then the mob would cut the throats of their masters and seize their property. In no time at all the country would become the scene of universal rapine and bloodshed. To avoid such a disaster the majority of mankind must be governed without their consent and, if necessary, positively against their will. (18)

This bitter attack on the claim of political equality based on equal rights in the state of nature was undoubtedly motivated by a deep-seated fear that, if this claim were conceded, it would lead to social revolution. The

alarming prospect of an attack on private property, which seemed so imminent to conservative Whigs in the late eighteenth century, provoked an ideological reaction to the whole notion of natural rights. The pre-political state of nature was rejected as historical nonsense and civil society was proclaimed to be both natural and necessary. The existing social order, based on an unequal distribution of property, was regarded as natural and divinely ordained. God had divided the world into rich and poor, masters and servants. (19) The appeal to natural rights was condemned as moral and rational nonsense resting on a non-existent contract and on pure speculation about a supposed state of nature. Abstract rights could not in fact be relied upon to preserve order and safeguard liberty. The conservative Whigs preferred to put their trust in English history, human experience and general utility. The existing constitution was praised as the most stable and most liberal system ever established. It represented directly the most important vested interests in the country — land, commerce and finance — while the whole population was virtually represented in Parliament, since all men were involved in some way with these basic economic interests. (20)

The assault on the radical interpretation of natural rights reached its height in the writings of Edmund Burke in the late eighteenth century. Burke completely rejected the notion of political rights which were universal — the same always, everywhere and for all men. He claimed that those who claimed such rights could provide no evidence for their demands. There was no proof that man had ever lived in a state of nature. Indeed, all the available historical evidence suggested that man had always existed in societies and, moreover, in societies where a minority had wielded political power. Burke refused to identify the natural with the primitive. He insisted that the development of highly complex civil societies was a natural process. To discover a man's rights it was necessary to examine the laws actually in operation in that individual's society. It was both idle and dangerous to appeal to abstract natural rights. Burke was appalled at the notion that the people could simply sit down and remake their constitution on the basis of the abstract rights of man. Such a claim would overthrow all governments, level all ranks, orders and distinctions in society, and reduce the civilised world to anarchy. Politics should be a debate about practical improvements and not about speculative perfection. Experience, utility and prescription, not rational deductions from an abstract state of nature, should determine men's political rights. Men must rest their political claims on the legal and historic rights which they enjoyed under their system of government. They only possessed those rights which they could make good in a court of law.

It is a mistake, however, to regard Burke as hostile to all natural rights. He certainly launched many bitter attacks on the radical demand for political power based on the claim to inalienable

42

natural rights, but he did recognise certain natural rights. These were very much the civil liberties claimed by Locke and allowed by conservative lawyers such as Blackstone. They included the rights to life, liberty, property, freedom of conscience and the fruits of one's labour, and they rested on an inalienable claim to equal justice under the rule of law. These rights, Burke allowed, belonged to all men regardless of nationality and irrespective of their personal merits. Although he regarded them as civil rather than as natural rights, Burke did not put them at the discretion of civil society. The right to active political power, however, was an entirely different matter. The franchise and the right to sit in a legislative assembly were not natural rights, belonging to all men as men, but were historic and legal rights to be determined as each civil society saw fit. In most societies real power was conferred on the minority who owned substantial estates. Immemorial possession and the actual terms of the British constitution legitimised the political authority of the property-owning minority. The reins of government ought to be in the hands of a natural aristocracy of substantial landowners and their actions should be judged by the men of independent means; perhaps some 400,000 smaller property owners who enjoyed the right to vote. (21)

III

It has been clearly shown that the influential, establishment Whig theorists and propagandists of the eighteenth century did not simply endorse the political ideology of John Locke. On the contrary, they steadily retreated from the moderately liberal views which he had expressed. The doctrine of natural rights, the contract theory and the right of resistance all came in for severe criticism. By the end of the eighteenth century an attack, bordering on the hysterical, was being launched by conservative Whigs against the whole concept of universal and alienable rights. The conservatives, though they carried most weight with the ruling elite, did not however have everything their own way. Throughout the eighteenth century a more radical ideology, stemming from Lockian principles but eventually going far beyond them, was developing. At first this political trend was confined to a small minority of campaigners on the fringes of the public debate on politics, but by the later eighteenth century the radicals had won a considerable hearing, at least beyond the narrow confines of Westminster. Inspired by both the American and French revolutions the radicals laid great stress on the rights of man. This, in turn, provoked the conservative backlash led by Edmund Burke.

Although they advanced far beyond Locke, the radicals of the later eighteenth century claimed to be the historical heirs of Locke's political philosophy. This was partly the consequence of interpreting natural equality, the contract theory and the right of resistance in a straightforward, literal sense, without the qualifications imposed by Locke, Sidney and other early Whig theorists. The radicals genuinely believed that these writers had campaigned for the rights of all men and that these rights included an equal right to an active voice in politics. They did not wish to see the positive right to give express consent to laws and to taxation restricted to a property-owning minority, but claimed it as a universal and inalienable right of all men. Their straightforward reading of Locke was encouraged by their acceptance of an older tradition which emphasised the liberties of Englishmen under the ancient constitution. This tradition traced the political rights of Englishmen to the Anglo-Saxon period before the Norman Conquest had placed an intolerable and unnatural yoke on the necks of free men. (22)

The appeal to Lockian natural rights and the traditional claim to English liberties were reinforced by several intellectual developments in the eighteenth century. Probably the most important of these was the long campaign for religious toleration which was based on the moral equality of man in the sight of God, on the right of man **qua** man to enjoy religious freedom. Locke and nearly all the other Whig theorists of the late seventeenth century had advocated liberty of conscience in religious matters and had campaigned for the removal of the religious disabilities facing Protestant Dissenters. The Toleration Act of 1689 was only a small step in this direction and throughout the eighteenth century a long, though unsuccessful, campaign was waged to repeal the Test and Corporation Acts. This campaign for religious liberty clearly spilled over into demands for an extension of political rights. (23) Both were regarded as universal and inalienable natural rights. It is no accident that nearly all the leading political radicals were Dissenters or were liberal Anglicans who wished to amend the 39 Articles. (24) A close scrutiny of the campaign literature of the Dissenters shows how the claim for liberty of conscience gradually changed from an argument about the superior validity of their ceremonies and modes of church organisation to a demand for the inalienable right of private judgment. The Rev. David Williams, for example, who was both a Dissenting minister and a political radical, urged his co-religionists to demand their natural right to complete intellectual liberty. Joseph Priestley regarded religious liberty as the most important natural or civil right of man, but he claimed that in order to safeguard this right all men must have a political voice. Richard Price was even more specific in allying demands for religious and political liberty. He maintained that all men must be free both to judge and to legislate for themselves in questions of religion and politics:

As no people can lawfully surrender their religious liberty by giving up their right of judging for themselves in religion or by allowing any human being to prescribe to them what faith they shall embrace or what mode of worship they shall practice, so neither can any civil societies lawfully surrender their civil liberty by giving up to any extraneous jurisdiction their power of legislating for themselves and disposing of their property. Such a cession being inconsistent with the inalienable rights of human nature. (25)

John Locke had been primarily concerned to limit the authority of the crown and to secure a representative system of government. He had not been overwhelmingly preoccupied with the pre-political state and indeed his argument did not depend on a clear demonstration that the state of nature had ever actually existed. The radicals were more concerned to justify extensive natural rights and in order to strengthen their campaign they claimed that the state of nature was an actual historical experience in which primitive man had enjoyed equal liberty. In this golden age most men had been naturally benevolent and well disposed and their reason had been unobstructed and uncorrupted. Only the ambitious designs of a few powerful men had rendered the creation of civil government a pressing necessity. Initially the compact which created civil government guaranteed the natural rights of all men, including the right to an active voice in decision-making. Unfortunately, democratic political institutions had been corrupted by an ambitious minority whose use of force and fraud had enabled them to monopolise power and to undermine the liberties of the subject. According to this radical interpretation of the state of nature and the contract theory, society was a natural blessing, but civil government was both artificial and corrupt. In order to recover his liberty and his natural rights man ought to return to his primitive past, to the political equality which he had enjoyed in the state of nature. (26)

Paradoxically, some of the radicals who appealed to the equal political rights men had enjoyed in the state of nature and who praised the virtues of primitive man also managed to adhere to a notion of unlimited future progress. (27) The concept of an historical state of nature and the conviction that civil government was the creation of an actual, express contract agreed to by all men were held in conjunction with an essentially rationalist belief in the unlimited progress of mankind. During the eighteenth century the enlightenment achieved a unique coming together of theological, philosophical and scientific assumptions which led to an optimistic vision of man's future. The radicals absorbed this confidence in unlimited progress. They became convinced that the future lay with them and that their political opponents appealed to the worst, most irrational passions in men. In their opinion human reason could master the environment and achieve a political system in which all men enjoyed equal and extensive liberties. The full potential of human reason could only be achieved if men were granted the fullest possible political liberty. Progress depended upon an equal right to self-determination. (28)

The intellectual foundations for a radical interpretation of the rights of man rested on a number of philosophical developments which occurred during the eighteenth century. Nevertheless, the case for an extension of popular rights might never have been so forcibly or so widely promoted if political changes had not brought the issue to the forefront of public consciousness. In the 1760s John Wilkes and his allies launched the first nationwide extra-parliamentary campaign. To a greater extent than any previous opposition campaign this movement appealed to the electorate and even to non-voters to defend their liberties against the encroachments of Parliament. At the same time the disputes with the American colonies raised a major political debate on the nature and extent of the political rights of man. The American demand for "no taxation without representation" encouraged reformers in Britain to press for the reform of Parliament. Moderate demands were made to reform the system of representation by eliminating rotten boroughs and transferring seats to the counties and larger towns. A reform of this kind would have reduced the influence of the crown and the nobility over the House of Commons, but it would still have restricted representation to a property-owning minority. The radicals, however, concentrated on extending the franchise so that the House of Commons would come to represent people rather than property. Their initial proposals suggested that the franchise should be extended to all taxpayers or ratepayers since they contributed to the national exchequer. By the mid-1770s the crucial step had been taken and reformers like Major Cartwright began to campaign for universal manhood suffrage. By 1780 the Society for Constitutional Information had started to disseminate propaganda advocating universal manhood suffrage, equal electoral districts, annual parliaments and the secret ballot. (29)

The campaign for parliamentary reform was based on a radical interpretation of the rights of man. Political liberty was regarded as a gift of God and as originating in the very nature of man. Hence these rights were inalienable and could be reclaimed under a political system which endeavoured to deny most men their natural heritage. The earlier radicals restricted their concept of active political rights, however, to an equal voice in electing members of the House of Commons. They still anticipated that the representatives chosen by the people would be substantial property owners and they made no attacks on the monarchy or the House of Lords. They wished the government to be more responsive to the desires of the people, but they did not expect the ordinary people to govern.

By the 1790s, however, a new impetus had been given to the campaign for the natural rights of man by the revolutionary events in France. Richard Price demanded for the whole body of the people: "The right to chuse our own governors; to cashier them for misconduct; and to frame a government for ourselves." (30) Tom Paine broke free completely from the intellectual inhibitions imposed on earlier radicals by their own admiration for the balanced constitution of King, Lords and Commons. He rejected piecemeal reform and condemned the existing political system as founded on force and sustained by fraud. In its place he wished to substitute a genuine democracy in which all unnatural distinctions between men would be abolished and in which all men would participate in the political life of the community. Both monarchy and aristocracy must be abolished and the sovereignty of the people must be proclaimed. The people should actually govern and their full natural rights should be clearly enshrined in a written constitution. No longer would a property-owning élite control the destiny of the nation. The only legitimate political system was a democratic republic under which all men enjoyed equal liberty and full political rights.

Paine's radicalism was based on the concept of the universal, inalienable rights of man. He denied that civil or political rights rested on historic or legal precedents. They were based on the natural inalienable rights enjoyed by all men by virtue of their humanity. He traced the rights of man back to the origin of human society when God made all men equal. Each succeeding generation deserved to enjoy the same natural rights no matter what political system was in force. When he entered political society each man retained certain rights from the state of nature, especially the rights of life and liberty. The one natural right which was clearly surrendered was the right of each individual to act as judge in his own cause. In going this far, Paine had not gone significantly beyond the position of Locke, though he did lay greater emphasis on the equal natural rights of all men. It was in his discussion on the origin of political society that he offered a radical interpretation of the contract theory. According to Paine the most important political contract was not the one between citizens and their ruler. Pride of place was given to the compact which established political society. This was an agreement made by every individual with every other individual. It was this agreement which established a constitution and it was this constitution which clearly marked out the limits of the government's power and expressly protected each individual's natural rights. In any legitimate civil society every man enjoyed an equal right to voice his political opinions. His natural right to protect his own interests was exchanged for a civil right which gave him an equal share in the political compact. Positive political power was shared by all men and this civil right could not be restricted by hereditary or property qualifications. All executive or legislative power was held in trust and could be revoked at will by the sovereign people. (31)

IV

By the 1790s Paine and other radicals had developed a concept of natural rights which extended far beyond Locke's civil rights of life, liberty and property to a more positive demand for every individual man to have an equal share in establishing a government which represented the sovereign will of the people. The doctrine of natural rights had clearly changed significantly during the eighteenth century, but as a means of improving the lot of the whole population it still suffered from some basic weaknesses. Close scrutiny shows that the radical version of the rights of man was still a limited vehicle for achieving substantial reform. Almost all the radicals ignored the claims of women to any share of political power. (32) Most of them also limited the positive rights of man to the possession of a vote in parliamentary elections and to the right to cashier a government for misconduct. Many of the radicals went out of their way to warn the public that they had no plans to attack private property or to overthrow the established social order. A radical meeting at Sheffield in 1794 resolved: "We are not speaking of that visionary equality of property, the practical assertion of which would desolate the world, and re-plunge it into the darkest and wildest barbarism." (33) A handbill, distributed in Liverpool and Manchester in the early 1790s, claimed:

The equality insisted on by the friends of reform is AN EQUALITY OF RIGHTS . . . The inequality derived from labour and successful enterprise, the result of superior industry and good fortune, is an equality essential to the very existence of Society, and it naturally follows, that the property so acquired, should pass from a father to his children. To render property insecure would destroy all motives to exertion, and tear up public happiness by the roots. (34)

Some radicals were, of course, conscious that political inequality and the abuse of power stemmed from the gross inequality of possessions, but very few were ready to advocate a major redistribution of wealth because they realised that this could only be achieved by a bloody revolution. William Godwin, for example, regarded the inequality of possessions as the greatest cause of social and political unrest and he hoped to see a more equal distribution of property; but he was unwilling to promote such a change even by peaceful legislation. He would go no further than urge the rich to treat their property as a trust which should be used for the welfare of the whole community, but he rejected the idea of achieving this by any form of compulsion. He hoped that men of property would eventually become so enlightened that they would voluntarily surrender their surplus wealth. (35)

Tom Paine was as concerned about the consequences of poverty as any radical of the late eighteenth century, but he still regarded private property as inviolable and refused to countenance any policy of confiscation. He was convinced that property would always be divided in grossly unequal proportions. In the hugely successful second part of the **Rights of Man**, however, he did put forward proposals for the alleviation of poverty. He proposed, in some detail, a scheme for family allowances, old age pensions, maternity benefits, and cash grants to newly married couples. In **Agrarian Justice** he suggested that property should be taxed so that enough revenue could be raised to give every man the sum of £15 when he reached the age of 21 and a pension of £10 p.a. from the age of fifty. (36) Other radicals suggested various means of improving the wages, working conditions and education of the poor, but only a handful put forward schemes for giving the poor some land of their own. James Oswald and an anonymous contributor to the radical journal, **The Cabinet**, suggested that waste and common land should be divided among the poor. William Ogilvie, in a confused, rambling work, suggested that every male over the age of 21 should be granted 40 acres of land which would come not only from waste land, but from the estates of the crown and the greatest landowners. Thomas Spence, in a much shorter and more incisive work, presented the only truly revolutionary scheme for redividing all the available land of the country equally among the entire adult male population. He was the only radical whose concept of natural rights led him to advocate a return to the state of nature when all men had enjoyed an equal claim to the fruits of the earth. (37)

All the radical proponents of the rights of man, whether they perceived these in purely political terms or were conscious of their social and economic implications, were agreed that sovereign authority lay with the whole body of the adult male population. Yet they never devised any effective means of implementing their demands. The ruling elite in Parliament would not surrender its political privileges, still less its economic advantages, without a fight. Faced with this situation most of the radicals rested their hopes on a prolonged propaganda campaign which would so educate the ruling class that reforms would be freely conceded. A few, however, were aware that such optimism was misplaced. They argued that the people must seize the initiative, establish a national convention and draw up a new constitution which would enshrine the rights of man. An attempt to do just this, in 1793-94, was promptly suppressed by the authorities. (38) When faced with such a determined and reactionary government, very few radicals were ready to contemplate a violent revolution on the French model. Thomas Spence did recognise that his scheme for a massive redistribution of property might well meet resistance from the great landowners and that force might therefore have to be used. (39) James Oswald was even more certain that substantial reforms could never be achieved by peaceful means. He, at least, was convinced that only violent revolution would secure the rights of man:

Let us not be deceived, for it is force alone that can vindicate the rights of the people. Force is the basis of right, or rather right and force are one . . . whoever shall dare to oppose the reformation of abuse, him let the besom of destruction sweep from the face of the earth; cursed by the eye that taketh pity on the enemy of the people; and may the tongue wither that shall plead in his behalf. (40)

Whilst most radicals were refusing to contemplate violent revolution, Edmund Burke and the conservative theorists were undermining the whole radical case built upon the concept of abstract natural rights. Thus, the doctrine of the rights of man was based on a claim to natural equality which could never be proved, was severely mauled by conservative thinkers, and was without a means of implementing its demands. A few radical propagandists, though committed to a programme of substantial political reform, realised that it was a mistake to base their claims on the theory of natural rights. William Godwin, for example, separated his commitment to democracy from any appeal to natural rights. He suggested instead that the criterion of reform should be the greatest good of the community. This utilitarian objective did more to impose duties on men than to confer rights. Godwin feared that the appeal to natural rights would obscure the more important obligation of achieving moral and intellectual progress. Men should concentrate on exercising their reason in order to discover and follow universal, immutable moral laws. These laws, if implemented, would achieve the greatest good for the whole community. Though he never developed a socialist philosophy, Godwin did come close to advocating a doctrine of "from each according to his ability, to each according to his needs". He certainly suggested that the fruits of the earth should be shared for the benefit of all, but he was not convinced that this could be achieved by the sovereign will of the people. Though he conceded the civil rights to life, liberty and property and though he was optimistic that reason would command attention and enforce conviction, Godwin was well aware that the voice of the people was not the voice of truth or the voice of God. Even universal agreement could not convert wrong into right. (41)

Jeremy Bentham was even more scathing in his denunciation of natural rights and even more committed to the utilitarian ethic of the greatest happiness of the greatest number. In his opinion political liberty was not a natural right, but a relative good: it was simply one possible way of achieving the greatest good. The objective must be to pass good laws. Men might be given equal political power and yet produce bad laws. Indeed, if men were allowed to possess equal natural rights this would certainly prevent the passing of any laws since subordination was based on differences in rights. If equality were truly an inalienable right, then all laws could be criticised as an infringement of someone's liberty. To live according to natural rights would be to live without society and without government. Thus, ironically, just when Paine was putting forward the most explicit defence of natural rights, the whole theory was being demolished by the conservative Burke and the radical Bentham. Among the radicals of the 1790s Paine undoubtedly enjoyed the greatest reputation and influence, but future reforms were to rest far more on the utilitarian arguments of Bentham than on the doctrine of natural rights. It was not Paine, but Bentham, though relatively unknown in the late eighteenth century, who was to inspire the philosophical radicals of the nineteenth century. His philosophy was completely at odds with the doctrine of Paine. According to Bentham, **"Natural rights** is simple nonsense: natural and imprescriptible rights, rhetorical nonsense, nonsense upon stilts." (42)

REFERENCES

* I am indebted to my colleague, Dr F. D. Dow, for her helpful criticisms of an earlier draft of this paper.

1. J. N. Figgis, **The Divine Right of Kings** (Cambridge, 1896; new ed., New York, 1965), pp. 148-60; **Patriarcha and Other Political Works of Sir Robert Filmer**, ed. Peter Laslett (Oxford, 1949); and J. G. A. Pocock, **The Ancient Constitution and the Feudal Law** (Cambridge, 1957), pp. 194-225.
2. **Patriarcha**, ed. Laslett, p. 93.
3. Gerald M. Straka, "The Final Phase of the Divine Right Theory in England, 1688-1702", **Eng. Hist. Rev.**, lxxvii (1962), pp. 638-58; and J. P. Kenyon, "The Revolution of 1688: Resistance and Contract", in **Historical Perspectives**, ed. Neil McKendrick (London, 1974), pp. 43-69.
4. C. B. Macpherson, **The Political Theory of Possessive Individualism** (Oxford, 1962), pp. 194-262. See also C. E. Vaughan, **Studies in the History of Political Philosophy** (2 vols., Manchester, 1925), i, pp. 167-68, 180-81; J. W. Gough, **John Locke's Political Philosophy** (Oxford, 1950), pp. 64-92; and John Dunn, **The Political Thought of John Locke** (Cambridge, 1969), pp. 120-47.
5. John Locke, **Second Treatise**, paras. 25-51, 124, 134, 138-40, 193, 222.
6. Ibid., paras. 63, 119, 122; and C. B. Macpherson, "The Social Bearing of Locke's Political Theory", in **Western Political Theory**, vii (1954), pp. 1-22.
7. Algernon Sidney, **Discourses Concerning Government** (3rd ed., London, 1751), p. 75; James Tyrrell, **Bibliotheca Politica** (London, 1694), advertisement; and **The Claims of the People of England, Essayed** (London, 1701), p. 106. The last is clearly by a Real Whig. For other similar definitions of "free men" see James Tyrrell, **A Brief Enquiry into the Ancient Constitution and Government of England** (London, 1695), p. 4; John Toland, **The Militia Reform'd** (London, 1698), p. 19; and (John Trenchard), **An Argument, Shewing that a Standing Army is inconsistent with a Free Government** (London, 1697), p. 4.
8. Algernon Sidney, **Discourses Concerning Government**, pp. 149, 423; and Locke's **Second Treatise**, paras. 131-34, 143, 150, 157-58, 243.
9. Daniel Defoe, **The Original Power of the Collective Body of the People of England, Examined and Asserted** (London, 1702), p. 19; Robert Molesworth, **The Principles of a Real Whig** (1711) in **The Memoirs of John Ker of Kersland** (3 vols., London, 1726), iii, p. 205; **Some Remarks upon Government** (London, 1689), pp. 24-26; and **Some Observations concerning the regulating of elections for Parliament** (London, 1689), pp. 9-12.
10. Walter Moyle, **An Essay upon the Constitution of the Roman Government** (c. 1699) in **Two English Republican Tracts**, ed. Caroline Robbins (Cambridge, 1969), p. 232. See also J. G. A. Pocock, "Machiavelli, Harrington, and English Political Ideology in the Eighteenth Century", **William and Mary Quarterly**, 3rd series, xxii (1965), pp. 549-83.
11. John Locke, **Second Treatise**, paras. 208, 225, 230; Benjamin Hoadly, **The Original and Institution of Civil Government Discuss'd** (London, 1710), p. 150; and James Tyrrell, **Bibliotheca Politica**, p. 808.
12. See my paper, "The Eighteenth-Century Debate on the Sovereignty of Parliament", **Trans. Royal Hist. Soc.**, 5th series, xxvi (1976), pp. 189-210.
13. **Free Briton**, 18 Jan. and 28 June 1733; **London Journal**, 23 June 1733, 12 and 19 Oct. 1734; William Arnall, **Opposition No Proof of Patriotism** (London, 1735), pp. 20-24; and (Henry Fielding), **A Dialogue between a Gentleman of London . . . and an Honest Alderman of the Country Party** (London, 1747). All these writers were in the service of the government.
14. **London Journal**, 5 May, 26 May, 2 June and 1 Sept. 1733; **A Letter to the Freeholders, &c. of Great Britain** (London, 1734), p. 5; **A Letter to a Member of Parliament, concerning the present State of Affairs at Home and Abroad** (London, 1740), pp. 2-6; **A Hint upon Instructions from the Electors to their Representatives in Parliament** (London, 1742), pp. 5-7; Hansard, **Parliamentary History**, xii, p. 474; and Lucy S. Sutherland, "Edmund Burke and the Relations between Members of Parliament and their Constitutents", **Studies in Burke and His Time**, x (1968), pp. 1005-21.
15. See Paschal Larkin, **Property in the Eighteenth Century** (Cork, 1930), pp. 82-136; and Daniel Boorstin, **The Mysterious Science of the Law** (Cambridge, Mass., 1941).
16. The contract theory was attacked by David Hume, "Of the Original Contract", in his **Essays Moral, Political and Literary** (London, 1741); **A Treatise on Government: Being a review of the doctrine of the original contract** (London, 1750); (Allan Ramsay) **Thoughts on the Origin and Nature of Government** (London, 1769), pp. 9-10; Jeremy Bentham, **A Fragment on Government** (London, 1776); (Soame Jenyns), **Disquisitions on Several Subjects** (London, 1782), pp. 119-51; William Paley, **The Principles of Moral and Political Philosophy** (London, 1785) in **The Works of William Paley**, ed. Edmund Paley (7 vols., London, 1825), iv, pp. 332-39; Adam Ferguson, **Principles of Moral and Political Science** (2 vols., Edinburgh, 1792), ii, pp. 218-27; Samuel Horsley, **A Sermon preached before the Lords . . . on January 30, 1793** (London, 1793), pp. 1-3; and George Horne, **Some Considerations on Mr Locke's scheme of deriving Government from an original Compact** in **The Scholar Armed against the Errors of the Time** (2 vols., 2nd ed., London, 1800), ii, pp. 289-96. The dangers inherent in the right of resistance were stressed by Lord Hervey, **Ancient and Modern Liberty stated and compared** (London, 1734), pp. 2-4; Josiah Tucker, **Four Letters on Important National Subjects** (2nd ed., London, 1783), pp. 96-97, 110-13; William Blackstone, **Commentaries on the Laws of England** (4 vols., 7th ed., Oxford, 1775), i, pp. 161-62; **An Essay on Constitutional Liberty** (London, 1780), p. 85 n; and Hansard, **Parliamentary History**, xxxiii, p. 467.
17. John Dunn, "The politics of John Locke in England and America in the eighteenth century", in **John Locke: Problems and Perspectives**, ed. John W. Yolton (Cambridge, 1969), pp. 45-80; and H. V. S. Ogden, "The State of Nature and the Decline of Lockian Political Theory in England, 1760-1800", **American Hist. Rev.**, xlvi (1940), pp. 21-44.
18. (Allan Ramsay), **Thoughts on the Origin and Nature of Government**, pp. 8-9; (Soame Jenyns), **Disquisitions on Several Subjects**, p. 137; **A Letter on Parliamentary Representation** (2nd ed., London, 1783), pp. 34-35; Robert Nares, **Principles of Government deduced from Reason, supported by English Experience and opposed to French Errors** (London, 1792), pp. 4-5, 12, 41-42; **Thoughts on the New and Old Principles of Political Obedience** (London, 1793), p. 32; and (Arthur Young), **The Example of France, a Warning to Britain** (London, 1793), pp. 41-43.
19. Hansard, **Parliamentary History**, xvi, p. 718; George Pitt, **Letters to a Young Nobleman** (London, 1784), pp. 226-27; **Thoughts on the New and Old Principles of Political Obedience** (London, 1793), p. 16; William Paley, **Reasons for Contentment, addressed to the Labouring Poor of the British Public** (London, 1793); Richard Watson, "Sermon V" (c. 1793) in his **Miscellaneous Tracts** (2 vols., London, 1815), i, pp. 448-93; and "Of the Necessity of Distinction of Ranks in Society", in **The Scots Magazine**, lvi (1794), pp. 241-42.
20. William Paley, **The Principles of Moral and Political Philosophy**, in **Works**, iv, pp. 379, 392-93; Josiah Tucker, **Four Letters on Important National Subjects**, pp. 68-71, 98; **Civil Liberty asserted, and the Rights of the Subject defended, against the Anarchical Principles of the Reverend Dr Price** (London, 1776), pp. 7-8; Joseph Wimpey, **Letters occasioned by Three Dialogues concerning Liberty** (London, 1777), p. 50; **Free Parliaments: Or, A Vindication of the Parliamentary Constitution of England** (London, 1783), pp. 66-67; (Francis Basset), **Thoughts on Equal Representation** (London, 1783), p. 21; John Andrews, **An Essay on Republican Principles** (London, 1783), pp. 45-46; **An Essay on the Polity of England** (London, 1785), pp. 239-40; Robert Nares, **Principles of Government deduced from Reason**, pp. viii-ix; and Hansard, **Parliamentary History**, xxiii, p. 831 and xxx, p. 900.
21. For Burke's views on natural rights, see C. E. Vaughan, **Studies in the History of Political Philosophy**, ii, pp. 1-63; Russell Kirk, "Burke and Natural Rights", **Review of Politics**, xiii (1951), pp. 441-56; Charles Parkin, **The Moral Basis of Burke's Political Thought** (Cambridge, 1956), pp. 6-29 and 54-82; Peter J. Stanlis, **Edmund Burke and the**

Natural Law (Ann Arbor, 1958), pp. 53-78, 125-36; R. R. Fennessy, **Burke, Paine and the Rights of Man** (The Hague, 1963), pp. 108-59; B. T. Wilkins, **The Problem of Burke's Political Philosophy** (Oxford, 1967), pp. 152-246; and Frank O'Gorman, **Edmund Burke: His Political Philosophy** (London, 1973), pp. 107-41.

22. Christopher Hill, "The Norman Yoke", in Christopher Hill, **Puritanism and Revolution** (London, 1958), pp. 50-122.

23. Caroline Robbins, **The Eighteenth Century Commonwealthman** (Cambridge, Mass., 1959), pp. 221-70; Anthony Lincoln, **Some Political and Social Ideas of English Dissent 1763-1800** (Cambridge, 1938); Richard B. Barlow, **Citizenship and Conscience** (Philadelphia, 1962); and Russel E. Richey, "The Origins of British Radicalism: The Changing Rationale for Dissent", **Eighteenth-Century Studies**, vii (1973-74), pp. 179-92.

24. Political radicals with a Dissenting background include, Richard Price, Joseph Priestley, Thomas Paine, John Cartwright, William Godwin, James Burgh, John Disney, Mary Wollstonecraft, Capel Lofft, David Williams, Andrew Kippis, Thomas Brand Hollis, Joseph Towers, Thomas Walker, George Dyer and William Enfield. Liberal Anglicans who advocated political reform include John Wilkes, Christopher Wyvill, John Jebb, John Horne Tooke and Granville Sharp.

25. David Williams, **A Letter to the Body of Protestant Dissenters and to Protestant Dissenting Ministers of all Denominations** (London, 1777), pp. 23-24; Joseph Priestley, **An Essay on the First Principles of Government** (London, 1768), pp. 54-55; and Richard Price, **Observations on the Nature of Civil Liberty** (London, 1776), pp. 21-22. On the same theme, see Joseph Fownes, **Enquiry into the Principles of Toleration** (1772; 3rd ed., London, 1790), p. 17; Andrew Kippis, **A Vindication of the Protestant Dissenting Ministers** (London, 1772), pp. 25-26; Joshua Toulmin, **Two Letters on the Late Application to Parliament by the Protestant Dissenting Ministers** (London, 1774), pp. 8-10; **Half an Hour's Conversation . . . on the Test Laws** (London, 1789), p. 2; **An Address to the Opposers of the Repeal** (London, 1790), p. 16; and George Dyer, **An Inquiry into the Nature of Subscription to the Thirty-Nine Articles** (1789; 3rd ed., London, 1792), pp. 60-61.

26. Richard Price, **A Review of the Principal Questions and Difficulties in Morals** (1758; 2nd ed., London, 1769), p. 345; idem, **Observations on Reversionary Payments** (London, 1771), p. 275; Mary Wollstonecraft, **A Vindication of the Rights of Man** (London, 1790), pp. 11-12, 40-41, 60-61; idem, **An Historical and Moral View of the Origin and Progress of the French Revolution** (London, 1794), p. 521; and John Thelwall, **The Rights of Nature against the Usurpation of Establishments** (London, 1796).

27. This link between primitivism and progress has been explored in detail by Lois Whitney, **Primitivism and the Idea of Progress in English Popular Literature of the Eighteenth Century** (Baltimore, 1934).

28. Joseph Priestley, **An Essay on the First Principles of Government**, pp. 3-8, 127-91; Richard Price, **The Evidence for a Future Period of Improvement in the State of Mankind** (London, 1787); Catherine Macaulay, **Letters on Education** (London, 1790), p. 10; William Enfield, **A Sermon on the Centennial Commemoration of the Revolution** (London, 1788), p. 17; James Mackintosh, **Vindiciae Gallicae** (Dublin, 1791), pp. 48-49; Mary Wollstonecraft, **An Historical and Moral View of the Origin and Progress of the French Revolution**, pp. 20-21, 72, 219; and William Godwin, **Enquiry concerning Political Justice** (2 vols., 1793; 3rd ed., London, 1798), i, pp. 69, 92-93, 109-19.

29. John Cartwright, **Take Your Choice!** (London, 1776), p.

19; idem, **The People's Barrier against Undue Influence and Corruption** (London, 1780), pp. 28-56; idem, **Give us our Rights!** (London, 1782), p. 5; James Burgh, **Political Disquisitions** (3 vols., London, 1774), i, pp. 36-38; (Capel Lofft), **An Argument on the Nature of Party and Faction** (London, 1780), pp. 43-46; **Report of the Subcommittee of Westminster, 27 May 1780** (London, 1780), pp. 3-4; (David Williams), **Letters on Political Liberty** (London, 1782), pp. 79-80; Hansard, **Parliamentary History**, xviii, pp. 1287-97. For the Society for Constitutional Information, see E. C. Black, **The Association** (Cambridge, Mass., 1963), pp. 174-212.

30. Richard Price, **A Discourse on the Love of Our Country** (London, 1790), pp. 28-29.

31. Thomas Paine, **The Rights of Man: Part One** (London, 1791). See also William Christian, "The Moral Economy of Tom Paine", **Journal of the History of Ideas**, xxxiv (1973), pp. 367-80; and E. P. Thompson, **The Making of the English Working Class** (London, 1963), pp. 93-110.

32. The idea of votes for women was explicitly rejected by John Cartwright, **Take Your Choice!** p. 46; John Longley, **An Essay towards forming a more complete Representation of the Commons** (London, 1795), pp. 4-9; and Charles James Fox, in Hansard, **Parliamentary History**, xxxiii, p. 726. Even Mary Wollstonecraft, in **Vindication of the Rights of Women** (London, 1792), laid no claim to the vote. The most favourable treatment of the question is in **The Cabinet** (3 vols., Norwich, 1795), i, pp. 178-84 and ii, pp. 42-48.

33. Hansard, **Parliamentary History**, xxxi, p. 738.

34. Thomas Walker, **A Review of Some of the Political Events which have occurred in Manchester during the Last Five Years** (London, 1794), pp. 46n-47n.

35. William Godwin, **Enquiry concerning Political Justice**, i, pp. 15-16, 134; and ii, pp. 93, 109, 423-69.

36. Thomas Paine, **Agrarian Justice** (1796) in **The Complete Works of Thomas Paine**, ed. Philip S. Foner (2 vols., New York, 1945), i, pp. 611-19.

37. James Oswald, **Review of the Constitution of Great Britain** (3rd ed., London, 1783), p. 59; **The Cabinet**, ii, pp. 215-19; and iii, pp. 281-95; (William Ogilvie), **An Essay on the Right of Property in Land** (London, 1782), pp. 74, 87; and Thomas Spence, **The Real Rights of Man** (London, 1793).

38. The calling of a national convention was suggested by James Burgh, **Political Disquisitions**, iii, pp. 428-34; Joseph Gerrald, **A Convention the Only Means of Saving Us from Ruin** (London, 1793); and Thomas Paine, **Letter Addressed to the Addressers on the Late Proclamation** (London, 1792), in **The Complete Works of Thomas Paine**, ed. Philip S. Foner, ii, pp. 499-500. The collapse of the National Convention of 1793-94 is described in G. S. Veitch, **The Genesis of Parliamentary Reform** (London, 1913), pp. 275-98.

39. Thomas Spence, **The End of Oppression** (London, 1795), in **Trial of Thomas Spence**, ed. Arthur W. Waters (Leamington Spa, 1917), pp. 112-16. See also T. M. Parssinen, "Thomas Spence and the Origins of English Land Nationalisation", **Journal of the History of Ideas**, xxxiv (1973), pp. 135-41.

40. James Oswald, **Review of the Constitution of Great Britain**, pp. 52-53.

41. William Godwin, **Enquiry concerning Political Justice**, i, pp. 144-47, 158-69, 186-93, 215-16, 256-57, 268-84; and ii, pp. 114-20.

42. **The Works of Jeremy Bentham**, ed. John Bowring (10 vols., Edinburgh, 1843), ii, p. 501. See also, ibid, ii, pp. 496-534. For evidence that Bentham was advocating radical reforms in the 1790s, see Mary P. Mack, **Jeremy Bentham** (London, 1962), pp. 409-66.

THE COMPLICITY OF CLIMATE WITH THE AMERICAN CAUSE

IAN H ADAMS

The American War of Independence and its attendant success has not lacked adequate analysis. Library shelves testify to the variety and detail of the countless studies in this subject. Yet one all-embracing element, the role of climate, has passed virtually without remark. The failure of the British, wrote Edward Curtis, was "due partly to inept generalship, partly to natural difficulties, and partly to mal-administration".(1) Of the natural difficulties he identified "bad weather" as one of the most important factors in the problem of transporta-tion. In this paper I want to address myself to the specific elements of climate and its handmaiden, weather, upon the progress of the war. My main object is to show that climate and weather were not just incidental nuisances to be borne with fortitude, but rather played a preordained role as a weapon, albeit unidentified, in the hands of the Americans. This linkage is not too far-fetched, for climate and weapons of war share the same physics of the kinetic energy of gas molecules — that is, the energy of motion. The atmosphere is a massive engine involved in the transfer of energy over the earth's surface. For the restricted area of importance during the American War — the British Isles, the North Atlantic route, the seaboard of North America from the St Lawrence to Florida — quite specific characteristics can be isolated (fig. 1). These are:

1. The Westerly Cyclonic Zone
2. Arctic ice and icebergs
3. Maritime tropical air masses
4. The Gulf Stream
5. Continentality

1. The Westerly Cyclonic Zone

Between the latitudes of 35 deg. and 60 deg. N. is the belt of prevailing westerly wind (the Westerlies). Moving from the subtropical high-pressure centres towards the subpolar lows, these surface winds can reach violent proportions, with frequent cloudy days and extensive precipitation. In many ways the cyclones of the North Atlantic were one of Washington's secret weapons. Before the British army could fire a shot at the rebels a journey of nearly 3,000 nautical miles had to be accomplished in the face of this cyclonic force.

Figure 1
The climatic elements significant in the American War.

Gales on the western seaboard of the British Isles today occur on 35 to 40 days in the year. For this purpose a gale may be regarded as any wind exceeding 45 miles an hour (force 8 or over on the Beaufort scale). The average number of gales occurring each month in the St George's Channel area is: Jan. 5.2, Feb. 4.7, Mar. 3.6, Apr. 2.0, May 0.9, June 0.7, July 0.7, Aug. 1.7, Sep. 2.1, Oct. 4.4, Nov. 5.2, Dec. 6.3. Average for the year 37.5.

However, the pattern of cyclones in the 1770s and 1780s was very different from that of today. The Atlantic summer storms were coming in over Ireland and Scotland, and even as far south as the Mediterranean, rather than tracking eastwards in the latitude of Iceland and northern Norway as they do today. This meant that any voyage across the Atlantic had a much higher probability of facing a force 8 gale, a circumstance which, in terms of late 18th century nautical technology, was fraught with anxiety and danger. Vessels could be dismasted and spring leaks, and the live animals penned on deck could be drowned or washed overboard. The shipping of added water spoiled cargoes and ships' stores, and called for extra pumping, which exhausted the men and could increase the chance of pumps being choked. Contact between ships was lost, leaving the separated vessels at the mercy of prey to privateers. Precise timetabling for disembarkation and other military activity was virtually impossible.

As an example I will examine in some detail the convoy carrying the Highland Brigade to reinforce Howe for the Manhattan campaign of the summer of 1776. (2) The story of this convoy starts in Glasgow on 13th April of that year, when 1,000 men of the 42nd Regiment (the Black Watch) marched the 32 miles to Greenock for embarkation. Even at this micro-scale, weather made an impact. Throughout the march they were buffeted by a vigorous cyclone which made the Firth of Clyde too rough for embarkation until 24 hours after they arrived. Indeed the winds were to remain in the south-westerly quarter, of sufficient strength to delay the convoy's start until 29th April.

On that day 32 transports bearing some 3,000 men of the 42nd and 71st Regiments set sail under the watchful eye of H.M.S. **Flora**, a fifth-rater of 32 guns (fig. 2). On the fourth day out, as the convoy under sail at a smart five knots turned out into the Atlantic south of Wexford, a frontal system approached, and the soldiers had their final glimpse of the British Isles as the ragged horizon vanished in a greying noon sky. For two days, while the gale raged, the convoy disintegrated from 32 down to 15 ships, then eight, until finally only five remained together to cross the Atlantic. By 10th May, in contrast, the decimated convoy was making but a single knot in a calm sea. As a result of this dispersal, the scattered vessels fell prey to the privateers infesting the American coast. The **Oxford** (42nd) and **Crawford** (71st) were captured by Captain Nicholas Biddle of the **Andrew Doria** some way out in the Atlantic on 29th May (later Biddle, a former midshipman in the Royal Navy, was to boast he captured them with a speaking trumpet). As a precaution, most of the troops were transferred to the **Oxford**, the masters, navigators, baggage and arms were taken on board the privateer and the **Crawford** was left with five subalterns, two officers' ladies and four privates. The three ships sailed in a small convoy towards Nantucket, but ran into H.M.S. **Mercury** shepherding another small convoy. The warship gave chase to the privateer, which left her captives unguarded, whereupon the **Crawford's** carpenter organised a party which overpowered the prize crew. On 12th June the **Crawford** was picked up by H.M.S. **Cerberus** and

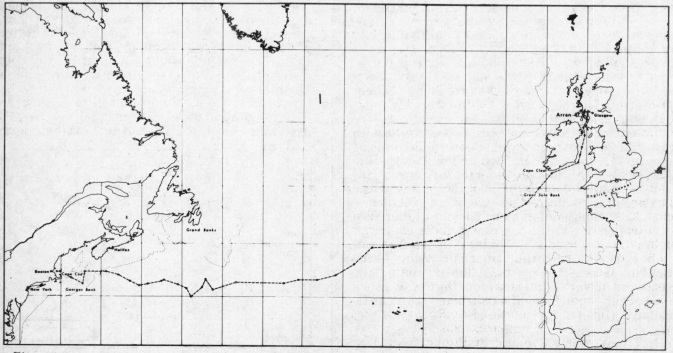

Figure 2
Chart of the Highland Brigade Convoy, 1776.

sent to the safety of Sandy Hook in convoy with an armed sloop, but south of Long Island they ran into the yankee privateer sloop **Schuyler,** which captured both vessels. And again the officers and their ladies found themselves the guests of a first lieutenant of the 19th Continental Army. As if this was not enough, the **Oxford** too was recaptured by James Barron in Chesapeake Bay, and the mixed bag of 217 Highlanders was landed at Jamestown. (3)

The first vessel to reach American shores was the **Ann**, carrying the Light Infantry Company of the 1st Battalion 71st Regiment under their officer, Captain Hamilton Maxwell, brother of the Duchess of Hamilton. Whilst near the coast they met the innocent-looking Jamaicaman **Lady Juliana**, London-bound but, so the master said, looking first into Boston because he had heard sugar was fetching a better price there. The master was invited to the **Ann** for breakfast and, claiming knowledge of the New England coast, offered to pilot the troopship into Boston. His audacious plan fell through when two over-anxious privateers appeared and the **Ann** hauled off. However, within 24 hours she had been taken by three of Washington's schooners.

Two transports of the 2nd Battalion, 71st Regiment — the **Annabella**, with Lieutenant-Colonel Archibald Campbell, and the **George**, with Major Menzies — arrived off Boston on 16th June. At first light they were engaged by five privateers in an action that lasted for eight hours. Then they made an unsuspecting dash to the safety of Boston harbour, only to find themselves again in action under the guns of Nantasket Point, aground and surrounded by rebel vessels. They fought with savage ferocity until Major Menzies was killed and all ammunition exhausted and only then, at 11 p.m., did they strike their colours. Next morning triumphant Bostonians lined King Street to watch the captives make their way from Long Wharf to General Ward's. Their jubilation rose to new heights with the capture of a further instalment of the 71st, when next day the transport **Lord Howe** sailed straight into Boston harbour and gave up without a fight.

Another transport was lost with all hands. On 23rd June 1776, George Washington observed: "If we get a few more of the 32 transports in addition to those we have already, the Highland Corps will be pretty well broken and disconcerted." (4) For the British the picture was grim, as a report of 9th July indicates: "The Highland Corps have been unlucky in the voyage out. Six of their ships taken that we know of, and but six companies of the 42nd and Frazer's arrived with us. The rebel privateers are indefatigable, and I fear will pick up a number of them." ((5)

The results of this disastrous convoy were fourfold. First, the direct loss of men and materials was highly damaging to the British. Some 800 men were killed or made prisoner in the seven vessels lost from the Highland Brigade convoy. This figure compares closely with the British losses at the battle of Bunker Hill, the bloodiest single engagement of the entire Revolutionary War, where 1,054 regular rank and

file and 27 officers were killed. Second, the delays that ensued resulted in the military campaign starting late and closing prematurely with the onset of winter. This gave rise to the view that "had they conducted themselves with more resolution, the British might have won the war in the first year of fighting" (that is 1776) — a view that was to take hold later when the problems of logistics and weather had been forgotten. Third, the Americans gained in confidence as a result of some easy captures which proved that British power was not omnipotent. And last, it encouraged privateers by offering struggling transports as easy pickings.

I would suggest that the cyclone of 3rd-4th April 1776 played as significant a role in the war as Benedict Arnold's superb delaying tactics on Lake Champlain in the October of that year. It has been claimed that delay in the British campaign on that occasion led to Burgoyne's surrender at Saratoga, which led in turn to France again taking up arms against the British; similarly, the delay in the arrival of the Highland Brigade led to the inconclusive results of the Manhattan campaign.

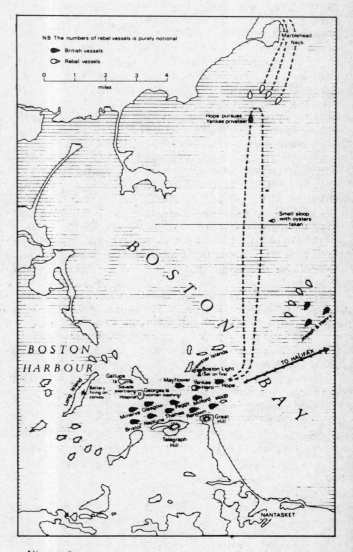

Figure 3
The remnants of the Highland Brigade Convoy gathering off Boston, June 1776.

2. Arctic Ice and Icebergs

The surface drifts and currents of the world's oceans play an important part in climatic regimes. In the western parts of the North Atlantic the Labrador Current brings cold water southwards and presents two hazards to the mariner. The first was the problem of icebergs brought southwards in the cold waters of the Greenland and Labrador currents, which combine to form a subpolar gyre off the coasts of Newfoundland, Nova Scotia and New England. The deep penetration of ice was especially marked from the 1770s onwards, for the northern hemisphere was entering the period known as the Little Ice Age. At that time, the Gulf Stream took a more southerly course across the Atlantic than it does now. (6) Arctic ice spread southwards, almost encircling Iceland, and remained on its coasts for more than nine weeks a year (compared to about ten days in the period 1920-50). It was as if nature provided **chevaux de frise** to force British vessels into a southerly track along 40 deg. N. latitude and thus become prey to American privateers. There was also the hazard of fog. The case I present here is that fog severely restricted communications, especially with the safe British headquarters at Halifax, so that a considerable amount of voyaging was wasted, often in sailing to the wrong destination. For example, the remnants of the Highland Brigade convoy gathered out of gunshot off Nantasket, three miles south-east of Boston (fig. 3). After blowing up Boston Light the fleet set sail northwards, hoping to join Howe at Halifax, but fog immediately enveloped them. For eight days they inched their way, occasionally colliding, and only catching fleeting glimpses of other vessels, whether friend or foe, until they reached Halifax, only to find they had unknowingly passed General Howe sailing south to New York. The convoy returned southwards, making only poor progress in the sultry weather — 31, 37, 50, 59, 39, 47, 45, 54, 50, 49, 48, 43 nautical miles a day — and a voyage which should have been completed in six weeks extended to nearly 16. Although casualties were few, the prolongation of any voyage was harmful and even if the men did not succumb to scurvy and other diseases, bad weather and sickness combined to produce enfeebled troops. (7)

3. Maritime Tropical Air Masses

The weather system on the east coast of North America, especially southwards from New York, was particularly savage and hostile to the sailing ship. This coastline is one of the six regions in the world prone to tropical cyclones (that is, hurricanes). These are the most powerful and destructive types of cyclonic storms. A terrible hurricane that struck Barbados in September 1780 tore stone buildings from their foundations, carried heavy cannon more than 30 metres and killed at least 6,000 people.

These storms develop over oceans in latitudes of 8 deg. to 15 deg. N. where there is a high sea-surface temperature. Warming of air at low levels creates instability and initiates the formation of a storm which moves westward and then poleward through the trade wind belt, often penetrating well into the belt of westerly winds (fig. 4c). Occurrence is mainly from May to November, with maximum frequency in late summer or early autumn. For this reason convoys south were restricted to November to March, but even then very strong gales, in the form of frequent middle-latitude cyclones, sweep over these seas (fig. 4a and 4b). Strong winds from the west and south forced the ships well off shore into the Gulf Stream. Passage times were extremely long for a relatively short distance. On 6th November 1778 an expedition under Lieutenant-Colonel Campbell embarked at New York for Savannah. The transports, delayed by bad weather, did not clear Sandy Hook until the 27th and arrived in the Savannah River on 24th December after a stormy passage. (8) In all, 28 days to cover 630 nautical miles.

The passage of the Charleston Expedition a year later repeated this experience and is worth looking at in more detail (fig. 5). In all, 100 square-rigged vessels plus luggers and schooners set out in stormy weather on 26th December 1779. On the third day the severity of the gale led to the dismasting of the **Anna** with 250 people on board. A line was put on board but snapped in a subsequent storm and the **Anna** drifted westwards for eight weeks until she was beached near St Ives in Cornwall. The rest of the fleet was scattered and each vessel was left to its own devices to reach its destination. The log of the transport **Margery** with the Grenadier Company of the 42nd Regiment on board shows that during the voyage barely three out of 36 days passed without reefing down, lashing the helm or laying to because of weather conditions. On 9th January 1780 the log reads: "The ship takes in some water at larboard

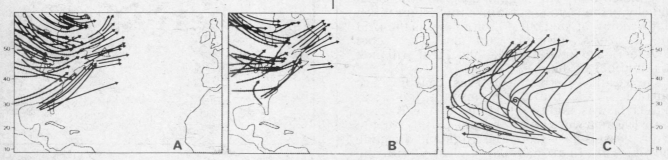

Figure 4
Principal storm tracks off eastern North America. Each track represents an average of four or five storms per year (after J. W. Watson).

(a) winter. (b) summer.
(c) Tracks of some typical hurricanes occurring during August (after U.S. Navy Oceanographic Office).

portholes which, being pumped out, runs down between decks and to the hold and wets our baggage. The gale, which has now lasted a week, has stretched our rigging and loosened the supporters of the flat boat but, except for living uncomfortably, has caused no damage, being a fine stout ship.''(9)

A similar tale was recorded by Captain Johann Hinrichs of the Hessian Jaeger Corps. "January 3rd. Left to the fury of wave and wind, we drifted southward with helm lashed and before one sail, the wind being westerly. Of the entire fleet we saw this morning only one man-of-war and 17 sail. It may be safely said that the most strenuous campaign cannot be as trying as such a voyage. . . .'' And two days later: "This morning we sailed for a few hours, but then the storm began to rage again so violently that toward noon it was necessary to lash the helm again and furl all sails except one. The entire day and night one could see and hear nothing but the flags and shots of ships in distress. However, no one could go to their assistance. At noon our ship, too, sprung a leak below the cabin, near the helm. But it was easily stopped since one could get to it without trouble.'' A few days later conditions had improved, but, "this morning we had a head wind (SW) and every inch we moved we went farther from our destination''.(10)

Ships began to founder under this constant battering. The store ship **Judith** sprung a leak and was abandoned on 14th January. A similar fate met the **George** and the **Swan**, and other vessels were reported missing. When the convoy ultimately made landfall at Tybee Island they were exhausted, without horses and much of their stores, and in little mood to fight. It was not until 12th March that the British began to invest Charleston.

To what extent was the rate of disablement through dismasting or the rate of loss of British transports in the North American theatre of war a normal nautical hazard of the age? Furthermore, were the voyage times similar to those faced in other seas? To answer these questions a comparative sample is taken from some of the convoys in the Mediterranean during the period of the French Revolutionary Wars, from May 1800 to the invasion of Egypt in March 1801 (fig. 6).(11)

To the first question the answer must be qualified by the paucity of the data.(12)

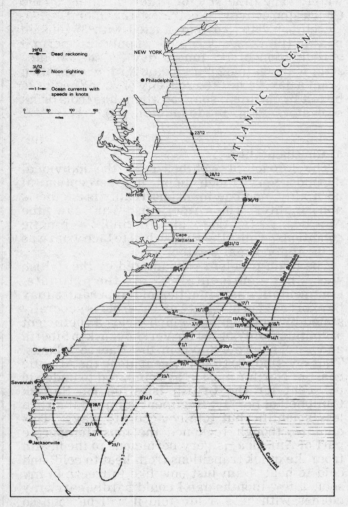

Figure 5
The erratic progress of the Charleston invasion convoy, December 1779-January 1780.

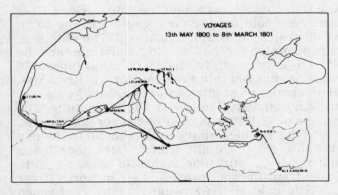

Figure 6
Comparative voyages in the Mediterranean, May 1800 to March 1801.

	North America	Mediterranean
Total loss (by weather)	4	—
Dismasting	7	3
	11	3

However, even taking into account the necessarily tentative nature of this comparison, there was sufficient ground to state that the American theatre of war posed a greater natural hazard than the Mediterranean was to be 20 years later. Foundering, stranding and dismasting were continual threats.

For the second question, a comparison is made of the average daily distances covered by the convoys. Although there are large differences between convoys, those in North American waters made only half the distances attained in the Mediterranean.

		Nautical miles	
North America (1776-80)	Days	Total	Av/day
Greenock-Boston	43	2745	63.8
Greenock-New York	150	2945	19.6
Boston-Halifax	8	383	47.9
Halifax-New York	30	580	19.3
New York-Charleston (1778)	28	630	22.5
New York-Charleston (1779-80)	36	630	17.5
			190.6
			av. 31.8
Mediterranean (1800-1)			
England-Gibraltar	24	1053	43.9
Gibraltar-Port Mahon	11	540	49.1
Port Mahon-Leghorn	8	324	40.5
Port Mahon-Malta	10	779	77.9
Malta-Rhodes	8	c.750	93.8
			305.2
			av. 61.0

(Distances from Reed's **Tables of Distances**)

4. The Gulf Stream

If the cyclonic activity of the tropical air masses was not enough to contend with, the Gulf Stream was a powerful ally to the Americans, pushing the British north and westwards whence they came. Although the nature of the Gulf Stream was first recorded off Florida in 1513, no chart of its location and magnitude was published until 1785.(13) The problems and opportunities of the Gulf Stream had long been appreciated by the New England whalers, but the masters of British vessels paid scant attention to it, even when their ships were sailing backwards. Benjamin Franklin, in his role as a Deputy Postmaster-General for the American colonies, tried to enlighten the packet captains about this ocean current, but to little avail.

To gain an appreciation of the somewhat mystifying nature of the Gulf Stream, one can return to the log of the **Margery**: "1st January 1780. From the noon observation it would appear that we have been retarded by a strong current — I suppose by the Gulf Stream." Again, on 11th January: "Good observation — looks as if we had got again in the influence of the Gulf Stream." By the 20th they really did not know where they were: "We have gone more to the southward than the whole distance on the logboard, by which it would appear that we are not only without the Gulf Stream but in a current that setts to the southward." (Presumably the ship was in one of the Gulf Stream's countercurrents, which can reach two knots.) Then, on the 26th: "Clear observation at noon, latitude 30.21, by which there is a difference of 35 miles more to the northward than by dead reckoning, which can only be accounted for by the influence of a strong current from the southward." Next day, the 27th, confirmed this: "Latitude 30.70 which proves that certainty of a current from the southward, but not so strong as yesterday."

The Gulf Stream played an important role in delaying passages to the South Carolinian theatre of war. This is clearly evidenced by the unpreparedness of the military transports. For example, the consumption of water on the packed transports could become critical if the voyage was prolonged, especially in semi-tropical waters. The timetable of water rationing on the Charleston convoy illustrates this point. 1779, December 29th: voyage started with 37 tons on board (that is, 24 days' supply at normal consumption of 1½ tons a day). 1780, January 20th: water ration 2 pints a day. 23rd: water ration 1 pint a day. 24th: "the scarcity of water begins to be felt by the men, some of whom like fools drink seawater." 30th: made landfall. (14)

5. Continentality

The impact of weather upon the individual depends very much upon his perception of normality, and one man's normality is another's abnormality. The American War saw the Americans fighting in "normal" climatic conditions, whilst the British had to face what was to them abnormal weather.

The main problem encountered by the British was the continentality of the climate. Continentality as a function of temperature may be expressed in a variety of ways, but is generally stated by a percentage which yields a coefficient of continentality of 100 for Verkhoyansk in Siberia and zero for Thorshavn in the Faeroe Islands. Thus one finds 30 to 40 per cent along the Atlantic coast of North America as compared to under 10 per cent for the British Isles. Major Patrick Campbell of the 71st Regiment summed it up in a less scientific but totally accurate way: "This climate, though reckoned the most temperate part of America, is very pernicious to the health from the quick transitions from heat to cold, and cold to heat. I am just now like to freeze in my seat, a few months ago I could hardly carry my clothes with heat. I am told it will be soon so again." (15)

The intense cold of the American winter was a condition unknown to most of the British soldiery. The 42nd Regiment took part in the invasion of Newport, Rhode Island, in December 1776, and Captain Peebles wrote on the 15th: "Hard frost and very cold for the poor soldiers in the barn, several sick, an hospital formed." The kilt, alas, was no match for the New England winter and the 42nd Regiment capitulated on 29th December 1776 when it changed into breeches for the first time. Both armies went into winter quarters, as was the military custom if not necessity of the time. The winter of 1779-80 was the most severe of the war and John Peebles' diary attests to the frequency of gales, snow, ice and frost: "December 3rd, a hard gale . . .6th, nine inches of snow . . .15th, snow from the southwest and ice in North River . . .17th, cold and raw wind . . .19th, cold sharp northwest wind and hard frost . . .20th, hard frost and strong wind at northwest . . .21st, this cold wind continues, more troops embarking but it is very tedious on account of the cold strong wind . . .22nd, very hard frost and much ice about the ships." On 26th December Sir Henry Clinton wrote to Admiral Arbuthnot: "The delay of some of the transports coming down was occasioned by the necessity of new arrangements, in consequence of seven ships being drove from their anchors by the ice and rendered unfit for sea."(16)

Many health problems arose from the extremes of climate. Troops were debilitated by poor food, and especially the accelerated decay of food in the hot humid weather of the summer months. Entries in John Peebles' diary tell a dismal story in 1779: "September 29th. The Queen's Rangers to Richmond to relieve the 37th who go to Newtown, on account of the very sickly state of that regiment . . . 30th. Wind northerly. Hope this weather will be of service to the sick and check the progress of the disease, which is still seizing on new subjects and but very few of the old recovering. The 37th Regiment, I am told, have not 30 men fit for duty" (on this day, of the 90 sergeants and men in Peebles' own company, the 42nd Grenadiers, 57 were sick)". . . October 1st. The number of sick still increases. . . . 4th. The number of sick does not yet diminish here in camp and, what is somewhat strange, those of the 44th increased at sea. . . . 9th. Two sergeants and 59 sick . . . 10th. If Mr Washington should come there" (Stoney Point) "in force, I'm afraid we shall have some difficulty in relieving that useless post, in the present sickly situation of the army".

Collapse through heat exhaustion of troops carrying heavy packs was a common occurrence. All in all, the British soldier had to face a climatic environment far more extreme than any encountered in his homeland. On the march from Elk Creek to Philadelphia on 6th September 1777, many of the troops complained of "pains and swelling in their knees and ankles". On the 11th, at the Battle of Brandywine, the Americans were saved because the British were "much fatigued with a long march and a rapid pursuit. Notwithstanding these disadvantages we briskly attack'd the enemy and after a close fire for some minutes charged them again and drove them into the woods in the greatest confusion, when the wearyness of the troops and the night coming on prevented any further pursuit and saved thousands of the rebels."(17) An even more debilitating situation arose on the march from Philadelphia during an engagement on 28th June 1778 when Clinton's force was intercepted at Monmouth Courthouse. "The 3rd Brigade came up after a very quick and fatiguing march of six or seven miles, and leaving their packs at the edge of the wood dash'd thro' that wood and a deep swamp and came upon a scatter'd body of the rebels whom the left of the 42nd drove before them. . . . These several manoeuvres and rapid marches with the excessive heat had so fatigued and knock'd up the men that a number of the several corps died upon the spot; while the 3rd Brigade halted a little while to breathe, the 1st Light Infantry and Queen's Rangers came up on their right and finding themselves likewise much fatigued and having drop'd a good many men, it was thought improper to advance any farther upon the enemy who were strongly posted and the troops were accordingly order'd to return to cover the village ot Monmouth."(18) Thus both these important engagements were brought to an inconclusive finish by the debilitating heat rather than the superiority of American arms.

Conclusion

The role of climate has passed virtually unnoticed by historians in assessing the outcome of the American War. The scholar may dismiss climatic factors but mariner and soldier alike do so at their peril. The armchair academic, in reviling "determinism" when one dares suggest that weather may play a significant role in the outcome of events, has not ridden out a typhoon in the China Sea as massive waves stove in the bows of his ship, nor crept out of the lee of Cape Gardafui into the teeth of the southwest monsoon. Throughout the ages weather has been a weapon of war: the soldiers of Napoleon and Hitler surrendered their leaders' ambitions in the face of the Russian winter; American technology and fire power in Vietnam never overcame the monsoonal tropicality of that country; one could go on. During the American War of Independence, the Americans dominated the land and left the British command of the sea. Whereas the Americans could regulate their movement over land with a degree of certainty, the British remained hostages to the vagaries of climate and weather.

To the Americans their climate was normal; to the British it was hostile. Climate, the universal provider of man, bestowed its blessings upon the American cause. It was indeed fortunate for the Americans that their country did not lie to the **east** of Britain.

REFERENCES

1. Edward Curtis, **The British Army in the American Revolution,** Yale University Press, New Haven, Conn., 1926 (reprinted by EP Publishing Ltd., 1972), 148.
2. Unless stated otherwise the ms references in this paper have been taken from the journal of Lieutenant (later Captain) John Peebles, Grenadier Company of the 42nd Regiment (henceforth Peebles Diary), which is preserved in the Frazer papers (GD.21), Scottish Record Office, H.M. General Register House, Edinburgh. There are 13 notebooks covering the entire war from 12th April 1776 to 2nd March 1782.
3. William Bell Clark (ed.), **Naval Documents of the American Revolution** (henceforth **Naval Documents**). U.S. Navy Department, Washington D.C., 15 vols. 1966-, iv, 1488-1503; v, 473, 626, 686.
4. **Naval Documents** v, 563, 576, 579, 618-20.
5. **Naval Documents**, v, 1011.
6. H. H. Lamb, **The Changing Climate**, Methuen, London, 1966; **Climate: Present, Past and Future**, Methuen, London, vol. 1, 1972.
7. Curtis, **op cit.**, 125-6.
8. Edward J. Lowell, **The Hessians and the other German Auxiliaries of Great Britain in the Revolutionary War**, Kennikat Press, Port Washington, New York, 1965, 239-40.
9. Peebles Diary, 9 January 1780.

10. Uhlendorf (ed.), **Siege of Charleston**, 117-25, quoted in Henry Steele Commager and Richard B. Morris, **The Spirit of 'Seventy-Six**, Harper & Row, New York, 1958, II, 1099-1101.

11. Data taken from papers of John, 4th Earl of Hopetoun, Hopetoun House, Queensferry, West Lothian.

12. A table of British Navy losses 1775-83 in A. Preston, D. Lyon and J. H. Batchelor, **Navies of the American Revolution**, London, 1975, p. 147 gives only two transports captured and three wrecked.

13. Louis de Vorsey, Jr., "Pioneering charting of the Gulf Stream: the work of Benjamin Franklin and William Gerard de Brahm", paper read at the VIth International Conference on the History of Cartography, The National Maritime Museum, Greenwich, September 1975.

14. Peebles Diary.

15. Letter from Major Patrick Campbell, 71st Regiment, to his father, Duncan Campbell of Glenure (S.R.O. Campbell of Balcaldine papers GD.170/1176/10/1).

16. William B. Willcox (ed.), **The American Revolution, Sir Henry Clinton's Narrative**, New Haven, Yale University Press, 1954, 437-8.

17. Peebles Diary.

18. Peebles Diary.

THE AMERICAN WAR OF INDEPENDENCE AND THE SCOTTISH ECONOMY

JOHN BUTT

Short-term fluctuations in economic activity tend to receive short shrift from historians if only because perspective becomes bemisted. About the influences of wars in the eighteenth century there has been perfunctory discussion, but beyond Ashton's conclusion that industrialisation might have occurred more quickly without them, little of broad interest has emerged. (1) Scottish economic development - and the influence of the American War upon it - has received greater attention, simply because the collapse of the tobacco trade seemed to scholars interested in Glasgow's history such as Gibson, (2) Denholm (3) and Cleland (4) of paramount importance. Henry Hamilton (5) in 1932 established an orthodoxy that capital transfers from the tobacco trade stimulated industrial investment, and in recent years scholars such as M. L. Robertson (6) and my colleague T. M. Devine, (7) have revised completely the Hamiltonian position without, however, attempting to assess the broad significance of the American War, simply because their principal concerns were deliberately more limited. This paper is essentially a preliminary salvo in what might well become a revival of the cut-and-thrust of historical controversy.

Recovery from the financial crisis of 1772 was well underway when the colonists began to prove more than usually troublesome. The banking structure had been savagely pruned already, and thus the war was not punctuated by bank failures. Only the house of Alexander, already bolstered by a loan of £160,000 from the Bank of England and heavily committed to the tobacco trade, failed. (8) Yet the War obviously had capital costs: (allowing for the difference between the peacetime and wartime cost of the armed services) it cost Britain £98 million and added a further £118 million to the national debt. British revenue increased, but deficits accumulated:

TABLE 1

Surplus and Deficit (£ thousands) on the Public Expenditure of Great Britain (1775-87)

Year ending Michaelmas		
	1775	747
	1776	—3,469
	1777	—4,154
	1778	—6,504
	1779	—7,861
	1780	—10,082
	1781	—12,630
	1782	—15,469
	1783	—10,832
	1784	—11,031
	1785	—10,305
	1786	—1,732
	1787	969

Source: T. S. Ashton, **Economic Fluctuations in England** 1700-1800 (Oxford, 1959), p. 186.

In fact, the government's intervention in the capital market was most marked from 1777, when a loan of £5 million was raised at 4 per cent. The approximate yield on 3 per cent consols (3.4 per cent in 1775 and 1776) rose to 5 per cent by 1780 and to 5.3 per cent in 1782. (9) New loan'stocks carried real yields of at least 5½ per cent by the latter year. (10)

As far as economic activity generated by public expenditure in Scotland was concerned, undoubtedly there were some gains - from transporting troops, for example, or from supplying ordnance and shot. Disadvantages, however, were more substantial. Fortunately, for Scotland there were a number of 'bull' features which at first minimised these. Capital flows into the country before interest rates began to rise markedly had been clearly noted by contemporaries. The non-importation agreements preceding the war tended to drive up the prices of Scots goods in America and allowed Scottish merchants to recoup some of their debts. (11) Dr Devine's estimate that slightly over £1.3 million was still outstanding in 1778 to Scottish merchants clearly indicates the difficulties of recouping debts rather than the full extent of Scotland's trading capital in America immediately before the War. (12) In a mixture of euphemism and blandness, David Macpherson commented: (13)

"The factors, whom the Glasgow merchants had established in America, by their prudent exertions, and the friendly terms on which they generally were with the planters, had been enabled to make large remittances . . . But very large sums still remained due . . ."

Before the switch of private capital into public expenditure began, the Government had released £800,000 in 1775 by redeeming £1 million for 3 per cent stock. (14) No doubt some of these funds crossed the Border for capital flows from England were very significant in 1775 and 1776. About July 1776 a glut of capital appeared to prevail:

"Money was now so plentiful in that country (Scotland) that above half a million was . . . lent out at an interest of **three per cent,** and more was ready to be laid out on good security". (15)

The banks lowered their rates to stem the flow of funds.

Consumption remained high even in those areas affected by a decline in exports. The harvests of the early war years were excellent, and employment remained at a high level until 1778. Imports of food were very low, and despite the fall in the re-export trade there was little or no pressure on the balance of payments. Inflation (ignoring American commodities) was relatively mild, the price index of 1783 probably standing 20 per cent higher than in 1775. Thus, domestic purchasing power was not so adversely affected by price changes as in the French Wars. Excise increases, as reflected in Table 2, were part of the fuel of inflation.

Undoubtedly, consumption was held back by increases in duties and excises, but this retarding influence on demand was only slight before 1779.

The increasing diversion of capital into government loans was principally at the expense of investment in agriculture, construction and capital goods production. In the easy money circumstances of 1775-7 port development at Grangemouth, Rothesay, Greenock, Dundee, Peterhead and Banff was begun - but terminated by 1779. Urban building in Glasgow, including the completion of the Hamiltonhill basin on the Forth and Clyde canal, had virtually ceased a year earlier, although the mansions making up Buchanan Street were not all finished before 1780. (16) However, merchants preferred, in general, to keep their funds liquid and secure and avoided speculation till the war ended.

The War lowered land prices, which were already depressed in the West following the extensive bankruptcies consequent on the failure of the Ayr Bank. The ill-fated York Buildings Company of 1779 added to the availability of land, as judicial sales of its assets were made. Mortgage rates rose in an attempt to offset the allure of investment in government stock. Good harvest brought low prices, as evidence from the Haddington and Renfrew fairs given in Table 3 reveals. In war land might appear an attractive investment, but circumstances combined during the War of Independence to make it a particularly illiquid asset. It was, therefore, generally foresworn, although extensive activity began to occur in an erstwhile sluggish land market in 1782 in anticipation of peace. (17)

Relatively low agricultural prices following good harvests temporarily reduced the pressure for improvement and almost certainly made investment in land less attractive. Agricultural

TABLE 2

Excise and Duties Revenue raised in Scotland 1774-83

Tax Year	Amount (£)
1774-5	139,713
1775-6	149,416
1776-7	161,586
1777-8	175,695
1778-9	191,444
1779-80	244,636
1780-1	271,523
1781-2	279,693
1782-3	247,520

Source: H. Hamilton, **Eighteenth Century,** Appendix III

TABLE 3

Oat Prices at Haddington and Renfrew, 1772-83

Year	H.	Price per boll	R
1772	14s. 2d.		13s. 6d.
1773	13s. 9d.		15s. 0d.
1774	13s. 4d.		16s. 0d.
1775	10s. 2d.		16s. 0d.
1776	10s. 1d.		14s. 2d.
1777	11s. 6d.		15s. 0d.
1778	11s. 4d.		15s. 1d.
1779	9s. 2d.		£1 0s. 0d.
1780	11s. 6d.		15s. 4d.
1781	10s. 0d.		£1 0s. 3d.
1782	17s. 9d.		15s. 0d.
1783	12s. 9d.		£1 1s. 10d.

Sources: Hamilton, **Eighteenth Century,** Appendix II; W. Hector, **Judicial Records of Renfrewshire** (Paisley, 1878), p. 46

employment did not suffer immediately for good harvests required all hands, but future employment was adversely affected - because improved agriculture commonly provided more jobs rather than fewer. Good cheap grain crops involved greater activity at the distilleries, breweries and corn mills, and, naturally increased opportunities for local carters and carriers. In so far as employment was concerned, gains were likely to be immediate and temporary. Thus the War did not affect immediately the recovery from the depression of 1772-3, but by 1779 the downturn in rural employment had begun.

The changes in the pattern of foreign trade are now familiar. Re-exports declined markedly, and since they were so significant in total Scottish exports, there was a fall in the aggregate performance, most apparent in 1778 and 1781-2. Naturally, imports declined, this feature being most apparent in 1776, 1778 and 1781-2. (18) There was a switch from commerce with the tobacco states to trade with the West Indies. Because this part of the story has received considerable attention, I will concentrate upon other important aspects. Table 4 is the statistical key, although it is based upon the official rather than the current values of imports and exports. (19)

consumption to exports. Occasionally, as in 1782 this expansion of home produced exports was arrested - but it was never reversed. Thus, effective export performance post-war was embryonic during the War itself.

Merchants made use of their opportunities within the British market as well as on the continent of Europe. South of the Border there was a widening market for Scottish textiles, particularly for linens and mixtures. Progressively the linen industry improved its economic performance during the War but became less dependent on foreign demand. (20) Partly this was a consequence of tariff policy but it is also an indication of improved distribution and marketing.

The Board of Trustees in 1776 reported an increase in linen stamped for sale:
"This Increase at the time when a total stop in the American Trade, occasioned by the present unnatural Rebellion ... had raised the most dismal apprehensions, gives real pleasure to every friend of this Country".
When the downturn came in 1778-9, it was exports and not domestic consumption that suffered; the domestic market in Britain, as again in 1782, was the main support of the linen industry (see Table 6).

TABLE 4			
Official Values (£) of Imports and Exports 1770-84			
Years	Average Annual Imports	Average Annual Re-exports	Average Annual Exports
1770-4	1,225,606	1,138,248	1,626,066
1775-9	866,350	439,211	905,541
1780-4	935,343	192,601	835,717
Source: PRO Customs 14			

TABLE 5			
Home Produced Exports in Relationship to Total Exports 1770-84			
Period	Annual Average Value (£)	% of total exports	Index 1780-4 100
1770-4	487,818	30	75.85
1775-9	466,330	51.5	72.5
1780-4	643,116	76.95	100
Source: Calculated from PRO Customs 14			

That the War severely damaged Scotland's foreign commerce cannot be denied. That there was a deficit on visible trade after 1780 is also inescapable. The question remains, however, whether these clouds had silver linings. The higher costs of foreign trade which the War engendered may have encouraged short-distance trade particularly with England. Moreover, the decline in re-exports certainly stimulated the growth of home-produced exports. Inevitably, there was some delay as merchants had to readjust to the instability in trade produced by the War. However, as a proportion of total exports - and also in terms of official values - home production became more significant from the beginning of the War, as Table 5 indicates.

Foreign trade was inextricably linked with circumstances prevailing in the domestic economy. The boom of the early years of the War occasioned some shift from exports to domestic consumption which low food prices and high levels of employment allowed and encouraged. The downward drift in later years - both in general economic activity and in the exchanges - stimulated a contrary movement from domestic

TABLE 6		
Linen Exports and Linen Stamped for Sale 1770-83		
	Exports	Stamped
Average 1770-4	1,983,200 yds.	12,164,000 (to nearest 1,000
1775	915,288	12,139,000 yds.)
1776	1,422,827	13,571,000
1777	2,257,035	14,793,000
1778	1,266,564	13,264,000
1779	1,973,825	12,867,000
1780	3,361,127	13,411,000
1781	2,038,211	15,178,000
1782	1,398,075	15,349,000
1783	2,771,055	17,075,000
Source: PRO, Customs 14; SRO, Board of Trustees Reports.		

What a revival of foreign demand could do for total domestic production is best indicated by the figures for 1783, but by that date a new industry was becoming established. Rising flax prices coincided with cotton as a 'drug on the market' because of the expansion of trade with the West Indies, the main source of raw cotton before 1800.

TABLE 7

Imports of Cotton Wool from America and the West Indies, 1776-83

Year	Amount (lbs.)	Value (£)
1776	84,280	4,214
1777	256,650	12,716
1778	216,870	11,060
1779	262,300	13,116
1780	222,939	11,147
1781	267,532	15,644
1782	289,832	14,165
1783	222,939	11,170

Source: PRO Customs 14.

Peter Brotherston, with the backing of the Edinburgh private bankers, Bertram, Gardner and Company, obtained a few of five acres from Sir James Clerk of Penicuik in 1776 and by 1778 had established the first cotton mill in Scotland. (21) The second, at Rothesay, was financed by Glasgow linen merchants and began in 1779. (22) To the mainland of the West of Scotland Robert Burns introduced Arkwright's waterframe in 1781 at Johnstone. (23) As peace approached, extensive plans were afoot to build more cotton mills. (24) Generally, it is fair to say that the longer the war lasted, the more deleterious it was to the expansion of the cotton industry.

Effects on the wider industrial structure were mixed. Carron Company benefited from demands for carronades and shot; (25) Wilsontown ironworks was founded in 1779. (26) Dumbarton Glassworks Company derived finance from the tobacco lord, James Dunlop, and began operations in 1776. (27) The production of leather goods, notably boots and saddlery, apparently gained ground during the War and there is scattered evidence of an expansion in shipbuilding, coal mining, and bleaching and dyeing.

However, it is possible that war-produced distortions in the capital and labour market, which varied widely according to region, were more serious obstacles to industrial growth than aides to it. The revival of the Scottish economy after 1772 was firmly established by the Declaration of Independence, and the checks which dear money imposed probably aborted a long and sustained boom which was, however, merely postponed.

REFERENCES

1. T. S. Ashton, **Economic Fluctuations in England, 1700-1800** (Oxford, 1959) 176.
2. J. Gibson, **History of Glasgow** (Glasgow, 1777) vi-vii.
3. J. Denholm, **History of Glasgow** (3rd edn. Glasgow, 1804). 83ff.
4. J. Cleland, **The Rise and Progress of Glasgow** (Glasgow, 1820), 89ff.
5. H. Hamilton, **The Industrial Revolution in Scotland** (Oxford, 1932), 118.
6. M. L. Robertson, "Scottish Commerce and the American War of Independence", **Econ. Hist. Rev.** 2nd ser. IX (1956).
7. T. M. Devine, **The Tobacco Lords** (Edinburgh, 1975) and his "Glasgow Merchants in Colonial Trade 1770-1815" (Strathclyde Ph.D. thesis, 2 vols, 1972).
8. S. G. Checkland, **Scottish Banking, 1695-1973** (1975), 134-5 and 155-6.
9. D. Macpherson, **Annals of Commerce** (1805), iii, 608: T. S. Ashton, **Economic Fluctuations**, 187.
10. D. Macpherson, op. cit., 708.
11. H. Hamilton, **An Economic History of Scotland in the Eighteenth Century** (Oxford, 1963), 269.
12. T. M. Devine, 'Glasgow Merchants in Colonial Trade', i, 203.
13. D. Macpherson, op. cit., iii, 581.
14. Ibid, 577.
15. Ibid, 593.
16. H. Hamilton, **Eighteenth Century**, 220 ff; **Glasgow Journal**, 3 April 1777 **Glasgow Mercury**, 5 Feb. 1778.
17. T. M. Devine "Glasgow Colonial Merchants and Land, 1770-1815", in **Land and Industry** (ed. J. T. Ward and R. G. Wilson), (Newton Abbot, 1971), 205-65.
18. PRO, Customs 14.
19. For an ingenious attempt to translate official into current values cf J. J. McCusker, 'The Current Value of English Exports, 1697 to 1880', **William and Mary Quarterly**.
20. SRO, N/G 1/7 series Reports of the Board of Trustees 1775-83.
21. Signet Library, session papers 449: 23.
22. SRO, Unextracted Processes, Adams Mask 01/40 Oliphant v. William Fleming & Co.
23. SRO, Unextracted Processes 1 Currie Dal C9/1 Corse & Houston.
24. SRO, N/G1/7 series Reports of the Board of Trustees 1783 and 1784.
25. R. H. Campbell, **Carron Company** (1961) 140f and 329.
26. I. L. Donnachie and J. Butt, "The Wilsons of Wilsontown: A Study of Entrepreneurial Failure" **Explorations in Entrepreneurial History** 2nd ser. IV (1967), 151 ff
27. J. C. Logan, "The Dumbarton Glassworks Company: A study in Entrepreneurship", **Business History**, XIV (1972), 67 ff.

THE AMERICAN WAR OF INDEPENDENCE AND SCOTTISH ECONOMIC HISTORY

T M DEVINE

There is a long-standing historiographical tradition that the American War of Independence was a turning-point in Scottish economic history. It is often asserted that the collapse of the lucrative tobacco trade was signalled by the outbreak of hostilities in 1775 and confirmed by the peace of 1783 when an independent United States was finally released from the constraints of the Navigation Laws. Since the old Virginia trade then seemed to have been eliminated, historians were concerned to explain what had become of the fortunes made from it, the capital employed in it and the enterprising merchants who had been responsible for its growth. (1) Until recently, for example, it was fashionable to explain the economic expansion of late eighteenth-century Scotland as the fruit of a transfer of capital from foreign commerce to domestic industry and, in particular, to the new cotton manufacture. (2) This view is certainly no longer favoured but the assumption persists that under-employed capital was available for new purposes after 1783: 'The collapse of the rich Glasgow tobacco trade after the War of American Independence is clearly associated with the movement of capital into cotton, coal and iron, though not usually in the form of crude transfers'. (3) Other writers have argued that an additional indication of diversification was the rise of the Caribbean trade when the American war came to an end, a development initiated by 'former' tobacco merchants striving to rebuild a new structure of colonial commerce on the ruins of the old. (4)

On the face of it, Scotland's profitable association with the thirteen American colonies **was** brought to an end in 1775. Imports of tobacco, which stood at an enormous 45 million lb. in that year, rapidly shrivelled to 294,000 lb. in 1777 and only recovered marginally to 5 million lb. three years later. (5) But U.K. customs figures can give only a very partial indication of the condition and dimensions of tobacco commerce during the war. Imports of tobacco to Scottish ports after 1777 represented only that proportion of the commodity meant for home sale since no tobacco was re-exported to Europe from then until April 1783. (6) Yet, before the war, the Scottish tobacco business had been essentially based on re-export with over 98 per cent of imports being shipped, after paying duty at the Clyde, to France, Holland and the German states. It is plain, therefore, that the supply of tobacco to U.K. **domestic** consumers not only persisted after 1775 but actually marginally increased in volume, possibly because Glasgow was now intervening in a sector previously controlled by London. There was an even more dramatic rise in the **value** of imports. Between 1770 and 1775 tobacco prices at the Clyde had averaged below 2d per lb. By Spring 1776 prices averaged between 8d and 1s 6d and by December 1777 had climbed further to 2s per lb. (7) Average prices in 1781 were between 2s 5d and 2s 10d per lb. (8) What is equally clear is that merchant houses carefully controlled the level of importation into Scottish ports in order to retain these inflated price levels. (8a) This was a strategy made possible by the oligopolistic nature of the Glasgow trading structure and the high costs of wartime commerce which confirmed the dominance of the larger firms. The low imports of the period 1776 to 1783 were therefore as much a token of business sense as proof of an interruption in trade. Certainly in themselves they are not informative about the true nature of tobacco commerce during the war. This was based on a combination of the clandestine supply of consumer goods to the embattled thirteen colonies and the sale of tobacco direct to continental markets.

Scottish exports to the thirteen colonies did decline from an annual average of £298,922 (official sterling values) between 1770 and 1774 to £24,193 in 1775, £905 in 1776 and £35,553 in 1777. (9) But the bulk of the trade was channelled through other routes. The official value of Scottish exports to Canada rose from £4,742 in 1774 to £12,882 in 1775 and to £28,215 in 1777. Nova Scotia, of little account before the war, took goods to the value of £126,136 in 1777-78. (10) But Canada was not the preferred intermediate market for long. Of the ten ships freighting for North America at Clyde ports between January 1776 and April 1777, seven sailed for Nova Scotia and two for Quebec. (11) By the end of 1778, however, there had been a marked shift in the direction of trade towards ports in the thirteen colonies under British control. During the period January-April 1779, for instance, only two vessels sailed for Nova Scotia from the Clyde while seven freighted for such ports as New York, Philadelphia and Charlestown. (12) As a consequence Scottish exports **direct** to the thirteen colonies rose from £35,210 in 1778, at official values, to £62,626 in 1778, £171,317 in 1780 and £147,508 in 1781, although **direct** exports to Virginia and Maryland remained at zero between 1775 and 1782. (13)

Probably even more significant was the emergence of the West Indies as the focus of a clandestine commerce between North America and the United Kingdom in both tobacco and goods, a development which was associated with tobacco's new scarcity value in international trade. In an important sense, war came as a blessing, not as a disaster, for the tobacco merchant. The period 1772-75 had been one of glut crops and sluggish demand and only when direct trade was cut off did market prices move markedly in favour of the seller rather than the consumer. (14) Throughout most of the war, production in Virginia and Maryland averaged between one-half and one-third of the levels prevailing before 1775 (15) while, on the European continent, demand for North American tobaccos proved only partially vulnerable to competition from indigenous substitutes. (16) At the same time, neither American nor European firms were able to organise a substantial transatlantic trade to satisfy this market. The blockade of the Royal Navy, the unfamiliarity of foreign sea captains with the Chesapeake and an intolerable rise in shipping costs combined to ensure its failure. (17) Ironically, however, war conditions accentuated not only the economic but also the strategic value of tobacco. Of all the major American export crops it lent itself more readily to development of trade with other powers, affording great possibilities of financing military operation and paying for much needed manufactured goods. The reality of the situation was, nevertheless, that only through utilising handled sales, could the American tobacco trade with Europe survive.

From the colonial side, the Caribbean was probably the most suitable area of exchange especially after France entered the war in 1778. The naval balance in the West Indies did not entirely favour the British, neutral Dutch (until 1780) and Danish islands there were obvious entrepots and the well-established provision trade with the thirteen colonies provided a ready-made channel for a rerouted tobacco commerce. Thus, the states of Virginia, Maryland and North Carolina began to maintain a regular correspondence with the mercantile firm of Harrison and Van Bibber in the West Indies. State authorities chartered ships, bought flour and tobacco, consigned the cargoes to their Caribbean representatives from whom they obtained in return military stores and consumer goods. (18) The principal centres of trade were the Dutch colony of St Eustatius and later, when Holland entered the war, the Danish islands of St Thomas and St Croix. When Admiral Rodney's forces took St Eustatius in 1781, John Adams saw the irony: 'There was found in that island a greater quantity of property belonging to the British themselves than to the French, Dutch or Americans. They have broken up a trade which was more advantageous to them than any of their enemies as it was a channel through which British manufactures were conveyed to North America'. (19)

Scottish merchants were able to enter this sector in a vigorous fashion. The early years of the American war and, in particular, the financial crisis of 1778, had not ruined their fortunes. Between 1775 and 1785 seven Glasgow tobacco firms did fail but their demise was not a catastrophic blow to Scottish enterprise. Only one bankrupt concern was numbered among the eleven large companies which shipped more than 500 hogsheads of tobacco in the years immediately before the war. Instead, four of the seven failures occurred among the ten firms which imported least. (20) Indeed, in the first two years of war the handful of great syndicates which controlled the Clyde tobacco business were able to achieve windfall gains which left them flush with capital and well able to adjust to the circuitous routes and high operating costs of Caribbean commerce at the time.

The direct purchase method of the Glasgow traders was very well suited to acquiring cargoes quickly in Virginia and Maryland during the crisis months of the summer of 1775. Evidence from the upper James River valley indicates that English merchants shipped approximately the same amount of tobacco in 1775 as in 1774. (21) Yet the larger Scottish firms managed to substantially increase their share. Cunninghame shipments rose from 1,654 hogsheads in 1774 to 1,771 in 1775; Speirs, Bowman and Co. cornered the lion's share, their exports rising from 4,853 hogsheads in 1774 to 5,451 the following year. As a result, Glasgow probably managed to secure more of the crucial 1775 crop than any other port in the United Kingdom. (22) In addition, the relatively sluggish demand of 1773-75 and the glut harvests of the same period meant that they had unsold stocks on hand anyway. The situation was even more favourable because the purchasing agents of the French monopoly in Scotland had cut back their orders before the war in an effort to push prices down. (23) Thus when the American ports were closed they were left in an exposed position with insufficient stocks and the possibility of an interrupted supply. Finally, the Glasgow houses benefited from the easy availability of credit in 1775-76. Unlike most wars, the early stages of the rebellion did not impair confidence in U.K. money markets. (24) So importers were not compelled to release their stocks because of pressure on credit. Instead those with sufficient nerve could await the anticipated rise in prices. Thus although only 1,521 hogsheads were landed at Clyde ports in 1776, there still remained 14,404 hogsheads, or about 25 per cent of the 1775 importation, in cellars there in August 1776. (25) In early 1777 one company estimated that there were 7,000 hogsheads at Port Glasgow and a further 8,000 at ports abroad 'belonging to this place and the whole quantity at market (in Europe) is reckoned to be about 30,000 hogsheads, so that half of the quantity at market belongs to this place'. (26) Inevitably, therefore, several of the great Glasgow houses did very well out of the ensuing bonanza as prices rose from around 3d per lb. in the autumn of 1775 to 10d by late 1776. (27). It was in this period that the financial resources became available to support investment in the Caribbean sector after 1778.

Not only did the larger merchant firms have the capital after 1775-77, they were also familiar with the West Indies. Some traders had always been more interested in sugar from that area than tobacco from West Virginia. Even companies normally more concerned with tobacco frequently made 'adventures' there when sugar prices merited it or when tobacco markets were sluggish. Furthermore, American traders had to retain correspondents to supply West Indian produce to their store outlets in Virginia and Maryland. But during the period 1775-77 contacts were sporadic because it was only when France entered the war that the commercial world finally adjusted to the possibility of an extended disruption in peacetime trade patterns. (29) By the end of 1777 the rerouting of Scottish exports via the Caribbean becomes apparent. Exports of plain linen to Virginia dropped from 700,000 yards in 1772 to zero in 1777, while exports to Jamaica rose rapidly from 250,000 yards in 1772 to 760,000 in 1777. (30) At the same time, Glasgow houses began to embark in the clandestine tobacco trade on a considerable scale. James Ritchie and Co., a medium sized concern, despatched an agent to the West Indies, gave him 'unlimited credit' and ordered him to engage in the purchase of tobacco. In 1779-80 he was spending £4,000 carrying out these directions. (31) Speirs, French and Co., one of the largest Scottish ventures, had, by 1781, secured a dominant position in this trade. By that date, their agent, Robert Burton, was reckoned one of the greatest merchants in the Caribbean. His annual outlay was an enormous £50,000 and he was dealing direct with European ports such as Hamburg, Ostend and Amsterdam in tobacco and employing neutral vessels as carriers. Manufactured goods came most often directly from London and the entire business was financed by Thomas Coutts and Sons, the Anglo-Scottish banking firm in the capital, with accounts later charged to Speirs, Murdoch and Co., bankers in Glasgow. (32)

Perhaps, in one sense, it might appear that the coming of peace in 1783 would pose a greater problem for Scottish tobacco merchants than the outbreak of war had done in 1775. Under the new relationship the independent United States were no longer compelled to send their export staples first to the United Kingdom, whatever their ultimate destination, or to acquire manufactures only from British traders. In other words, the legislative framework of the old tobacco entrepôt trade had been dismantled. In consequence, Scottish imports of tobacco in the following decade never reached more than a quarter of pre-war levels.

But when looked at in the round the overall commercial connection between Scotland and the United States after 1783 was much stronger. Scottish exports direct to the U.S.A. quickly regained the levels prevailing before 1775. Official sterling values of exports between 1784 and 1788 averaged £243,244 per annum compared with £222,497 from 1765 to 1769, and £298,922 between 1770 and 1774. (33) Moreover, while the number of vessels from the former thirteen colonies to Clyde ports fell from 136 to 84 between 1772 and 1790 (a drop of 38 per cent), the number to the U.S.A. only diminished from 103 to 95 (a drop of 11 per cent). (34) In addition, Glasgow merchants managed to maintain a substantial role in the American tobacco trade to Europe. The city's trading houses described four years after the war ended how the supply of American tobacco to the Continent employed 200-250 ships of all nations. But more than three-quarters of this number were British owned and, even more significantly, at least two-thirds of the tobacco cargoes carried in them were on British account. (35) Plainly, therefore, Scottish customs data can give only a partial indication of the survival of the Scottish tobacco trade after 1783.

Because, when peace came, the Scots factors returned in force to Virginia and Maryland. By the middle of 1784, on one estimate, there were 80 stores in Petersburg and as many in Richmond. (36) In Georgetown the Scots controlled 17 or 18 outlets. (37) As one contemporary remarked: 'the Glasgow goods continue still to be much liked . . . and Glasgow may yet have a great share of the trade'. (38) Both long-established and new organisations were involved in the revival. The three most famous 'tobacco lords' of an earlier generation, Alexander Speirs, John Glassford and William Cunninghame had all disappeared from the scene. Cunninghame seems to have retired from a dominant role in his firm but remained a sleeping partner in Robert Dunmore and Co. (39) Both

Speirs and Glassford had died before peace was signed. Yet their three great syndicates survived and continued to play a major role in the Chesapeake after the war. Robert Findlay, Cunninghame's kinsman and protégé, became associated with the Hopkirks and a branch of the Buchanan clan to form Findlay, Hopkirk and Co., while the Speirs and Glassford organisations continued under the leadership of men long experienced in the trade before 1775. (45) In 1785, these three groupings, together with Colin Dunlop and Sons and Corbett, Russell and Co. shipped more than 90 per cent of the Clyde's tobacco imports. (41) In the Chesapeake, therefore, Scottish business ability once again became a factor of consequence. In Petersburg in 1784, 'Messrs Donalds have been grasping all the trade' and, a year later, Patrick Henry complained to Thomas Jefferson that Scottish hegemony had not come to an end: 'We are much disappointed in our expectations of French and Dutch traders rivalling the British here. The latter engross the greatest share of our trade, and was it not the Irish bid up for our produce, the Scotch would soon be on their former footing'. (42)

The Glasgow merchants were very eager to re-establish themselves in order to recover the enormous pre-war debt (reckoned in 1778 at over £1,300,000) owed them by American planters. (43) Ironically, however, the only practical way of doing so was to provide further credit and consumer goods to their former clients in order to support a revival in tobacco cultivation. Indeed the Scottish firms were more necessary than ever to the economies of Virginia, Maryland and North Carolina after 1783. Put simply the British commercial role in North America had begun to function independently of the Navigation Laws by the later eighteenth century. Whatever changes had occurred in the political sphere a powerful alien merchant class remained vital to the efficient disposal of the produce of the agrarian economy in European markets. For investment capital planters still depended on U.K. sources and, moreover, the consumer habits of generations could not be broken by the accident of constitutional change. After 1783 it was only the British merchants who could supply the range of commodities in demand, at attractive cost and on long credit. (44) If anything, in fact, in the era of the Industrial Revolution, British goods were even more competitive than before. Therefore,

seven years after independence was granted to the former colonies, their commercial dependency lingered on: '. . . there are not imported into all the United States from Europe five thousand pounds value of manufactures but what comes from Britain; the French and the Dutch are quite drove out of the trade by the superior quality and cheapness of British articles'. (45)

There was thus no need or desire for Scottish disinvestment from the American sector. Certainly, over the 1780s and 1790s the Scottish economy expanded rapidly and Scottish involvement in the West Indies trade was consolidated but neither of these two developments were associated with changes in the tobacco trade. Tobacco merchants invested in industry after 1783 but they had always done so and there is no evidence of an acceleration in the diversion of trade resources to the domestic economy. Between 1780 and 1795 colonial merchants took up shares in 21 new industrial partnerships but between 1796 and 1815 this figure declined to nine. Moreover, colonial merchants supplied at most about 17 per cent of the total capital in the Scottish cotton manufacture in 1795 but of the 25 merchants concerned, 17 were primarily involved in Caribbean rather than North American commerce. (46) The fact that needs to be stressed surely is the new strength and maturity of the Scottish economy which allowed **both** a renewal of the American link **and** substantial investment in indigenous industry.

Similarly, after 1783, the growth in the West Indies trade was related to industrial needs for cotton and increased consumer demand for sugar rather than to new strategies by tobacco firms. Although these concerns were associated with the Caribbean during the war this was primarily because they sought to continue the American connection. When peace came, the importation of West India commodities was controlled by companies long experienced in that trade (such as Alexander Houston and Co. and Somervell, Gordon and Co.) or by relatively new concerns with no previous interests in tobacco commerce. The link between the American and Caribbean sectors remained close but it was based on the diversified nature of the Glasgow business community which allowed wealthy merchants, long before 1775, to retain commitments in both areas. (47)

REFERENCES

1   M. L. Robertson, 'Scottish Commerce and the American War of Independence', **Economic History Review**, 2nd ser., IX (1950), 123-31; B. Crispin, 'Clyde Shipping and the American War', **Scottish Historical Review**, 41 (1962), 124-133.

2   For the older view see H. Hamilton, **The Industrial Revolution in Scotland** (Oxford, 1932), 121; L. G. Saunders, **Scottish Democracy: the Social and Intellectual Background** (Edinburgh, 1950), 98. For the modern reassessment, Robertson, **loc cit**, 130; R. H. Campbell, **Scotland Since 1707** (Oxford, 1965), 40; S.G.E. Lythe and J. Butt, **An Economic History of Scotland 1100-1939** (Glasgow, 1975), 147-8.

3   B. F. Duckham, **History of the Scottish Coal Industry** (Newton Abbot, 1970), 179-80.

4   Campbell, **op cit**, 78; Crispin, **loc cit**, 128-9; A. Slaven, **The Development of the West of Scotland** (London, 1975), 6; Lythe and Butt, **op cit**, 147-8.

5   Public Record Office (PRO), Customs 14.

6   Scottish Record Office (SRO), Collector's Quarterly Accounts, Port Glasgow and Greenock, E.504/28/22-36; E.504/504/15/22-38.

7   SRO, Oswald Papers, GD 213/53, John Anderson to Richard Oswald, 22 September 1776, 4 October 1776; **Edinburgh Evening Courant**, 20 November 1776; **Caledonian Mercury**, 9 June 1777.

8   Library of Congress, Washington (LC), Dunlop Family Papers, Box 1, James Ritchie and Co. to James Dunlop, 28 April 1780; Henry Ritchie to James Dunlop, 2 November 1781 (I am very grateful to Mr Stuart Butler for kindly lending me his transcripts of these papers); Strathclyde Regional Archives (SRA), Speirs Papers, TD131/9,

Alexander Speirs to J. G. Martens, 11 October 1781.

8a LC, Dunlop Family Papers, James Ritchie and Co. to James Dunlop, 29 January 1779.

9 Jacob M. Price, 'New Time Series for Scotland's and Britain's Trade with the Thirteen Colonies and States, 1740 to 1791', **William and Mary Quarterly,** 32, 2 (April 1975), 307-325.

10 PRO, Customs 14; SRO, RH 20/22, Customs Account Book, Newfoundland, 1771-85.

11 SRO, Customs Accounts, E,504/28/29-35; E.504/15/28-37.

12 Ibid.

13 Price, **loc cit,** 320-1.

14 SRO, GD 247/59/Q/1, William Cunninghame to John Turner, 18 July 1774; to J. Robinson, 13 August 1774; to Thomas Gordon, 15 July 1774; Sir William Forbes, **Memoirs of a Banking House** (London, 1860), 45-6.

15 R. W. Coakley, 'Virginia Commerce during the American Revolution', University of Virginia, PhD (1949), 380.

16 Jacob M. Price, **France and the Chesapeake** (Michigan, 1972).

17 Coakley, **op cit,** 166-7, 335.

18 L. C. Gray, **History of Agriculture in the Southern United States to 1860** (Washington, 1933), II, 578; David Macpherson, **Annals of Commerce, Manufactures, Fisheries and Navigation** (London, 1805), III, 719-20.

19 Quoted in C. B. Coulter, **The Virginia Merchant** (University of Princeton PhD, 1944), 152. In fact official acquiescence had been given a year earlier when the U.K. Parliament legalised the trade in American tobacco from foreign islands in the West Indies and placed a special duty on it (20 Geo. III, c 39).

20 This is a brief summary of T. M. Devine's 'Glasgow Merchants and the Collapse of the Tobacco Trade, 1775-83', **Scott. Hist. Rev. LII** (1973), 50-74.

21 R. P. Thomson, 'The Tobacco Export of the Upper James River Naval District 1773-75', **William and Mary Quarterly,** 3rd ser., XVIII (1961).

22 T. M. Devine, **The Tobacco Lords** (Edinburgh, 1975), 108-9.

23 SRO, GD 247/59/Q/1, William Cunninghame to John Turner, 18 July 1774; to James Robinson, 13 August 1774; Price, **op cit, 646.**

24 Robertson, **loc cit,** 123.

25 SRO, CE 60/1/9, Account of quantities of tobacco in the hands of each importer, 5 August 1776.

26 SRO, Oswald Papers, GD 213/53, John Anderson to Richard Oswald, 18 February 1777.

27 Ibid, John Anderson to Richard Oswald, 1 February 1776; **Edinburgh Evening Courant,** 4 September 1776.

28 Ibid, John Anderson to Richard Oswald, 22 September 1776. For details of mercantile profit at this time see Devine, **op cit,** 110-111.

29 Devine, **op cit,** 106-7.

30 PRO, Customs 14.

31 LC, James Dunlop Family Papers, Hugh Wylie to James Dunlop, 22 December 1779; James Anderson to James Dunlop, 15 March 1780.

32 Strathclyde Regional Archives (SRA), Speirs Papers, TD 131/9, Letterbook of Alexander Speirs, **passim.**

33 Price, **loc cit,** 320-321.

34 SRO, Collector's Quarterly Accounts, E.504/28; E.504/15, Port Glasgow and Greenock.

35 PRO, B.T.6/20, Answers to the several questions respecting the commerce and shipping between Great Britain and the United States of America, 16 December 1789.

36 LC, James Dunlop Family Papers, James Dunlop sen. to James Dunlop, 20 July 1784.

37 Ibid, Thomas Montgomerie to James Dunlop, 10 August 1784.

38 Ibid, David Buchanan to James Dunlop, 5 April 1784.

39 SRO, GD 247/140 (Copy) Memorial and queries for the Trustees of the late Mr Cunninghame of Lainshaw.

40 SRO, RH 15/2237, Contract of Findlay Hopkirk and Co., S.R.A., TD 131/3, Sederunt Book of the Trustees of Alexander Speirs of Elderslie, 1782-85. **Glasgow Advertiser,** 22 January 1790; **Glasgow Mercury,** 19 January 1790.

41 SRO, E.504/28/38-40, Port Glasgow Customs Accounts, October 1784-April 1786.

42 LC, James Dunlop Family Papers, James Dunlop sen. to James Dunlop, 16 September 1784. Patrick Henry to Thomas Jefferson, 10 September 1785 in **Jefferson Papers,** VII, 509.

43 For the figure quoted as the pre-war debt see SRA, Speirs Papers, TD 131/10-12, Diary of Alexander Speirs, 2 March 1778. For company motivation see PRO, AO 12/9/35; LC, James Dunlop Family Papers, Box 6, Instructions from Messrs James Ritchie and Co., 31 March 1784; SRA, Speirs Papers TD 131/13, Sederunt Book of the Trustees of Alexander Speirs of Elderslie, 8-9.

44 Price, **op cit,** 728-31; Gray, **op cit,** II, 597; W. A. Low, 'Merchant and Planter Relations in Post-Revolutionary Virginia, 1783-1789', **Virginia Magazine of History and Bigraphy,** 61 (1953), 208-17.

45 Extract of a letter from Philadelphia, 10 October 1789, in **Glasgow Advertiser,** 8 January 1790.

46 T. M. Devine, 'The Colonial Trades and Industrial Investment in Scotland, 1700-1815', **Econ. Hist. Rev.,** 2nd ser., XXIX (1976), 1-13.

47 Devine, **op cit,** 165-7.

THE AMERICAN REVOLUTION IN THE SCOTTISH PRESS

D. B. SWINFEN

Given the fact that contemporary Scots had considered access to England's colonies to be one of the principal attractions of the Union, and given the profitable exploitation by Scots of such access through trade and emigration, (1) it would be surprising indeed to find a majority of opinion in Scotland in support of the American rebellion, and opposed to its suppression. Yet some historians would seem to disagree. D. I. Fagerstrom, in an Edinburgh Ph.D. thesis presented exactly a quarter of a century ago, (2) laid great emphasis upon the extent of Scottish opposition to the war and the war effort, and linked this opposition tentatively with subsequent political developments in Scotland. More recently, Dr N. T. Phillipson has spoken of "the remarkably widespread sympathy with which Scotsmen viewed the cause of the Americans", and linked this with Anglo- Scottish friction and Scottish disenchantment with the Union. (3) There were of course some individuals and groups in Scotland, as there were in England, who approved of the principles upon which the American rebels took their stand. Some elements of the Presbyterian Church, of the literary fraternity in Edinburgh, and of the legal profession made their opposition to the war perfectly plain. (4) There were still more who attacked North's ministry, not because they disapproved of the war, but because they were angered by the failure of government and the military to prosecute the war successfully. It is the argument of this paper that, on the evidence afforded by the contemporary Scottish press, the large majority of educated Scots deplored the American rebellion, urged the vigorous prosecution of the war, and only in the later stages, when the loss of the American colonies was seen to be unavoidable, turned to resignation and indifference. At the same time, the war did exacerbate anti-English feeling in Scotland, though not, it will be argued, because of the underlying affection for the American cause.

On one point there will be no disagreement. The Scots it is clear were vitally interested in the issues raised by the Revolution, as well as in the day to day progress of the military campaign, and in this they were extremely well served by the press. In the period spanning the American troubles - from the early 1760's to the Peace of Paris - a total of around 50 newspapers and periodicals were at one time or another in existence. (5) While the vast majority of these were produced in Edinburgh, newspapers and magazines were published also in Glasgow, Aberdeen, Dundee, Kelso and Dumfries. Although there is insufficient evidence to plot with accuracy the distribution of readership, it probably extended considerably beyond the limits of the town of origin. The short lived **Dundee Weekly Magazine,** for example, had agents in Brechin, Forfar and Montrose, (6) yet one of the reasons given for its demise was competition from the higher quality Edinburgh papers. (7) Statistics of circulation are also hard to come by, though most authorities agree that actual readership must have greatly exceeded the numbers printed. (8) Significantly, the sharpest increase in new publications came in the second half of the 1770's, while many of the weaker journals foundered in the later stages of the war, or after the Peace, when interest in the American scene was at a low ebb.(9) While the rapid development of the British periodical press in this period might be attributed to other causes, such as the facility after 1771 to publish Parliamentary debates,(10) it does seem that in Scotland interest in American affairs was crucial. And, of course, Parliamentary debates themselves would frequently and inevitably centre around American questions in this period.

Any Scottish newspaper publisher who wanted to survive had to cater for the healthy appetite for American news. The publisher of the **Caledonian Mercury,** launching a plan to turn the thrice-weekly paper into a daily, undertook to "omit no American information that he can procure and depend upon as authentic". On the other hand, there was the ill-fated **Mirror,** whose proud parent, taking a stroll around Edinburgh in the hope of hearing some praise of his new offspring, was mortified to come across only one who had even looked at it. This individual "after glancing over the pages ... said he could have wished they had set apart a corner for intelligence from America; but having taken off his spectacles, wiped, and put them into their case, said, with a tone of discovery, he had found out the reason why there was nothing of that sort in the **Mirror;** it was in order to save the tax on newspapers".(12)

In failing to offer coverage of American affairs, the **Mirror** was unusual, and it may be significant that it lasted no more than a year. In most other periodicals the American section was the largest of all, and even news entered under "Scotland", "England", or the local city was frequently in the form of letters about American matters. An extreme example was **Ruddiman's Weekly Mercury** in which, with the bombshell of Saratoga, the American section took over the entire publication.(13) In other papers, American affairs often took precedence over major items of domestic news; as when in 1775 the **Caledonian Mercury** delayed its report on the General Assembly to bring the news of Lexington and Concord.

There can be no doubt then that the contemporary Scottish newspaper reader was kept remarkably well informed about the issues and the progress of the war. Nor was this information confined to the British side of the conflict. Rebel proclamations, intercepted letters, even Witherspoon's treasonable sermons were printed in full or in lengthy extracts - a fact which prompts important questions as to press censorship and editorial policy.

No evidence has come to light of direct government interference in the press, though this may simply be because the most likely source for such evidence, the correspondence between Lord Advocate Dundas and the Home Office, has not been preserved for the period before 1782.(15) Such interference, in the later eighteenth century, was largely confined to government subsidy to 'loyal' newspapers.(16) In any case, late eighteenth century publishers prided themselves on their impartiality,(17) and this required at least some coverage of the anti-establishment position. Thomas Colville, the Dundee publisher of three ephemeral journals contemporaneous with the American war, asserted in a new venture first published in 1799 that "the Editor is of no political party, and means to take no side in political discussions".(18) The **Caledonian Mercury,** taking the Prime Minister to task in 1776 for "his facetious remarks upon newspapers", reminded him "that these publications have been as much at the service of his advocates as of enemies, that they have extolled his great abilities as well as declaimed his egregious blunders and, in short, have manifested the greatest impartiality".(19)

The real question, however, is not what was claimed but what was practised. The modern editorial was not of course a feature of the **eighteenth century press in Britain,(20) though an** impression of editorial policy can be gleaned from the occasional remark, the opinions of reviewers employed by the paper, and the selection of items by correspondents and contributors. Judged by this evidence, there was no such thing as a radical press in Scotland at this time - the most we can discern are slight variations in the degree of attachment to the ministry of the day. The **Scots Magazine** took impartiality to the length of employing two reviewers, identified as "C" and "M", who regularly adopted quite opposite stances in their reviews of books and pamphlets on the American question.(21) The most candid statement of editorial policy on the **American war** was that offered to its readers by the **Caledonian Mercury** in 1780. The **paper's** publisher, John Robertson, reminded them that "the period which the present publisher has occupied has been a most important and eventful portion of the annals of Great Britain and America. It has during this time been his study, in the insertion of Essays and Letters upon the subject, to pay a proper deference to the several opinions which have prevailed even on this side of the Tweed. While one of the most learned and respectable societies in Scotland" (i.e. the **Faculty of Advocates**) "**refused to subscribe supplies or testify their** approbation, it would well have become the publisher of a newspaper, **however clear in his own opinion,** to treat all opposition to the measures of government as factious or unwise ...."(22)

No other editor at this time offered such a clear statement as to where his own personal sympathies lay, and attempts to assign a particular character or bias to particular journals are fraught with danger. For one thing, as is well known, it was common practice for newspapers to take in each other's washing - to fill their columns not only with news but also with letters reprinted from other papers. This practice was bound to encourage some uniformity, or apparent uniformity, of view throughout the nation's press. Against this, it was always possible for a publisher to select which items to reprint, and in any given region there would usually be some special interest which would affect the view taken of a particular issue. For example, letters in the

Aberdeen Journal on the question of recruitment into the navy centred on the problem of maintaining the strength of the local fishing fleet. (23) Other examples of local differences could be cited.

Obviously local interests and personal inclinations helped to produce a variety of views on certain issues. But out of this variety it is possible to discern some dominant trends, and, tentatively, outline perhaps three fairly distinct phases. During the first of these, from the early skirmishes at Lexington and Concord to the publication of the Declaration of Independence, opinions were expressed by correspondents to the papers both in support of the American cause and denouncing the American rebellion. With the news of the Declaration and the earlier announcement by government that a state of rebellion now existed, opinion coalesced rapidly and firmly behind the ministerial policy. Support for the war, though given a severe blow by the disaster of Saratoga, was reinforced by the news of the Franco-American alliance of 1778, and the need to defend the empire, possibly even Britain herself, against attack. In the third phase, as defeat followed defeat, enthusiasm waned significantly, attacks on the ministry and the military leadership became more frequent and outspoken, until towards the end the whole country, with only a few exceptions, seemed to lapse into a state of apathy - resigned to American independence, possibly also to the loss of other parts of Britain's overseas empire.

The response in Scotland to the American crisis in its early stages may be said to have been characterised by public enthusiasm and some private doubts. Cities like Edinburgh and Dundee, smaller towns like Arbroath, offered Loyal Addresses to the Crown, calling for the firmest measures to be adopted to put down the rebellion. (24) The press was one medium for the publication of recruitment notices, which offered to the lucky recruit the chance to become a landowner in the colonies, or to escape a "termagent and cross" wife at home. (25) Such appeals to self interest and good sense attracted a ready response in Scotland. General Fraser's new Highland regiment was completed in only six weeks. (26) Scotsmen were proud of the readiness of their countrymen to enlist, and so help to suppress what was generally termed "this unnatural rebellion in America". One correspondent to the **Caledonian Mercury** observed with satisfaction that "even the women of Scotland are so fully satisfied of the justice of the cause, that they have endeavoured to be enrolled in General Fraser's new regiment", and he cited the case of such a woman who was discovered "only after her husband thought proper to claim her", noted that even then "as a proof that her abilities were in no wise inferior to many who had enlisted in that corps, she offered to fight, by single combat, either by fists or any other way they would think proper, half a dozen they should pitch (sic) out of these recruits". (27)

Other writers to the press denounced the Americans as inferior beings, and warned government of the consequences of leniency. A Strathspey Farmer,' writing to the **Aberdeen Journal** in February 1775, claimed to have located in America the seat of "the Popish purgatory", (28) while 'Coriolanus' in the **Caledonian Mercury** traced the development of American demands which, he claimed, had fed upon the lack of ministerial resolve. "The mask", he declared, "is at last thrown off; an exclusive power of legislation is now maintained to be the inalienable right of America, and its independency essential to its happiness'. If the "impartial reader ... dreads the prospect of having the colonies torn from the mother country, and erected into a separate and independent state, he will confess the necessity of a speedy and vigorous opposition to the present and unnatural rebellion". (29)

On the whole, however, calls in the press for vigorous action to put down the rebellion were matched if not outweighed in this early period by calls for leniency, or by reasoned defences of the American position. 'Pacificus' in the **Aberdeen Journal** in August 1775 proclaimed "the impiety of attacking men who own their allegience to the King, but appeal to the sword only in defence of their liberties ". "How?" he asked, "can we go against such a people with any shadow of hope of succeeding?". Nay, we are rushing headlong in the support of a bad cause, to the ruin of both countries, and our own perdition". (30) In the same issue 'Juvenis' lamented "to see with what malignant venom some writers deprecate the Americans, and treat them with the greatest contempt; and also express an ardent desire for their utter and final destruction". Yet the American cause was not without merit. "The Americans cannot", he argued, "consistent with propriety, allow their" (i.e. the British Parliament's) 'right of taxing them, unless they are represented as a body politic. Some of the ablest men that Britain can produce have plainly proved, by cogent and nervous reasoning, that taxation and representation are inseparably connected". (31)

While it might be difficult to estimate precisely the relative weight of the two sides in this debate, the fact remains that there were two sides. This was true even amongst those who had a common financial interest. As Dr Devine has recently shown, the Glasgow tobacco lords at this time adopted a low profile - petitioning the Crown for a policy of leniency, and instructing their factors in America to avoid antagonising local opinion. (32) Yet others, also with an admitted interest, wrote to the press calling for firm retaliatory measures against American non-intercourse, and arguing that the interests of men like themselves were bound to be "much safer in the hands of a British Parliament, than in the Americans under no government". (33)

The point about this early period surely is this - that so long as the Americans merely contended for their rights **within** the British imperial system, these rights could be legitimately, often sympathetically, debated. But once they moved on from claiming the rights of British citizens to proclaiming their independence from Britain, the nature of the debate in Scotland, and in the whole country, was forced to change. The effect of the Declaration of Independence on former sympathisers was put forcefully in an article in the **North British Miscellany** (another of Colville's Dundee Journals) of September 1779. "Whatever might be the opinion of different parties, with regard to the resistance which America made to the claim of taxation, the declaration of independence staggered her most zealous friends. A declaration which was to throw off all the authority of this country over America, to expunge from our books every statute concerning her, to annihilate our commerce, to shut up our nurseries of seamen, and taking from us those great resources pour them into the lap of a powerful rival and inverterate enemy - such a declaration can hardly be supposed to have been favourably received". (34)

The Declaration, and the declaration by Britain that the colonies were now in a state of rebellion, thus cut the ground from under many of those who had supported the American view of British parliamentary authority. Arguments which hitherto had been acceptable as contributions to the debate now smacked of treason, and when Dr John Erskine reprinted in 1776 his controversial pamphlet "Shall I go to war with my American brethren?" he was roundly condemned by the **Edinburgh Magazine and Review** for publishing "this treasonable paper". (35) That an entirely new situation now obtained was widely recognised. "As to the subject that gave rise to the present dispute, viz. the right of the British Parliament to tax America", wrote 'Monitor' to the **Caledonian Mercury** in August 1776, "I shall neither affirm nor deny anything concerning it. This is now no longer the question. The point now to be determined is, whether it is now most for the interest of Great Britain, that the Americans should be allowed to continue in the same footing on which they have hitherto stood, . . . or that the British Empire in America should be finally extirpated". (36)

The issues between Britain and her colonies had, by the late summer of 1776, been resolved into one - who would win? There were always a few pessimists around who doubted Britain's capacity to subdue a determined and energetic people in America, but for the moment they were outshouted by the jingoists who took every opportunity to raise morale and cast doubts about the Americans' ability to wage a successful war. In March 1776 the **Dundee Weekly Magazine** had drawn attention to the Americans' "want of ammunition and other necessaries requisite for war", and claimed that "a very great desertion had taken place in the Provincial army, on account of their not receiving their pay regularly". (37) Hopes of a quick and successful conclusion to the war were high. Almost on the eve of Saratoga the following poem appeared in the **Caledonian Mercury,** addressed to General Burgoyne, on reading his Proclamation to the Americans:
"From Rebels hide the Pen you drew,
Keen as your Sword, as polished too,
Nor still more desp'rate make 'em,
Lest, ere your march can be begun,

The Heroes should so stoutly - run,
You'll never overtake 'em!" (38)

In the face of such confidence, Burgoyne's defeat at Saratoga with the capture of his entire army came as something of an unwelcome surprise. Dundas for one changed from being a stalwart supporter of the war, to doubting whether it should be proceeded with. (39) His new pessimism was widely reflected in the press. 'A.B.', writing to the **Caledonian Mercury** in December, argued that the only possible hope now lay in an all out effort to crush New England, but that "if the subduing of that province is impracticable, we ought to take the Dean of Gloucester's advice at the beginning of the American disputes, i.e., to leave America to itself". (40)

That such a course - simply to abandon the Americans to their independence - was not and could not be followed, was the consequence of the Franco-American alliance of 1778. Opinion in Scotland was at once outraged at and contemptuous of this move. By enlisting the aid of Britain's old enemy, the Americans had added treachery to rebellion. By allying themselves with a Popish depotism they had betrayed their own religion and their belief in democracy. They would in any case soon find to their cost that such an ally would inevitably become a master. In August 1778 the **Scots Magazine** came out with an ingenious poetic version of the King Log and King Stork fable, with France cast as King Stork and the American rebels as the Frogs. This poem is too long to be given here in full, but the last few lines give a flavour of the whole:
"Say Yankees, don't you feel compunction,
At your unnatural rash conjunction?
Can love for you in him take root,
Who's Catholic, and absolute?
I'll tell these croakers how he'll treat 'em;
Frenchmen, like Storks, love frogs - to eat 'em". (41)

The transformation of the war into an international conflict had at least one tangible effect - a massive recruiting drive in which Scotland took or believed she took, the lead. "In this part of the kingdom", the **Scots Magazine** reported early in the year, "the exertions in support of government have even exceeded the exertions in the southern part". (42) The **Magazine** went on to detail the efforts of the big landowners, like the Dukes of Atholl and Hamilton, and of the towns and burghs, to raise regiments and companies at their own expense. Of the leading societies in Scotland, only the Faculty of Advocates in Edinburgh refused to take part in the general enthusiasm for raising them - and this for a variety of reasons, of which opposition in principle to the American war was probably the most important. (43) When the supply of recruits seemed to be running low, ingenious proposals were advanced to make up the deficiency. The recruitment of women was perhaps an obvious suggestion, and we have seen how some women eagerly responded to the call. There is no evidence, however, that a solution proposed earlier in the **Dundee Weekly Magazine**, that new companies be formed of imported Orang

Utangs, (44) was ever put into practice.

No amount of enthusiasm for recruitment, however, could disguise the fact that the war was going badly, and that the cause of imperial integrity was probably already lost. 1778 was a year of confusion, when calls for national unity were matched by counsels of despair; when fierce recrimination was directed against the ministry either for embarking on the war or, having once embarked on it, failing to bring it to a successful conclusion. The point is an important one that the lack of military success brought together into the opposition camp individuals who had hitherto been opposed to one another on the question of the American war. Criticism of the ministry and of the military leadership mounted in 1778 and 1779. Of the army commanders, Howe bore the brunt, and a lengthy letter attacking his conduct of the campaign point by point was so well received by readers of the **Caledonian Mercury** that the publisher had to reprint it in the next issue to satisfy the demand. (45) But the severest censure was reserved for the ministry. One of the most outspoken letters on the subject appeared in the **Caledonian Mercury** under the name of 'Horatio'. "The Ministry", the writer alleged, "have lost us America, for a point of honour and a pound of tea. They have lost us the islands of Grenada and St. Vincent, and the dominion over Ireland.... They entered into a war with America, without deliberating sufficiently on the justice of the measure or knowing any more concerning the strength or inclinations of the Americans than I do of what is transacting in the Turkish Divan". Amongst other blunders, 'Horatio' included the failure to find allies, the increase in taxation, the choice of Germaine as Secretary for War, the appointment of Howe, Keppel, Burgoyne and others to senior military and naval commands. (46)

The Ministry was subjected not only to criticism but also to an abundance of good advice. By this stage most commentators recognised the impossibility of securing the original objective of subjugating all the American colonies, and proposed lesser objectives - partition of the thirteen colonies, holding on to key ports like New York, securing the British West Indies. (47) A rare lighter note was struck by the writer who suggested that the war be brought to an immediate end, and that the British and American armies be amalgamated into a single "INVINCIBLE ARMADA" to descend on the gold and silver colonies of South America. The spoils from this expedition were to be divided between the Americans and the British, the latter's portion being applied to pay off the National Debt and various other deserving uses, leaving only a small stipend, by way of reward, for "your servant, Jacob Henriques". (48)

Even if we accept, however, that the volume of criticism mounted sharply from 1778, it must be emphasised that opposition to government was still only a minority view. When the 'Ghost of Wallace' issued a call for national unity in the dark days of the spring of 1780, (49) commentators on his letter admitted that his appeal was likely to meet with majority support. "It must be

acknowledged", wrote his principal critic, "that Scotland had, to appearance, all along encouraged the minsterial war against our fellow subjects in America", (50) while another, less critical, estimated that "nine-tenths of the inhabitants would approve the programme" of sending loyal addresses to the Crown. (51) Unless we accept that such was the opinion of very many Scots at the time, and try to explain it, we shall be in danger of distorting the true picture.

While the response of individuals or groups to the American crisis would to some extent be dictated by special interests or circumstances, all these must be set against the general view of the colonial relationship as seen through Scottish eyes. While differing views on the subject certainly existed, and were given a thorough airing in the press, the consensus must be described as thoroughly orthodox, even, or so it was sometimes alleged, reactionary. In a long letter to the **Caledonian Mercury** in January 1775, one correspondent faced up squarely to the "question of right", and set "to examine on what principles the Americans ground their objections to the right of the British Parliament to tax them; the establishment of this right being the foundation of that conduct which, I think, parliament ought to hold to her Colonies". "The principal ... objection to which it will be requisite to give a formal and direct answer is this: That the Americans are not represented in Parliament, and therefore are not subject to taxes imposed by it, representation being, by the constitution of this realm, a necessary ground of taxation. To this I answer, that by the constitution, representation is not necessary to taxation, and that if it was, the Americans are represented". (52) 'Q in the corner', writing to the **Aberdeen Journal** in the following month, strongly deprecated the repeal of the Stamp Act, since to have done so implied "an acknowledgement of right in the colonies, which is a monstrous idea. The very word 'colony' implies 'dependency'. An absolute right in a dependent state is an absurdity in terms; it can be no other than a right derived from a superior, whose superior authority should therefore be acknowledged". (53)

That there were opponents of this view within Scotland can scarcely be denied, but the best known of the pamphleteers who sympathised with the American position was Dr Richard Price, an Englishman. Many of Price's writings on the American question were reviewed in Scottish periodicals like the **Edinburgh Magazine and Review,** generally in terms of vigorous condemnation. Price, according to one such comment, had " acquired importance from the number of pamphlets which have been published against him, from the blind and factious approbation of the city of London, and from the anxious industry of administration to prevent its influence". (54) On another occasion a correspondent to the **Caledonian Mercury** ironically expressed his gratitude to Price for making taxation depend on representation - if applied to his own case, the argument would effectively discharge him from the obligation of paying taxes. (55)

A survey of opinion as it was reflected in the Scottish press suggests that, while there were some sympathisers with the American interpretation of their rights as regards parliamentary taxation, these were outnumbered by their opponents. In any case, as pointed out before, the American leap from a claim to rights within the British constitution to, in the Declaration of Independence, a complete rejection of that constitution dismayed their friends and infuriated their enemies.

The **Scots Magazine** ran a series of lengthy articles under the heading of "An Answer to the Declaration of Independence", (56) which displayed very clearly where the real sympathies of that periodical lay. The articles began by adopting an almost pedagogical tone, examining the Declaration clause by clause, and exposing tis weaknesses lf logic and historical accuracy. In a final review of the document, however, the author turned to the preamble, which he declared he was tempted to dismiss, since "the opinions of the Americans on Government, like those of their good ancestors on witchcraft, would be too ridiculous to deserve any notice, if, like them too, contemptible and extravagant as they are, the had not led to the most serious evils. In the preamble . . . they attempt to establish a theory of government; a theory as absurd and visionary as the system of conduct in defence of which it is established is nefarious. Here it is that maxims are advanced in justification of their enterprise against the British government. To these maxims, adduced for the purpose. It would be sufficient to say, that they are repugnant to the British constitution. But beyond this, they are subversive of every actual or imaginable kind of government".(57) Given the **Scots Magazine's** usual attitude of cool detachment, this was a remarkable indictment.

The Scottish attitude to American claims and ultimate rebellion was derived not only from a general view of the imperial relationship, but also, it might be suggested, from a general view of domestic politics. In the opinion of the Lord Mayor of London, this general view amounted to a predilection for despotic government, and while this charge was indignantly repudiated, there is clear evidence in the press of widespread distrust in Scotland of republicanism, the opposition factions, and individual radicals from Chatham to Wilkes.

Not surprisingly, former Jacobites and their sympathisers condemned Wilkesian radicalism and upheld the virtues of the monarchical system. In a remarkable letter to the **Dundee Weekly Magazine** in 1775, Hector Stuart of Lochaber, claiming to have fought in both '15 and '45, launched a harsh attack on Wilkes. (58) Admitting that his own generation had been deluded into believing in the **jus divinum** of the House of Stuart, the writer pointed out that "we were for **some** King, but erred in our choice; but you and your Myrmidons are enemies to **Monarchy** - to a regular and mild establishment, and to civil society". More significant here is the charge laid against Wilkes that "You have endeavoured to deprive your country of those colonies which she has been establishing ever since the reign of Elizabeth". In many Scottish minds there existed a complex and many sided connection between republicanism and the American rebellion. The Rev. John Witherspoon tried to explain this connection in an address to his fellow countrymen, in America, which was reprinted in the **Scots Magazine.** Witherspoon admitted that the real friends of America in Great Britain were very few, and this was as true of the Scots as it was of the English. But he tried to excuse Scottish opposition to the American cause as a reaction to Wilkes, despite the fact that that cause "was as different from that of Wilkes as light is from darkness". The blame for this confusion lay with "that gentleman and his associates", who "thought proper to found the whole of their opposition to the then ministry upon a contempt and hatred of the Scottish nation; and by the most illiberal methods to stir up a national jealousy between the northern and southern parts of the island".(59)

Scottish affection, then, for the monarchical principle, displayed by several other writers besides Stuart,(60) their hatred of Wilkes, and their identification of American republicanism with Wilkesian radicalism, may help to explain in part their hostility to the American cause. But Stuart had carried the connection further by blaming Wilkes for trying to deprive Britain of her colonies. Charges of this kind were constantly being levelled against the so-called "Patriots" - that is American sympathisers in Britain - on two main grounds. Firstly, there was the charge that they had encouraged the Americans to rebel by their example. As an "Epigram" in the **Caledonian Mercury** put it:
"Twas Wilkes's low self centred knav'ry
Taught mobs all government is slav'ry.
Twas he our Britons taught to jar,
Abroad, our Yankies fired to war,
Ye gods, what mighty evil springs,
From most contemptible of things".(61)
Secondly, it was a common charge that, by destroying public morale and governmental authority at home, the "patriots" severely impeded the war effort. Explaining the humiliating position in which his country found itself by the spring of 1778, 'An Indignant Briton' in the **Caledonian Mercury** asserted "that it was want of unanimity that ruined us: there were adders in our bosom that gave us much more mortal wounds than the swords of our enemies; the worm of faction nipped our measures in the bud, and blasted all our hopes". (62)
Another aspect of the imperial relationship which this time was less clearly concerned with constitutionalism, though still with paternalism, is reflected in the frequent application of the term "unnatural" to the American dispute. The word was used by both supporters and opponents of the war, but it suggests that on both sides the relationship between the colonies and the 'mother country' was seen as a familial one, and that within the imperial family it was as 'unnatural' for the child to rebel against the mother, as it was for the mother to destroy the child. A noteworthy example of this concept is to be found in a long

allegorical tale, published in the **Dundee Weekly Magazine** in 1777, in which the whole dispute is retold in the form of a family quarrel, involving "Mrs Albion" and her four sons. America, by a neat **double entendre,** is renamed "Benjamin". (63)

In addition to these general views of the imperial relationship, Scottish opinion was influenced by particular consequences and characteristics of the American rebellion. High on this list must come considerations of trade, and the effect of the war on the Scottish economy, though the picture revealed by the press is confused. Some sectors of the economy benefited from the war, others, most obviously the tobacco trade, appeared to have been adversely affected. The effects altered also through time, as the initial 'windfall' gains of the tobacco trade were not repeated, or as the attacks of privateers become bolder and the losses they inflicted more severe. (64)

In the early months of the war, we can detect a remarkable degree of optimism. Attempts to collect debts owed to Glasgow merchants in the colonies were reported as having been successful, although the recently published researches of Dr. Devine have cast doubts on the accuracy of these claims. (65) In August 1775 the **Dundee Weekly Magazine,** amongst other papers, printed a letter from Glasgow which claimed that "More than half a million of the debts due from America to Glasgow have, by the activity and prudence of the storekeepers, been recovered and sent home in the course of the month past. What is owing to this country is very trifling", and the letter went on to assert that "while this anarchy and distraction distress America, liberty, concord, and a trade beyond our hopes, bless this corner of happy Britain". (66)

Of course the war offered special opportunities to some industries involved in the production of war supplies, and the **Caledonian Mercury** in January 1776 noted with satisfaction the large order for ship's cannons, field pieces and other weapons won by the Carron Company. (67) The same paper reported in the following month the imminent arrival at Leith of 17,000 Hessians and Hanoverians. "The money so great a body of men behoved to spend would ... be highly advantageous to this city", while "the farmers and others would also be greatly benefited, as they could not fail of finding a ready market for grain". (68) Reports from Glasgow and Paisley in March 1776 continued in this optimistic vein, despite the difficulties of the American trade. "The demands for all our different manufacturers", noted the **Dundee Weekly Magazine,** "still continue brisker than when the American trade was open. The orders from England and abroad are so very large, that it will not be in our power to complete them for many months to come". (69)   In September, the **Edinburgh Advertiser** printed a letter which noted that "it is a matter of curious speculation to enquire why the annihilation of the American trade, which has been set forth as of vast importance to this kingdom, has had so little effect upon our manufactures?" (70)

The truth was, of course, as in most wars, that war-based industries thrived, while the vulnerable trans-Atlantic trade suffered. As early as November 1775 the **Aberdeen Journal** reported, possibly inaccurately, that large numbers of seamen at Port Glasgow had been thrown out of work, and that a subscription had been opened for their relief. (71) Short term factors which had cushioned the effect of the war on Scottish trade, had, by the late '70s, ceased to apply. Even so, the gloomy picture presented by a correspondent to the **Caledonian Mercury** in 1778 was probably an exaggeration. "Upon a little reflection, the justice of the cry 'Alas, poor Scotland', will be very obvious. We appear on the brink of ruin. One half of our merchants have lost their fortunes, and will involve many individuals in ruin. One million five hundred thousand pounds cannot be lost by 30 companies only. Tradesmen and money lenders, in great numbers, must be ruined". (72)

An accurate statement or not, the resecuring of the old monopoly of the colonial trade was seen by many as one of the main reasons for continuing the war. "One of the greatest benefits" of (the possession of colonies) wrote 'D.T.' to the **Caledonian Mercury,** "is an exclusive trade with all our colonies on the continent of America; the only possible way now left to secure which is to act with the utmost vigour against the rebels there, as well as domestic enemies here". (73) Some writers saw the commercial implications of the American question, and the likely consequences of American independence, in a wider imperial context. "The question now", wrote 'A Patriot' in 1778, "is not the right of levying a tax . . . but the dependence and subjection of your old colonies and provinces on the continent of America upon the executive and legislative government of Great Britain, and in consequence your maintaining the possessions of all your colonies and plantations in that quarter of the world, nay of those in Asia and Africa, and your very existence as a commercial state". (74) It is interesting to note that in March 1783, when such was the feeling in Scotland over the peace negotiations that the subject of America had all but disappeared from the correspondence columns, the last word lay with 'A Glasgow Merchant'. Through the pages of the **Glasgow Mercury** he urged his fellow merchants and trades to abstain from offering an address to the Crown in support of the peace proposals - at least "until you see whether the recommendations of Congress to the different States of America will operate in your favours or not". (75)

Finally, amongst the major factors influencing Scottish opinion towards the American cause, we may consider the revulsion, on the part of many liberal minded Scotsmen, at the reported oppressive policies of the provincials against the loyalist opponents. The effect of these reports on the minds of those who had hitherto sympathised with American claims against Parliamentary tyranny were well expressed in a letter to the **Aberdeen Journal** in the autumn of 1776. "I confess", wrote 'Apius', "I was once an advocate for the Americans: their claim to be exempted from Parliamentary taxation seemed to me to be founded in justice; and I thought that it was equitable at least to give them a security against the oppressive exercise of it. But some of their late proceedings have convinced me, that their opposition is not dictated by true patriotism, but a spirit of tyranny and despotism''. Amongst American tryrannical acts he cited their destruction of the liberty of the press, curtailment of free speech, denial of trial by jury and punishment under **ex post facto** laws. (76)

It would not be difficult to identify other factors which had some influence on contemporary attitudes to the American Revolution. But in the time which is left let us turn to a different aspect of the question - what we might call the 'Scottish Dimension'. Having chosen to examine the Revolution in the Scottish press, can we now identify any peculiarly Scottish aspect of the debate?

To investigate this question thoroughly would require a comparative study of the English press far beyond the scope of this paper. I would suggest, however, that in the matter of sympathy for the American cause, Witherspoon's assessment - that there was little to choose between the Scots and the English – was substantially correct.

To some extent, the nature of the press itself helped to blur the lines of national demarcation. For its news of the American situation, the press in Scotland was heavily dependent on English sources - for example the news coverage of the **Aberdeen Journal** was made up almost entirely of a summary taken from the latest English papers. Even the correspondence was to a large extent national - letters to the London press were frequently reprinted in Edinburgh, Glasgow and Aberdeen. Many correspondents within Scotland made it clear that when they spoke of ''the nation'', they meant the whole of the United Kingdom. ''The unhappy contest with America is not'', objected one Scots writer, ''as has been most impudently and unjustly held forth by the trumpeters of treason and sedition in our neighbouring kingdom a **Scots** war. It is the cause of Great Britain at large''. (77) Many Scots believed, however, that it **was** a Scots war, in the sense that Scotland bore the brunt of recruitment, and in the process denuded herself of useful inhabitants, and rendered herself vulnerable to foreign invasion. ''Our nobility and gentry'' claimed 'A Scot' in 1778, ''have voluntarily raised a number of regiments for the defence of the united kingdoms. How have they been disposed of? It will not be alleged that many of them have been allowed to remain in the country where they were raised, though it was never in a more

defenceless state''. (78)

It was this feeling of vulnerability, not only to possible French invasion, but also to actual attack from privateers like John Paul Jones and Commander Fall, which stimulated demands in Scotland for a national militia. The persistent refusal of the ministry to give in to this demand was an important source of Scottish grievance, and the militia question became the dominant theme of correspondents in most newspapers during the second half of 1782. (79) Unlike other grievances, like the failure to win the war, which the Scots shared with the English, the militia issue brought out expressions of violent Anglo-phobia, and was the primary cause, I would suggest, of that dissatisfaction with the Union noted by Dr Phillipson. 'Vox Populi', writing in the **Caledonian Mercury** as early as April 1776, drew attention to the small number and poor quality of troops stationed in Scotland, and urged with considerable cogency the dissolution of the Union. (80) At the same time, the Scots themselves were not united on the issue, and the aristocracy, none too keen to see arms in the hands of those over whom they had insufficient control, would perhaps have preferred to place their trust in the Duke of Buccleuch's Anti-Gallican Society, which sought to repel the French threat by offering prizes for archery and route marching. (81) Certainly the militia question revealed some of the tensions and political disagreements within Scotland herself. In Pittenweem, to take perhaps a minor example, the local citizens used the alternative offer of a volunteer force to back their demands for the annual election of magistrates. (82)

The picture of Scottish involvement with and attitudes towards the American Revolution which emerges from the contemporary press is, then, a full one. In it the Scottish people are seen to be directly affected by the war in a variety of ways, intensely interested in its day-to-day management, and in the fundamental principles of empire involved. While majority opinion was opposed to American claims, and would have wished for outright victory, Fagerstrom is right to draw attention to the growing disillusionment with the national leadership as the possibility of that victory receded. But the point must be emphasised that Scottish anger, as reflected in the press, was directed not so much against the basic principles of the existing government, as against its malfunctioning. The Scots emerged from the war in a mood to demand reform, but not their own revolution.

REFERENCES

1. See e.g. Campbell, R. H., **Scotland Since 1707** pp. 39 et seq.
2. Fagerstrom, D. I., ''The American Revolutionary Movement in Scottish Opinion, 1763-1783''. Unpubl. Ph.D thesis. Edinburgh 1951.
3. Phillipson, N. T., ''Public Opinion and the Union'', in Phillipson and Mitchison (eds), **Scotland in the Age of Improvement**, p. 126.
4. Fagerstrom D. I., **op. cit. passim**, and ''Scottish Opinion and the American Revolution'', **William and Mary Quarterly** 3rd ser. vol. XI 1954 pp. 252-76.
5. See Craig, M. E., **The Scottish Periodical Press 1750-1789** (Edin. 1931) and Ferguson, J. P. S., **Scottish Newspapers held in Scottish Libraries** (Scottish Central Library Pamphlet, Edin. 1956).
6. **D.W.M.**, vol. 1., no 25 back cover.
7. See 'F. La Bar---S.' in **D.W.M.** 3 Nov., 1775, p.292.
8. According to Fagerstrom, ''The American Revolutionary Movement'' p. 189, **R.W.M.**, had a sale of around 1400 copies a week in 1779. The **Mercury's** predecessor, **The Weekly Magazine**, had a circulation of 3000 per week, which was claimed to be almost as many as all the other Edinburgh papers put together. **R.W.M.** vol. 1, no. 1, p. 1. But Fagerstrom puts the **C.M.** at the top of the circulation table. (''American Revolutionary Movement'', p. 189).
9. See the very useful Chart of Periodicals current between 1750 and 1789, in Craig, **op. cit.** pp. 87-89.

10. Aspinall, A., **Politics and the Press, 1780-1850** p. 351.
11. **C.M.** 31 May, 1776, p. 1.
12. **S.M.** v. 41, Jan. 1779, pp. 1-4. By a decision of the Court of Exchequer in 1777, the newspaper tax was extended to 'magazines' if they contained regular news items. This decision was described by the Dundee publisher, Thomas Colville, as "so fatal to all weekly publications in this country", and was certainly the direct cause of the demise of his **Dundee Weekly Magazine,** and also of **The Weekly Magazine,** published in Edinburgh by Walter Ruddiman and Son, defendants in the case.
See **D.M.** No. 24, 1800, quoted in Millar, A. H., **Dundee Periodical Literature** (n.d., unpaginated), and **C.M.** 18 June 1777, p. 3.
13. **R.W.M.** vol. II, no. 13, 1777.
14. **C.M.** 3, 5, 10 June, 1775.
15. i.e. Home Office Papers (Public Record Office, London) H.O. 102/...
16. Aspinall, A., **op. cit.** p. 351.
17. On claims to 'impartiality' in the English press of the period, see Hinkhouse, F. I., **The British Press and the Preliminaries of the American Revolution,** pp. 13 et. seq.
18. **D.M.** Jan. 1799, quoted in Millar, **op. cit.** (unpag.).
19. CM. 1st May, 1776 p. 2.
20. On the early "editorial" see Hinkhouse, **op. cit.** pp. 11-12.
21. See for example the reviews of Dr Price's "Additional observations on the nature and value of Civil Liberty, and the war with America ...", in which the author announced his intention of withdrawing from politics:
M: "We cannot take leave of this respectable writer, without expressing our concern to see a person of his amiable character so reviled and unworthily treated as he has been by some of his numerous opponents".
C: "We congratulate the public and Dr Price on his resolution of retiring into obscurity; whence he ought to have been restrained, by the strongest bonds of civil duty, from ever emerging, as the partisan of a rebellious and infatuated people".
(**S.M.** vol. 39. 1777, p. 98).
22. **C.M.,** 1st Jan. 1780, p. 2.
23. e.g. **A.J.,** 15 Nov. 1779, p.4.
24. Typical of such addresses were those from the Provost and Town Cuncil, and from the Gentlemen, Clergy, Merchants, Manufacturers, incorporated Trades and principal Inhabitants of Dundee, in respectively, **A.J.** 13 Nov. 1775, p. 3, and **D.W.M.,** 24 Nov. 1775, p. 384.
25. **D.W.M.** vol. 1, no. 23. Notice on back cover.
26. **C.M.** 11 March, 1776, p. 2.
27. **C.M.** 20 Jan. 1776. p. 2.
28. **A.J.** 6 Feb., 1775, p. 4.
29. **C.M.** 17 April, 1776, p. 1.
30. **A.J.** 28 Aug., 1775, p. 3.
31. **Ibid.**
32. Devine, T. M., **The Tobacco Lords,** p. 103.
33. **S.M.** Jan. 1775, p. 8. 'H.S.' to the Printer.
34. **N.B.M.,** vol. II, no. 6, 13-19 Sept., 1779, p. 176. "Considerations upon granting independence to America".
35. **E.M.R.** vol. V 1776, p. 267-271.
36. **C.M.** 31 Aug., 1776, p. 1.
37. **D.W.M.** 22 March, 1776, pp. 163-166.
38. **C.M.** 13 Sept., 1777, p. 3. 'Foresight' to the Printer.
39. Mathieson, C., **Life of Henry Dundas.**

40. **C.M.** 17 Dec. 1777, p. 3. 'A.B.' to the Printer.
41. **S.M.** vol. XL Aug., 1778, p. 439.
42. **S.M.** vol. XL Feb., 1778, 48 **et seq.**
43. **Ibid.** See also Fagerstrom, "The American Revolutionary Movement . . .", pp. 322 **et seq.**
44. **D.W.M.** 5 July, 1776, p. 514. According to the author of this pleasing "Ode addressed to Lord Barrington", such recruits would have certain clear advantages over other foreign mercenaries :
. . ."With envious glance shall Germaine see,
These Tory troops skip up a tree,
Firing as quick as Prussians,
He'll find the loyal Ourans far,
The fittest for his Yankey war,
And scorn the aid of Russians".
45. **C.M.** 30 Dec.,1778, p. 1, and 6 Jan., 1779, p. 1.
46. **C.M.** 24 May, 1780, p. 3.
47. See for example, **A.J.** 14 Sept., 1778. 'Nerva' to the Printer.
48. **C.M.** 13 Jan., 1777, p. 1.
49. **C.M.** 17 April, 1780, pp. 1-2.
50. **C.M.** 24 April, 1780, p. 1. "One of the People of Scotland".
51. **C.M.** 19 April, 1780, p. 1.
52. **C.M.** 2 Jan., 1775, p. 1. "A Speech . . . on the Bill for altering the charter of the colony of Massachusetts Bay".
53. **A.J.** 20 Feb., 1775, p. 3.
54. **E.M.R.** vol. V, 1776, pp. 316-325.
55. **C.M.** 8 April, 1776, p. 3.
56. **S.M.** vol. 39, 1777, pp. 122-128, 177-186, 233-248.
57. **Ibid.** pp. 288-293.
58. **D.W.M.** 15 Dec., 1775, pp. 438 **et seq.**
59. **S.M.** vol. 39 1777, pp. 93-6. "Dr Witherspoon's address to his fellow countrymen in America".
60. e.g. by 'The Ghost of Wallace' in **C.M.** 17 April, 1780, pp. 1-2.
61. **C.M.** 6 July, 1776, p. 3.
62. **C.M.** 2 March, 1778, p. 1.
63. **D.W.M.** vol. I, no. 1, 1775, p. 149.
64. For an account of the impact of the American war on Scottish overseas trade, see Ferguson, W., **Scotland, 1689 to the Present,** cap. X., and Robertson, M. L., "Scottish Commerce and the American War of Independence", **Econ. H. R.** 2nd ser. iX, no. 1 (1956) p. 123.
65. Devine, **op. cit.,** pp. 112-115.
66. **D.W.M.** 25 Aug. 1775, p. 69.
67. **C.M.** 8 Jan., 1776, p. 2.
68. **C.M.** 17 Feb., 1776, p. 2.
69. **D.W.M.** 22 March, 1776, pp. 164-165.
70. **A.J.** 27 Nov., 1775, p. 2.
71. **C.M.** 29 Apr., 1778, p. 1.
72. **C.M.** 24 Aug., 1776, p. 1. See also **Ibid** 28 Aug., 1776, p. 1. 'X' to the Printer. ". . .it is necessary for Great Britain to reduce America that it may not infringe upon her navigation".
73. **C.M.** 14 Jan., 1778, p. 1. 'A Patriot' to the People.
74. **G.M.,** 6-13 March, 1783, p. 86.
75. **A.J.** 30 Sept. 1776, p. 3.
76. **C.M.** 7 Jan., 1778, p. 3. 'Censor' to the Printer.
77. **C.M.** 27 April, 1778, p. 3.
78. For a very full statement of the various plans for a militia in Scotland, see **G.M.** No. 246, Sept., 1782, pp. 297-298.
79. **C.M.** 13 April, 1776, p. 8.
80. **C.M.** 28 Jan., 1780, p. 3.
81. **C.M.** 10 July, 1782, p. 1. 'A Burgess' to the Printer.

SCOTTISH ENLIGHTENMENT, AMERICAN REVOLUTION AND ATLANTIC REFORM

C DUNCAN RICE

As a matter of self-defence, I shall begin this paper by taking some pains to explain what it is not. It is not any of things which might reasonably be expected at a conference held in Edinburgh, a city swarming with Scottish historians, to celebrate the bicentennial of American independence. I am not, for instance, concerned with adding to our information on specific contacts between Scotland and America. I shrink from the Herculean task, indeed the impossible task, of demonstrating that my countrymen contributed significantly to the success of the American Revolution. I shall not attempt to differentiate between what was Scottish and what was merely enlightened about the Scottish Enlightenment, and those aspects of it which were absorbed by American learning. I have no intention of presenting my head on a pike by coming to any conclusions, and my approach as a whole is not in any way comprehensive. This is not because I believe, with a Victorian Historiographer Royal for Scotland, that the study of Scots abroad is so far off the beaten track that it leaves one "free from the responsibilities for exhaustive completeness which attend on history-making".(1) But I do consider myself excused from the obligation to describe the whole Scottish-American relationship before, during, and after the Revolution. My only intention is to suggest some questions about that relationship which we have so far avoided asking. In short, I shall spend this contribution indulging in the delicious vice of telling other historians where they have gone wrong.

My premise is that our research and writing in this field is still trapped within the framework provided by a national inferiority complex. Perhaps, indeed, this is a weakness to which all forms of ethnic history are prey. Certainly there seems to be little writing on the enterprises of the Scots overseas which is free from it. All I can speak for specifically, however, is work on Scottish contacts with and influences on North America, in the period from, say, 1760 to 1830. Here the whole thrust of research is still towards finding more and more detailed evidence of interaction, apparently on the premise that he who finds the greatest number of Scottish bricks in the fabric of the American building will be the most successful historian. There are some notable exceptions, for instance the modern immigration historians like Mr Graham or Mr Gray.(2) But most of us still seem to be driven by an unconscious conviction that if we could once and for all demonstrate the scale and importance of Scottish contributions to other nations, we would redeem our country from the historical stigmas of its size, its poverty, and its undignified status as a province to an English metropolis. The school of students trained here by Professor Shepperson, among whom I include myself, has not escaped from this malaise.(3) Even Mr Hook's recent volume, which is the most sophisticated work we now have in the field, tends to make the presentation of evidence an end in itself, partly at the expense of explaining what it all means.(4)

Actually it is not at all necessary to be a Scot

to become besotted by the view that finding more Scottish-American contacts means writing better history. There have been few worse examples than Thomas Jefferson Wertenbaker, the historian of Virginia. (5) Wertenbaker may have been driven by the assumption that what was for the greater glory of Scotland was for the greater glory of Princeton. The same cannot have been true of Wallace Notestein, a great though eccentric Yale teacher, whose **Scot in History** is one of the most deplorable cases of the kind of hagiography I have in mind. (6) The point is that the volume of Scottish-American contacts in the late eighteenth and early nineteenth centuries really **is** colossal, startlingly so to anyone who comes to the field for the first time. Americans obviously did use Scottish educational models; the circulation of Scottish works in the colonies and the young republic never ceases to be surprising: and the complexity of personal ties between the two countries is extraordinary. There is no need to be a professional Scot to develop a macabre fascination with demonstrating these phenomena for their own sake. The result has been the accumulation of a great deal of raw evidence, with precious little explanation of what it signifies. I would like to suggest, too, that asking fruitful questions about the dynamic behind the Scottish-American relationship in this period, has been inhibited by the inherent shortcomings of the specialist approaches of the historians who have worked on it. I shall therefore begin with some remarks on studies already produced. I shall divide them under four headings according to the interests of their writers - first the interest in the libertarian or revolutionary tradition, and thereafter the interests in emigration, in education, and in the world of letters.

The first specialist approach is the one we are all busily engaged in this weekend, the approach of tracing Scottish contributions to the American libertarian tradition, and in particular to the American Revolution. I do not wish to imply that anyone here takes the view that all Scots have peculiar genetic virtues of rugged individualism which lead them to align themselves unfailingly on the side of progress and liberty. That view is demonstrably grotesque. (7) Jefferson's identification of Scottish with Hessian mercenaries in the first draft of the Declaration of Independence is well known, and Scottish revolutionary sympathisers like Witherspoon and James Wilson, or like Alexander Garden, the South Carolina botanist, are so atypical as to be irrelevant. The overwhelming majority of Scots became loyalists in 1776, and were pillaged for their pains, by governments already strongly biased against them, whom they regarded as "a lawless and unprincipled faction". (8)

Nevertheless, there are some isolated instances in which texts of the Scottish enlightenment were used for libertarian purposes in America. Miss Robbins, for instance, has pointed out that the first statement on the right of colonists to revolt appears in Francis Hutcheson's **System of Moral Philosophy** (1775), which we know circulated in the colonies. (9) More specifically, Mr Davis has shown that radical material on slavery was taken from George Wallace's **System of the Principles of the Law of Scotland** by Anthony Benezet, for use in one of his pamphlets, and that it was therafter lifted without acknowledgement to be used in the 'Slavery' entry of the **Encyclopedie**. (10) Mr Adair, too, has tried to demonstrate the American debt to Hume's experimental conception of history, and Madison's use of a section from his **Political Discourses** in the Tenth **Federalist**. (11) Yet there are serious problems about this method, quite apart from the scatter-shot form in which it provides information. First, as I have already hinted, it is often impossible to distinguish between what is Scottish and what is merely enlightened. Moreover, revolutionary scholars doubtless often did what we do ourselves, and used quotations from established scholars to give respectability to perfectly viable ideas they had thought for themselves. Much more important, the tracing of Scottish influences on America is infinitely reductionist. Though the Americans had borrowed from Hutcheson and Hume, both in turn were heavily influenced by Harrington's **Oceana**. To give another example, it is easy, on a first reading, to jump to the attractive conclusion that Jefferson lifted the Query XVIII of his **Notes on the State of Virginia,** where he talks about the corrupting effect of slavery on masters, from Hume's Discourse 'On the Populousness of Ancient Nations', which we know he had in his library. (12) Walter Scott, in the **Heart of Midlothian,** makes very much the same assumption. (13) But the coup-de-grâce to any potential paper on the subject is that it is an assumption that goes back to the classical literature in which all three men had been educated.

In fact it would have been most surprising if a society as profoundly conservative as late eighteenth century Scotland had knowingly contributed to the American or any other revolution. Certainly there were pockets of sympathy for the Americans, and isolated individuals like the Rev. John Erskine wrote in their favour. Mr Fagerstrom has shown that in purely Scottish terms, the Revolution played an important role in a political reawakening which began the organisation of opposition to the Tory ascendancy of the Dundas machine. (14) But what is more impressive than the emergence of Scottish political liberals, was the strength of the conservative backlash against it. By the time of the Sedition Trials of 1793, shocked back to their normal distrust of change by the more terrifying French Revolution, few Scots saw anything to be alarmed at in Lord Braxfield's comment from the bench to a prisoner who claimed that Jesus Christ had also been a reformer - "Muckle guid it did till him - he was hangit!" (15) Even something relatively as innocuous as the attack on the slave trade was quickly abandoned because of its jacobinical overtones. (16) Whatever the immediate excitement of the American Revolution, it was not enough to build a tradition of liberal opposition able to survive the repression of the early nineties. I shall suggest presently, in fact, that the Revolution, or at least the existence of a society which had survived a revolution, had a much more significant impact in the nineteenth than the eighteenth century. But for the latter, in conclusion, it seems to me that there is only a limited amount of scope for illuminating the Scottish-American connection through the interaction between the libertarian and revolutionary traditions in the two countries.

At the first sight there is a good deal more future in approaching the relationship between the two countries through tracing the movements of those Scots who actually went to America. Mr Graham, the principal modern historian of emigration, has at least confronted the principal question about the problem he is dealing with: why Scots should have gone to America in the first place. (17) His answer, that they went there to get more money and raise their standard of living, is persuasive. Indeed the nature of Scottish emigration before the Revolution gives a number of clues to the role of Scots as loyalists. Both in the island and mainland colonies, Scotland had used temporary emigration as a democratising mechanism to absorb, and in some cases enrich its surplus of poor but over-educated young men. There were two corollaries. The first, in the Southern colonies at least, was that Scottish immigrants, like West Indians and East Indians, but unlike all other American settlers, expected to return to Scotland once they had made their fortunes. Moreover, they maintained systematic ties of ethnicity, kinship and business throughout the colonies, to an extent which made them a successful, threatening, and identifiable out-group. They were even popular with colonial women, and turned their marriages, like everything else, to good business account. In Port Royal, for instance, one Scottish clerk noticed that his countrymen had "been extremely lucky in trade and at making connections and generally make good Husbands which makes the ladyes like them so". (18)

It is not surprising that Scots were hated throughout the tropical colonies. The emigrant whom I have just quoted found he could not become a schoolmaster in Port Royal, since it was inconceivable that he would not fail his exams, "the name of a Scotsman being almost enough for that". (19) As a much distrusted out-group, who had thrust their tentacles into the colonial bureaucracy as well as the purely commercial structure, it is not surprising that Scots became loyalists. They badly need further serious study, and the documentation for it is fully available. They formed a chain of economic pressure-groups throughout the colonies, marrying into colonial society for their own advantage. Yet they retained a distinctly European frame of reference, and normally expected to prosper and return to Scotland or England. Their story cannot fail to tell us much about the evolution of colonial business practices, and, equally important, about the way in which the self-image of Scots changes in an alien or hostile environment.

In either case, the story of these Scots expatriates, and with it much of the value of the approach to the Scottish-American relationship through immigration, comes to an end with the Revolution. They had been too successful, and remained too distinctly culturally, to have gathered the kind of friends who could save them from the consequences of their loyalism. Many were ruined. Some managed to transfer their assets into West Indian agriculture, some into the fish and lumber businesses of Nova Scotia, New Brunswick, or Newfoundland. They had long had family and commercial contracts in all these areas. Quite a few, like Dr Garden of South Carolina, did remain. Indeed, when Henrietta Marchant Liston, the daughter of the Attorney General of Rhode Island, sister of an Antiguan planter and wife of a poor boy from Kirkliston who became first British ambassador to Philadelphia, noted in 1796 that Glasgow friends called on them in every town they passed through on their way to inspect General Washington's agricultural experiments at Mount Vernon. (20) But the old Scotch mafia was swept away. Emigration had almost stopped, and the Scots still in America expected to remain there and to become absorbed into the wider American society. In spite of their annual effusions of sentiment at St Andrew's Society meetings and the like, their existence as Scotsman had become irrelevant to their everyday lives as Americans. Further work on Scottish emigration will give only limited help in exploring the relationship with America after the Revolution.

Scottish influences on American higher education, on the other hand, clearly persisted into the nineteenth century. Using them as a means of approaching Scotland's relationship with America also has the advantage of providing great names whose work in American colleges was demonstrably influential - James Blair at William and Mary, William Smith at Penn, Charles Nisbet at Dickinson, John Witherspoon at Princeton, and Cullen's students John Morgan and William Shippen at the University of Pennsylvania Medical School. (21) In structure and curriculum both, the work of these teachers meant that their colleges clearly followed Scottish examples. This does not solve the problem of why men of such distinction were prepared to make their careers in the colonies, or why that example was attractive in the first place. Moreover, as Samuel Eliot Morison has pointed out, the apparent clarity of such borrowings is blurred by the similarity between eighteenth century European universities, and their common descent from Paris and Bologna. They "were all concerned in the common task of inducing more or less reluctant youth to absorb learning". (22) The particular Scottish influences which Mr Sloan and others have traced are perhaps specific enough for this college cousinage not to be a problem, but there is one much more serious methodological difficulty.

Given the attitudes of "reluctant youth", we have no hard evidence that what was taught in American classrooms, or the way in which it was taught, had the slightest effect on anyone. Even Charles Nisbet felt he had so little influence on anyone at Dickinson, that he lived there "like a Pelican in the Wilderness". (23) After some years of teaching, I have still to be convinced that what men in their middle and late teens absorb under compulsion in the classroom in equal importance to what they draw from general reading done voluntarily in later life. Clearly these educational contacts did leave a substantial institutional legacy, in the form taken by American colleges, and it stands to reason that they must also have had an impact of some sort on the luckless youths who passed through them. No one, however, has yet explained what form this influence took, or speculated as to its scale. All this approach can tell us, in itself, is that many educated Americans spent two to four years of their lives in institutions modelled partly on Scottish colleges, and staffed partly by Scottish dominies.

This in turn brings us to a final common approach to the Scottish-American relationship. It is the attempt to trace Scottish works read and responded to in America, both inside and outside the walls of the classroom. It is perhaps the most fruitful tack, and apart from the emigration one, it is the one which has been followed up most thoroughly. In Mr Hook's recent work we have a valuable survey of Scottish literature used and reviewed in America, for the whole period from 1750 to 1835, as well as a good deal of material on the personal contacts between Scottish and American scholars and literateurs .(24) What emerges is that the relationship may be divided into two themes, the theme of Scotland as land of learning, and the theme of Scotland as land of romance. The two do interact, but they may be distinguished throughout Mr Hook's period. Neither was interrupted by the Revolution of 1776, and indeed American enthusiasm for the scholarship and literature of Scotland heightened as the young nation moved into adolescence. This work will not have to be done again. Unfortunately, however, Mr Hook's sheer success in tracing the unseemly American lust for Scottish letters still leaves questions which sooner or later confront anyone working in the field, and which none of us has yet been able to answer. It is still unclear why Americans became enthusers over some works of learning, and not over others. As for Scottish works of romance, which they gobbled up quite without discrimination, we do not yet know why they should have wanted them at all. Until these questions are seriously addressed, the literary approach will also have its shortcomings.

Unfortunately these questions are only genteel offshoots of another and greater one: so what? It is a vulgar question, but it refuses to go away. We have not managed to answer it fully by using the Revolution, emigration, education, or letters as pivots for inquiry, but at least we have amassed much of the information needed to do so. It does indeed seem to be true that Scotland's influences on the colonies and the young republic were out of all proportion to her size. What I shall do in the rest of this paper is speculate as to the function which this kind of interaction fulfilled for the societies involved. I shall again focus my remarks on four areas. First I intend to glance at the years before and during the Revolution. I shall then speculate in greater and more startling detail about the philosophical connection in what I shall call the period of the second American

Revolution: about the role of images of America in Scottish society: and finally about Scotland's American function as Mr Hook's land of romance.

I shall dwell only briefly on Scottish-American connections before and during the Revolution, for the problems they raise are less puzzling than those of the early national period. By the 1760's, the Scottish universities were demonstrably able to give a more effective practical education than their English sisters, and it is not at all surprising that mainland colonists who could afford it so frequently sent their sons to them. Nor is it odd that their colleges were often modelled in part on a university system which was clearly the most vital example offered by the mother country to which they habitually looked for guidance. Again, it was only natural that Scotland, an underdeveloped country which produced more scholars than it could absorb at home, should send a number of them out to make careers in whatever part of the English-speaking world had teaching posts available. (25) The reception and circulation of Scottish works in the colonies is also unsurprising. The colonists normally read books in English. If they were to read moral philosophy at all, it would have been extraordinary if they had not chosen the Scottish authors who had a dominant share of the British market in the field, and whose deep concern over problems of taste, style, and aesthetics was so similar to their own.

It is not even surprising that the most pressing Scottish and American interests in moral philosophy were so close. Scotland was in many ways as distant a satellite of London as Boston or Philadelphia. At least one Scot, as late as 1830, thought the Atlantic passage safe enough to ship a pipe of Madeira uninsured, but carefully covered it in the smacks on the London to Leith leg of its journey. (26) Both Americans and Scots were British provincials, in a state of confusion about their own cultural identity, and ambivalent about their relationship to the metropolis. The colonists' distrust of Scots on the ground did not prevent them from admiring and absorbing the speculations of Scottish moralists who were struggling in the same way as themselves to find independent canons of manners. (27) The modest scale of Scottish influence on revolutionary political theory is itself circumstantial evidence that what Americans found attractive about Scottish writing was not its libertarian content, but its guidance in developing local standards of judgment in matters of taste and morality. This explains the only surprising thing about the richness of Scotland's educational and literary influences on America before 1776 - that there are only a tiny number of specific instances where they had any demonstrable impact on the coming of the Revolution or its outcome. (28)

The American Revolution of 1776, in fact, is the wrong revolution. Perhaps, to put it another way, it is the wrong part of the right revolution. To go on to my second area, I would like to suggest that the time when Scotland did make genuinely important contributions to the development of the United States was in the fifty years after the Peace of Paris. This was the time when Americans worked to lay foundations of a moral republic, in a way which many of them conceived as the completion or securing of the first Revolution, or the launching of a second one. Although many of us would now see their work as counter-revolutionary, their own self-image was explicitly progressive. The ultimate dymamic behind their activities was religious, and it strengthened in the period of ante-bellum reform, but it had its origins before the Second Great Awakening. In the years immediately after the Revolution, the archetypical reformer of this sort was Benjamin Rush. He has recently been characterised as a Christian revolutionary, who saw the political separation from Britain as a mere precondition for developing a society based on universal principles of Christian morality, a society which would become the hub of the divine plan for human regeneration. (29) Rush himself has been educated at Edinburgh. His work at the University of Pennsylvania Medical School, and his personal influence over Witherspoon at Princeton and Nisbet at Dickinson, made him the most important carrier of Scottish educational ideals and practices to America. What is much more important is that the moral philosophy and ethics which he and his contemporaries adopted was fundamentally Scottish. The same is true of James Wilson, another of the Founding Fathers, whose post-revolutionary writings clearly use a Scottish frame of reference. (30)

After the Second Great Awakening, when a new religious urgency speeded up the drive to a second revolution, the adoption of Scottish philosophy also gathered pace. It would be easy to trace the specific transmission of Scottish concepts into American writing on morals, much easier than in the eighteenth century, but the influence goes deeper than mere specific borrowings. Much of the whole moral frame of reference of progressive Americans was drawn from Scottish sources. (31) It was not just a matter of Scottish works being read in college classrooms, though they were, for this had been going on for over half a century. As Mr Meyer has shown, Scottish thought became a major component in developing the country's official moral philosophy, a nationalising philosophy which was industriously preached outside the classroom in popular works on morals, in sermons and in religious and reforming periodicals. (32) It was already dominant by about 1820, and it provided a backdrop of technical uniformity for the age of ante-bellum reform. Like Rush, though they were much his junior, the leaders of the new benevolence conceived their work as a revolution in morality which went beyond the more restricted goals of the political and military revolution fought by his generation and their fathers'. (33) The Scottish philosophy, which contributed heavily to their outlook, retained a central influence on the reform mentality until the rise of the social gospel at the end of the century.

The function of this Scottish adoption for nineteenth century America is well illustrated by the particular aspects of philosophy which it turned to its own use. This is partly obscured by our tendency to perceive the Scottish Enlightenment as a whole. Contemporaries,

whose anxieties were more immediate, were more discriminating. In brief, Americans drew only upon those Scottish writings which were free from the taints of infidelity and scepticism, and which had indeed been written in large part to overcome them. Aside from commentaries on the canons of taste and style, which continued to attract their attention, their principal interest was in the synthetic philosophy of common sense, which they absorbed most commonly through the semi-popular work of Dugald Stewart. (34) Common sense had many attractions for Americans, as indeed it had for Scots. Perhaps the greatest was its reassurance that society had not been cast loose from its moral sheet anchors by the idealism of the enlightenment proper. The horror of Berkeleyan and Humean scepticism was not simply that it called faith into question, though that in itself was bad enough. It also implied a moral scepticism which left the individual adrift in a determinist world. He was ruled only by laws always beyond his comprehension. He was unable to take bearings on the knowable moral constants which had always guided human conduct and morality. Common sense, except in the bastardized form presented by James Beattie, was not a simple effort to shore up faith. It also announced decisively that man was a free moral agent because he knew himself to be free. Above all, by expanding on Hutcheson's conception of moral sense, it provided an intuitive underpinning for moral rules which were discernable and uniform throughout human societies. If the philosophers sophistically denied the obvious and fixed rules of behaviour, **tant pis pour eux.** Though Thomas Reid was by far the best mind of the school, it required little intellectual equipment to repeat his **cri de coeur** on the idealist opposition - "I renounce philosophy, and flee its guidance. Let my soul dwell with Common Sense". (35)

No philosophy could better have suited the needs of early nineteenth century America. Mr Ahlstrom has correctly pointed to the static nature of common sense, to the effect of its conception of intuitive moral universals in putting nineteenth century American theology, and by inference morality, into a sort of intellectual holding pattern. (36) By the same token, however, common sense was an indispensible weapon in the **jihad** of middle class ante-bellum reform. Not only did it protect the flank of the warriors in this second American Revolution from sceptical and deistical guerillas. It was also a valuable support in imposing their ethnic on American society as a whole. The moral imperative which spurred them on was in my estimation a religious one, and their ethic of respectability was, whether they knew it or not, ideally suited to the evolution of nineteenth industrial society. But the value of common sense was that its stress on the universality of moral rules gave a fundamentally emotional movement, which was deeply concerned with the irrational basis of faith, all respectability of a grounding in a philosophy which was, at least superficially, rationalist, secular, and even enlightened. Nothing could better justify a movement determined to impose its ethic on a total society.

indeed on a whole world, whether across the barrier of race, class or region. Even better, the Scottish philosophy served admirably to soothe the deep anxiety of benevolent evangelicals over free agency. From conversion onwards, the behaviour of the Christian was based on a series of free choices. Much of the thrust behind ante-bellum reform was to remove the barriers to imposed moral autonomy raised by drunkenness, ignorance, war, and slavery. The benevolent empire could not have dreamt of a finer handmaiden than a system of secular philosphy which demonstrated so fully that man was indeed free. It is not surprising that early nineteenth periodicals are so full of references to the Scottish philosophy, or that common sense became so major a component in the formation of Mr Meyer's instructed conscience. (37)

To move on to the influence of America on Scottish life, it seems to me that it was also in the period after the revolutionary war, and into the nineteenth century, that the relationship was most dynamic. Professor Shepperson's most memorable epigram is that "One of Scotland's favourite games was to use events in the New World to bring into focus its own situation in the old". (38) In spite of the extraordinary amount of evidence gathered by Mr Fagerstrom, I would suggest that this was much more the case in the nineteenth century than in the eighteenth. (39) The occurrence of a revolution was and is all very interesting, but for observers in Europe it probably had less force than the process of creating a society based on that revolution. The existence of an American republic, and its struggles to mould itself in various directions, was an ongoing phenomenon which required an ongoing response. The response itself, however, had important functions for the societies or parts of societies from which it came. This is nowhere clearer than in the case of Scotland in the period between independence and the American Civil War. On one level, the phenomenon Professor Shepperson refers to just involves the choosing of views on American issues as means of projecting standing rivalries between different elements of Scottish society. It is no surprise to find Scottish, or for that matter British conservatives pointing triumphantly to maladjustments in the American republic, such as slavery - or to find progressive and liberal elements glossing over such defects, or working furiously to help American friends remove them, as a smudge on the mirror of the perfect commonwealth. This phenomenon is not unique to Scotland, and there is a huge literature on it. (40) What does seem to be unusual in the Scottish case, however, is that the use of American images goes beyond the simple polarisation between right and left, between progressive and reactionary. Within the structure of Scottish reform movements themselves, predominantly liberal and fundamentally pro-American though they all were, infighting often went on by means of making alliances with different factions of corresponding American movements. To take the anti-slavery example once again, the latter half of the forties saw elements in the Scottish established church, and

in the voluntary secession churches, which were as alike as chalk and cheese, join in an unlikely alliance with the radical wing of the American anti-slavery movement. Their sole reason for doing so was to express their shared hostility to the Free Church of Scotland, which was in alignment with more conservative abolitionists on both sides of the Atlantic. The Free Church affair was the most spectacular of this sort, but there are many others. (41)

Although these phenomena are all very interesting, and at times sufficiently droll, I am left with a suspicion that we have not gone quite far enough in the questions we have asked about them. Everyone who writes in the field has observed Scots using American examples for short-term advantage in their habitual squabbles, or as an ongoing means of projecting long-standing tensions between different groups in Scottish society. I cannot quite bring myself to the vulgar level of suggesting that some Scots expressed strong opinions on American situations because they actually believed what they said. However, they may have done so less to smite their enemies, than as a means of soothing their own internal anxieties about the pace of change in Scottish society. At the end of the eighteenth century, and during the first half of the nineteenth, Scotland was going through a process of extraordinarily rapid social and institutional transformation. Such change must inevitably have created strains, doubts, and anxieties.

The American example had an important psychological role to play both for conservative and progressive Scots. For instance, it is hard to avoid the suspicion that a conservative Scottish clergyman, who announced in 1830 that slavery was just "another of the brutal deeds of republicanism and voluntaryism" was saying something about himself as well as about Americans and about his enemies in the secession churches. (42) This radical flaw in American society was reassuring proof that the threatening forces in his own society, which were symbolised by the American experiment, were ultimately doomed, that he and the ordered society he dreamt of were still on the side of history. Ambivalences about change, at home, too, could also be expressed through the American example, as they were, for instance, in the **Edinburgh Review.** (43) At the other end of the scale, to go back to the late eighteenth century, it is intriguing that those Scots most deeply committed to improvement, to progress, and to the values on which the nineteenth century was to be based, were greatly enthused over the future of American society. This was true of James Fletcher, the burgh reformer; of John C. Millar, Jr., the Whig lawyer who eventually died in America; of James Anderson, the editor of the **Bee**; and of the ghastly Earl of Buchan. They had no tactical gain to make by pointing to the virtues of American republicanism, for the society in which they lived was still too deeply conservative to be impressed by them. America had a more intimate function for them, for it enabled them to handle unavoidable doubts as to whether their own progressive views were manageable in reality.

Buchan did so by sending Washington boxes made out of the oak under which William Wallace sheltered at Selkirk. He could do so more easily, and more typically for his group, by taking refuge in improbable superlatives about the triumphs of American social engineering. As the culmination of an epic design, the Americans, and the Americans alone, had "furnished an example of what constitutes the cement for erecting the true and lasting edifice of government, **knowledge mixt with virtue building upon the platform of real property, and agricultural industry and simplicity of manners**". (44) For Buchan, and for other Scots who responded in one way or another to America, the republican experiment, in its success or failure, provided a means of self-assurance as to the speed of progress and modernisation at home. America could provide a psychological shorthand for reaffirming personal faith, whether that faith was placed in change or in the status quo.

The tensions created by rapid social change may also provide a clue to some of the problems raised by the evidence Mr Hook has presented on Scotland as the land of romance. (45) He has made it absolutely clear that Americans were fascinated by the Scottish past, particularly as it was depicted in Scott. But it is still not entirely clear why that particular past should have been of interest to them, or indeed why they felt the need to romanticise any past at all. It is call the more puzzling, in that the fad for Scott and his imitators was just as great in the North as in the South. (46) A possible solution is that Americans were responding to a static version of Scottish history in much the same way, and for much the same reasons, as Scots responded to the dymanic American present and future. For Southerners the equation is simple, for it was obviously cheering to a people who were in many important respects outside the stream of nineteenth century history to identify with an idealised and pleasingly stable past. Yet not even the most sober reformers were immune to the spell of Scott: even Lucretia Mott felt obliged to visit Abbotsford in 1841. (47) Perhaps they too suffered from the kind of subconscious doubts about change which I have suggested for the Earl of Buchan. Determined to impose a new, progressive system of values though they were, they cannot have been safe from fears about the speed with which they were parting from a similar and apparently more stable past. (48) Absorption in a romanticised history, which their own country broadly speaking lacked, could provide a helpful crutch for them in a time of turmoil.

This hypothesis fails, of course, to explain why the particular romantic model chosen by Americans was the Scottish one. I have a splendid speculative explanation, which also helps solve the paradox that Scots were detested in America before the Revolution and adulated after it. I would suggest that the Revolution was only fought and won at the cost of considerable subliminal guilt, given the extent to which images of fatherhood and motherhood were used to define the relationship between colony and metropolis. It was therefore tempting, before independence, to express irritation with the English as hatred for the Scots. Nationhood, however, subtly inverted this relationship. Whether Americans were looking for a romantic past, or an evangelical model of morality, it was natural that the examples they chose should be English-speaking. By the nineteenth century, however, a new generation of Americans were unable to use England as a model without suffering from serious guilt feelings, both over declension from patriotic ideals, and over disloyalty to their fathers of the revolutionary generation, whom they already regarded with some Freudian antipathy. During the period of the second revolution, which I have largely discussed today, it was only too easy to solve the problem by moving towards extreme enthusiasm for all things Scottish. Scotland was all the more attractive because its historical glamour could not overshadow the extent to which it was committed to an ethic of improvement. She was eschatalogically unique in being anchored in history's past but tacked towards history's future.

After this statement, I am brought back to reality only by the necessity for ending my paper. My conclusion is that the most dynamic phase of the Scottish American connection comes during the second American Revolution, and not the first. During this period, a special aspect of Scottish philosophy provided the ethical framework within which Americans might modernise. Scottish romance, at the same time, provided the opiate which enabled them to handle the strains of doing so. In both ways, the Scottish world of letters was contributing to the age of reform. At the same time, Scots were able to use America, as they perceived it during that age, to help them adapt to the transition of their own society.

I have spoken a lot today about the function of various kinds of writing. I once heard it said that the function of a conference paper was to give one's colleagues something to criticise. I hope I have not been derelict in my duty.

REFERENCES
1. J. H. Burton, **The Scot Abroad**, 2nd ed. (Edinburgh, 1881) p. viii.
2. I. C. Graham, **Colonists from Scotland: Emigration to North America, 1707-1783** (Ithaca, 1956); M. Gray 'Scottish Emigration: the Social Impact of Agrarian Change in the Rural Lowlands, 1775-1875', **Perspectives in American History**, VII (1973) 95-176.
3. My own dissertation, 'The Scottish Factor in the Fight against American Slavery, 1830-1870', is a glaring example, which may be used as a bogey to frighten future graduate students in the field.
4. A. Hook, **Scotland and America, 1750-1835** (Glasgow, 1975).
5. **Early Scotch Contributions to the United States** (Glasgow, 1945).
6. **The Scot in History** (New Haven, 1946).
7. For an example, see J. H. Fairley, **The Coming of the Scot** (New York, 1940).
8. A. Ogilvy to Pegie Ogilvy, Feb.(?), 1779, Box 20, uncatalogued, Ogilvie-Forbes of Boyndlie Papers, AUL. See also J. Ross to R. Herries, 25.6.1782, GD 186, Box 4, Leith-Ross Papers; SRO; Various letters from Scottish episcopalian minsters to Dr Cooper, Box 82, Acc.4796, Fettercairn Papers Deposit 1, uncatalogued SNL; Graham, **Colonists from Scotland**, p. 150-177; W. Brown **The King's Friends. The Composition and Motives of the**

American Loyalist Claimants (Providence, 1965) passim.

9. C. Robbins, '"When it is that Colonies May Turn Independent": An Analysis of the Environment and Politics of Francis Hutcheson (1694-1746)', WMQ 3rd. Ser. XI (1954) 214-251.

10. D. B. Davis, 'New Side Thoughts on Early Anti-Slavery Radicalism', WMQ 3rd. Ser. XXVIII (1971) 585-594.

11. D. Adair, '"That Politics May be Reduced to a Science": David Hume, James Madison, and the Tenth **Federalist'**, HLQ XX (1957) 343-360. See also H. T. Colburn, **The Lamp of Experience. Whig History and the Intellectual Origins of the American Revolution** (Chapel Hill, 1965), passim.

12. D. Hume, 'Of the Populousness of Ancient Nations', **Political Discourses,** 2nd. ed. (Edinburgh, 1752) p. 161. Cf. **Notes on the State of Virginia** (Harper edition, New York, 1964) pp. 155-156. Jefferson is known to have possessed a late edition of Hume's **Essays,** and he had read and approved of the **Political Discourses.** See E. Millicent Sowerby, comp. **Catalogue of the Library of Thomas Jefferson,** 5 vols (Washington, 1952) II 14. Miss Sowerby, however, takes pains to stress Jefferson's contempt for Hume as an historian.

13 Collins edition, London, 1952, pp. 313-314.

14. D. I. Fagerstrom, 'Scottish Opinion and the American Revolution' WMQ 3rd. Ser. XI (1954) 252-275. See also Mr Fagerstrom's unpublished doctoral dissertation, Edinburgh, 1960.

15. On this period of repression, see H. W. Meickle, **Scotland and the French Revolution** (Glasgow, 1912).

16. T. Somerville, **My Own Life and Times, 1714-1814** (Edinburgh , 1861) pp. 263-266.

17. **Colonists from Scotland.**

18. A. Cumine to A. Ogilvy, 17.6.1763, Box 9, uncatalogued, Ogilvie-Forbes of Boyndlie Papers, AUL.

19. A. Cumine to Mrs A. (Forbes) Ogilvy, 1.4.1763, ibid.

20. H. Liston to J. Jackson, 6.9.1796, Ms.5589 f. 159, Liston Papers, SNL.

21. See D. Sloan, **The Scottish Enlightenment and the American College Ideal** (New York, 1971); G. S. Pryde, **The Scottish Universities and the Colleges of Colonial America** (Glasgow, 1957).

22. S. E. Morison, **The Founding of Harvard College** (Cambridge, 1935) .p. 128. .

23. Nisbet to C. Wallace, 19.8.1791, **Bulletin of N.Y. Public Library** I (1897) 183. I am obliged to Miss Pamela Atkins for drawing this reference to my attention.

24. **Scotland and America,** passim.

25. See, for example, L. P. Eisenhart, 'Walter Minto and the Earl of Buchan', PAPS XCIV (1950) 282-294, though this is an example from the after the Revolution.

26. D. Mackay to J. Grant of Bught, 27.3.1830, GD 23.6.391, Bught Papers, SRO.

27. B. Bailyn & J. Clive , 'England's Cultural Provinces: Scotland and America', WMQ 3rd. Ser. XI (1954) 200-213; R. Mitchison & N. T. Phillipson, **Scotland in the Age of Improvement** (Edinburgh, 1970); A. Hook, ''Scottish Contributions to the American Enlightenment', TSLL VIII (1967) 519-532.

28. Setting aside the few personal Scottish contributions to the Revolution, like those of Witherspoon and Wilson, the only specific Scottish influences on revolutionary thought so far identified are those mentioned in the works cited above by Adair, and, more tenuously, Robbins. A close reading of periodical literature would certainly reveal others, but it is unlikely that they will emerge on a scale which bears any relationship to the mass circulation of Scottish books in America.

29. D. J. D'Elia, 'Benjamin Rush: Philosopher of the American Revolution', TAPS New Ser. LXIV (1974).

30 A. B. Leavelle, 'James Wilson and the Relation of the Scottish Metaphysics to American Political Thought', PSQ LVII (1942) 394-410.

31. I am much indebted to Miss Marta Wagner for sharing the results of unpublished work in which she has thoroughly surveyed early nineteenth century periodicals as a means of demonstrating the massive infiltration of Scottish concepts. See also S. Ahlstrom, 'The Scottish Philosophy and American Theology', CH XXIV (1955) 257-272.

32. D. H. Meyer, **The Instructed Conscience. The Shaping of the American National Ethic** (Philadelphia, 1972) pp. 35-42; D. Howe, 'American Victorianism as a Culture', AQ XXVII (1975) 525.

33. I have been particularly influenced, on the tension between the generations, by the unpublished work of Mr William Breitenbach, who specially stresses the nature of ante-bellum reform a a parallel revolutionary experience. See also F. Somkin, **Unquiet Eagle, Memory and Desire in the Idea of American Freedom, 1815-1860** (Ithaca, 1967).

34. The American absorption of common sense philophy has been fully studied in the unpublished doctoral dissertation, American University, 1963, by R. J. Petersen, 'Scottish Common Sense in America: an Evaluation of its Influence'. The specific use of common sense authors is discussed in Hook, **Scotland and America,** pp. 86-89 and passim.

35. **An Inquiry into the Human Mind, on the Principles of Common Sense,** 2nd ed. (Edinburgh, 1765), p. 14.

36. Ahlstrom, loc.cit., p.269.

37. **The Instructed Conscience,** pp. 35-42.

38. G. A. Shepperson, 'Writings in Scottish-American History: a Brief Survey', WMQ 3rd Ser. XI (1955) 173.

39. Cf. Fagerstrom, loc.cit.

40 See for instance G. A. Shepperson, 'Frederick Douglass and Scotland', JNH XXXVIII (1953) 307-321; idem, 'Thomas Chalmers, the Free Church of Scotland, and the South', JSH XVII (1951) 517-537; idem, 'The Free Church of Scotland and American Slavery', SHR (1951) 126-143; G. D. Lillibridge, **Beacon of Freedom. The Impact of American Democracy upon Great Britain** (Philadelphia, 1954), passim; D. P. Crook, **American Democracy in English Politics, 1815-1850** (Oxford 1965).

41. On the Free Church affair, see the articles by Professor Shepperson, cited in n.40 above, also my unpublished Ph.D. Dissertation, Edinburgh, 1969, pp. 272-346. I have treated the problem in shorter and less inelegant compass in a recently completed manuscript on **The Scots Abolitionists, 1833, 1861.**

42. **Picture of Slavery in the United States of America: Being a Practical Illustration of Voluntaryism and Republicanism** (Glasgow, 1835) p.5.

42. **Picture of Slavery in the United States of America: Being a Practical Illustration of Voluntaryism and Republicanism** (Glasgow, 1825) p. 5.

43. See P. W. Mowbray, **America through British Eyes; a Study of the Attitude of the Edinburgh Review toward the United States of America from 1802 until 1861** (Rock Hill, 1935); Hook **Scotland and America,** pp. 93-105.

44. D. S. Erskine, 11th Earl of Buchan, **Address to the Americans at Edinburgh, on Washington's Birth-Day** (Edinburgh, 1811) p.7.

45. **Scotland and America,** pp. 116-173.

46. Ibid; cf. R. Osterweis, **Romanticism and Nationalism in the Old South** (New Haven, 1949).

47. See F. B. Tolles, ed., 'Slavery and the ''Woman Question''. Lucretia Mott's Diary of her Visit to Great Britain to Attend the World's Anti-Slavery Convention of 1840', **Journal of the Friends' Historical Society, Supplement No. 23** (London, 1852), entries for 3.8.1840, 4.8.1840. See also H. B. Stowe, **Sunny Memories of Foreign Lands** (London, 1854) passim.

48. On the tensions created by adopting a new value system I have been influenced, for better or worse, by F. Weinstein & G. M. Platt, **The Wish to be Free. Society, Psyche, and Value Change** (Berkeley, 1969).

SCOTLAND AND AMERICA REVISITED

ANDREW D. HOOK

Since my account of Scotland and the American Revolution is already in print any contribution from me to this volume may well appear more than somewhat superfluous. The editors, however, in their wisdom, have suggested that I might like to avail myself of the opportunity to say something more — either about my thesis on the Scottish dimension of the Revolution or, more broadly, about my version of the whole Scottish-American connection from the revolutionary and post-revolutionary periods well on into the nineteenth century. In what follows I shall attempt to comply with both of these generous suggestions, dealing with the first quite briefly, with the second at rather greater length.

II

The view I have taken of the role of the Scots in the Revolutionary period is broadly a demythologizing one. Despite the existence of various distinguished and deservedly famous Scots patriots, both soldiers and statesmen, the Scots in Revolutionary America seem generally to have sided with the Tory, loyalist cause. Furthermore, in American patriotic circles, and among those English "country" Whigs who opposed the American war, there clearly existed a widespread belief that at least since Bute's brief period of power the Scots in Parliament and government were peculiarly responsible for those anti-American policies that had made war inevitable. This general thesis is one that I see no

reason to modify. On the contrary. Such evidence as has emerged since it was offered has tended to confirm it. Dr Swinfen's careful survey of the Scottish press in the Revolutionary period provides little or no evidence of anything other than widespread Scottish support for the government in the American dispute. (1) The Beattie letters, in King's College Library, Aberdeen, give a similar picture. Of course it is perfectly fair to argue — as some Scottish historians and economic historians are quick to do — that there is little or no evidence of the feelings about the American revolutionary cause of the mass of ordinary Scottish people either in the Lowlands or in the Highlands. But as the case now stands, the burden of proof rests with those who wish to contend for Scottish working-class solidarity with the American revolutionaries. Until such time as evidence of popular support for America is forthcoming, the general thesis that the Scots, both in Scotland and America, showed little sympathy for the revolutionary Americans must stand. Of course there were individual Scots, and even certain groups of Scots, who spoke out in favour of the American side in the dispute with the mother country — particularly in the period before 1776 — but their existence does nothing to transform the basically "loyalist" position of the Scots.

Let me cite one amusing piece of evidence I have recently come upon which seems to me to point to a positive lack of popular Scottish sympathy for the American cause. It concerns John Witherspoon. Before leaving his own country to become president of the College of New Jersey, Witherspoon had been a minister in two towns in the west of Scotland: Beith and Paisley. Possibly because the economic prosperity of this part of the country suffered as a result of the outbreak of the American war, Witherspoon's role as a leading spokesman for the rights of the colonists does not seem to have caused him to be remembered there with much affection. At least affection is hardly the emotion suggested by the following story which was still current in the area around 1830. As a young clergyman in Beith, Witherspoon acquired a considerable reputation as an enthusiastic and aggressive curler. On one occasion in 1746 he led the Beith curlers against their Lochwinnoch opponents. With the game going against his side, the story goes, he made all his players stand together in such a way as to make the ice dip and allow the water underneath to flood the playing surface. "This reckless trick, not suitable to the mild character of a Christian minister, was the cause of the ending of the sport as a draw-game. . . ." But it is the conclusion of the story which really suggests how Witherspoon survived in the communal memory:

When the news of the turbulent priest of Beith being elected as representative for New Jersey, for the Congress, arrived at Lochwinnoch, his antagonists remembered his dangerous prank near the Peill, and they were red that he was in a far wider field than the Lochwinnoch bonspiel, and he would play a more dangerous game; he would spill a horn or make a spune, and to make a republic; or cause many men hing in a wuddie. (2)

Witherspoon's reputation as a revolutionary leader does not seem to have cut much ice in the popular memory of that part of Scotland where he was best known!

III

In **Scotland and America** I discussed the Scottish dimension of the American Revolution as only one traumatic chapter in the larger story of the cultural relationship between the countries in the eighteenth and early nineteenth centuries. Thus to have no serious second thoughts about that particular chapter in no way implies a similar self-satisfaction with the story as a whole. The subject itself is a large one, and one which seems to get still larger all the time. Inevitably, then, there is plenty of room for second thoughts, not to mention third, fourth or fifth ones. I shall restrict myself, however, to some account of how I approached the subject in the first place, and then go on to comment on some of the comments the book has provoked since its publication a little over a year ago.

What I mean by the first point is an admission that I did not approach the topic of Scottish-American cultural relations from the position of a specialist in Scottish history or even Scottish literary history. Basically I was working as a student of American literature; what I knew of eighteenth-century Scotland was no more or less than had come by way as a student of English literature at the University of Edinburgh in the 1950s. In other words, and as I believe quite significantly, I did not approach the Scottish side of my subject with any very definite views of eighteenth-century Scotland and its culture. What I did have, very quickly, was a great mass of material, mostly from eighteenth and early nineteenth-century American sources, which seemed to reflect the tremendous range and depth of America's Scottish connection in the Revolutionary and post-Revolutionary periods. But a mass is precisely what it was — undifferentiated, unstructured, without any coherence or meaning. I was then in the classic position of the researcher, confronting a mountain of "facts" but lacking any kind of hypothesis or "model" which might begin to make some sense of the still-accumulating body of research material. It was at this point that I began to realise that the material seemed to be classifying itself into two broad categories. The first was concerned with Scotland and the intellectual life; here the material was about education and educationalists, about religion and philosophy, about the Scottish universities, about the **Edinburgh Review** and **Blackwood's Magazine,** and so on. It was a body of American material that seemed to recognise in Scotland a pre-eminent land of learning. The second category was about Scotland and romance; here the material was about Scottish poetry and song, about Scottish landscape and scenery, about Scottish novelists and dramatists, about Scottish history and legend - Wallace and Bruce, Mary Queen of Scots, Rob Roy and the Jacobite Rebellions. It was a body of American material that seemed to recognise in Scotland a pre-eminent land of romance.

It was at this point that I began to look more closely at modern historical accounts of eighteenth-century Scotland. In the work of standard Scottish historians I found little to help me; neither the Scottish philosophical Enlightenment nor Scottish romance seems to have engaged their attention. From a cultural point of view they did not provide me with any kind of coherent account of eighteenth-century Scotland. It was left to Scottish literary historians to fill the gap. In G. Gregory Smith's idea of "the Caledonian antisyzygy", the characteristically self-contradictory nature of Scottish culture, and even more in David Daiches's account of the divided nature of the culture of eighteenth-century Scotland, I found suggestions in terms of which my two broad categories of Scottish-American material began to make excellent sense.

Such, then, was the background out of which **Scotland and America** acquired the shape and form it has. Let me repeat, though, that my body of Scottish-American research material seemed increasingly to take this shape of its own accord. There is no question of an imposed structure arising out of a prior commitment to one particular view of Scottish cultural history in the eighteenth century. I repeat the point because of course I am conscious that the structure of the book does seem to embody just such a particular view. Rather than ultimately depending on that view I would like to think that my work simply confirms its accuracy, or at least its usefulness. In any event, the literary-historical account of the essentially divided nature of Scottish culture in the eighteenth century remains the only coherent and fully comprehensive account that has been advanced. To some more recent proposals in this field I shall return below. Meantime, one further point needs to be made. The concepts of Scottish "learning" and Scottish "romance" I do regard as valuable because they provide both a useful principle of organisation and an important insight into the nature of Scottish culture in the eighteenth and early nineteenth centuries. But the distinction between them is less clear-cut than I may perhaps have made it sound. They do not point towards two wholly incompatible areas of Scottish cultural life; nor do they imply a necessary dichotomy in the Scottish psyche between reason and emotion, thought and feeling. There is clearly a sense in which the reading and writing of literature, however romantic, are as much intellectual pastimes as the reading and writing of philosophy. Thus, for example, those Americans who visited the "classic ground" of romantic Scotland in the early nineteenth century were no less "enlightened" than their fellow-countrymen who read the histories of William Robertson or David Hume and studied Dugald Stewart. Very frequently, of course, these groups were one and the same.

So much for the background to the structure and organisation of **Scotland and America**. Before leaving this subject, however, I should like to acknowledge that I do now recognise that something more in the way of explanation of the theory and methodology behind the book's structure would have added a useful dimension to it. The basic concept of cultural exchange or transmission itself does require examination at a theoretical level. How do ideas or values pass from one society to another? Is cultural influence dependent on economic or political dominance? What can be accepted as evidence of cultural transference? The tobacco trade between the Chesapeake Bay and the Clyde can be expressed in terms of sets of economic statistics; cultural exchanges cannot be quantified so readily. Yet if economic statistics illuminate a society's "base" structure, culture is the crucial element in its "super-structure"; historical understanding requires attention to both.

In fact the case of Scotland & America presents the cultural historian with an ideal example of the process of cultural transmission in action. No one now doubts that between these two countries a considerable cultural exchange did take place. Hence out of the laboratory of this particular relationship it should be possible to construct or deduce a general theory of cultural transmission. My own view is increasingly that, except in situations where one society's culture is imposed upon another by the exercise of sheer power, the one essential requisite for cultural exchange is the receptiveness or responsiveness of the one society to the cultural values of the other. Economic links, political links, migrations, personal relationships, the availability of books, individuals from the one society in positions of authority and influence in the other — none of these are of much significance except in a situation where there is already in existence a set of circumstances which make a positive reaction to influence possible. Because someone owns or has read a particular book does not mean he was influenced by it; what is needed is evidence that the book was read with understanding and sympathy.

What, then, in the case of societies, are the kinds of "pre-existing circumstances" required for cultural transmission to occur? I would now argue that what is needed is some form of shared pattern of consciousness itself; the structures of thought and feeling in the two societies have to have at least a strong similarity before any kind of cultural influence can be properly assimilated. In relation to Scotland and America it is the nature of this shared consciousness which needs to be explored further. It was a commonplace, for example, in the early nineteenth century, that the New Englander was the "Scot" of America; perhaps it is this kind of clue that needs to be followed up. Of course consciousness itself, ways of perceiving reality, of making sense of one's self and one's world, are modified by a variety of factors, internal and external. Language is one such factor, and that Scot and American shared a common language is, however obviously, a vitally important link between them. Religion is another immensely important consideration; and the religious assumptions and habits of mind of large and influential sections of America had much in common with those of Scotland. Again, Scot and American shared a consciousness of their provincial status in relation to the dominant culture of England; this of course is the burden of Clive and Bailyn's influential thesis on Scotland and America as England's cultural provinces. And Dr N. T. Phillipson has helped us to see how the cultural élites of Scotland and America may well have occupied a somewhat similar social and political position. (3) Furthermore, it may be true that the societies of both Scotland and America in the eighteenth century were caught up by a process of fairly rapid and fundamental change, while at the same time remaining deeply conservative: both are progressive, forward-looking, modern, enlightened, but both are reluctant to allow revolution in any sense to sweep them too far too fast. No doubt there are many other factors involved in producing the kind of shared consciousness, shared structures of thought and feeling, between Scot and American which I am postulating, and more work needs to be directed towards establishing what they are. But however it was brought into being, I would maintain that it is a sharing at this level that makes the penetration of American culture by a remarkable range of Scottish intellectual and literary influences finally explicable.

IV

If I may now turn to the general reception over

the last year of **Scotland and America**, there is one basic point which recurs in discussion of the book with which I agree. The book is by intention something of a pioneering study; it tries to provide a reasonably comprehensive account of the Scottish-American connection, particularly in the post-Revolutionary period, bringing together diverse kinds and bodies of information, some of it already available in more specialised studies, some of it new. Beginning in the colonial period, carrying through the revolution, and focusing on the post-Revolutionary period, it aims at narrative rather than analytic unity. A broad survey, mapping out the territory, it covers many topics without exhausting any of them. Thus I broadly accept the criticism (if one regards it as such) that it is more concerned to present the evidence than to explain or interpret it. Here are the ingredients, it seems to say, that make up the pudding: it invites other scholars to eat and digest it. Not, of course, that I would agree that the book presents nothing in the way of explanation and interpretation: to a degree greater than most reviewers and commentators seem to have noticed a line of interpretation, in relation both to Scottish and American cultural history, is suggested. But I would hope that as a result future scholars of the Scottish-American connection will find it easier to base their interpretative theories on a well-documented basis.

That such a basis is required is suggested by some of the speculative comment that **Scotland and America** has already inspired. Examining the work of earlier scholars who had taken an interest in some aspect of Scottish-American relations, I was much struck by the regularity with which their focus fell either on the colonial period or on the first half of the nineteenth century. Both these periods were seen as ones in which Scotland had made significant contributions to American culture; but apparently there was no connection between them. In my own work I tried to show how in fact the earlier period prepared the way for the later one. Today, both Dr Phillipson and Professor Duncan Rice, influenced particularly perhaps by Daniel Howe's study, **The Unitarian Conscience**, apparently once again wish to see the middle decades of the nineteenth century as the most important period of Scottish influence upon America. (4) Such a view is in fact the received one in terms of American intellectual history: such scholars as Perry Miller, Merle Curti, Howard Mumford Jones, and Roy Harvey Pearce have always recognised that the single most powerful influence on American thought in this period was that of the Scottish school of philosophers. So Rice and Phillipson are right; but perhaps in only a limited sense. What they are talking about is the period when American professors of philosophy, American college presidents, American seminarists, American clergymen, and many American essayists, critics and reviewers, recognised in Scottish common sense philosophy the best and surest defence of the religious, moral and social orthodoxy of their own society. Certainly to recognise the Scottish origins of this conservative American philosophy in the ante-bellum period is important; but one

may wonder whether the Scottishness of common sense philosophy, now domesticated on the American scene, is in any way significant.

What is equally important is the recognition that the massive infiltration of American thought by the values and attitudes of the Scottish common sense philosophers in the middle decades of the nineteenth century is only the consequence of a transmission of values whose origins go back to the colonial period of Scottish-American relations and whose progress is already marked by 1800. In other words, even if we are thinking only of American intellectual history, the evidence points to a unified pattern of developing Scottish influence. This is not to deny that between the Revolution and the Civil War Americans at different times took different things from the Scottish philosophical Enlightenment; but it is to argue for continuity of influence, and continuity not only in New England, where Howe's emphasis falls, but, largely through the fast- and wide-spreading influence of Witherspoon's Princeton, through the South and West as well.

What is more surprising is that neither Phillipson nor Rice - nor for that matter Howe — seem to recognise how Scottish influence on the intellectual and religious history of America was renewed and revitalised within the very period they regard as crucially important. That is to say, they have nothing to say about Carlyle. In fact in the middle decades of the nineteenth century the main challenge to the conservative religious and social orthodoxy of New England and beyond came not from Humean scepticism but from Emersonian transcendentalism. And in his struggles with his establishment opponents, Emerson's most formidable ally was Carlyle. Deeply offensive to the New England conservative establishment, and bitterly attacked by the Unitarian Andrews Norton and other defenders of the social and religious status quo, "Carlyleism" quickly became a source of excitement and inspiration to a new generation of restless, emotionally and spiritually dissatisfied Americans. What Carlyle, Emerson and his transcendentalist followers had in common was a compelling need to break free from the comfortable straightjacket of the Scottish common sense tradition in which all of them had been educated. All are reacting against the Enlightenment, and against the Scottish "counter-Enlightenment" as well; they are seeking to break out of the world of cool and moderate common sense to find a deeper sense of spiritual fulfilment and, as Daniel Howe puts it, "to revive the fervent emotions Jonathan Edwards had aroused a century before". It is beautifully appropriate that it should have been Carlyle, another Scot, who did as much as anyone actually to undermine the hold of Scottish common sense philosophy on the American mind towards the end of the ante-bellum period. (5)

One further point remains to be made. If the subject under discussion is the transmission of cultural values from Scotland to America in the eighteenth and nineteenth centuries, we should remember that more is in question than Scottish common sense philosophy. The American sensibility, the American imagination, these are involved quite as centrally as the American mind. Just at the time when Americans were coming increasingly under the influence of Scottish thought and philosophy, Scottish medical and scientific studies, Scottish college and university education, Scottish rhetoric and literary criticism, so they were responding with increasing enthusiasm to Scottish poetry and song, Scottish history and legend, Scottish fiction and drama. The American taste seems to have been not only for a specific philosophy, but for Scottish culture as a whole. And indeed it was from this broad spectrum of Scottish cultural achievement that many Americans felt their own new nation could learn. It can only be misleading, then, to regard the penetration of orthodox New England academic philosophy by the Scottish common sense school as a discrete cultural phenomenon.

V

During my earlier discussion of the structure of **Scotland and America** I mentioned that some alternative views on the essential nature of eighteenth-century Scottish culture had recently been put forward. Since one's views of Scottish culture itself is bound to affect one's view of its influence elsewhere, I should like now to comment on these new accounts of the Scottish cultural situation in the context of Scotland's connection with America. Dr Phillipson, then — and Professor Rice seems broadly to go along with him — dismisses the literary historians' account of the divided nature of Scotland's eighteenth-century culture. It is not, he believes, the division between North British learning and more native or national romance that really counts. What does count is another kind of division: that in Scotland between "Enlightenment" and "counter-Enlightenment". In this account the Enlightenment is represented by the radical metaphysical and moral scepticism of Hume, Smith, Kames and their Edinburgh circle, while the "counter-Enlightenment" is created by the common sense rebuttal of such attitudes and values by Thomas Reid and his disciples such as James Beattie and Dugald Stewart. (6) Now the importance of this major philosophical dispute is beyond question; and my own work, like that of other scholars, makes it abundantly clear that it was indeed the philosophy of the Scottish "counter-Enlightenment", the common sense philosophy of Reid and Stewart, and their followers, which permeated American intellectual life up to the Civil War at least. To recognise this is also to go far towards understanding why these Scottish thinkers exercised so much influence in America. A set of philosophical principles specifically designed to answer the dangerous scepticism of Hume appealed to a post-Revolutionary society much more interested in preserving and conserving social and religious stability than in pursuing further radical change in new directions.

Whereas in the later eighteenth century American intellectuals in Philadelphia and elsewhere could see in the post-Humean Scottish Enlightenment a system of values at once modern and progressive and free of the taint of scepticism or moral relativism, in nineteenth-century New England and beyond it was the second set of considerations that really mattered. As we have seen in relation to Carlyle and transcendentalism, it was the older American establishment that stuck firmly to its common sense principles.

Nevertheless, how true is it that "the crucial internal tension in Scottish culture in the eighteenth century" is that between "scepticism and its critics"? (7) Has enough evidence been brought forward to substantiate such a view? Surely such a tension can only be identified as operative within a cultural élite rather than within Scottish culture as a whole? At those points where philosophy, religion, morality and social conduct come together in Scottish culture is there not a much more obvious and simple tension between traditional Presbyterian Calvinism, with its immense grassroots, popular support, and the new "Moderation" within the Church of Scotland? How does this widely recognised division relate to the philosophical argument over Humean scepticism? Finally, **pace** Dr Phillipson, surely it is not only literary historians who would regard the crisis over language — the choice between English English and vernacular Scots in some form — as at least one of the major determinants of eighteenth-century Scottish culture? In any event, I regard it as quite significant that neither Dr Phillipson nor Professor Rice, arguing from the position I have described, are able to provide a really convincing account of American responsiveness to Scottish literary romanticism. Professor Rice argues that American readers found in Scottish romance reassurance: disturbed by the pace of change in their own society they responded enthusiastically to the romanticised picture of an older, static world. But Professor Rice recognises that this account does not explain why it was to Scottish romance that Americans turned. His answer is that Scottish romance appealed because it was not English — in the post-Revolutionary period it would have been unpatriotic and disloyal of Americans to become enthusiastic about English writers.(8) But one wonders whether the actual nature and characteristics of Scottish literary romanticism could ever have been quite so irrelevant as this account implies; and how does one explain America's enthusiasm for the works of Byron, Bulwer Lytton and Dickens?

Dr Phillipson's account of why America responded so positively to Scottish romance is different but no more convincing. Trying to link this literary enthusiasm with American assimilation of Scottish common sense philosophy, he argues that the one complemented the other in such a way as to provide Americans with a comprehensive and satisfying view of man and society to which they were more than willing to give their assent. Scottish romance, he argues, supplied the American reader with that reminder of man's mortality, his relative helplessness in confronting the inevitability of change and decay, which the secure and confident world of common sense philosophy took no account of. (9) This is clearly an interesting hypothesis; but it is nothing more. Where is the evidence that it was this one dimension of some Scottish writing (**Douglas, Ossian,** some of Scott's novels) which accounts for America's general enthusiasm for the products of Scottish literary romanticism?

In **Scotland and America** I do at least point towards an explanation of what I document: the remarkable vogue enjoyed by Scottish literature in America from the 1790s until at least the death of Scott. I would agree that there is indeed a connection between the American vogue of Scottish romance and that of common sense philosophy. But it is not a question of the romance in some way qualifying the comfortable optimism of the philosophy. In their different spheres the two rather represent facets or dimensions of the identical impulse; both satisfy the same basic American need. I have already argued that particularly in the earlier period of major Scottish influence in the post-Revolutionary years, Scottish common sense philosophy while reassuringly free of scepticism and moral relativism was nonetheless modern and progressive; without being offensive to religious and moral orthodoxy it was enlightened and improving. Scottish romance answered the needs of the American sensibility in exactly the same way. From **The Gentle Shepherd**, through **Douglas** and **Ossian** to Walter Scott, Scottish romance was something new and different; it appealed to the feelings, it touched and refined sensibility in a way that the works of Augustan neo-classicism did not. But at the same time it kept its romanticism under fairly tight control; the more radical or revolutionary brand of romanticism hardly makes an appearance. More specifically, Scottish romance offered little or nothing in the way of a challenge or threat to the rationalism, moderation, or morality of enlightened modern society; it may present the reader with a vision of another, more dangerous, world of colour, excitement and high passion — but the location of that world is safely remote both in space and time. It is scarcely surprising that a society which had embraced the broadly conservative system of values enshrined in Scottish common sense philosophy should also

have found Scottish romance peculiarly to its taste.

In **The Instructed Vision: Scottish Common Sense Philosophy and the Origins of American Fiction** — a book which I much regret omitting from the bibliography of **Scotland and America** — Terence Martin provides an acute analysis of the consequences for American fiction of the dominance of the common sense philosophy in the early nineteenth century. His argument is broadly that the committment of the Scottish philosophers to a "metaphysics of actuality" — to the actual as the measure of reality — inclined them towards a devaluation of "fiction" or any other imaginative creation. (10) Perhaps we can see here another reason why an American audience, guided by critics and reviewers whose own aesthetic and critical values and attitudes derived from the common sense school, should have preferred Scottish romance to other less imaginatively inhibited forms of romanticism.

These then are some thoughts on the problems of explanation and interpretation which the facts of the Scottish-American connection seem to raise. I recognise the tentative and sometimes speculative nature of some of the points I have made. I recognise, too, that so far it has been the Scottish side of the question that has occasioned most debate; perhaps in time more comment will be forthcoming on the American dimension. One hopes at least that the debate will continue; as long as it does Scottish-American studies will remain in a healthy condition.

VI

A postscript. One or two readers of **Scotland and America** seem to regret that the evidence it presents is not other than it is. They would have wished Scottish romance to be less sentimental, Scottish criticism to be less conventional, Scottish philosophy to be less conservative, and Scotland's Gaelic culture to be less neglected. What one culture takes from another, however, seems to be less a question of what is "good" or "admirable" than of what it believes it needs. For better or for worse, in the eighteenth and early nineteenth centuries, it was Scotland that answered more than one of America's cultural demands.

REFERENCES

1. See D. Swinfen, "The American Revolution in the Scottish Press".
2. The story in full appears in Andro Crawfurd, **Cairn of Lochwinyoch** Ms., Vol. XXX, pp. 91-92, in Paisley Public Library. The following notes on vocabulary may help some readers: **Peill:** a ruined tower beside Castle-Semple loch in Lochwinnoch; **red:** afraid; **spill a horn or make a spune:** strive hard whether successfully or not; succeed or fail in a big way; **wuddie:** gallows.
3. N. T. Phillipson, "Culture and Society in the Eighteenth Century Province: The Case of Edinburgh and the Scottish Enlightenment" in Lawrence Stone, ed., **The University in Society** (Princeton, 1974), II, pp. 407-48.
4. See C. Duncan Rice, "Scottish Enlightenment, American Revolution, and Atlantic Reform", above; and Nicholas Phillipson, "The Export of Enlightenment", **Times**

Literary Supplement, July 2, 1976, pp. 823-4.
5. For a fuller discussion of these points, see Andrew Hook, **Carlyle and America,** Occasional Papers No. 3, The Carlyle Society, Edinburgh, 1970.
6. N. T. Phillipson, "Towards a Definition of the Scottish Enlightenment", in P. Frotz and D. Williams, eds., **City and Society in the 18th Century** (Toronto, 1973), 125-47 and op cit., "The Export of Enlightenment", p. 823.
7. "The Export of Enlightenment", p. 823.
8. Duncan Rice, "Scottish Enlightenment, American Revolution, and Atlantic Reform", p. 81.
9. "The Export of Enlightenment", p. 824.
10. See Terence Martin, **The Instructed Vision: Scottish Common Sense Philosophy and the Origins of American Fiction** (Bloomington, 1961), chapters 2 and 3 in particular.

SCOTTISH AND AMERICAN PRESBYTERIANISM
Their Relations in the Revolutionary Age

RONALD G CANT

In commemorating the bicentennial of the American Declaration of Independence it is natural to attempt to identify factors or influences which contributed to this historic event. And there is certainly much in Scottish history of the sixteenth and seventeenth centuries that provides precedents for the conduct of the Americans in 1776. Beyond this it is well known that the actual signatories of the Declaration included, in James Wilson and John Witherspoon, two native-born Scots of outstanding ability and influence, and there were others in this group or high in revolutionary councils having close family ties with Scotland. At the same time even the most perfervid Scot must recognise that all this was no more than a contribution to an achievement that was mainly of English derivation or that special development of English ideas along very different lines from those prevailing in England itself that one many call Anglo-American.

Yet it is still worthy of comment that the only clergyman among the signatories of the Declaration of Independence was a Scottish presbyterian, John Witherspoon. Despite the common belief that the Reformation was a movement of liberation - and this was undoubtedly true of its religious aspirations - in only a very few places in Europe was it accomplished as part of a political revolution. In England, Germany, and Scandinavia reform came under the control of the civil government. In Scotland, however, the reform of religion came in 1560 through a revolt against constituted authority in church and state. And although the

reformed church was in theory committed to a partnership with the civil government it approached it on the basis of its own inherent independence. On two further occasions, in 1638 and 1688, the Scots repeated what they had done in 1560, overturning an episcopal and monarchist regime and replacing it by a system more answerable to the community both in its ecclesiastical and political aspects. If the new presbyterian establishment of 1690 was more dependent on the civil authorities than fifty years before it still enjoyed substantial autonomy in its courts and equality between the ministers and elders who constituted them, an equality that was made still more effective by a provision for universal elementary education in 1696 and the general accessibility of high schools and universities to all qualified persons.

It was within a church and society of this kind that John Witherspoon received his upbringing. His own family background made him particularly aware of the traditions of Scottish presbyterianism, his father being minister of the parish of Yester in East Lothian where John was born in 1723 and his mother being the daughter of another minister. As the young Witherspoon was himself preparing for the ministry a division had developed within Scottish presbyterianism between what came to be called the 'moderate' and 'evengelical' parties. The 'evengelical' criticism of the moderates was that while protesting their Calvinist orthodoxy they reduced religion in practice to a form of Christian stoicism and that while claiming to adhere to the principle of the independence of the church from the state they tolerated interference in such fundamental matters as the appointment of parish ministers. In 1733 a group of evangelical ministers headed by Ebenezer Erskine left the Established Church on these issues to form what was to grow into the 'Secession Church'.

This controversy was well known to Witherspoon and it is clear that his own sympathies were strongly evangelical but by the time of actual entry to the ministry in 1744 the Secession Church was itself about to divide on the somewhat technical issue of the Burgess Oath, and if there was one characteristic in his career more consistent than any other it was a refusal to become involved in such technicalities. He had a particular admiration for Thomas Gillespie, uncharitably expelled from the Established Church in 1752 for evangelical heterodoxy and eventually the founder of the 'Relief Church' of 1761, publishing his **Ecclesiastical Characteristics** in his defence in 1753. When Witherspoon acknowledged the authorship of this work ten years later he was minister of the important urban parish of Paisley and one of the best known evangelicals in Scotland. But respected as he was in his own country it was obvious that his ecclesiastical standpoint made it unlikely that he would achieve the kind of academic preferment there, as principal or professor of divinity, for which his attainments qualified him. Hence in 1768 he accepted the invitation, pressed on him for a second time, to become President of the College of New Jersey.

This college, at Princeton, had been promoted some twenty years earlier by the presbyterians of New Jersey and the neighbouring colonies of Pennsylvania and New York as a centre of higher education associated with their ecclesiastical viewpoint. At the time of Witherspoon's arrival, however, it had still to establish itself as a serious rival to other colonial colleges. This Witherspoon enabled it to do in a remarkably short time, reorganising and extending its curriculum on the lines with which he was familiar in Edinburgh and the other Scottish universities. What is particularly interesting is the way in which he sought and obtained the co-operation of fellow-Calvinists in the Congregational and Dutch Reformed churches in securing students for both the philosophical and theological courses. In this he was helped by the distinctive tradition of American presbyterianism, largely re-united just ten years before his arrival under the Synod of New York and Philadelphia. From a study of his own ministerial career in Scotland it would seem that he had already developed a warm and generous outlook rare among his fellow-evangelicals there but it was the ecclesiastical situation in America that enabled him to realise his ideals so effectively and to give them a prestige and influence, even at long last in Scotland, that they would not otherwise have had.

On an ideological level superficially more recondite but inherently more fundamental it was mainly through Witherspoon that the Scottish 'Philosophy of Common Sense' became established in America. Its most characteristic exposition was in Thomas Reid's **Inquiry into the Human Mind** published four years before Witherspoon's departure for the new world. Like Witherspoon, Reid was a member of the Scottish presbyterian establishment, his academic career as Professor of Moral Philosophy at Glasgow (1764-96) running parallel to that of Witherspoon as President at Princeton (1768-94). Under Witherspoon 'Scottish Realism' became a prominent part of the Princeton curriculum. But its development into the principal means of defending Calvinist thought in America against 'deism' and the more extreme forms of scepticism that emerged in the revolutionary period reached its climax in the presbyterian theological seminary established in association with the College of New Jersey in 1812.

While Witherspoon was busy with his educational and ecclesiastical commitments the great crisis in the relations between the colonies and the British government was advancing towards its climax. From the beginning he was a strong supporter of colonial claims but it was some time before he altered the accepted Scottish view that ministers, while entitled to express political opinions, should not become directly involved in politics. In 1776, however, he yielded to pressure to participate in the New Jersey constitutional convention and to represent his colony in the Continental Congress. Having taken this step he then became one of the most outspoken supporters of independence, an issue on which his own church held a more reserved position, hailing the actual Declaration as a 'noble instrument' and urging its immediate adoption. Once again one can see the way in which a Scottish upbringing prepared a public man to sympathise with any movement that seemed to offer greater political liberation but also how American conditions induced a more pragmatic approach than Scottish conventions. In Witherspoon's case not only did he become involved in the work of Congress but served on all its important committees throughout the war. His example of public service was reflected in the extent to which Princeton alumni participated in the deliberations attending the birth of the American republic, the Constitutional Convention of 1787 containing more such than from any other college.

When the war ended Witherspoon was a man of sixty, an advanced age in the conditions of the time, and although he was to live on until 1794 he felt that his remaining energies must be devoted to restoring his college, closed during hostilities and its buildings severely damaged. But he went least part of the way with his presbyterian colleagues in re-defining their attitude on the relations of church and state within the new republic. In 1783 the Synod of New York and Philadelphia, riled by suggestions that it had supported independence to secure establishment status for itself and its allies where they were in a majority, issued a statement expressing its belief 'that every member of civil society ought to be protected in the full and free exercise of their religion'. From here it was a short step to the provision in the Bill of Rights of 1791 that

'Congress shall make no law respecting the establishment of religion or prohibiting the free exercise thereof'.

These proceedings were viewed with somewhat mixed feelings in Scotland. From its earliest days American presbyterianism had looked here more than anywhere else for help and encouragement. But when Witherspoon came back in 1785 to seek support for his church and college his reception was something less than cordial. Despite the important role played by him and other Scots in the American Revolution and the natural support in the home country for a movement of this kind, this was countered by sympathy for the plight of the numerous Scottish 'loyalists' dispossessed by the revolution. On ecclesiastical matters, moreover, even those with whom Witherspoon had been associated in earlier life were far from happy about the 'lax' attitude of American presbyterians to 'Westminster standards' and the relationship of church and state. Scottish suspicions regarding these matters persisted in both parties in the Established Church and both branches of the Secession Church. But in the Relief Church there was considerable support alike for a more liberal doctrinal theological standpoint and for the notion of 'voluntaryism' as the basis of ecclesiastical organisation.

Admittedly the American example was not the only source of such opinions in Scotland. Voluntaryism in particular had a long history among English dissenters with whom Scottish ministers, even of the Established Church, had more contact than is often realised. But it was the close and continuous association between Scottish and American presbyterians and the prestige attaching to the latter as the dust of conflict cleared and the scale of their achievement became apparent that the growth of liberal and voluntary opinions in Scotland mainly proceeded. In this development the special link between the Scottish Secession Church and America played a curious and critical part. First formed in 1753 to sustain conservative attitudes in the new world and still being used for the same purpose in the 1780's, by the 1790's it became the vehicle for the introduction of liberal ideas into Scotland. The immediate consequence was to produce a split, in 1799 and 1806, in both branches of the Secession Church, but the majority who supported the 'New Light' grew steadily, combining in 1820 as the United Secession Church. Throughout this period this element maintained very intimate relations with the 'Reformed Associate Synod' of America, particularly after the visit to Scotland in 1801-2 of its leading minister John M. Mason. Himself the son of one of the Secession pioneers he had taken his theological training in Edinburgh and in 1804 founded a divinity school in New York on the Scottish model. Distinguished from the outset for its doctrinal liberalism, this was to grow into the famous Union Theological Seminary of later years.

When the United Secession Church came into being it did so very much under the impact of the maturing liberal ideas derived from the New Light, itself derived in great part from America. These ideas were already strongly developed in the Relief Church, mainly as an indigenous growth. Yet it was from within the United Secession Church that the first formal advocacy of voluntaryism took place in Scotland in 1829. Needless to say it was denounced by both the moderate and evangelical parties in the Established Church, as well as by the persisting Old Light Seceders, and when the majority of the establishment evangelicals left it to form the Free Church in 1843 they still adhered to the 'establishment principle'. But voluntaryism and liberalism were fundamental elements in the United Presbyterian Church resulting from the combination of the United Secession and Relief churches in 1847.

EDINBURGH UNIVERSITY IN THE AGE OF THE AMERICAN REVOLUTION

ANAND CHITNIS

My contribution to this symposium entitled "Edinburgh University in the Age of the American Revolution" consists of an inquiry. I am struck by three matters — first, that originally the University of Edinburgh was part of that impetus to education that arose from the Reformation in Scotland, and that as the years wore on to, say, 1776, that original religious inspiration appears to have been less overt or to have diminished, and to have evolved into, or to have been replaced by, more worldly concerns. Charles Webster's book, **The Great Instauration: Science, Medicine and Religion 1626-1660**, published late last year, has prompted some thoughts about the similarity between the interest in religion, knowledge and education shown by Puritans in England and that shown by reformers in Scotland. And so these thoughts have led to a third matter, an inquiry, which I would turn over to panel participants for discussion after I have said a little about the first two, and the question is did American institutions of higher education display the same tendencies? Were they founded from a religious base and by the time of the Revolution had they too become more overtly secular institutions? I will use the University of Edinburgh as a case study in Scotland of the question I wish to pose. In short, I want to take one view of the University of Edinburgh in the 18th century as a point of departure for a much more wide-ranging inquiry into the fate, by 1776, of religious reformers' ideals in Scotland, England and America.

The celebrated Glasgow professor of law, John Millar, in his major work, **Historical View of the English Government**, first published in 1803, was one of the first analysts of that distinguished philosophical age in Scotland that was contemporaneous with the age of revolution in America. Millar pointed to the importance of the century or so between the union of the Crowns and the union of the Parliaments, when Scotland lacked the patrons of and stimuli to trade, industry and the liberal arts. It was a century when manufactures and the elegant arts in Scotland were all discouraged, retarded and prevented, and when the Scots tongue was regarded as a corruption of English. But despite the disadvantages, Scotland had been able to make advances in knowledge herself and to appreciate the scientific and literary achievements of other nations. The Scots "were directed into the road of general science" rather than poetry and literature by the circumstances in which they found themselves. More significantly, the way in which they had carried through their Reformation also dictated the nature of their intellectual interests. Roman Catholicism had been regarded as a deep-laid system of superstition, which the Scots countered by a disposition to inquire and by a refusal to accept anything without examination. Energy was required to accomplish the Reformation, said Millar, and the impulse to examine most actively not only religious opinions, but more general matters, continued long after the Reformation. The active, vigorous mentality was supported in Scotland by educational institutions which concentrated on utilitarian subjects. Educational institutions were, in short, the means of reinforcing the reformed religion not only by the continuous process of elaborating knowledge but also by training ministers and schoolmasters to inculcate young and old in godly ways. The University of Edinburgh, a Reformation foundation, must be seen against the background of Millar's historical analysis. It arose from a commitment to reformed religion, to intellectual inquiry and to winning over the congregations to these causes.

Let various facets of the history of the University bear witness to the function of the institution as an agent of the reformed religion that later became more secular. Like its sister universities, its character was a mixture of the academic and professional, concentrating on philosophy and on training ministers and school-masters. Two trends, one academic, the other professional, became evident well before the end of the 17th century. Newtonianism entered the Scottish universities — a major intellectual development that benefited mathematics and the sciences immensely, and as far as the professions were concerned, the foundations were laid in Edinburgh for medicine and medical education. In 1670, for example, was established the Edinburgh Botanical Garden, in 1681 the Edinburgh Royal College of Physicians, the appointment of Edinburgh's first three professors of medicine was made in 1685, and from 1687 systematic anatomical instruction began to be given in the Surgeon's Hall. From 1699 the College of Physicians published a pharmacopaeia whose formulae were binding on Edinburgh apothecaries.

The abolition of regenting which was first undertaken at Edinburgh in 1708 also helped academic development in the long term because it ultimately permitted the fashioning of new disciplines out of traditional subjects — new disciplines like political economy or logic whose elaboration was encouraged by the professorial system. Nevertheless, professors themselves moved within subjects and were not narrow intellectual specialists but the most distinguished among them owed their position to intellectual ability and not to their status as kirk ministers. The abolition of regenting, then, made possible the creation of new chairs at Edinburgh and since chairs of Divinity were already in existence, it is instructive to note that the character of the new chairs founded in the 18th century was totally secular. Mathematics, botany and medical chairs had all been created in the late 17th century; seven more, four in law, three in medicine or allied to it, were established between the treaty of Union and 1726. Six more were created between 1760 and 1790, three in medical or allied subjects, and the others in rhetoric, astronomy and agriculture — the last two being little more than sinecures. Nonetheless, it is significant that the bulk of 18th century chairs were in the worldly science of medicine and that no further chairs of divinity were founded in the metropolitan university.

The chairs were supported by improved facilities and apparatus that testified to the emphasis being given, as the 18th century wore on, to worldly rather than divine matters. Again medicine is the outstanding example in Edinburgh: the founding of the Royal Infirmary in 1729, which made possible clinical lectures as part of the medical curriculum from 1746, may be cited. Museums, laboratories and elaborate equipment of various kinds were also fairly lavishly provided by the Town Council throughout the 18th century. Declining provision was made for Divinity in relation to other disciplines. The universities as a whole, but Edinburgh in particular, were concentrating increasingly throughout the 18th century, on mundane matters such as medicine, political economy, chemistry, natural history. Indeed medical education consumed more resources than the education of ministers.

The Edinburgh medical school to which Benjamin Rush and many other Americans came had, therefore, assumed a particular significance in the development of the social function of Scottish institutions of higher learning and training.

A non-medical barometer of the decline of overt religious inspiration in informing the work of the University of Edinburgh was the principalship of an historian of America, William Robertson. Despite his place as Moderator of the General Assembly and powerful leader of the Moderate Party in the Kirk, his major emphases were not (as with Leechman during his principalship earlier at Glasgow) in developing Divinity teaching, but in securing the services of outstanding professors of non-Divinity subjects, in raising better salaries for the professoriate, in carrying out a major building programme (a new anatomy theatre, chemistry classroom and laboratory, and the construction of the Old Quad), in providing new facilities and in reorganising the library. Material considerations were his concern.

The adaptation to a wholesale professorial system at Edinburgh coincided with the Scottish intellectual affinity for such crucial English thinkers as Bacon, Newton and Locke. The affinity shown for Bacon by so many eighteenth century Scottish philosophers, notably Dugald Stewart, is interesting not least because it mirrors Bacon's intellectual influence amongst some Puritans in 17th century England.Locke bolstered the Scottish Reformation's professed concern for the unshackled use of reason, pointed out, as I mentioned earlier, by Millar. Newton found in the 18th century Edinburgh mathematics professor Colin McLaurin, one of his earliest disciples and clearest exponents, as evidenced by the account of McLaurin published in 1748 of Newton's philosophical discoveries. At that time, McLaurin was still professing that natural philosophy was the search for causes in and a description of the operation of the universe and as such, subordinate to natural theology. As the 18th century wore on, however, there was much less profession of this sort of faith, and an increase in the concern for more overtly scientific or medical matters by the Edinburgh professors who came after McLaurin.

One such science that benefited from Newtonian observation and experiment was earth science, specifically Geology, which in the decade after the American Revolution became so consuming an intellectual subject in such forums as the Royal Society of Edinburgh, the University's Museum and various periodicals. Before then, though, it had been of interest for economic reasons in Scotland's age of improvement, since agriculture was so vital a concern, since the Scottish coal mining industry was expanding and since surveys of the Highlands and Islands by the Board of Trustees, the Commissioners for the Forfeited Estates and the S.P.C.K. were frequent.

It is worth exploring the developing connection between learning, religion and secularism in 17th and 18th century Scotland as evidenced (to take but one example) in the foundation and progress of the University of Edinburgh. Religious objectives gave an important place to matters that were apparently to our eyes, worldly, — namely to medicine, to chemistry, to political economy, to geology, and so on. Yet they had a place in the reformers' godly scheme of things and it is almost as if their own self-generation made them in the 18th century, ends in themselves. The post-Reformation social programme in Scotland, in other words, paved the way for the material age which characterised the post-American Revolution age or the age of industrialisation.

This causation of the distinguished Scottish intellectual age that preceded the American Revolution has emerged for me in my studies thus far of the Scottish Enlightenment. And I was, therefore, interested to read Webster's book on the attitude taken to learning, medicine and science in mid to late-ish 17th century England by some Puritans, for there was much that had a familiar ring. A large body of puritan opinion believed that the reformation of the church would be accompanied by a "Great Instauration" of learning. Several matters lay behind that belief. The glorification of God was linked to the idea of the most efficient exploitation of human and material resources. Insights to God, who to some, such as the Calvinists, was distant and inscrutable, could be given by the patient and accurate methods of experimental science. In other words, learning, science, medicine could all be espoused by man to bring about dominion of man over nature, and the new paradise on earth. Bacon was one of several major intellectual influences on this Puritan espousal of a number of educational, scientific and medical ventures which were all undertaken for religious reasons, just as he was to be important to 18th century Scottish intellectuals. Universal education would enable the young to understand the evils of paganism and to be steeped in Christian philosophy; medicine would counter disease, a manifest exposure of man's Fall that showed up the relationship between spiritual guilt and physical corruption; agricultural innovation could restore the plenty of the Garden of Eden — and so on. Knowledge was to undo the Fall and the resultant renewed state was called by Bacon, the Great Instauration. The people Webster has

studied are virtually all millenarians which separates them in a major way from the promoters of the Scottish concern for philosophic, scientific and medical learning of the late 17th and 18th centuries. Despite this difference, the kinds of schemes they advocated were remarkably similar — new universities, schools and universal education; scientific organisations; colleges of physicians; new chairs and lectureships in scientific and medical subjects; the promotion of such subjects as botany, chemistry and mathematics; a general concern for social amelioration and utilitarian schemes. Both countries in the two periods showed a distinct concern to glorify God by exploiting efficiently human and material resources. It is clear how the concern with religious motivation, evolved into preoccupation with the secular results of the exploitation, in the ensuing era of the mid-17th century English period studied by Webster, and the late 17th to 18th century period in Edinburgh that I outlined earlier.

I have deliberately not discussed today the obvious matters that might be expected to arise from a paper entitled "The University of Edinburgh in the Age of the American Revolution". I have not attempted to assess the impact of a period of study at this institution on those who subsequently signed the Declaration of Independence, not least because I am not convinced of the value of such an exercise. Certainly much has been written about the connections between Edinburgh and Philadelphia medicine but the value of that exercise must be shown to be more than a mere catalogue of names who studied in Scotland and then went or returned westwards. Features of Edinburgh medicine which may have been incorporated in American medical schools have to be shown to be distinctive to Edinburgh and more than merely obvious and sensible means at the time of fulfilling the function of medical education.

Yet a third, well-worn and perhaps obvious way of treating of the topic of Edinburgh University in the Age of the American Revolution would be to look at such matters as the advice Dugald Stewart gave to the fledgling University of Virginia and the regard in which Scottish philosophy and Scottish philosophers were held by such as Jefferson, but that would be to focus on individuals who were, in their professional life not acting for nor on behalf of their institution. Hence, I have here tried to pose questions pertaining to the function and development of an institution in an improving society in which reformed religion was so potent a force. The question is whether American learning, too, shows similar trends to the British, and whether American colleges, founded by men of religion with religious objectives, had also by 1776 found their original inspiration secularised. As the mid-to late 18th century University of Edinburgh faced the overtly secular future of industrialisation after 1776, were American colleges to find the post-independence era to be worldly also? Why did the ideals of religious reformers become so mundane by the late 18th century?

SCOTTISH SCIENCE IN AMERICA IN THE REVOLUTIONARY ERA

ARTHUR DONOVAN

I think it would be well to admit at the outset that the phrase 'Scottish Science', while useful, invites a certain misunderstanding of our subject. None of the eighteenth-century Scots who achieved renown as natural philosophers would have identified their work as Scottish science. They considered themselves and their studies of nature part of a cosmopolitan endeavour to establish the laws that govern the universe and all that dwells in it. The fact that they happened to be British had little bearing on the way they went about their investigations and none at all on the significance of their conclusions. Of course we need not their view of science when studying their works for our own purposes, but we should at least be aware that when we characterise their achievements in terms of their national origins, we are neglecting the more generous faith in science that inspired much of their work.

We, of course, have our own reasons for focusing on the less inspirational aspects of science. The history of science was long dominated by a triumphal concentration on individual achievements and cumulative progress. Since the reaction against the heroic and 'Whig' interpretations of science is now in full spate, it may not be amiss to note that although often overstated, the older view did have some merit. The community of first-rate creative scientists is at any given time very small and great achievements in science owe as much to the tradition of their appropriate speciality as they do to a particular national culture. Scottish s cientists in the eighteenth century established a distinguished record when judged by international standards of achievement. The contributions of Joseph Black to chemistry, James Hutton to geology, William Cullen to medicine and James Watt to technology are well known and justly celebrated. In America only Benjamin Franklin reached comparable heights and he worked in the new field of electrical experimentation, a subject the Scots largely ignored.

When speaking of the impact of Scottish science in America we must therefore avoid the trap of looking for particular achievements of world-historical significance and focus instead on the connections between science, culture and society. Such an approach also has the advantage of speaking to the questions that are presently of greatest interest to historians of American science. Charles Rosenberg has argued, in an essay titled "On Writing the History of American Science", that "the institutionalisation of the academic disciplines was as important an event as there has been in the history of American intellectual life". (1) Did the Scottish inheritance influence the way in which the scientific disciplines attained institutional status? Indeed it did, but to appreciate exactly how its influence was felt we must keep in mind that the cultivation of scientific studies had to be justified in terms of the larger purposes of the institutions that supported them. Disinterested curiosity may be the eternal motive for the study of nature, but certainly in the era of the American Revolution it would have been considered an insufficient, if not irrelevant, reason for committing individual or social resources to the support of such activity.

The university was the key institution in the transmission of Scottish scientific influence to America. In Scotland, as is too well-known to require recapitulation, the universities, particularly the Town's College in Edinburgh, became during the eighteenth century the foremost centres for science education in the English-speaking world. Rather than listing the new professorships created and dilating on the eminence of the men who filled them, I would like to draw attention to two aspects of this revitalisation of Scottish university life that were to be of great importance in America. In the first place, the leaders in the reformation of the Scottish universities set out to reconstruct the university philosophy curriculum in general, and not just the study of natural philosophy or medicine or law. Secondly, the reforms offered had to be acceptable to the kirk, speaking through the General Assembly, before they could be accepted as the basis for education within the nation's universities. I realise that this latter statement glosses over the complex patronage and governance struggles that disturbed and enlivened Scottish university life in the eighteenth century. The kirk had a great deal to say about university matters at the beginning of the century; much less at the end. Yet throughout, the traditional belief that the kirk and the universities were jointly responsible for sustaining and transmitting the cultural heritage of the Scottish nation never lost sway. In this sense the Scottish universities were national institutions, fulfulling the role assigned to them by the Scottish Reformers of the sixteenth century. The philosophy and theology taught within their walls changed radically but their social function, and their commitment to fulfilling that function, endured. Wasn't this the commitment that Woodrow Wilson, that eminent American Presbyterian and university president, was honouring when, at dawn of the Progressive Era, he spoke of Princeton in the nation's service?

I suppose if we could formulate a convincing utilitarian theory of intellectual creativity we could afford to ignore the close relations between science and religion in Scottish philosophy after the middle of the eighteenth century. There were, of course, plenty of philosophical utilitarians in Scotland, or at least many philosophers who occasionally advanced utilitarian arguments. Francis Hutcheson, long before Joseph Priestley, argued in behalf on the greatest good for the greatest number, and David Hume freely admitted that he thought "the only immediate utility of all sciences is to teach us how to control, and regulate future events by their causes". (2) Arguments such as these were commonplace in the Enlightenment, but mask much of the significance attached to the study of nature in that era. For those who looked towards the transformation rather than the abandonment of the Christian doctrinal tradition, science had to be understood in a way that acknowledged its distinctive features without rendering religious belief untenable. Utility alone could not satisfy the deeply searching soul who continued to believe in nature's design and life's larger meaning, and it was men of this stripe, and not the witty club men of international fame, who established the Scottish teacher-preacher tradition in America.

Scottish science impressed itself upon American culture, as opposed to individual Americans, not as a research tradition distinguished by a brilliant record of achievement but as a central concern of an integrated and purposeful university curriculum. The point could be put more concisely by saying Scotland gave American a profound and enduring philosophy of science were it not that today we see the task of the philosophy of science as explicating the processes of discovery and verfication within science. Scottish natural and moral philosophers did take up these questions, as Professors Lauden and Olson have recently demonstrated, (3) and their analyses of science gave rise to the great nineteenth-century British tradition in the philosophy of science. But the overriding concern among Scottish moral philosophers, and also among natural philosophers who, like James Hutton, ranged far beyond science, was to define the limits of natural knowledge and its relations with other kinds of human understanding. Hume's critique of natural theology forced educators such as Thomas Reid to be thorough and profound; their own sense of their place in a national tradition of didactic philosophy obliged them to be comprehensive. In the lectures and writing they combined a sharp sense of the logical limits of inductive arguments with a non-naturalistic belief in the dignity of the individual's struggle for perfection through the cultivation of his intellectual capacities. In a century in which the propertied, privileged and professional joined in promoting and celebrating economic improvement, these earnest figures combined to weigh knowledge on the social and cultural scales of an earlier age. They understood and championed the science of Newton and his successors, but what is of singular importance from our point of view, they did so in a way that enabled their disciples to establish the pursuit of science as a deeply rooted tradition in the new republic in America.

In emphasising the contribution of Scottish didactic philosophy, I do not mean to imply that the many Americans who studied scientific subjects in Edinburgh had no impact on the pursuit of science in their native land. It is difficult, however, to make a reliable general statement about the effect of study abroad upon a student's attitudes. Although the Revolution led to a political break between Great Britain and the United States, it does not seem to have significantly altered the assumptions American medical students brought to Edinburgh or their reasons for going there. As many of you will recall, going abroad to study is an exhilarating but wrenching experience. The student, made vulnerable by age, ignorance and foreignness, opens himself only to that thin yet nourishing stream of special knowledge that cannot be obtained at home. Historians have drawn a great deal of attention to the American medical students in Edinburgh, too much, I suspect. Listen again to a famous passage from a letter Benjamin Rush wrote in 1766, in which he unburdens himself to his mentor, Dr John Morgan, shortly after arriving in Edinburgh. After asking how Morgan's medical lectures at the College of Philadelphia had been received, Rush wrote: "Science planted in a spot so advantageous as Pennsylvania methinks cannot help flourishing when reared by your careful hand. Physic had long sought some new abode in the wilds of America, and sought in vain till, invited by you, she fixed her residence in Philadelphia. Methinks I see the place of my nativity becoming the **Edinburgh of America.** The student now no longer tears himself from every tender engagement and braves the danger of the sea in pursuit of knowledge in a foreign country. Methinks I see the streets of Philadelphia crowded with sons of science whom your fame has brought from the remotest confines of the continent, while future ages rise up and hail the name of Morgan". (4)

Of course this is an outrageous piece of flattery, but it also reveals the perfectly understandable homesickness of a young student newly abroad. Science must be mastered and therefore we must study in Edinburgh, but how wonderful it would be if these harsh realities could be avoided by the development of a comparable centre in America. Naturally when Rush got home merciful memory soon obliterated the uncomfortable feeling of dislocation he had experienced, and in later life he recalled his years of study under Cullen, that shining oracle, with great fondness. But while actually attending his lectures, Rush confided certain troublesome doubts about the great man to the privacy of his journal.

"There is", he wrote, "One thing . . . wanting in Dr Cullen to constitute his character a complete One, viz: a Regard to Religion . . . A Man Who has long been in a Habit of thinking for himself & of doubting the Truth of every Principle of Science until ^{t} it is proved to him by the usual Laws of Demonstration is very apt to carry the same thirst of free inquiry with him to religious matters which will by no means admit of the same Demonstration that is to be found in Matters of Science . . . I am not fully acquainted with Dr Cullen's Principles, nor do I believe he has formed any regular System for himself. He believes in the Immateriality & Immortality of the Soul. This I have heard him frequently declare in his Lectures. But with regard to revealed Religion he professes himself a sceptic". (5)

Although by the middle of the eighteenth century the material and cultural resources of the British colonies in North America had developed to such a point that Rush and others could dream of an Edinburgh of America, American scientists continued to depend upon European leadership until well into our own century. American students continued to go overseas, therefore, both to complete their education and to certify their professional standing. Although David Hosack had already received his medical degree from the

University of Pennsylvania, he felt compelled to continue his studies abroad because, as he later explained, of "the distinction which our citizens . . . made between those physicians who had been educated at home and those who had had additional instruction at the universities of Europe". (6) If, as John Greene has written, American science 'came of age' between 1780 and 1820, it did not in any sense become self-generating or self-contained. Since political independence did not cut American scientists off from the traditional sources of inspiration and instruction, it is difficult to determine exactly what effect the revolution had upon the study of nature in America. A flush of patriotism is evident in the claim made in Samuel L. Mitchell's **Medical Repository** for 1802 that medical education in America had advanced to the point that "among the graduates of Edinburgh (in that year) . . . there was not a single one from the United States". (7) But the fact was anomalous, and during the early decades of the nintettnth century Edinburgh continued to attract young Americans who, like Benjamin Silliman, wanted a glimpse of the frontiers of their subject before settling down to teaching or medical practice.

What careers were open to these young men when they returned home after their periods of study abroad? If we restrict our examination to institutional positions, and neglect for now the possibilities available to individuals of private means, we see that the colleges of America were the seedbeds of science in the new nation. In the twentieth century science has achieved the status of a highly developed profession of great social importance, and the history of the professionalisation of science in America has therefore become, to borrow a phrase, a hot topic. But according to George Daniels, throughout the nineteenth century the budding profession of science was nourished by the educational institutions. "In 1802", Daniels tells us in his **American Science in the Age of Jackson,** "there were about twentyone full full-time jobs in science in the United States, all academic positions . . . By the 1820s the demand for teachers of science had actually outrun the supply". (8)

Today we find the intermingling of professional science and university education unexceptional and, on balance, constructive. But before the middle of the nineteenth century there was no separate profession of science in the United States and thus our current vocational arguments in behalf of science education cannot be used to explain the colleges' support for science in this pre-professional era. But their support can be understood, I believe, largely as a successful transplanting to America of the ideal of liberal education that had been articulated and realised in Scotland during the eighteenth century. To be convinced that Scottish educational models were profoundly influential in America, one need only read Douglas Sloan's recent book, **The Scottish Enlightenment and the American College** Ideal. (9) And to appreciate the importance of science in the liberal arts curriculum during the first half of the nineteenth century, one can now turn to Stanley Guralnick's **Science and the**

Ante-Bellum American College.(10) On a more general level, both books direct our attention to the religious and cultural significance of natural knowledge in the decades before science became the hand-maiden, if not the mistress, of industry. In this way they help us rediscover the powerful impact that Scottish science had upon American culture in the Revolutionary era.

REFERENCES

1. Charles E. Rosenberg, "On Writing the History of American Science", in **The State of American History**, ed. Herbert J. Bass (Chicago, 1970), p. 185.
2. David Hume, **Enquiries concerning the Human Understanding and Concerning the Principles of Morals**, ed. L. A. Selby-Bigge (2nd ed., Oxford, 1902), p. 76.
3. L. L. Lauden, "Thomas Reid and the Newtonian Turn of British Methodological Thought", **The Methodological Heritage of Newton**, ed. R. E. Butts and J. W. Davis (Toronto, 1970); Richard Olson, **Scottish Philosophy and British Physics 1750-1880** (Princeton, 1975).
4. **Letters of Benjamin Rush**, ed. L. H. Butterfield, vol. I: 1761-1792 (Princeton, 1951), pp. 28-29.
5. Benjamin Rush, "Scottish Journal", a MSS record of his visit to Edinburgh, 1766-68, Indiana University Library, pp. 58, 66-68.
6. Quoted in John C. Greene, "American Science Comes of Age, 1780-1820", **The Journal of American History**, 55 (1968): 22-41, p. 28.
7. Quoted in George H. Daniels, **American Science in the Age of Jackson** (New York, 1968), p. 42.
8. Daniels, **American Science**, p. 34.
9. New York, 1971.
10. Philadelphia, 1975.

THE SCOTS IN COLONIAL VIRGINIA DURING THE REVOLUTIONARY WAR

CHARLES H HAWS

Old Dominion University has become the centre of Scottish Studies in the United States of America with its Institute of Scottish Studies, Annual Conferences and published **Proceedings.** This year the Fifth Annual Conference had the Bicentennial theme, Scotland and the American Revolution and attracted scholars, from Scotland, England, Canada and the USA. This paper is an outgrowth of that conference as it seeks to discover the Scottish influences on the Old Dominion, Virginia, especially at the time of the American War of Independence. This preliminary study will attempt to show the reactions to the war of some of the Scottish clergy, physicians, merchants and tradesmen who were living in colonial Virginia. Although the majority of the Scots in this study appear to be loyalists, it is important to realise that a significant number of patriots and still others remain neutral or their ultimate stand on the issues is unknown.

On the eve of the American War of Independence there were at least thirteen Scots serving in Episcopal Church of Colonial Virginia. Of these, five were loyalists and the remaining eight sided with the patriots. The five loyalists were the Revs. Alexander Cruden, William Douglas, John Agnew, Alexander Gordon and Christopher MacRae. Rev. Alexander Cruden, a student of Marischal College, 1736-40 was the son of Alexander, a maltster in Aberdeen. Later he was minister of South Farnham Parish, 1752-1774. Rev. Alexander Cruden returned to Scotland at the outbreak of hostilities and this was usually interpreted to mean that he had loyalist leanings.

Rev. William Douglas received the Long's Bounty in 1749 and was a tutor in Westmoreland the same year. He became minister of St. James Northam Parish in 1750 and was there in 1777. He resigned the parish and lived on the glebe. He was known as a Tory in Goochland County with loyalist sympathies, perhaps one of the most interesting loyalists and was minister of Suffolk Parish, 1754-75. The sign outside the church today reads: "In 1775 the parish minister, Parson Agnew, was driven from the Church for preaching loyalty to the king". After this unpleasant encounter, he joined the Queen's Rangers, was captured, and finally, ended up in prison in France. He remained imprisoned in France for twenty-one months. The loyalist claim he submitted later, included lots, and houses in Portsmouth, lots in North Carolina and a number of slaves. (2) Rev. Alexander Gordon was minister of Antrim Parish in 1763 and until 1775. At the outbreak of the war, he indicated loyalist sympathies, left the parish and moved to Petersburg. Finally, Rev. Christopher MacRae was licensed for Virginia in 1765 and was minister of Littleton Parish before 1773 and until after 1787. (3) He refused to take the oath of allegiance to the Commonwealth. On one occasion he was severely beaten, but refused to leave his parish. Bishop Meade records his death at seventy-five in 1808.

In these cases, the Scottish clergy who were loyalists either left the country, or joined the King's forces, or quit their parish, or remained in their parish conscious of the consequences of their decision. The majority of their fellow clergy, especially the Englishmen, were either patriots or neutral in their allegiance.(4) However, at least eight fellow Scottish clergy joined the American cause.

Rev. David Currie, sometime of Edinburgh, came to Virginia about 1730 and was a tutor in the Lee family with Richard Henry Lee as one of his pupils. He was ordained for Virginia and served fifty years, 1741-42 to 1791-92, as minister of Christ Church Parish. To the American cause, he was both devoted and enthusiastic. Rev. Archibald McRoberts received the King's Bounty in 1761, was minister of Dale Parish, 1769-75 and during the early part of the Revolution was minister of St Patrick's Parish, 1776-79. He served as Chairman of the Committee of Public Safety in Chesterfield County which is one of the ways he demonstrated his loyalty to the American cause. In 1779 he dissented from the Anglican Church in Virginia and joined up with the Presbyterians. Rev. James Thompson was licensed for Virginia in 1769 and was minister of Leeds Parish, 1769 until his death in 1812. He served his new country with dedication and remained in his parish during the Revolution. Rev. John Cameron, a highland Scot who graduated from King's College, Aberdeen, was minister of St. James Parish, 1770-84; Bristol Parish, 1784-93; Nottoway Parish, 1793; Cumberland Parish, 1806 until his death in 1815. He too was a Patriot. Rev. John Braidfoot was licensed for Virginia in 1772 and was minister of Portsmouth, 1774 until his death about 1785. He served in the American forces as a chaplain throughout the Revolutionary War. In 1772, Rev. Alexander Balmaine was licensed for Virginia and upon arriving he temporarily was tutor for the family of Richard Henry Lee. He was minister of Augusta Parish, 1773-75 and was on the Committee of Public Safety for Augusta County when the war broke out. The records of the 13th Virginia Regiment show that he was a chaplain throughout the Revolution. After the war, Rev. Balmaine was elected minister of Frederick Parish in 1785 and remained there until his death, about 1820. Rev. John Buchanan was born in Scotland in 1743 and received the King's Bounty for Virginia in 1775. It is not known exactly when he came to Virginia; however, he was minister of Henrico Parish and remained there until his death in 1822. It is likely that he came to Virginia shortly before hostilities made it difficult to come; having decided to come at all, he apparently made up his mind to support the American cause. In any case, he was treasurer of the Diocese of Virginia for twenty-nine years and a leading member of the Convention. Lastly, Rev. William Willie, who was minister of Albermarle, 1740-76, may have been sympathetic to the American side.

These Scots, who were patriots and sympathetic to the American cause, were largely young men when they came to Virginia. They were idealistic enough to see the vision of a free and independent country and to take the risks which every revolution brings to those willing to accept the challenges and the consequences. Being clergy, they took places of leadership on Committees of Public Safety and became chaplains to the American forces. Some obviously believed that they could best serve their new country by remaining in their parishes performing their spiritual duties. It was a time of change and turmoil and these Scottish clergymen provided much needed spiritual leadership when it was needed most on the battlefield and at home during both defeats and victories. Even after the Revolutionary War was won, these Scots in particular continued to serve in the no longer established church, with the exception of Rev. Archibald McRoberts, for the rest of their lives.

To these Scottish clergymen, who took sides during the War of Independence, can be added the known Scottish physicians who likewise became the loyalists or patriots or neutral in their allegiance. The three Scottish physicians, Drs McCaw, Campbell and Gordon, who were loyalists, all practised medicine in Norfolk prior to the war. Dr James McCaw came from Wigtownshire in Scotland and settled in Norfolk, Virginia in 1765. He dispensed drugs and practised medicine for ten years in the town until the outbreak of the Revolution. When Lord Dunmore left Williamsburg to take refuge in the waters off Norfolk, Dr McCaw joined his forces and served as captain of militia.(5) After the defeat at Great Bridge and the bombardment of Norfolk, he and his family fled to Great Britain. His testament at Register House, Edinburgh indicates that he was married to Elizabeth Brough and had a son, James Drew McCaw. Apparently after the war his son took his medical degree at the University of Edinburgh and later returned with his mother to practise medicine in Richmond, Virginia.(6)

Dr Archibald Campbell eventually fled to Bermuda. In his claim which is at the PRO in London, he stated that "he followed the Profession of Physick and Surgery for upwards of twenty years and afterwards until the time of his leaving that country he was engaged in Trade". While in Norfolk Dr Campbell was a very controversial figure and was involved in the inoculation riot of 1768 which resulted in some anti-Scottish feeling in Norfolk.(7) His medical and business activities were extremely successful and he had a considerable fortune in lands, houses and slaves. According to his report, he "demeaned himself as a loyal and faithful subject ... that he was appointed by his Lordship to administer the oathes of allegiance to such persons as came in under the Proclamation". Because of this loyalty Dr Campbell was claiming recompense for his wharf and stores which were set fire to and destroyed by a party from his Majesty's fleet, and for the rest of his property which was later destroyed by the American troops. By May, 1776, he "received information that American Independence would soon take place, and that unless he would conform to their measures, he could not remain longer in that country".(8) It was then that Dr Campbell, like other Scottish Loyalists in Norfolk, decided to leave Virginia.

Dr Alexander Gordon was a druggist and surgeon in Norfolk before the war. In 1775 he was censured for violating the articles of the Association by importing a consignment of medicines and refusing to give them up. In his loyalist claim Dr Gordon states that he was a Colonel in the Militia and fought with Lord Dunmore when he was taken prisoner. His imprisonment was from Dec. 14, 1775 until March 26, 1777 at which time he was exchanged for a Colonel of the Rebel Army. Upon his release, he was taken on board the **Emerald** for passage back to Britain. He wanted to bring his family, wife and four children, back from Virginia to Scotland where his eldest son had been studying for these past seven years. The doctor made a claim for three new houses, stock in trade and spices and furniture valued at over £2000. Two known Scots, James Parker and William Calderhead in Norfolk before the war, witnessed to his statements as being true. (9)

It is not surprising that the Scottish physicians in Norfolk were loyalists; Norfolk was considered a "hotbed of Toryism" having had the largest concentration of Scottish merchants who likewise were loyalists. Nevertheless, there was a significant number of Scottish physicians who were patriots, in fact, one of the greatest heroes of the war, Dr Hugh Mercer, was a Scot.

Dr Mercer, born in Pitsligo, Aberdeenshire, on Jan. 16, 1726 was educated at Marischal College in Aberdeen. His father, William, was a minister in the Scottish Kirk. After his medical training, Dr Mercer joined the forces of young Charles Edward Stuart. When the battle of Culloden was over he had to take flight to avoid punishment. He fled from Leith to Philadelphia and finally to the Virginia frontier to a place called Green Castle (which is the modern Mercerburg) where he did more fighting than practising of medicine. (10)

The French and Indian War gave him an opportunity to develop his leadership in the line. Mercer served under Braddock during the disastrous march on Fort Duquesne and was among the fortunate few who survived. He went from captain to major while acting as post surgeon. In 1758 he was involved in the successful attack on Fort Duquesne and was later left in charge of the fort. During this campaign, Dr Mercer became a good friend to George Washington and decided to move to Fredericksburg so that he could be near to Mount Vernon.

Upon his arrival in Fredericksburg, Dr Mercer set up an apothecary shop and returned to the practice of medicine. He married Isabella Gordon and had four sons and a daughter. Within a short time, he became the leading physician of the community and in 1771 took Dr Ewen Clements as his partner. Among his friends in Fredericksburg was William Paul, the brother of John Paul Jones. (11) Dr Mercer was a member of the Masons and had the opportunity to meet Thomas Jefferson and Arthur Lee, who were friends of George Washington, a fellow Mason. This comfortable lifestyle ended with the outbreak of the American Revolution.

Dr Mercer was elected colonel of the third regiment of Virginia and was sent to Williamsburg to train the raw recruits, after a test of leadership with Captain Gibson which showed Mercer at his best. The colonel was sent to Gwynn's Island where Lord Dunmore, another Scot, had taken refuge with the Loyalists from Norfolk and Portsmouth areas. It was while Mercer was pursuing Lord Dunmore that he was notified of his appointment as brigadier-general. He joined Washington's command and was with him at Trenton on January 2, 1777 when it was decided to give General Cornwallis the slip. This led to the battle of Princeton where General Mercer fought bravely and was seriously wounded. He was taken from the battlefield and attended by Drs Rush and Alexander, who were sent by General Washington. However, General Mercer, one of the first Scots to become an American hero, died of his wounds on January 12, 1777. He was first buried at Christ Churchyard in Philadelphia and later removed to Laurel Hill Cemetery.

Another Scottish physician who was an officer of the line for the patriots was Dr Adam Stephen. He was born in Scotland in 1718, and he graduated from University of Aberdeen in 1740. Then he went on to do his medical training in Edinburgh. After various duties on the high seas, he settled first in Maryland in 1748 and later came to Fredericksburg where he was practising medicine until 1754. (12) It was at this time that his medical career was augmented by a series of military commands. He developed into an outstanding fighting man and served under Washington in both the French and Indian War and the Revolutionary War. He rose to the rank of major-general and served with honour at Brandywine. At the battle of Germantown General Stephen was intoxicated and was later dismissed by General Washington. This was an unfortunate end for a man who had fought so bravely for the American cause. Washington's decision was criticised, but General Stephen left the army and retired to his plantation in the Virginian frontier. He was a member of the Virginia Constitutional Convention in 1778 and was a strong advocate of the constitution. He died in 1791 with respect and honour.

Unlike Drs Mercer and Stephen, Drs Riddell, Forbes and French were Scottish physicians who served the American cause as surgeons rather than officers of the line. Dr Riddell was from Kinglass, West Lothian and was the son of Captain George Riddell and Christian Paterson Riddell. He first settled in Yorktown where he was advertising drugs in 1751. He later moved to Williamsburg where he was practising medicine when the war came. (13) Dr Forbes came to America in 1774 and finally settled in Fredericksburg. He was married to Lady Margaret Sterling from Edinburgh. Dr French also set up practice in Fredericksburg and was eventually elected mayor. (14)

There is no doubt that these Scottish physicians were patriots for they devoted their leadership and medical skill to the American cause. However, Dr James Currie, who was born in Annandale, Scotland in 1745, and was a leading physician in Richmond, may have been neutral. His name fails to appear on any of the known lists of Virginia Revolutionary doctors. He remained in Virginia and counted Jefferson among his friends.

If the Scottish clergymen and physicians appear to have a balance in their numbers of known loyalists and patriots, then the Scottish merchants are obviously lopsided because almost all of them are either loyalist or neutral. The largest concentration of loyalism in Colonial Virginia was in the Norfolk-Portsmouth area. A few other Scottish merchants from Nansemond and outlying counties filed loyalists claims. (15) For Scottish merchants like Archibald Ritchie and William Allasoun there are no records of any claims; however, they did not serve in the American cause and appeared to have loyalist leanings. On the other hand, the two James Hunters of Fredericksburg were patriots. (16)

It has been estimated that there were about forty Scottish merchants in the Norfolk-Portsmouth area before the hostilities erupted. (17) Charles Stewart, who had come to Norfolk and Portsmouth and returned to Scotland just before the outbreak of the war. His correspondence with his friends along the Elizabeth River clearly indicated loyalist leanings. The majority of the Scottish merchants who stayed after Stewart's departure were loyalists and later filed loyalist claims. James Parker, who was from Port Glasgow, was an an ardent supporter of the Scottish Governor of Virginia, John Murray, better known as Lord Dunmore. Parker encouraged Lord Dunmore to leave Williamsburg in 1775 for Norfolk where he could rely on the loyalty of the Scottish merchants. Lord Dunmore accepted the invitation and proceeded to establish the Norfolk-Portsmouth area as a coastal base for future operations against the rebels.

Lord Dunmore in his testimonials on behalf of the Scottish merchants who filed loyalist claims stated that the Scots of Norfolk and Portsmouth rendered him and the King loyal service above and beyond the call of duty. Neil Jamieson and Andrew Sproule aided Lord Dunmore by giving him financial aid and by quartering his troops. Both of these Scottish merchants could afford it because they had accumulated large holdings of warehouses and other real estate. (18) George Rae, who came to Norfolk in 1771 with £600 to set up his own business helped Lord Dunmore build the fort at Great Bridge. (19) Benjamin Bannerman, a Portsmouth merchant who came from Scotland in 1763, gave intelligence to Lord Dunmore; refused to take a commission in the rebel army and to take the oath of allegiance to the American cause. He was accused of high treason by the Americans and eventually ended up as a prisoner of war in France. (20)

A number of the Scottish merchants took part in the victory at Kemp's Landing and the subsequent loss at Great Bridge in 1775. John Crammond, one of the two loyalists who suffered being tarred and feathered for his loyalism, fought in the Battle of Great Bridge, was taken prisoner and later escaped to Newport, Rhode Island. (21) John Cunningham was taken prisoner and later escaped on the **Roebuck.** Having escaped from the patriots, John Carmont fled to the Bahamas. Either the patriots in Virginia were lenient towards the loyalists they captured or they were very poor guards. (22)

After the defeat at Great Bridge, Lord Dunmore retreated back to Norfolk and on New Year's Day, January 1, 1776, bombarded the town destroying property along the waterfront. Shortly after this the patriots burned the rest of the buildings leaving Norfolk in ruins. William Chisholm had his two houses destroyed by Lord Dunmore's forces and in his claim he valued them at £500 Virginia currency. (23) The Brown Brothers, John and William, saw their buildings go up in smoke and later valued them at over £2000. John fled to Jamaica and then returned to Britain while his brother, William, returned to Britain, but later fought for the King in Charleston. (24)

A few months after the complete destruction of Norfolk, most of the Scottish merchants fled with Dunmore to Gwynn's Island and then on to various parts of the British Empire. Robert Shedden, who came to Norfolk in 1759 from Beith, Ayrshire, went first to Bermuda and then on to Britain. He filed a claim of over £11,000. David Ramsay was with Lord Dunmore, and James Parker, Robert Shedden and James Ingram testified on behalf of his claim. James Ingram, who came to Norfolk in 1753, returned to Glasgow and filed a claim for losses of over £10,000. (25)

Next to the Norfolk-Portsmouth area was Nansemond County with its own contingent of Scottish Loyalists. Anthony Warwick came to Virginia in 1761 and was later tarred and feathered for his loyalism. After refusing to give his gunpowder and tea to the rebels, he was obliged to quit Virginia. (26) His loyalty was rewarded with a stipend from the King of £50 per annum. Samuel Donaldson filed a claim for over a £1,000 for the losses he suffered in Suffolk. (27) Thomas Jack, a planter and merchant, stated that he was the only Nansemond Country magistrate loyal to the King. He was induced to sign the agreement of the association to avoid being tarred and feathered. (28)

The final battle of the American War of Independence at Yorktown, Virginia included a few Scottish loyalists who had served throughout the war. William Calderhead managed the distillery in Norfolk before the war and fled with Lord Dunmore. After going to Maryland he joined the King's forces and was captured at Yorktown. James Tait, who lived on the eastern shore of Virginia, served under Cornwallis and was taken prisoner at Yorktown. He was later awarded £20 per annum for his loyalty and service. Captain William Hamilton, sometime of Nansemond County, was taken prisoner at Yorktown. His claim for a stipend was considered unreasonable because he was receiving half pay as captain in 1785 while living in Scotland. (29)

To these Scottish loyalists must be added other Scots who were tradesmen and remained loyal to the crown. John Ewing, who came from Scotland to Portsmouth in 1776, was a baker. He valued the loss of his bakehouse at £1,055. (30) Alexander McGregor came from Scotland in 1772 and settled in Blackwater, Isle of Wright, Virginia. He considered himself both a tailor and schoolmaster. The committee on loyalist claims questioned his being a schoolmaster and awarded him a single £10 of the £150 he requested. This is one of the many claims which the committee either gave a small amount of what was requested or awarded nothing at all. John Muirhead, a shoemaker in Norfolk and Portsmouth, joined Lord Dunmore's forces and lost an arm and his left eye. In 1786, he was awarded £20 per annum for his service to the King. A master cooper, William Donaldson, came to Portsmouth in 1763. During the war he left the Tidewater area and later settled in Nova Scotia. William Hunter, the printer of Dixon and Hunter's **Virginia Gazette,** had taken oaths on both sides of the issue. In 1781, he finally joined the British because he thought that they would prevail. When his claim came before the committee it was considered most difficult; however, Hunter was awarded £30 per annum. Finally, John and Michael Wallace were listed as milners of Nansemond County. (31)

In conclusion, this preliminary study indicates that the known Scottish professionals, clergy and physicians, were split in their reactions to the war. Mercer and Stephen were outstanding leaders of the patriotic side. Additional research will undoubtedly uncover a few more on both sides of the issue, but work must be done on the known Scottish teachers, lawyers and other professionals. As far as the Scottish merchants are concerned, it appears that the vast majority of them were loyalists; many of them served with Dunmore and Cornwallis. Although the loyalist claims do not include all the known Scots because some of them did not file claims, they are an excellent source for determining Scottish nationality and the size of individual holdings in Virginia. Also, they indicate the type of involvement by the claimant in the war and any subsequent reward. The Scottish merchants were, on the whole, wealthy and clannish. The large concentration of so many of them in the Norfork-Portsmouth region with their obvious mercantile interests at stake helps to explain their loyalty to the King at a time when commerce was threatened. Their coastal position, the overwhelming strength of the British Navy, the possibility of support from the freed slaves and the fact that some of them never had any intention of making Virginia their ultimate home must be some of the other possible reasons why they remained loyal. On the other hand, the Scots who joined the American cause did so for other political and economic reasons. Lastly, the Scots who were neutral or had leanings one way or the other must have felt enormous pressures from both sides.

REFERENCES

1. Part of this study was made possible by a grant from the Carnegie Trust for the Universities of Scotland.
2. PRO, London, AO/13/27/958.
3. E. L. Goodwin, **The Colonial Church in Virginia,** (Milwaukee, 1927), p. 290.
4. I. S. Harrell, **Loyalism in Virginia,** (Durham, North Carolina, 1926), p. 63-4.
5. **Virginia Magazine of History and Biography,** XXII, 160-172.
6. Edinburgh Testaments in SRO, Edinburgh, CC8/8/128/2; **List of the Graduates in Medicine in the University of Edinburgh** (Edinburgh, 1867), p. 23.
7. PRO, London, AO1)12/55/70; P. Stewart, "Norfolk's Scottish Loyalists during the American Revolution", **Proceedings of the Conference on Scottish Studies,** No. 2, 23-25.
8. PRO, London, AO/12/70/10.
9. **Ibid,** AO/13/29/Part II.
10. H. Scott, **Fasti Ecclesiae Scoticanae** (Edinburgh, 1915-), VI., 235.
11. Blanton, **Medicine in Virginia,** p. 223. William Paul was a tailor in Fredericksburg and his brother, John, came from the family home in Kirkcudbrightshire to visit him. Later he became the famous John Paul Jones of the American Navy.
12. **Ibid.,** p. 238.
13. **Scottish Notes and Queries,** III. 342; Blandon, **Medicine in Virginia,** 319, 325.
14. O. H. Darter, **Colonial Fredericksburg and Neighbourhood in Perspective** (New York, 1957), pp. 169-70.
15. W. Brown, **The King's Friends** (Providence, Rhode Island, 1965), p. 332.
16. R. W. Coakley, "The Two James Hunters of Fredericksburg", **The Virginia Magazine of History and Biography,** Vol. 56, No. 1, pp. 3-21.
17. P. Stewart, "Norfolk's Scottish Loyalists", p. 26.
18. PRO, London, AO/12/75/235.
19. **Ibid.,** AO/12/99/21.
20. **Ibid.,** AO/12/100/200.
21. **Ibid.,** AO/13/28/C; AO/12/95/6.
22. **Ibid.,** AO/12/102/152.
23. **Ibid.,** AO/13/28/C; AO/12/74/216/95.
24. **Ibid.,** AO/12/102/115; AO/12/101/224.
25. **Ibid.,** AO/12/99/315.
26. **Ibid.,** AO/12/100/359.
27. **Ibid.,** AO/12/70/119.
28. **Ibid.,** AO/12/99/222.
29. **Ibid.,** AO/12/74/293; AO/12/99/312.
30. **Ibid.,** AO/12/70/1; AO/12/55/15.
31. **Ibid.,** AO/12/101/37; AO/12/102/42; AO/12/70/14; AO/12/101/96; AO/12/55/110.

NOVA SCOTIA AND THE AMERICAN REVOLUTION

G A RAWLYK

In 1776 most residents of what is now Canada chose not to become American Republican Revolutionaries. It was a collective decision based partly upon their indifference to the ideological and social forces which had helped to precipitate the Revolution and partly upon their unwillingness to shatter the existing framework and unity of the British North American Colonial Empire. Obvious strategic, military and economic realities, moreover, appeared to strengthen the prevailing resolve to reject the American Revolution and all that it seemed to represent. And the arrival of over 40,000 Loyalists during and immediately following the War of Independence further consolidated the pro-British and anti-Republican thrust of British North American development especially in the Atlantic region. "Of greater moment than the boundary settlement was the parting itself", Professor A. R. M. Lower has perceptively pointed out. "Here surely was the profoundest depth of the Revolution. For the parting had been in bad blood. The race was broken. Neither Englishmen nor Canadians, especially Canadians, have realised to this day what Revolution really means, how wide and enduring is the gulf that it opens up between the winning and the losing sides". (1)

Nova Scotia's response to the American Revolution has long intrigued historians. And what is widely considered to be the definitive answer was provided by J. B. Brebner in his influential and ground breaking study, **The Neutral Yankees of Nova Scotia,** published in 1937. According to Brebner, the recently arrived Yankee settlers of Nova Scotia, like the Acadians during various periods of Anglo-French conflict, resolved to walk the knife-edge of neutrality. Even though he warned his readers of the great danger of relying - as he put it - "on a single explanation for Nova Scotia behaviour", Brebner nevertheless concluded that the colony's "insulation from the rest of North America" provided the "principal clue" to Nova Scotia's pragmatic response to the Revolution. Brebner implicitly and explicitly emphasised what he felt was the striking theme of continuity in Nova Scotia's 18th century experience. The Yankees, he contended, despite their New England origins and ties, were forced two decades later into the same frustrating predicament of their predecessors, the French-speaking Acadians. When war came to the northeastern extremity of the Thirteen Colonies, whether it was the Imperial struggle between France and Great Britain or the Revolutionary War between the United States and Britain, it seemed, for Brebner natural and almost inevitable, that Nova Scotians would have no capacity for any kind for positive action. They were - as he graphically expressed it - passively "ground between the millstone of contending imperial forces". (2)

Locked into what to some might appear to be a restricting "neutrality paradigm", Brebner suggested that the English-speaking Nova Scotians of 1776 had transformed by the twin forces of geography and history, into "Acadian Neutrals". He had thus imposed a brilliant and illuminating overview of over 150 years of Acadia-Nova Scotia - New England development. Brebner had, at last, made sense of an extremely confused historical relationship. His "neutrality thesis" has been described recently as the only "classic and satisfactory" interpretation and all historians were warned that there was nothing further to say about the topic.(3) Despite Professor W. S. MacNutt's warning a handful of scholars led by Gordon Stewart of Michigan State University and Jack Bumstead of Simon Fraser University, have re-examined Brebner's Nova Scotia. And even though they may not have succeeded in demolishing Brebner's "neutrality paradigm", they have, nevertheless, extended significantly the parameters of the debate. And, in the process, they have challenged Brebner's central argument that "neutrality" alone was at the core of Nova Scotia's response to the Revolution. Moreover, they have shown that Nova Scotia was not simply a "Yankee" colony in 1776 and that religion was of primary importance in shaping the contours of Nova Scotia's response to the Revolution. And, in particular, Professor Gordon Stewart has made excellent use of the insights from Cultural Anthropology and Social Psychology in an attempt to come to grips with some of the situational pressures which impinged upon the inhabitants of Revolutionary Nova Scotia.(4)

By 1770, it should be kept in mind, the influx of Yankee fisherman and farmers into Nova Scotia had virtually come to end, and an outflow back to New England had begun. Immigration from Great Britain, however, continued and even expanded. As a result, a little more than 750 Yorkshiremen, some destitute Scots and some Irish Roman Catholics entered the colony before the outbreak of the Revolution and substantially strengthened the non-Yankee element of the population. By 1776, of an estimated total population of 17,000 to 20,000, only approximately 60 per cent was of New England origin. Nova Scotia in 1776, therefore, was not a homogenous New England colony as J. B. Brebner implied. Rather, it was little more than a political expression for a number of widely scattered and isolated communities stretching from Pictou on Northumberland Strait, to the Acadian villages on Cape Breton Island, to Canso and then to Halifax and Yarmouth, along the Bay of Fundy coast to Maugerville on the St. John River and to the tiny outpost of Passamaquoddy on the St. Croix.

During the Revolutionary decade, there were at least, two distinct Nova Scotias, Halifax and the out-settlements. The actual influence of the capital was largely restricted to the Bedford Basin region. Petty political squabbling, graft and corruption, economic and social stagnation seemed to characterise Halifax life in the pre-Revolutionary years. Governor William Campbell, and Francis Legge who replaced him in 1773, were in constant trouble with the Halifax commercial élite and both were eventually hounded out of the governorship by their persistent and unscrupulous critics. Being forced to leave the capital was, in many respects, something to be looked forward to. Halifax which

in 1775, had a population of almost 2,000, was described by one eyewitness as being—
"little more than a hamlet; at best it was a miserable village, inhabited chiefly by fishermen . . .most of the houses were in a dilapidated state, letting in the bleak winds of the season through maniford chinks, hardly a room having ever known the luxury of being plastered.(5)"

Apart from the Yorkshiremen and Scots-Irish residing in the Chignecto-Minas Bay region, and the Scots of Pictou and the "Foreign Protestants" of Lunenburg, the outsettlements were dominated by the Nova Scotia Scotia "Yankees". These inhabitants of the coastal strip of the southern half of peninsular Nova Scotia and of the Valley of the Saint John River had strong cultural and economic ties with their former homeland. They also were sullenly suspicious of the small clique of Halifax merchants who controlled the legislative and executive functions of government and who attempted to impose centralised control over the isolated townships. Consequently, when the Revolutionary crisis engulfed North America, the Halifax authorities, not without reason, expected their "bitter bad subjects" to flock to the American side. Only in the two western frontier settlements of Maugerville and Cumberland, however, was there any indigenous Revolutionary activity. And the so-called "contagion of disaffection" inflicted merely a minority of the population of these two regions and for only a period of a few months in 1776. Even then, the "disaffection" was probably more than anything else proof, as the Maugerville rebels put it, of "our . . . Desire to submit ourselves to the government of the Massachusetts Bay".(6) But there was little interest in Massachusetts in liberating what John Adams once contemptuously referred to as "a set of Fugitives and Vagabonds".(7)

The major Massachusetts expansionist thrust during the early years of the Revolution was direct north-westwards against Quebec. The centre of organised activity against Nova Scotia during this same period was the tiny isolated lumbering and fishing outpost of Machias, a few miles west of the St. Croix River. And this fact underscores New England's indifference to the liberation of neighbouring Nova Scotia. In the summer of 1775 the Machias settlers proposed to General Washington that they would "liberate" Nova Scotia if supported by a force of 1000 soldiers and four armed vessels. Washington tactfully refused the offer and carefully underlined his strategic reasons for doing so. It was "the Enemy's Strength at Sea".(8)

During the Spring and Summer months of 1775, quite independently of one another, indigenous Revolutionary movements came into being at Maugerville and the Chignecto Isthmus. The first was led by the Reverend Mr Seth Noble, a recently arrived Congregational minister who had been able to convince his parishioners, "That as tyranny ought to be Resisted in its first appearance . . . the united Provinces are just in their proceedings".(9) On the Chignecto Isthmus Jonathan Eddy and John Allan, leading public figures and successful farmers, were the ringleaders.

Towards the end of November and in early December of 1775, Noble, Eddy and Allan were certain that the Nova Scotia government had prepared the way for Revolution by passing two extraordinary unpopular acts. The first stipulated that one-fifth of the militia was to be called out to defend the colony, and the other imposed a tax for the support of the militia. Almost immediately the legislation was denounced throughout the "Yankee" regions by those who violently objected to the new tax and the the possibility of being compelled, as one petition emphasised, to "march into different parts of arms against their friends and relations". (10) Just at the moment when it seemed likely that the profound discontent would be channelled into a violent confrontation, Governor Legge promptly suspended the two contentious acts.

Failing to grasp the significance of Legge's decision in undermining the base of their political support, Eddy and Allan decided in early 1776 that the time was up for formenting a major insurrection. They badly misjudged public opinion. When they sounded out their neighbours regarding the viability of rebellion, they were apparently genuinely shocked to discover that most "Yankees", even though they would have welcomed an army of invasion, had no enthusiasm for participating in an independent insurrection. (11) Pressed between the millstones of contending forces and values, most of the Chignecto "Yankees", like those New Englanders in other areas of Nova Scotia, did not at that moment in time want to commit themselves. The well-known petition from the Yarmouth inhabitants to Governor Legge cogently expressed this point of view—
"We do all of us profess to be true Friends and Loyal Subjects to George our King. We were almost all of us born in New England, we have Fathers, Brothers, and Sisters in that Country, divided betwixt natural affection to our nearest relatives, and good Faith and Friendship to our King and Country. We want to know if we may be permitted at this time to live in a peaceable State. . . "(12)
The "Yankees" would patiently wait, aloof from the conflict, until they were either "liberated" and absolutely certain which side would gain effective control of Nova Scotia.

In February, 1776, Eddy, with fourteen supporters, left Chignecto to persuade Washington and the Continental Congress to send on "army of liberation" to Nova Scotia. Eddy's mission failed but he, nevertheless, refused to abandon his scheme. In early August he was at Machias where he was able to recruit a twenty-eight man liberating army for the planned invasion of Nova Scotia. After picking up a few more volunteers at Passamaquoddy and Maugerville, at which latter place the inhabitants were "almost universally to be hearty in the cause", (13) Eddy's eighty-man army made its way to the Chignecto Isthmus. The immediate military target was Fort Cumberland, the British fort on the Bay of Fundy side of the narrow Isthmus.

The supporters of Eddy and Allan on the Isthmus understandably "expressed their uneasiness at seeing so few (invaders) . . . and those unprovided with Artillery". (14) They vehemently argued that, taking everything into account, there was no possible chance of success. Eddy was therefore forced to resort to outright intimidation in order to prevent his former supporters from drifting into the enemy camp. And even in spite of all sorts of fantastic rumours as to the size of Eddy's invading force, which rumours spread throughout the colony in October and November, almost all of the "Yankees" on the peninsula were content to wait patiently to see what would eventually happen before committing themselves. In late November the invading force was driven from the Chignecto by British troops and Eddy and his men retreated westwards to Maugerville. The inhabitants, under British pressure, abandoned their American sympathies and submitted themselves once again to George III. In the Chignecto, by 1777, most of the overt supporters of Revolution had been compelled to emigrate to Massachusetts, thus destroying the local movement. (15)

In both areas there were four phases in the collective response to Revolution on the part of a large number of inhabitants. There was, prior to 1775, a prevailing apathy concerning the political and economic questions that were disturbing New Englanders. The Nova Scotia "Yankees", by emigrating in the early 1760s, had missed a critical decade in the ideological development of the New England colonies. And consequently, most of them were incapable of comprehending the arguments used during the immediate pre-Revolution period. In a sense then, their political thinking had congealed before the Stamp Act Crisis. What was required in the colony, according to one American contemporary, before Revolutionary ideas could influence large numbers of "Yankees" was an "ecclaircisement". (16)

Another suggested that until all the Patriot pamphlets were read by the Nova Scotians and inwardly digested they would remain in an unlightened state. What was needed, Alexander McNutt contended in 1778, was a massive propaganda effort that would telescope the transformation that had apparently taken place in American values between 1765 and 1775 into one great act of Revolutionary understanding. (17)

The second phase of Nova Scotia's collective reaction to the Revolution occurred in late 1775 and early 1776. During these months, the government Militia policy had precipitated a crisis, which, together with the underlying sympathy for family and friends in New England, was used by politically aware leaders like Eddy and Allan to bring the local Revolutionary movement into public view. Then there followed a period of a number of months when the leaders attempted to broaden the base for support, in the Chignecto, by bringing in an invading force, and by intimidation and in Maugerville by persuasion. Then in 1777, the fourth phase, most of the remaining settlers quickly reverted to their special kind of British allegiance.

Most other Nova Scotians, even though they probably never passed beyond the first phase of the Maugerville - Chignecto reaction to the Revolution still must have shared the basic vacillation and confusion of the response. In a very real sense the essence of Nova Scotia's response to the Revolution was acute confusion. The activities of American privateers and British press-gangs merely added to the existing chaos. Almost every Nova Scotia settlement, with the exception of Halifax, was ravaged by American privateersmen. This was a strange way to make American converts of Nova Scotians. And large numbers of Nova Scotians were either impressed or threatened by impressment. And this, too, was a strange way to persuade Nova Scotians to remain loyal to the British Crown.

But it is too simplistic, I think, to conclude (as some historians have), that the New England privateering raids drove the wavering Nova Scotia "Yankees" into the welcoming arms of the Mother Country. Some of the well-to-do merchants, who bore the brunt of these expeditions probably did move in this direction. But the majority of "Yankee" inhabitants, who had little of any value to lose to freebooters, certainly did not. These men must have been able to distinguish clearly between the rapacious privateersmen and the people and governments of the independent states. Moreover, the ordinary Nova Scotia inhibitant had much more to fear from the press-gangs than he did from the privateer. For example, even after having lost a number of their ships to American privateers and having suffered depredations ashore, the people of Liverpool "much Discouraged" wanted to return to New England. They blamed their plight, it should be noted, not on the Americans but on the irresponsible apathy of the British authorities in Halifax who seemed far more interested in impressing Nova Scotians than in defending them. (18)

As in Quebec, the Revolution brought to Nova Scotia a sudden burst of economic prosperity. Halifax, as always during periods of war, sucked in huge sums of money for military purposes and some of this money made its way to the outsettlements as did revenue from the considerable illicit trade carried on with the Americans. But unlike many of the inhabitants of Newfoundland and present-day Prince Edward Island, large numbers of Nova Scotians, especially the Yankees, from 1775 to 1783, experienced a general feeling of intense uneasiness, fear and puzzlement concerning the War. Of course, they were much closer to hostilities in terms both of distance and personal attachments and consequently far more involved. John Allan observed in September 177 that "the whole province is in Confusion, Trouble and Anguish" and almost a year later he referred to the persistence of "Trouble and Confusion". (19) Until local leaders were able to make some sense out of the confusing contemporary situation, the Nova Scotians were bound to have remained in a troubled frame of mind, as they desperately searched for a new sense of identity and new relationships to replace their disintegrating dual loyalty. As one contemporary observer noted in the autumn of 1776:
"(the) inhabitants ... were reduced to the shocking dilemma of Being Either plundered and butchered by their friends or of incurring the highest displeasure of the own Government". (20)

Henry Alline was one Nova Scotian who was able to perceive a special purpose for his fellow colonists in the midst of the confused Revolutionary situation. He was the charismatic leader of the intense religious revival which swept the colony during the war period. This revival was not merely a "retreat from the grim realities of the world to the safety and pleasantly exciting warmth of the revival meeting", and "to profits and rewards of another character." (21) Nor was it basically a revolt of the outsettlements against Halifax or an irrational outburst against all forms of traditonalism and authority. (22) The Great Awakening of Nova Scotia may be viewed as an attempt by many Yankee inhabitants to appropriate a new sense of identity and a renewed sense of purpose. Religious enthusiasm in this context, a social movement of profound consequence in the Nova Scotian situation, was symptomatic of a kind of collective identity crisis as well as a searching for an acceptable and meaningful ideology. Resolution of the crisis came not only when the individuals were absorbed into what they felt was a dynamic fellowship of true believers but also when they accepted Alline's analysis of contemporary events and his conviction that their colony was the centre of a crucial cosmic struggle. (23) Alline was born in Newport, Rhode Island in 1748 and in 1760 he moved with his parents to Falmouth in the Minas Basin region of Nova Scotia. Like most young people in the settlement, he was brought up in a pious Christian atmosphere. His finely developed morbid sense of introspection and the pressure he was under to commit himself one way or another in the Revolutionary struggle probably helped to precipitate in March, 1775, first a profoundly disturbing psychic crisis and then an unusually intense conversion experience. The young farmer observed in his **Journal:**
"my whole soul seemed to be melted down with love; the burden of guilt and condemnation was gone, darkness was expelled, my heart humbled and filled with gratitude, and my will turned of choice after the infinite God . . . . my whole soul seemed filled with the divine being . . . my whole soul was filled with love, and ravished with a divine ecstasy beyond any doubts or fears . . . for I enjoyed a heaven on earth, and it seemed as if I were wrapped up in God." (24)
Compelled to have others share with him this traumatic religous experience, Alline resolved "to go forth, and enlist my fellow mortals to fight under the banners of King Jesus". (25) Alline considered himself to be more than an evangelist or even a prophet; he was, rather, Nova Scotia's and the world's second John the Baptist. It was Jesus Christ and Alline and not George III or George Washington who were alone worthy of blind obedience.

Eventually Alline visited almost every

settlement in Nova Scotia; and Halifax and Lunenburg were the only major centres unaffected by the revival he largely articulated into existence. The Lunenburg area was peopled by Foreign Protestants who understood neither Alline's brand of Christianity nor the Patriot ideology of independence. Their loyalty was a mixture of self interest, indifference and splendid isolation. In Halifax, economic and military ties with Great Britan together with the heterogeneous nature of the population and the influence of the élite created a consensus violently opposed both to Revolution and to Alline. Throughout the war years, Halifax witnessed periodic outbursts of mob violence. And the evidence suggests that the violence was encouraged, if not manipulated, by the elite of the community. In Halifax the community consensus (the dynamic which E. P. Thompson has argued was the "legitimizing notion") (26) blended into the élite's fear of change to produce a powerful conservative force in the capital. The community consensus and élite self-interest merged, for example to protest vociferously against impressment, the forced expropriation of goods and supplies, and also against the arrival of trouble-making Evangelical preachers. In this manner, the status quo in Halifax was being assiduously protected at a time of acute disorientation and anxiety.

Between April, 1776 when Alline first preached in public and his ordination as an itinerant preacher three years later the young evangelist concentrated his attention to the area he knew best - that lying between the Minas Bay settlement and Annapolis Royal. On building a strong base in his home territory, after his ordination, Alline extended his activities to the Saint John River Valley where the inhabitants were without a regular minister. It was only after 1780, it should be pointed out, that he visited the Yarmouth-Liverpool region.

Almost single-handedly Alline was able, by his frequent visits to the settlements, to draw the isolated communities together and to impose upon them a feeling of oneness. They each were sharing a common experience and Alline was providing them with answers to disconcerting and puzzling contemporary questions. For Alline, the Nova Scotia revival was, among other things, an event of world significance. The social, economic and political backwater that was Nova Scotia had been transformed into the new centre of the Christian world. Alline thus was attempting to lift Nova Scotians from their parochial surroundings and to thrust them into the middle of the world stage.

In his sermons preached as he crisscrossed the colony, Alline developed the theme that the Nova Scotia "Yankees", in particular had a special predestined role to play in God's plan for the world. It must have required a special effort for Alline to convince Nova Scotians of their special world role. But Alline, striking deep into the Puritan New England tradition that viewed self-sacrifice and frugality as virtues, contended that the relative backwardness and isolation of the colony had removed the inhabitants from the

prevailing corrupting influences of New England and Britain. As a result, Nova Scotia was in an ideal position to lead the world back to God. As far as Alline was concerned the revival was convincing proof that the Nova Scotians were "a people on whom God had set his everlasting Love: and that their colony was 'as the Apple of His Eye'". (27)

The implication of the conjunction of events, of civil war in New England and an outpouring of the Holy Spirit in Nova Scotia was obvious to Alline and the thousands who flocked to hear him. God was passing New England's historical mantle of Christian leadership to Nova Scotia. With New England gone madly off course, there was apparently no longer any solid basis there from which true Christianity could spread throughout the world. With two powerful Protestant nations furiously battling one another, the whole course of events since the Reformation seemed to be ending in a meaningless tangle. In the world view of those New Englanders fighting for the Revolutionary cause, Old England was corrupt and the Americans were engaged in a righteous and noble cause. There was therefore some meaning for hostilities. But to Alline the totally "inhuman War" had no such meaning. (28) Rather, along with all the other signs of the times, it could only indicate one thing, that the entire Christian world, apart from Nova Scotia, was abandoning the way of God.

What was regarded as the tragic backsliding of New England had presented Nova Scotia with an opportunity to put things right. Alline was determined that the new "City upon a Hill" would lead to the world back to the pristine purity of the Christian faith. By permeating his Evangelical preaching with this mission-oriented rhetoric, Alline provided his audience with what he termed "an omniscient eye" to read the "map of the disordered world". (29) He was helping them find a new collective identity - an awareness of being Nova Scotian. Alline was also pointing the way to a new kind of lasting relationship at a time when traditional relationships were disintegrating . In an intuitive yet penetrating perception of the realities of Nova Scotia existence, he began the process of extricating the Yankees from the cultural dominance of New England that had, among other factors, placed them in such a confusing predicament during the Revolutionary War. Instead of being a mere outpost of New England on the remote fringes of the continent, Alline argued, the Nova Scotia Yankees could now regard themselves as being important parts of a distinct society. The ideology which emerged during the period of Alline's leadership made the revival a movement with somewhat broader implications that has hitherto · been acknowledged. By generating a religious ideology that was specifically relevant to the situation and problems of the northern colony the revival began the process of turning Yankees into Nova Scotians.

This evolution was reflected clearly in the case of Alline who was, naturally enough, most convinced by his own reasoning. In March 1775, shortly after his conversion experience, Alline whose parents had lived most of their lives in Boston and Rhode Island, felt he must travel to New England "to get learning there". (30) Instinctively Alline assumed New England to be the source of all true Yankee religous culture. Eight years later his views had completely changed. The success and extent of the revival had persuaded him that Nova Scotia was no longer inferior to New England. When, in August 1783, Alline once again decided "to go to New England" he did not intend to travel as a diffident backwoods convert seeking a religious education in an environment he considered in every aspect to be superior to his own. Alline had preached throughout Nova Scotia and had seen the firm establishment of his revivalist doctrines; it was now time, he felt, to spread the movement beyond the northern colony. By 1783 "the word of God", he felt, had to be taken from pristine Nova Scotia to corrupt New England. Nova Scotia was no longer merely a receiver of religious values as she had been throughout the pre-Revolutionary period. The northern Yankees had produced a leader who could transmit ideas back to New England.

Even after Alline died in New Hampshire early in February, 1784, many of his followers remained persuaded that their Nova Scotia was superior in every respect to the New England they had abandoned. They were keen therefore to contrast their "vital piety" with the "vice and immorality" which seemed to thrive in the United States. They were not eager - as some of them expressed it in November 1784-"to throw away the fruits of many years of painful industry and leave the place where God in his próvidence has smiled upon us both in our spiritual and temporal affairs". (31)

The Yankees in Nova Scotia, it should be pointed out became increasingly loyal to Britain during the Revolutionary War but they were an unusual breed of Loyalists. During the Seven Years War when Britain and her American colonies were struggling against French power in Europe, India and Canada, American colonists had possessed a loyalty to Britain as well as to their colonies in America. In the "intense political heat" of the 1760's and early 1770's this dual loyalty was, in the case of the Patriots, gradually transformed into a single loyalty to what were regarded as "American" or colonial values and institutions and the war for independence consolidated these newly perceived loyalties to the states and the American nation. As the debate with Britain reached the crisis stage, in 1774 and 1775, Tory pamphleteers diverged sharply from the Patriots. Whereas the Patriot spokesmen glorified colonial history and gave most credit for the rise of colonial prosperity to colonial efforts, the Tory pamphleteers, in 1774 and 1775, disparaged colonial contributions and insisted that without British aid and protection, the American colonies would never have flourished. Thus, while the Patriot loyalties were transformed into a new American loyalty the Tory pamphleteers assumed an exaggerated or distorted loyalty towards Britain. (32)

In pre-Revolutionary Nova Scotia, the Yankees followed neither of these paths. They did not undergo the transformation of the Patriots nor did they exaggerate their loyalty to Britain as did the Tory pamphleteers . When the war came many of the Yankees experienced a complete breakdown in loyalties. As the British in Halifax threatened to use the militia against New England invaders and as the British navy used the press; as American privateers plundered Nova Scotian vessles and threatened the Yankees with Indian attacks and loss of property, the Nova Scotia Yankees found it difficult to retain their former loyalties. For the first time since their emigration loyalty to both New England and the British colony of Nova Scotia became incompatible. In Yarmouth and Cumberland county some Yankees, for a brief period of time, attempted to overcome these problems by suggesting the possibility of neutrality. But neither Halifax nor the American privateers would recognise this solution and the Yankees did not long persist with it. In such circumstances, as many contemporaries observed, the predominant characteristic of Yankee society was a feeling of insecurity, confusion and disorientation.

It is common in such situations of cultural and sociopsychological disequilibrium for new ideologies to emerge and this is what apparently occurred in Nova Scotia during the revival under Alline's leadership. In a recent analysis of this type of social process Clifford Geertz has argued that "it is a loss of orientation that most gives rise to ideological activity". This disorientation creates a feeling of insecurity in the society it effects and "brings with it conceptual confusion as the the established images of political order fade into irrelevance or are driven into disrepute". In these fluid circumstances, Geertz suggests, new ideologies emerge which "attempt . . . to render otherwise incomprehensible social situations meaningful to so construe them as to a new synthesis in a confusing situation that "accounts both for the ideologies highly figurative nature and for the intensity with which, once accepted, they are held". (33)

Nova Scotia during the Revolutionary period, for example, presents an example of these social processes at . work. The war between New England and Great Britain had shattered the traditional political world of the Yankees, for it had brought about a relatively sudden and drastic change in the external circumstances facing the Yankees and had led to a crisis of identity as Yankee society desperately attempted to make appropriate responses. This made many Yankees susceptible to the new ideology popularised by Alline which could "explain" the contemporary world and help in coping with the changed conditions. By accepting the highly figurative ideology and forming new churches and separate meetings in which solidarity could be established the pro-revivalist sections of the population in particular believed they had found a coherent pattern to events, a pattern which brought some semblance of stability into their society.

The Great Awakening of Nova Scotia was, it seems clear, one of the most significant social movements in the long history of Nova Scotia. It was, among other things, the means by which a large number of Nova Scotians extricated themselves from the domination of New England. By creating a compelling religious ideology that was specifically geared to conditions in the northern colony, the Great Awakening enabled some residents to regard themselves as a people with a unique history, a distinct identity, and a special destiny. In a very real sense, even before the arrival of the Loyalists, the Great Awakening, at one level of experience, had begun to turn the Yankees into Nova Scotians. At yet another level - the more traditional perhaps - it provided the opportunity for many inhabitants of New England's Outpost to experience the ultimate Evangelical Christian experience - the "New Birth". (34)

REFERENCES

1. Quoted in G. A. Rawlyk, **Revolution Rejected, 1775-1776** (Scarborough, 1967), p. 9.
2. See J. B. Brebner, **The Neutral Yankees of Nova Scotia: A Marginal Colony During the Revolutionary Years** (New York, 1937) and J. B. Brebner, **New England's Outpost: Acadia Before the Conquest of Canada** (New York, 1927).
3. See in particular Professor W. S. MacNutt's introduction and historiographical note in the Carleton Library, No 45 (Toronto, 1969) reprinting of Brebner's **Neutral Yankees.**
4. Professor Stewart originally developed these arguments in his brilliant Ph.D. thesis, "Religion and the Yankee Mind of Nova Scotia during the American Revolution" (Queen's University, 1971)
5. See T. C. Haliburton, **A Historical and Statistical Account of Nova Scotia** (Halifax, 1829) I, p. 256.
5. Massachusetts Archives, Vol. CXLIV, Maugerville Committee of Safety to the Massachusetts General Court, May 21, 1776.
7. L. H. Butterfield, (ed.), **Diary and Autobiography of John Adams** (Cambridge, 1961) I, p. 285.
8. J. C. Fitzpatrick, (ed.), **The Writings of George Washington** (Washington, 1931) III, p. 416.
9. Massachusetts Archives, Vol. CXLIV, Maugerville Committee of Safety to the Massachusettes General Court, May 21, 1776.
10. This reaction is examined in greater detail in G. A. Rawlyk, "The American Revolution and Nova Scotia Reconsidered", **Dalhousie Review,** XLIII (1963) pp. 383-384.
11. See G. A. Rawlyk, **Nova Scotia's Massachusetts: A Study of Massachusetts - Nova Scotia Relations, 1630 to 1784** (Montreal, 1973) pp. 232-240.
12. Public Archives of Canada, Series A, Vol. 94, Memorial of the Inhabitants of Yarmouth, December 8, 1775.
13. D. C. Harvey, "Machias and the Invasion of Nova Scotia", Canadian Historical Association **Report** (1932) pp. 22-24.
14. Massachusetts Archives, Vol. CXLIV, John Allan Petition, Feb. 19, 1777.
15. See Rawlyk, **Nova Scotia's Massachusetts,** pp. 239-246.
16. E. C. Burnett, (ed.), **Letters of the Members of the Continental Congress** (Washington, 1928) IV, p. 246, James Lovell to Horatio Gates, June 3, 1779.
17. Public Archives of Canada, Mss. Group 23, B-2, Box 1, Fol. 2, A. McNutt to James Lovell, William Whipple and John Witherspoon, Dec. 23, 1778.
18. This general theme is developed at considerable length in G. Stewart and G. Rawlyk, **A People Highly Favoured of God** (Toronto, 1972), pp. 64-70.

19. F. Kidder, **Military Operations in Eastern Maine and Nova Scotia** (Albany, 1867), pp. 228-231, 253-255, "Extract of a letter from John Allan," Sept. 22, 177 and "Report of John Allan", Aug. 17, 1778.
20. Massachusetts Archives, Vol. 195, Massachusetts Committee of Safety in the Massachusetts Council, Nov. 27, 1776.
21. M. W. Armstrong, "Neutrality and Religion in Revolutionary Nova Scotia", **New England Quarterly,** Vol. IX (1946) pp. 50-62.
22. See in particular S. D. Clark, **Movements of Political Protest in Canada, 1640-1840** (Toronto, 1959) pp. 69-70.
23. This thesis is developed in much greater length in Stewart and Rawlyk, **A People Highly Favoured of God.**
24. H. Alline, **The Life and Journal of the Rev. Mr Henry Alline** (Boston, 1806) pp. 34-35.
23. **Ibid.,** p. 44.
26. E. P. Thompson, "The Moral Economy of the English Crowd in the 18th Century", **Past and Present,** 50, (Feb., 1971) p. 78.
27. This theme is developed in the sermons preached by Alline. See for example, **A Sermon Preached ... Liverpool, on the 19th of November 1782** (Halifax, n.d.); **A Sermon on a Day of Thanksgiving ... on the 21st of November, 1782** (Halifax, n.d.). This aspect of Alline's message is examined in Stewart and Rawlyk, **A People Highly Favoured of God,** pp. 154-178.
29. H. Alline, **Two Mites ...** (Halifax, 1781), p. 265.
29. H. Alline, **A Sermon on a Day of Thanksgiving ...** 21st November, 1782, p. 23.
30. Alline, **Life and Journal,** p. 42.
31. J. Hannay, "The Maugerville Settlement", New Brunswick Historical Society **Collections I,** no. 1 (1894), pp. 84-86.
32. See in particular J. C. Potter. "The Lost Alternative: Loyalist Ideology and the American Revolution", (Unpublished M.A. thesis, Queen's University, 1970).
33. G. Geertz, "Ideology as a Cultural System", in D. Apter, (ed.), **Ideology and Discontent** (Chicago, 1964), pp. 52-56. For an interesting discussion of dual loyalties as well as multiple loyalties and the breakdown of loyalties see H. Buetzkow, **Multiple Loyalties: A Theoretical Approach to a Problem in International Organization** (Princeton, 1955).
34. See A. Heimert, **Religion and the American Mind** (Cambridge, 1966) pp. 27-58, "The Nature and Necessity of the New Birth".

EDMUND BURKE AND THE AMERICAN REVOLUTION

CONOR CRUISE O'BRIEN

Let us begin by considering two well-known lines from W. B. Yeats' poem **The Seven Sages**:

American colonies, Ireland, France and India Harried, and Burke's great melody against it.

What was it? I shall come back to that question. For the moment let us note the implied acknowledgement of Burke's consistency: a just acknowledgement of something that has been unjustly impugned. In other ways I think Yeats's lines somewhat misleading. The key words 'harried' and 'melody' suggest a Burke concerned to stir emotions by his eloquence on behalf of the persecuted. Burke could do that; he did it for the victims of the Irish Penal Laws, for the Begums of Oudh and, most famously, for Marie Antoinette of France. He knew well how to play on the emotions, but on the whole he used this skill sparingly. The great bulk of his writings and speeches consists of reasoned arguments. And nowhere is this more evident than in his speeches aimed at averting the conflict in America.

In all his great campaigns there was, as Yeats discerned, one constant target. That target — Yeats's 'it' — was **misuse of power**. But the forms of the misuse of power differed in the different cases mentioned, and Burke's manner of approaching the different cases differs also. In his impeachment of Warren Hastings he used rhetorical devices to excess: in his last writings on the French Revolution — the Letters on a Regicide Peace — there is a reckless abandonment to crusading fury. Emotions

perhaps equally powerful, or even more so, working generally under greater restraints the famous Burkian veils — are often present in his writings on Ireland. But in none of the great themes which he treated is he more consistently rational and free from pathos as in his speeches and writings on America in the period before the outbreak of war.

The sufferings of the colonists are not his theme, nor does he dwell on the brutalities of the agents of George III. In the most striking of the rare cases (before the war, that is) in which he backs his case by an appeal to an emotion on behalf of the Americans, the emotion he appeals to is not pity. It is admiration. It is also by implication, fear. 'Timidity, with regard to the well-being of our country', he had written, 'is heroic virtue'. The passage I refer to is the famous one about the whalers in **On Conciliation with America**, 1775. It will be familiar to many of you: I quote a part:

"No sea but what is vexed by their fisheries. No climate that is not witness to their toils. Neither the perseverance of Holland, nor the activity of France, nor the dexterous and firm sagacity of English enterprise, ever carried the most perilous mode of hard industry to the extent to which it has been pushed by this recent people; a people who are still, as it were, but in the gristle, and not yet hardened into the bone of manhood".

Burke's concern, in relation to America, was not primarily with the Americans, though it was also with them. It was primarily with the interests of

Great Britain(including Ireland). His objection to the policies of Grenville, or North, or George III himself, in relation to America, was not that these policies were oppressive or unconstitutional, but that they were dangerously foolish. The particular form of misuse of power with which he was concerned in this case was misuse through folly, ignorance and complacency, rather than through greed or cruelty. Basically, he thought that, if military conflict could not be averted, Britain would be the loser — not necessarily on the field of battle but in relation to its long-term interests. 'Victory', as he wrote during the war, 'would only vary the mode of our ruin'.

In reaching this conclusion he had taken into account not merely the resources of the colonies, and the energies of the colonists, but also the **feelings** of the colonists. He does not share those feelings, but he has taken the measure of their force. Thus, he has this to say, on the tea tax:

"No man ever doubted that the commodity of tea could bear an imposition of threepence. But no commodity will bear threepence, or will bear a penny, when the general feelings of men are irritated, and two millions of people are resolved not to pay".

(I may add in parenthesis that this passage is much more characteristic of Burke's usual manner than the 'melody' of that too-famous flourish about the Queen of France; or even than the whaling passage, one of the purplest patches in his American writings.)

This common sense, down-to-earth Burke, concerned with practical interests and assessment of forces, may perhaps seem and indeed be, a less noble figure than the lamenting harpist of **The Seven Sages**. Yet, if one has come to distrust the plangent strain in politics, one turns with relief from that distorted Yeatsian Burke — recognisable though some of his features are — to the real Burke of the American Revolutionary period. I have spoken of his common sense, but this is not quite the right word. It comes out as common sense, especially as we read it in retrospect, because the plain and robust style in which it is often (though not always) expressed can make his propositions appear to be obvious. But they were not obvious at the time to most people, and it took a quite uncommon energy of mind to lay hold of those propositions, and to state them so that they now seem obvious. It also took uncommon largeness of mind in the contemplation of the great scale of the interests involved, uncommon industry in the mastery of detail, and uncommon deftness in the passage from great to small.

Considering all these qualities, and considering also the lucidity and generosity of mind — even in the weighing of interests — which shine out from, for example, the speech **On American Taxation (1774)** and **On Conciliation with America (1775)** I for one do not wonder at the admiration which so many nineteenth century thinkers had for Burke's political wisdom. Other views have to be taken into consideration, however. In general, in relation to Burke, Sir Lewis Namier's frequent

disparagements **en passant** — rather like those of T. S. Eliot on Milton — have exerted a certain influence. People like to quote biting remarks made by one eminent person about another. What interests us here specifically however is Burke's view of America, and that has been forcefully criticised by modern writers, including Burke's American biographer, Carl B. Cone.

As is well known, Burke's Party, the Rockingham Whigs, when in office in 1766, had accompanied their concession to American feeling — the repeal of the Stamp Act — by a Declaratory Act asserting the supremacy of Parliament, and its **right** to tax. This combination is believed to have been Burke's idea, and he defended it for years afterwards, notably in his great speech **On American Taxation** of 19 April 1774. In **Burke and the Nature of Politics the Age of the American Revolution,** Dr Cone finds that this speech has been praised extravagantly. He thinks its 'gorgeous rhetoric' and 'wonderful imagery' have combined with other factors, such as its 'apparent reasonableness and magnanimity' to persuade men that Burke's recommendations offered a solution to the American colonies. Dr Cone considers this judgment 'open to question'. He notes that Burke offered, at this time, only one specific proposal: the removal of the tax on tea. He wonders how long Americans would have remained satisfied with that concession, and also 'how far men in control of a government should withdraw from a position they believe is constitutionally sound'. He thinks that Burke's 'gliding over the matter' ignored 'the basic problem'. 'Either the colonies were subordinate in all cases whatsoever, or they were not. Burke tried to have it both ways'.

Dr Cone concludes: "The imperial constitution needed amending by granting to the colonial assemblies not merely the privilege, but indeed the right to tax. Even the Rockingham party, under whose guidance Burke thought the quarrel could be ended, was not prepared to grant this".

I think this line of argument worth considering, both directly on its merits and for two other reasons. The first is that it is characteristic of a certain current of twentieth century academic depreciation of what nineteenth century Englishmen thought of as Burke's **wisdom**. And the second is that this depreciation, both in the degree that it is justifiable, and in the degree to which it is excessive, encourages us to think again about the nature of Burke's political thought and action, the question of his **wisdom**.

The language of Burke's biographer about Burke's language reveals a distance between the biographer and his subject. 'Gorgeous rhetoric' would apply well enough to some of the anti-Jacobin writings of Burke's old age. It fits only isolated passages in his writings and speeches on America. Nor is the reasonableness of **On American Taxation** only 'apparent', it is incontrovertibly there, and reasoned argument and the fire of conviction, not gorgeous trappings, make the force of the speech. Judgments about magnanimity have to be more subjective, but I do not know where anyone who would deny real magnanimity to Burke's American utterances would look for examples of that quality in political history.

It is true of course that there is something sophistical, and even slightly ludicrous, in the combination of an insistence on the right to tax, with an equal insistence on the inexpediency of exercising that right.

It reminds one a little of that Catholic theologian who reconciled the strict eschatology of his Church with his personal humane feelings by managing to believe in 'an eternal Hell eternally empty'. As compared with Burke's balancing act, Chatham's rejection of the right to tax Americans **at all** seems more consistent — just as the same Chatham was more consistent during the war itself when he continued to refuse to contemplate independence for America, long after Burke and his friends had dropped the right to tax, and resigned themselves to the inevitability of independence. But Burke was not trying to win competitions in intellectual consistency; he was trying, in the first place, to avert a war, and then, when that failed, he was trying to shorten one. The propositions that were needed to shorten the war were not the same as those which, if adopted, might have averted it. The price of the Sibylline books was subject to inflation.

As I have indicated, I think Burke's nineteenth century admirers were right in speaking of his wisdom. Where they were wrong — and most unBurkian — was in tending to minimise the importance of the contexts in which that wisdom had to express itself. We may properly say that Burke was a **wise** politician, but we have also to redistribute the emphasis and say that he was a wise **politician**. The noun also qualifies the adjective. Burke worked in a particular political context, with particular political friends and enemies, for particular political objectives. His words should be judged by political standards and not just by academic ones. If a student 'glides over' something in an exam paper, his examiners will rightly conclude that this is because the student doesn't know the answer. But a politician may well 'glide over' a particular question because he **does** know the answer. Politicians talking among themselves like to use the word 'political' as a term of praise, and I have observed that they are especially apt to use this term about statements which successfully glide over those themes over which the speaker wishes to glide. We have Burke's own word for it that he thought such glidings permissible.

Falsehood and delusion are allowed in no case whatsoever', he wrote in the first of the **Letters on a Regicide Peace**, 'but as in the exercise of all the virtues there is an economy of truth. It is a sort of temperance by which a man speaks truth with measure that he may tell it the longer'. I might add that if a politician claims to be more truthful than that, it may safely be inferred that he is in fact showing himself to be less truthful.

In emphasising the need for the repeal of the tea tax, Burke was concentrating on a step which he thought within the bounds of political possibility in Britain, and among things politically possible in Britain, the most likely, to abate the fever in America. On the question of rights, he 'economised'; the Rockingham Whigs who had carried the Declaratory Act as an adjunct deemed necessary to a conciliatory measure, were not well placed to ask North to repeal it, although its repeal would have served the end of conciliation. Burke believed in party, and he accepted the limitations placed on him by party. 'Party divisions', he had written in 1769, 'whether on the whole operating for good or evil, are an inseparable part of free government'. The assertion of the **right** to tax in the Declaratory Act is unBurkian **if taken by itself.** The repeal of the Stamp Act, on the other hand, was the most important achievement of Burke's policy of practical conciliation. I believe it is legitimate to infer that a number of Burke's associates in the Rockingham party would not have gone along with the repeal of the Stamp Act if it were not combined with the Declaration. And Burke had to defend the policy, and the record, of his party — a policy and record which he had strongly influenced, but had not been alone in influencing. Wisdom informs his speeches, but the practical restraints of political action, and the very nature of the objective which both wisdom and practicality dictated, filtered the expression of that wisdom. Burke had to take account of the views and the prejudices both of those whom he was trying to persuade, and of those with whom he acted.

Dr Cone, very oddly, rebukes Burke simultaneously **both** for not going the whole way with the colonists — by advocating the repudiation of the right to tax, in 1774 — **and also** for failing to convince the majority of the House of Commons. But if he had gone the whole way with the colonists he would have failed to convince his own friends, let alone a majority in the House of Commons. The idea that any opposition speech could have convinced such a majority at that time is a strange one, and Burke certainly entertained no such notion. He showed clearly, near the beginning of his speech, that he knew how the vote would go, when, having appealed to 'experience' he added 'and would to God there was no other arbiter to decide on the vote with which the house is to conclude this day'. By the 'other arbiter' he meant, of course, the influence of George III and his Ministers over the parliamentary majority.

On that April day, Burke did not hope to sway the majority in the House of Commons. He did believe that, as time revealed the folly of North's course, and thereby also the wisdom of the conciliatory policy of the Rockinghams, Rockingham would come back to power. That did happen, but only after the total defeat of Britain in the war, and when it happened Lord Rockingham promptly died. In the meantime Burke had lost his own seat at Bristol, as an indirect consequence of the war he had sought to avert. In his political life Edmund Burke had much wisdom, but little luck.

In an essay on Burke's writings on the French Revolution, I have stressed the relevance of Burke's Irish origins. I believe these origins are also relevant to his writings and speeches on the American Revolution, but relevant in a different way. In the case of the French Revolution, what was mainly relevant were Burke's Catholic associations and sympathies: the Catholicism of his mother and her Nagle relatives, of his wife's father, and possibly the abjured Catholicism of his own father. (One of Burke's American editors, Elliott Barkan, defines his religious background in rather quaint language. Burke, he says, 'was reared in his father's religion, Anglicanism, but his mother, a Roman Catholic, nevertheless managed to instil in him a deep belief in the existence of God'.)

With these connections — and the word connection is always a key word with him — he was incensed by the triumphant anti-Catholicism of the initial British welcome for the news of the French Revolution. A sermon by Dr Price in that vein provided the detonator for the great explosion of Burke's **Reflections on the Revolution in France.**

In the case of the American Revolution it is Burke's general Irishness, not specifically his Irish Catholic connections, which is relevant. There was no Irish Catholic welcome for the American Revolution, corresponding to the English Protestant welcome for the French one. In Ireland, it was Protestants, not Catholics, who welcomed the agitation which preceded the American Revolution. I confess that if I were addressing an Irish-American audience in this Bicentennial Year, that is one topic on which I might well practise an economy of truth, that my address might last the longer. Irish Protestants tended to favour the American cause, in that period, both on Whig principles and as favourable to the winning of concessions from England — the process that led to the relative autonomy of Grattan's Parliament, which was of course an exclusively Protestant body. The Irish Catholic leaders on the other hand saw in the proceedings which led to the revolution the possibility of winning concessions for themselves, as against the Protestant Ascendancy, by the directly opposite course; that of demonstrating their loyalty to the Crown. The whole justification of the Penal Laws and the Protestant Ascendancy had been the presumption that Irish Catholics were disloyal, because of their Jacobite past. The proceedings in America, and the response of many Irish Protestants to those proceedings, seemed to the Catholic leaders a golden opportunity of demonstrating that the boot was on the other foot: that it was **Catholics** who were loyal and **Protestants** disloyal. This was the response of Catholic leaders; it need not of course be assumed that the mass of Catholics were praying for victory for George III.

We do not know what the mass of Catholics felt about the matter, but given the state of relations between Catholics and Protestants in Ireland at the time it would not be altogether surprising that a course which aroused demonstrative enthusiasm among Protestants should receive at best a tepid reception among Catholics. These were the conditions that permitted the Catholic leaders safely to display so much loyalty at this period to the British Crown and its dealings with the American rebels.

Burke was a moderate Whig, with strong Irish Catholic connections and affections. This involved tensions, since Whiggery generally was anti-Catholic, and Irish Whiggery vehemently and vindictively so. One might say loosely, but I think meaningfully, that in the case of the French Revolution the Irish Catholic side of Burke won, while in the case of the American Revolution the Whig won. It is instructive to compare the use of the word 'Protestant' in the two relevant periods of Burke's life. In the context of the period preceding the American Revolution it is a term of praise: the virtues and achievements of the settlers are linked to their Protestantism. But by the time of the French Revolution, Burke is using the term in hostile and derisive ways: not of course hostile to the Church of England, but hostile to those who emphasise the divisions between that Church and Rome.

There were, of course, differences in his personal situation. At the time of his major speeches aimed at averting the American Revolution, Burke is in his mid-forties, ambitious and hopeful of the return of the Rockinghams to power. He was mindful of Whig orthodoxy, and knew that his own was suspect because of his Catholic origins. By the time he came to write the **Reflections** the need for such economies was no longer so pressing. Burke was over sixty, Rockingham was dead, Pitt was Minister, Fox leader of Burke's party, Burke himself derided in the House of Commons.

He had lost his seat at Bristol in 1780 for reasons connected both with Ireland and with Catholicism, and in attempting to defend himself in these sensitive areas had revealed his real opinions much more openly than he had thought prudent — or than actually **was** prudent — in the period before the American war. By 1790 the pressures of party ties and of ambition, and indeed of hope, were relaxed. He could express much more of his personal feelings, even those connected with his Irish Catholic origins, covered in the mid seventies with that 'politic well wrought veil' of whose propriety he spoke in another context.

This is not, however, to say that, if he had felt free to express such feelings on the eve of the American Revolution, his response to the American events would have been different in substance. In comparing his responses to the two revolutions, the differences in his personal situation has to be noted. But there is also a difference in the nature of the challenges. The character of the French Revolution itself, and of British responses to it, involved attacks on Catholicism. No such direct challenge was involved in the process leading to the American Revolution, although such a challenge did emerge during that American war and partly in consequence of it. As between George III and the colonists — two contending sets of Protestants — the Irish Catholic leaders took the line which they thought most advantageous to themselves and their people, which was the line of loyalty. Burke might well have approved, for people in their position, a tactic so obviously dictated by 'prudence, the god of this lower world'. But his own position was different. He was a member of the British Parliament and of the Established

Church. He might, and indeed certainly did, share many of the feelings of the Irish Catholics — of the class from which they drew their leadership — but he did not have to be swayed by their tactics. As far as Ireland was concerned, what he hoped to see, as appeared a little later, was a kind of double enfranchisement: Ireland itself treated on an equal footing with England, and Irish Catholics on an equal footing with Protestants, distinctions being based on social class and property, not on religion. As far as he was concerned, the cause of concilation with America was fully consonant with the first of these objectives — which indeed in **On Conciliation** he misleadingly presented as if already attained — and not inconsistent with the second.

The discriminatory laws against Irish trade were analogous to the laws to which the colonists objected, and were applied by the metropolis with uniform indifference to the feelings of the dependencies. Irish resentment against the discriminatory laws was not affected by religion. Catholics of the class to which Burke's Nagle relatives belonged hated these laws quite as much as Protestants did. Burke's Irishness — however guarded its expression at the time of his writings of the mid-seventies — gave him a first-hand understanding of how people in dependencies can feel about such laws, and about the indifference which such laws at best reflect. His American writings are reasonable but they emphasise the importance of **feelings**, while his adversaries, and some of his friends, emphasise intellectual concepts: duties, rights.

Burke was conscious that the state of feelings would be decisive in the circumstances. Both as agent for the New York Assembly (1770-75) and as a conscientious legislator, he had studied America enough to know that it could not be governed against its will. He knew that if American feelings continued to be ignored and trampled on, the result would be a disaster for Britain. No one knew better than he the importance of feelings in political affairs. And he had to share some of the feelings of Americans. In his American writings of before the war, these feelings are masked where he refers to Ireland. At one point he goes beyond 'economy of truth' and seems to fall into that 'falsehood and delusion' which he thought 'permitted in no case whatever', and which indeed he very rarely falls into.

The passage I refer to is that idyllic picture of Anglo-Irish constitutional relations which he draws in **On Conciliation**:

"Ireland has ever had from the beginning a separate, but not an independent, legislature; which, far from distracting, promoted the union of the whole. Everything was sweetly and harmoniously disposed through both islands for the conservation of English dominion, and the communication of English liberties".

Nobody knew better than Burke — as his later writings reveal and indeed not very much later — how far the sweet harmony described was from the reality. But that that reality was present to Burke's mind, in the American context, is evident from, among other passages the following generalisation in the **Letter to the Sheriffs of Bristol** (1777).

"When any community is subordinately connected with another, the great danger of the connection is the extreme pride and self-complacency of the superior, which in all matters of controversy will probably decide in its own favour".

The American Revolution, **in its inception**, had not touched the nerve of the Catholic question. But the reverberations of the American war did so. Ironically that war both stimulated policies towards Ireland which Burke favoured, and also severely damaged Burke's career. Keeping Ireland quiet for the duration became an important part of British policy.

Ireland at the beginning of the war was more than quiet: it was helpful. Not only did Catholics enlist but — more surprisingly — the Protestant Parliament, to Burke's indignation, voted supplies for the war in America although these were opposed by the Patriot party, whose influence later grew. Burke, who had hoped to see Ireland become, by mediation, 'the balance of the Empire', was disappointed and embittered by that vote. Yet a war of which he disapproved, and Irish reaction to it of which he also disapproved, produced consequences which he could not help supporting although they hurt him politically.

As a result of skilful or fortunate combinations of displays of loyalty and implied threats in Ireland, it became expedient to allow concessions — some of them proposed by Burke's friends — to both Irelands: some economic and later constitutional concessions, beneficial in practice mainly to Protestants, and some relaxations of the anti-Catholic penal code.

The combined concession, both sets of which Burke was known to favour, were unpopular in his Bristol constituency, as in other parts of Britain. Anti-Irish and anti-Catholic feelings became inflamed. The Gordon riots in the summer of 1780 put Burke's life in danger. The linked questions of Burke's Irishness and of his (suspect) attitude to Catholicism now became painfully relevant. When he had been elected for Bristol in 1774, his attitude towards America had been popular in a city whose trade with the colonies was important. But already by 1778 and even more by 1780, he was in trouble because of the Irish consequences, which he favoured, of the war he had sought to avert. His previous 'gliding over' of the Irish reality, and his own relations to it, will no longer serve. He stops gliding and defends himself manfully, from 1778 to 1780. In defending his vote to his constituents, in 1778, he both departs from his earlier idyllic picture of Ireland — he now refers to 'the vicious system of its internal policy' — and reveals the real, though partly subterranean, continuity of his thinking on Ireland and America. '

"I oppose the American measures upon the very same principle on which I support those that relate to Ireland. God forbid that our conduct should demonstrate to the world that Great Britain can in no instance whatever be brought to a sense of rational and equitable policy, but by coercion and force of arms''.

By 1780 he was speaking even more plainly. ''To read what was approaching in Ireland in the black and bloody characters of the American war, was a painful but a necessary part of my public duty'' (speech at Bristol previous to the election).

The prevailing tone of the England of George III in relation to America had to remind such an Irishman as Burke of that England's tone towards Ireland also, and indeed his Bristol constituents reminded him of it: a tone which boded no good for any of the countries concerned.

Burke's counsels in relation to America went altogether unheeded after 1766, and he came to be honoured only in retrospect. The policies he favoured for Ireland were partially implemented, but as near panic measures under the pressures of the American war, and Burke was damaged by the backlash against those measures. More than a decade later, under the pressures of the war with France, similar but greater concessions to Ireland were followed by a recoil, the dismissal of the reforming Lord Fitzwilliam in 1795. Burke, who had forseen the disaster in America, in the closing years of his life foresaw disaster in Ireland. That disaster came in the year after his death, 1798. In that sense, Yeats was right.

Because of America and of Ireland, Burke lost his seat at Bristol, and with it much of the weight he had acquired in the practical politics of Great Britain. During the remainder of his political life, as a member for a pocket borough, he never recovered the standing and contemporary influence which he enjoyed from 1774 to 1780 as the representative of a great trading city.

It was a heavy loss to him: but he knew also that he had won something. I shall conclude by quoting possibly the most moving words that even Burke ever spoke. Those in which he acknowledged his probable impending defeat on the eve of the election on 9 September 1780 must move us still:

''And now, Gentlemen, on this serious day, when I come, as it were, to make up my account with you, let me take to myself some degree of honest pride on the nature of the charges that are against me. I do not here stand before you accused of venality, or of neglect, of duty. It is not said, that, in the long period of my service I have, in a single instance, sacrificed the slightest of your interests to my ambition, or to my fortune. It is not alleged, that to gratify any anger, or revenge of my own, or of my party, I have had a share in wronging or oppressing any description of men, or any one man in any description. No! the charges against me are of one kind, that I have pushed the principles of general justice and benevolence too far; further than a cautious policy would warrant; and further than the opinions of many would go along with me. In every accident which may happen through life, in pain, in sorrow, in depression, and distress — I will call to mind this accusation; and be comforted''.

IRELAND AND THE AMERICAN REVOLUTION

OWEN DUDLEY EDWARDS

"As a dog returneth to his vomit, so a fool returneth to his folly" (Proverbs, xxvi. II). Like most of us, I have illustrated this adage by my conduct often enough to be sensitive about it. I do not propose, therefore, to repeat what I have written elsewhere about the uses to which the American Revolutionaries put Ireland and to which the Irish put the American Revolution. (1) In the context of a Scottish recognition of the bicentennial of the American Revolution, it may be useful to look at the Irish case in the light of what my colleagues who have commented on Scotland have been saying.

The first point, I think, which strikes one in any such test, is that Ireland, like Scotland, interested the American literati in 1765-85 very greatly, and that their idea of Ireland, like their idea of Scotland, was chimerical. Dr Andrew Hook has shown in his **Scotland and America** how American comment saw little distinction between Highland Jacobites and Lowland Hanoverians, the latter in that view being merely a more cunning version of the former. And Dr Duncan Rice, earlier in these pages, has asked why. The case of Ireland may add something to his speculations, if only a further complication. The same monolithic image is evident, although not the same urgency. If we accept the view - as I think we should - that the American Revolution was in many ways derived from an impulse against Scotland, we will not find much evidence of comparable fears of Ireland. It would have made some sense, or at least similar nonsense, to have seen an Irish conspiracy as an extension of the Scottish one. Irish Protestant

supporters of the American rebels had no difficulty in seeing Jacobite bogeys in any conciliatory movement of the North government towards the Catholics. But despite these fears, with their corollary that concessions to the Papists would bring uprising, massacre and Papist repossession of the land - precisely the kernel of the American rebels' theory of government concessions to the Amerindians - they did not succeed in transmitting them to their American correspondents.

One suspects that the American literati had become rather good at seeing what they wanted to see. We do need a book probably entitled **O Strange Old World,** concerning what vision of Europe the Americans chose to retain, and what parts of it to cultivate. Their view of Scotland dissolved the central fact of Scottish history at that moment of time - the division between Highland and Lowland - but it was useful to them to do so. Their view of Ireland dissolved the central fact of Irish history in that century - the tripartite caste system based on religious difference and repressive legislation - but it would not have been useful to them not to do so. They had created a symbolic drama: it is important to remember how strongly **political** drama often revealed itself to be at this time and what anti-Scottish strains Dr Hook has observed in it. (2) The revolutionaries were thinking in highly dramatic terms, and melodramatic at that. (3) England, Scotland and America had obvious roles. But since the development of events ranged Scotland, the villain, and England, her irredeemable victim, against virtuous America, dramatic balance suggested a friend for America. Ireland filled that slot.

As friends go, Ireland was, on the most charitable analysis, a pretty poor specimen. Her elitist Protestant episcopalian parliamentarians produced a flourish of trumpets in opposition to the war, but they also produced a majority in favour of the government. Her most famous expression of quasi-revolutionary activity, the Irish Volunteers, actually commenced as a defensive exercise against the Americans, specifically the raids of John Paul Jones. (4) Her Catholic denizens, in particular, flocked to the King's colours in noteworthy numbers. (5) The Americans would dearly have liked the compliment of an Irish variation on their Revolutionary theme, and would have even more richly prized the strategic advantage of an Irish upheavel to divert the British troops. But they maintained a kindly view of Ireland, that is, of the Ireland they had invented.

We think of countries in terms of people from them we know, and of public figures associated with them. Dr Hook has shown how the poor opinion of the Scots was enhanced by their skill in business. The Irish do not seem to have had that reputation, although the late eighteenth century witnessed considerable advance in Irish commercial life, among Catholics as well as Protestants. (6) At the same time it is clear that whatever Irishmen were encountered by the Americans, they were readily identified with the whole country. And since the most visible Irish element· in the American colonies was the Scotch-Irish , the American image of Ireland was largely constructed around them. It was an image later to be imposed on the Irish-American Catholics, but by 1775 Irish Catholic immigrants to the United States were not sufficiently numerous or sufficiently effective to elicit reaction. As a downtrodden caste, it is hardly surprising that they made so little impact on colonial American history. Because their spirit was broken, they lacked the motivation to assert an identity as the Highland Scots did. An occasional figure captures the limelight on one side or the other during the Revolution, but it is primarily a story of silent acquiescence and a hope of avoiding trouble. Irish Protestant episcopalian migrants to North America were of course conscious of being a master caste, and hence carried their heads high, but they were so successful that they largely blended into the general English-descended elite groups of the colonies. It was the Scotch-Irish who offered a real notion of Ireland. And, indeed, the close links which they maintained with Ulster probably gave them a title to persistent Irishness which neither the largely illiterate Catholics nor the assimilationist episcopalians then possessed.

In terms of public figures, to the Americans Scotland, noted Dr Hook, meant Bute and Mansfield, and Ireland must have meant Burke. His work as New York agent, his oratory, his American correspondence, fixed him firmly in American minds as their friend. Dr Cruise O'Brien points out in these pages precisely how

near to and how far from the American rebels Burke actually was, but the Americans, above all needing to convince themselves, raised few questions about him. Many of them came close enough to the reality of Burke to recognise the greatness of intellect he brought to their ranks. It was, after all, a highly intellectual revolution, for all of its mythologising. Hence in identifying Scotland with Mansfield and Ireland with Burke, America, however unsound in its assumptions, at least paid the other provinces the compliment of judging them by the assessment of intellectual figures.

Ireland possessed another item in the very small list of her credentials to be Revolutionary America's friend.

Dr Duncan Rice, while cogently presenting us with the evidence for Scottish ideological influences on post-revolutionary America, argues that there was no notable Scottish icon in the ideological pantheon to which the American revolutionaries turned for inspiration. As Mr Cant, Professor Shepperson and Dr Rice himself testify, major Scottish intellectual contributions to the revolution are contemporary; and if, as Dr Rice so justly says, they are neither numerous nor representative, James Wilson and John Witherspoon at least exhibited a stature which places the quality of that contemporary Scottish gift to the American revolution in inverse proportion to its quantity. In this sphere, the Irish contribution offers the converse case, as far as icons and activists are concerned. Not even the fiercest Irish-American filio-pietist can make a case for a contemporary Irish contribution to the ideology of the American Revolution. If Ireland supplied a birthplace to more signatories of the Declaration than did Scotland, the intellectual force of the Scots throws the obscurity of the Irish into stark relief. Until such time as a rash man may emerge to argue that Conway of the Cabal brought a new ideological dimension into the Revolution, the matter may be left there.

But the Irish past did produce one, or possibly two, figures for the pantheon so frequently visited by the American revolutionary ideologists. The pantheon was very important. The Americans were, in most cases, rebelling against Britain while appealing to, and being stimulated by, major names in the British ideological heritage. It was essential for them to heal the psychological wound which their rebellion induced by seeking to convince their tortured selves even more than a candid world that the noblest of their traditions, by which they meant British traditions, vindicated them. And, with scant thought for the preoccupations of future America-centred historians, they wasted little ink in delving into the colonial past for icons, however necessary they found it to study colonial history for precedents. It was the common heritage of the English-speaking world which supplied their icons . An admirer of Puritan culture would be no more likely to put Anne Bradstreet and Michael Wigglesworth before Milton and Marvell than were the ideologists of the American Revolution to aggrandise Daniel Dulany, senior, at the expense of John Locke. Unlike America, Ireland had in the early eighteenth century produced two political thinkers of the first rank, in the persons of Jonathan Swift and George Berkeley, albeit that their prior claims on posterity have been with regard to literature and philosophy, respectively.(8)

The names of Swift and Berkeley suggest an obvious reason for Americans to look to Irish intellectual inspiration. Dublin, the second city of the empire, was an obvious point of reference for peoples within that empire who with respect to its metropolis were coming to "think otherwise", as Berkeley so happily defined the Irish ratiocinative processes. What the Americans did not do, curiously, was to appeal to these two men specifically. This is not only true in the matter of direct citation. The style of American literary protest in the era of the revolution, ferociously alienated though it could show itself (in Adams's **Novanglus,** Paine's **Common Sense** and the Declaration of Independence, to name but three examples), bore a less corrosive, and indeed more impatient, form than could be found in the black satire of Swift and the ironic queries of Berkeley. For all of Swift's savage indignation and Berkeley's profound scepticism, their writings hold a conviction of pessimism wholly foreign to the American revolutionary writers, whose tone generally holds an implication that results are to be expected. Berkeley's cold exposition of misgovernment in **The Querist** and Swift's powerful questioning of the rights of the British Parliament to bind the Irish legislature should, one would think, have had every relevance for the Americans. Whether for stylistic, philosophical or temperamental reasons, they did not. They chose instead figures of more congenial, or at least, less abrasive mentality. They turned to William Molyneux and Charles Lucas.(9)

Molyneux in 1698 asserted the case of the Irish Parliament for not being bound by acts of the English legislature, and Lucas in the third quarter of the eighteenth century reasserted his claims. The colonial publicists, perhaps influenced by Molyneux's friendship with Locke, made a good deal of his arguments, especially when their denial of parliamentary supremacy while still accepting Royal rule left them without a direct basis of appeal to Locke himself. Lucas's interest in American expressions of dissent, and hospitality to Franklin during the latter's visit to Dublin in 1771, kept himself and his arguments before American eyes.(10) The Americans seemed much less aware of the arguments of Patrick Darcy in the 1640s along similar lines, although it was an American scholar, Robert Livingston Schuyler, who was ultimately to give them their place in the historiographical debate of the 1920s.(11) In any case Molyneux as a representative of the self-consciously English stock in Ireland had obviously more in common with the Americans than had the Catholic Darcy. One would not assert the rights of the colonial assemblies by an appeal to Hiawatha.

Behind the use of Molyneux and Lucas lay a deeper point. The American idea of Ireland was of relevance in the matter of justification. The American idea of Scotland was useful to sharpen the Englishness of American protest, but Scottish history offered weaker analogies. Certainly Americans could argue that the Anglo-Scottish settlement of 1707 involved the creation of a contract whereby the Scots, in return for representation, agreed to be bound by Parliament and that hitherto the Scots, while under royal rule, remained outside the control of Parliament. When one detached this argument from theory, it was evident that in the seventeenth century the English Parliament had exercised a considerable sway over the fortunes of Scotland, apart from Cromwell's famous Union of the Kingdoms. But Scotland was not, in a formal sense, a colonised country. It had not been conquered. Its King had added the English and Irish kingdoms to his dominions. Its Parliament had voluntarily merged itself with that of Westminster. The American revolutionaries made much of America not being a conquered country either, with that insouciance to the Amerindian experience which characterised American revolutionary utterances when the Amerindians were not being directly singled out for denunciation. But it was taking the tortuous to extremes to see parallels between the historic kingdom of Scotland and the early colonial settlements.(12)

Had the American vision of Scotland been more complex and more realistic, it would certainly have been possible to see parallels between the Lowland-Highland hostility and the settler-Amerindian relationship. But since Scotland was proving much more valuable as a conspiratorial and treasonable unity, little was made of that. Lowland Scots in America may have told themselves that courageous destruction of aboriginal treason at Glencoe and Culloden was a principle still being fulfilled on the American continent despite the evil restraints of the London government, now in less reliable hands than those of William III and the Duke of Cumberland. But if they did, they failed to bring the point before the mass of American revolutionary public opinion.

The American view of Ireland was equally vague, but its use created an analogy. The colonists, in fact, had very little choice in coming to terms with Ireland. Government had, rightly or wrongly, imposed an Irish, and not a Scottish, solution on the colonies. If one read the arguments of the colonists one way, they did demand some equivalent of the Act of Union of 1707. If they demanded representation, well, the Scots had obtained it, for what it was worth. But the Irish had not been given representation at Westminster (although, many Irishmen, of whom Burke was but the most illustrious, were to sit for English seats). Yet the Declaratory Act of 1720, on which the Declaratory Act of 1766 was explicitly based, had asserted the supremacy of Parliament over Ireland. The American publicists, when they came, somewhat belatedly, to deny the validity of the Declaratory Act of 1766, found themselves uncertain as to whether to question also the validity of its Irish predecessor, or to argue that what had been justified with respect of Ireland was not so with respect to America. Some took one stand, some took the other. John Adams, who probably knew more about Irish constitutional history than any other man in America, took both. But whether they accepted the parallel or questioned it, the remonstrations of Molyneux and Lucas were accepted as possessed of every relevance to the American cause. (13)

It had been English authority which had first fixed the Irish-American analogy and, as Professor David Quinn has shown so well, the first expressions of this analogy emerged in Elizabethan times. (14) The economic expectations of America which, as John Donne should remind us, (15) at times reached erotic heights, can be duplicated in English comment on the potential wealth Ireland could realise for them, Edmund Spenser offering us, a case in point. (16) The plantation system, introduced initially into Ireland by the Catholic Mary I, was used in the light of that experience when Government turned its attention to America. Contemporary commentators in the eighteenth century, once the caste system had been established in Ireland, commented frequently on similarities between the native Irish Papists and the Amerindians. (17)

Even the monolithic vision of Ireland had an English origin. Cromwell and William III made pointed distinctions between their Irish Protestant supporters and their Irish Catholic opponents, but in the eighteenth century vulgar comment was very ready to homogenise Ireland as a term of opprobrium. And this often arose, not from ignorance, but from acquaintance. A bigoted Protestant episcopalian Irish country gentleman in London would nevertheless often exhibit, notably in accent but also in provinciality of dress or manners, an alien quality which elicited assumptions that all Irish were rebellious and slightly subhuman. The eighteenth century version of the Irish joke turned no more on distinctions of caste among the Irish than does its twentieth century counterpart. It should be the aboriginal who is being attacked, but the Irish visitor to London - who in the eighteenth century was often likely to be Protestant, at least as far as moving in literate society was concerned - found to his dismay that aboriginal qualities were ascribed to him rather than to the unknown Papists at home in their hovels. It was the constant misfortune of the Irish of English stock that the distinction between themselves and the natives, in their view their trump card of identity, seemed unrecognised in casual speech among the English. This again probably goes back to Elizabethan times. When Shakespeare portrayed the Irish Captain Macmorris in **Henry V** as responding in most violent, if confused, language to an allusion to his nation, (18) was this because he was an aboriginal with a chip on his shoulder or because he was a colonist dismayed at being taken for an aboriginal? The name suggests the former, but the indignation might be consistent with the latter. If Shakespeare had heard such sentiments from men with Irish accents, it was natural for him as an Englishman to apply the aboriginal name to a settler's complaint.

It might be felt that the Americans were surely spared that particular paralle. given the obvious

racial distinctions between colonists and Amerindians, but they were not. The London inconography cheerfully depicted Americans in Amerindian dress and possessed of putative Amerindian manners. The nineteenth century cartoonist may have often been unflattering with his emphasis on cigar, rapacity and slave driver's whip, but the eighteenth century cartoonist, amiably or abrasively representing America as an Amerindian, must surely have irritated the colonists far more. Thus the Americans had learned both a monolithic manner of thinking, and a monolithic view of Ireland, from their English tutors.

The mythical Ireland invented by the Americans ultimately became very important. It was adopted by, among others, the Irish themselves. It was an American invention, given that its English antecedents arose in a spirit of hostility hence proving unconducive to Irish acceptance. It is very much alive at the present day. Professor Daniel Boorstin, in his Reith lectures in 1975, asserted it in his third chapter suggestively entitled 'The Therapy of Distance'. "In the seventeenth century, while Englishmen in America were building colonies, the Irish separated by only a few miles of water, were trying without success to assert their right to legislate for themselves. ... The irony of this situation, which escaped most English statesmen, was vivid enough to the dyseptic Irishman Jonathan Swift, who called 'government without the consent of the governed ... the very definition of slavery'. The Irish, Swift noted, were well enough equipped with arguments, 'but the love and torrent of power prevailed ... in fact, eleven men well armed will certainly subdue one single man in his shirt'. Ireland was too close to England, and the stakes of the Irish Empire too great, for the Irish prophets of Revolution to prevail. ...while Cromwell's Army could master next-door Ireland, neither he nor his successors could preserve the power of the English Parliament over these thirteen colonies of transatlantic Americans. Three thousand miles of ocean accomplished what could not be accomplished by a thousand years of history. The Atlantic Ocean proved a more effective advocate than all the constitutional lawyers of Ireland". (19)

It is of course regrettable to have so wide a dissemination of a farrago of nonsense from so eminent a person and platform. But what is of more importance to our enquiry is to see why and how a myth has thus been set in the crown of scholarship. The theory would seem to be this. Ireland, an island in proximity to Britain, was conquered at some point by the English between 921 A.D. and 976 A.D. (it is clear that Professor Boorstin does not assume the conquest to have been successfully accomplished by the well-known British immigrant, St. Patrick, whose date, however uncertain, is at least about 1500 years ago). The Irish at some point in the seventeenth century demanded legislative independence apparently through the use of constitutional law, although they also had the services of prophets of Revolution. Cromwell mastered Ireland, thus presumably ending the legal action and, one assumes, the prophets then in business. His settlement proved permanent, given the point at which Ireland was situated in the Atlantic Ocean. The Irish therefore contracted dyspepsia.

The Atlantic certainly played a part in giving American history a different course to Irish, although we are on rather firmer ground in following Dr Ian Adams than Professor Boorstin on this point. It would not be fair to John Adams and his associates to ascribe to them the degree of ignorance with which Professor Boorstin has chosen to shroud himself. They knew, for instance, that the disappearance of Irish constitutional quasi-independence under Cromwell - a disappearance which, after all, did allow for Irish representation, of a kind, at Westminster - did not survive the Commonwealth. But the germ of Professor Boorstin's theory is certainly present in the American Revolutionary view of Ireland. The Irish Parliament was in fact a Norman innovation in Irish life after the conquest. The independence of conduct exhibited by the Norman-Irish nobility, particularly evinced during the Wars of the Roses, ultimately led Henry VIIl to ensure the enactment of Irish constitutional subordination to the English Government. Its corollary, the right of the English Parliament to legislate for Ireland, was not asserted in theory unti. the reign of George I, when the Declaratory Act stated what had long been existing in practice. By this time the 'Ireland' against whose being bound by English Parliamentary Acts Molyneux had protested was the Protestant episcopalian caste, who alone could be represented in Parliament. The American constitutionalists there had to assume a continuum for Ireland which did not exist. The Parliament whose powers were circumscribed by Henry VII did not contain a single person who was not officially a Roman Catholic. The Parliament whose powers were circumscribed by George I did not contain a single person who was not officially a Protestant episcopalian. Neither Parliament derived from the Gaelic world into which the Normans formally intruded in 1169, although by Henry VII's time the frontiers of Gaelic and Norman civilisations had been considerably blurred. To be sure Parliament in Ireland was as conscious of precedent as any other legislative body. But its balance had shifted sharply from a geographical to a religious perspective. Prior to the Tudors it had effectively spoken for as much of Ireland as it could, which was often very little. In the eighteenth century it spoke for the uppermost caste across the entire country. The primary purpose of the Parliament was to ensure that the three castes, Protestant episcopalian, dissenter and Roman Catholic, maintained their relative positions. And in order to do so it acquiesced in the primary English objective, that of economic control of the archipelago. It was in the era of the American Revolution that pottage began to prove more important than birthright.

The work of Professor Barnard Bailyn and others has brought us to see how powerful a force

rhetoric could be, to the point where, in the 1770s, it is possible to see the American publicists acting much more under the dictates of ideology than by any economic motivation. The 1760s supplied economic causes for American protest. The 1770s brought a climate in which ideological commitment often transcended immediate economic motivation. The Declaratory Act of 1766 asserted a principle with the unspoken codicil that it would not be enforced in practice. The Americans were happy to abide with that in the 1760s, but not in the 1770s. This point of ideological 'take-off' was of course different in time for different Americans, but we can fairly argue that it was in the ascendant for the vociferous American dissidents by 1775.[20] There was no such point of 'take-off' for the Irish Parliament, although we may see evidences of it among certain Presbyterians. A middle caste has more reason to listen to the siren songs of revolutionary ideology than an upper caste. The Irish Parliament was, of course, famed for its rhetoric. But having such long familiarity with it, they took care to keep it their prisoner, and not become its. When they spoke of 'Ireland,' they meant themselves. The Americans also meant **Them**selves when they spoke of America, but they had achieved a genuine degree of representation of American whites in their assemblies and Continental Congress. The Irish Parliament, even among the Protestant episcopalian caste, could make no such claim.

The analogy between Ireland and America was enhanced by the existence of rule by viceroy, and again a contrast with Scotland. But the analogy broke down on the question of self-definition. The Irish use of rhetoric enabled the word 'Ireland' to mean a wholly contrasting series of things to Jacobite Gaelic poets, Presbyterian ministers and Irish Parliamentarians. But Ireland had been defined. It was a Kingdom, declared as such by Henry VIII to show his superiority to the status of Lordship given to it by the Pope when he entrusted to Henry II, and confirmed for Mary Tudor by another Pope who found it easier to sanctify the Henrician secular claims when dealing with Henry's daughter than to gainsay them. As a Kingdom, it therefore had a corporate unity which the thirteen colonies certainly did not possess before independence. In practice the Kingdom of Ireland in the mid-eighteenth century was effectively administered by English officials supported by an Irish establishment of varying individual degrees of ancestral longevity in Ireland. It involved a convenient mechanism by which charges could be made in furtherance of individual Royal needs not likely to receive kind consideration from the British Parliament. The overawing of the Irish Parliament was substantially a matter for each viceroy to effect by a judicious exercise of patronage, diplomacy and dictation. So far as the Catholics were concerned, they preferred more rather than less Royal domination, given that London had less direct reason to enforce penal laws against them than had the Irish upper caste. The separate identity which many of the Gaelic poets gave to Ireland, by means of personification in godlike feminine form, in practice meant very little by 1775. Certainly any songs declaring the permanent fealty of that kingdom of Ireland to the exiled Stuart were now composed and sung as a matter of poetic form only. In the early eighteenth century the songs and poems had been more genuine in sentiment, although without hope, or even perhaps desire, for the vindication of Stuart claims by anything other than a faraway miracle. (21) And certainly the identification of the kingdom with the Stuart cause was of very little more ancient antecedents than the Protestant episcopalians' identification of it with themselves.

So the Kingdom of Ireland meant everything and nothing. It had no ancient origins: the country had never been united beyond brief moments when the transient power of an ancient local ruler had enforced reluctant acquiescence in his pretentions by potential rivals while he was within striking range of them. The Pope, with Lordship or Kingship, had simply legitimised what the King could hold. The Parliament had been wholly dependent for its existence on English power, and during the Williamite wars that status had been further compounded by the question of what kind of English power was at hand. The caste system, for all the rhetorical pretentions of its aristocracy, depended utterly on British military support.

But the Kingdom of Ireland had one overwhelming call on American interest. It was, in theory, the most important area of sovereignty - however constitutionally uncertain the independence of that sovereignty might be - within the British Empire outside of Britain. It had a theoretical identity which America lacked, even if America possessed, an increasingly practical identity which Ireland did not possess. The Americans could therefore envisage the concept of a separate Kingdom within the empire by the visible existence of the island of Ireland supported by its legal Kingship. This, of course, passed out of the reckoning in 1776, but up to that point the nominal Irish identity as well as the pretentions of Irish independence offered Americans a means of declaring their own identity. Nor could they afford to move to the closer parallels of British settlers in Ireland and America **versus** an aboriginal population. The Kingdom of Ireland embraced all its subjects, in theory, even in the eighteenth century when a judge could say on the Bench that the law did not presume an Irish Roman Catholic to exist. (22) Would it be unkind to suggest that the Irish Protestant ability to assume an existence for Catholics when necessary, and to assume their nonexistence when preferable also offered its analogies with respect to the American Revolutionaries' view of the Amerindians? If so, the lesson was learned silently. It had to be, for the Lordship of Ireland as originally constituted had assumed a totality, and the Americans looked at that originality.

There may have been some identity of attitude between Irish and American Protestants in 1774, when the colonists, in the initial session of the Continental Congress, revealed so strongly their

fears of Catholic establishment under the Quebes Act and beyond. But while the Anti-Catholic origins of the American Revolution are very important, and were quickened by American appeals to the memory of 1688, they had been swept from blatant view by the time of the Declaration of Independence. Charles Carroll of Carrollton and others must have undertaken some of the work of convincing their Protestant fellow-Revolutionaries of the need to make their appeal palatable to American Catholic opinion, much as Witherspoon and Wilson would ensure the removal of anti-Scottish sentiments from the text of the Declaration itself. (23) Irish Protestant episcopalians who responded to the Revolution with enthusiasm remained ignorant of that change, and found an identity of bigotry as well as liberty: had not William III, after all, formally identified the causes of English liberties and the Protestant religion? Here again, one can see the Americans, anxious to place behind them the earlier anti-Catholic phase, carefully ignoring its more permanent counterpart in Ireland.

There remain two problems in examining the American Revolutionary view of Ireland and the Irish view of the American Revolution. With respect to the Irish reaction, we may return to Dr Swinfen and Dr Duncan Rice. Examination of Irish newspapers suggests that, as with the Scottish press, Irish publicists were much more concerned to use the Revolution for their own ends, than to respond to it. Pamphlet literature also bears out this argument. But the Irish newspapers were much more noticeably partisan than were the Scottish, as the severity of the caste system would imply. The form of Irish government meant that the influence of the Viceroy dictated the content and attitudes of certain newspapers through patronage: accordingly expressions of Irish support for the Government, and arguments in its furtherance, were at once more partisan, less heartfelt and more statesmanlike. It is possible to see a shrewd use of propaganda to convince the Catholics that American rebellion was inimical to their liberty. Similarly, given that the Irish Protestant supporters of the Americans somewhat resembled the Americans in being conscious of the justification for their attitudes accorded by English political tradition, Irish journalists were ready to give some strong support to the American cause, even after the Declaration, albeit on a very narrow construction of the American case. The Irish newspapers were fairly sensitive to the English debate on America, and in general one sees here a further illustration of the theme that Ireland reflected English influence more than did Scotland. After all, Irish politics was by now much more of an English export commodity than was Scottish politics.

As to Dr Duncan Rice's argument that the American Revolution was of much greater consequence to 19th-century Scotland, it is tempting to pursue the same point with respect to Ireland. In a formal sense it is not true. One can argue that the American Revolution finally truly found ideological disciples in Ireland via the French Revolution, and that that vanished also after the rebellions of 1798 and 1803, much as the verbal imitations of the American Revolution evident in the Irish Parliament properly concluded for good with the Act of Union passed in 1800. But of course Dr Duncan Rice's argument has every relevance to Ireland. Irish revolutionary nationalism, when it existed, naturally looked to the fish that got away from the British imperial catch, especially when the fish began to consume large quantities of Irish emigrants. Much more important was the development of mass political democracy in Ireland. This owed more to specific Irish circumstances and British forms of government than to American influences, and if its great midwife, Daniel O'Connell, acknowledged American influences, he also owed much to European liberal Catholicism - to be sure a beneficiary in some degree of the American Revolution in its turn - as well as to British utilitarianism and radicalism. But the case of O'Connell reminds us that the American Revolution, as ultimately realised by the liberal world, raised expectations of America itself which accounts for the urgency with which he and others attacked American slavery. (24) A word here is needed in defence of European critics of America, who have been assailed by sensitive defenders of America and insensitive flatterers of it. We in the twentieth century have seen apologists for other revolutions much abused for their failure to acknowledge stains on the records of the new regime. Those who looked to America for vindication of liberal-democratic principles often showed themselves men and women of honour in their insistence in being first with denunciation of their exemplar's shortcomings. To O'Connell in particular the preaching of democracy which was alien to both British and Irish alike had to be reinforced by an insistence on ideological integrity. To say this is not to negate his hatred of human suffering as revealed in slavery. But it does serve to show how antislavery to O'Connell was an integral part of his politics, not an additional side-issue.

As Professor Kiernan has so ably stressed, the European responses to the American revolution were generally well mixed by the preconceptions the Europeans brought to their examination. Thomas Moore, as he justly implies, was too conditioned by his upper-class drawing room English environment to adulterate his elitist romantic Irish utterances with American revolutionary fervour. But, granting this, it is possible to see in Moore's view of America a more muted version of O'Connell's dismay at the inconsistencies in America's vindication of her revolution. Was it, one wonders, wholly a preference for English manners which elicited his bitter lines against Jefferson:
The Patriot, fresh from Freedom's councils come,
Now pleas'd retires to lash his slaves at home,
Or woo, perhaps, some black Aspasia's charms
And dream of Freedom in his bondsmaid's arms
. . . (25)

Perhaps there lay behind the self-indulgent poet's

gibes a note of pain that America had failed to show him an integrity in its idealism worth imitating. And this, also, is a strain which may be found in other Irish writers. One can see in their resentment of America a resentment also that it failed in its duty to give them a whiter hope.

Once the U.S.A. had established itself as the Irish Eldorado, with American dollars for private and public relief, revolutionary dreams and constitutionalist realities, the Irish in Ireland, so far as they thought about it, eagerly adopted the myth of Irish support for the American Revolution. Irish-Americans, anxious to establish their American credentials, vociferously claimed a grandiose participation by the Irish Catholics in the American Revolution. Their action in this respect was all the more urgent in view of the prevalence of Anglo-Saxonist historiography. When the Irish Catholics thought of the point, they readily accepted it. In part, they simply politely swallowed the Irish-American argument: when the poor relation is being stood a good dinner, he is careful to agree with his host's conversation. In part, it derived from the myth of the Kingdom of Ireland, which the Irish Catholics, struggling to achieve constitutional independence, thankfully adopted. Those Irish Protestants who had opposed the Union, which Irish Catholics now wished to repeal (with the important addition of Catholic emancipation), had in many cases supported the American Revolution. Wishing to court British and Irish Protestant support, the Catholic constitutionalists declared that they only sought to prove themselves the heirs of Henry Grattan and his pro-American friends in the Irish Parliament. It was hardly tactful to suggest that their actual ancestors had been bitterly opposed to the American cause, especially since its most canonised Irish Parliament had produced its most vigorously patriotic speeches in its support. This mythologising was part of a great good: by identifying their cause with the defunct Irish Parliament, Irish nationalists also nailed their colours to the democratic and constitutionalist mast. The Irish Parliament had been undemocratic: but its cult became a great means for asserting democratic principles.

In the 19th and 20th centuries the revolutionary rhetoric of Irish nationalism also infected even the strictest constitutionalists and hence gave dangerous hostages to fortune. But these revolutionary theorists also needed to assert Irish Catholic support for the Revolution. Irish republicanism came increasingly to depend on a historical myth as insistent on its thousand-year life as Professor Boorstin could wish. Hence whatever the quarrel, especially a nice, fashionable quarrel like the American Revolution, it could not be admitted for a moment that the Irish Catholics turned their backs on the anti-British cause. It is important to notice the existence of these myths. Today the Scottish Universities American Bicentennial Conference revealed no readiness to question the new consensus, that the American detestation of Scotland was far more important to the Revolution than any small Scottish expressions of support, but let us not forget that only a few years ago, such finding would have elicited general horror. Similarly at the subsequent Irish American Bicentennial Summer School, under the auspices of Cumann Merriman, a range of scholars as divergent in other respects as Professor John Murphy, Dr Conor Cruise O'Brien, Dr David Doyle and myself acknowledged that our independent investigations had all moved to the same conclusion of Irish Catholic hostility to the American Revolution, but that new consensus is also in danger of clouding our minds to the vigour of the earlier myth of Irish Catholic support for it.(26) Dr Cruise O'Brien's joke at his own expense in his paper in this volume reminds us how much the Irish-Americans cherish that myth today, although he does himself less than justice in implying he would not speak in the same vein to such an audience. But of course it is in the Irish-American and Scottish-American communities that the myths of reciprocal love affairs between their ethnic groups and the American Revolution must be strongest. They cannot permit their American shadows to grow any less than two hundred years' stature. And a society by now uneasily conscious of the dangers of questioning ethnic versions of the past finds it wiser and easier to perpetuate the myth. If Professor Boorstin's resurrection of Cromwell and citation of a thousand-year struggle sit oddly with the shade of Lord Reith, it will do him no harm in American establishment circles as balanced among their present compromises.

Yet in a sense the finding of this paper does offer one line of support for Professor Boorstin's famous thesis of environmentalism as the determining factor in the American experience. The American Revolution certainly was an event undertaken with Europe in mind - the European heritage, the European sources for American Revolutionary ideology, the European diplomatic potentialities for assisting America, the European missionfield for future American ideas. And in the cases of certain Revolutionary Americans, one is left very deeply amazed at the profundity of their knowledge of the European past. Certainly the men of 1776 in most cases reveal a European sense which their heirs, for all the technological leaping of continents, have never achieved. But the selectivity, mythologising, ignorance and unreality which American views of Scotland and Ireland in the Revolutionary era revel does suggest a point for the Boorstin thesis. They made their Europe what they wanted it to be. They made Ireland nice and Scotland nasty and England degenerate and France miraculously transformed from bad to good within a decade. In the fullness of time individual ethnic groups would play comparable games with the homelands whence they had derived. In giving, therefore, this modicum of support to Professor Boorstin, perhaps one could adopt his term, in a somewhat different sense, and find in the American use of Ireland, Scotland and Europe "The Therapy of Distance".

REFERENCES

1. Owen Dudley Edwards, "The American Image of Ireland: a Study of its Early Phases", **Perspectives in American History**, IV (1970), Owen Dudley Edwards, "The Impact of the American Revolution on Ireland", in R. R. Palmer **et. al.**, **The Impact of the American Revolution Abroad** (Library of Congress symposium, Washington, D.C., 1976).

2. Professor Kiernan's remarks on Beaumarchais which appear earlier in this volume give an instance of the subtle operation of this political use of drama. The mass of political drama in the late eighteenth century English speaking world was crude, emotive and blatant. I am not giving specific references to Dr Hook's work, since his book, especially chapter 3, is essential reading in its entirety for the student of the American connection with that world in this period: even where the Scottish dimension does not directly obtrude it must be considered for the light it throws on events and attitudes elsewhere and for its comparativist potentialities.

3. The American dissident's response to England, Scotland, and Ireland was of course manifested across the whole spectrum of communications, from the supremely intellectual contributions to constitutional theory of John Dickinson, James Wilson, John Adams, and to a lesser degree, Thomas Jefferson, through the pragmatic publicism of Benjamin Franklin, the tough economic realism of Alexander Hamilton, the emotive cadences of Tom Paine, the crowd manipulation of Sam Adams, the forest of controversial pamphleteering high-, middle-, and low-brow, the incessant newspaper warfare from journalists and correspondents, the varieties of private correspondence, the satires, lampoons, speeches, cries and mutterings, to the anonymous inflammatory handbills and placards. Political drama was only one of these innumerable media. But however limited its extent, dissemination and audiences, it must be seen as conditioning the mind of the era far beyond the determinable limits of its specific impact.

4. The Irish Volunteers were much more conservative than subsequent Irish nationalist mythology found it expedient to recognise, but as with many other conservatives the revolutionary era induced a greater liberalism in their ideology if only by leading them to see more political options than their initial perspective suggested. Even their initial anti-Catholicism was very remarkably eroded, in some instances. In the cases of relatively few of them the era did its work by drawing them ultimately into support of certain French revolutionary ideals. But to say this is not to grant them the status of Irish Washingtons, Jeffersons and Adamses, either in character or in ideology. See Maurice R. O'Conell, **Irish Politics and Social Conflict in the Age of the American Democratic Revolution** (Philadelphia, 1965). Their legacy was specifically appealed to in the second decade of the 20th century, when Edward Carson, Eoin MacNeill and John Redmond produced their different varieties of "Volunteers". What is not thought about in Ireland was that during the Revolutionary war in America, the term "Irish Volunteers" referred to a regiment raised by the British forces in America, allegedly from Irish deserters from the American ranks, initially formed in early Summer, 1778 under the command of Lord Rawdon. They played a part in Virginia in May 1779, in the Charleston Campaign of 1780 and at Hobkirk's Hill, S.C., in April 1781. It is probable that many of them were not, in fact, deserters from the Americans but recent Irish arrivals within the colonies whose first service was under Rawdon. The deserter element probably proved ultimately very undependable: Rawdon ran into difficulties with serious desertions himself, in the Carolinas.

5. It was, of course, the more pessimistic Protestants, fearful of the domestic effects of arming Papists, who found the numbers particularly noteworthy.

6. And where Americans did acknowledge Irish business enterprise, they often viewed it in a spirit of kindly

contrast to such activity on the part of the Scots. Dr Thomas Devine's very interesting quotation from Patrick Henry, printed in his essay above, gives us a perfect illustration. Henry's evident partiality for the Irish as symbolic adversaries to the Scots is highly suggestive to the student of the dramatic mentality in the American Revolution.

7. A necessarily superficial glance at Dublin and Ulster publications of American interest during the period suggests a much closer Atlantic community mentality among the Scotch-Irish than among either Protestants or Catholics in the South. I am thinking less in terms of Irish or American republication of works originating from the other side of the Atlantic, which ever side it was, as of subscription lists for books on either side. Admittedly, very few of these survive. There are, of course, Dublin exceptions, such as Mathew Carey, who when commencing his Philadelphia career went to pains to sell or republish interesting Dublin items, but the Scotch-Irish were probably more infected by the deeper ideological sentiments of the American Revolution than anyone else in Ireland, and may also give a clue as to why new readiness to sympathise with the Catholics emerges towards the end of the American war most genuinely on the Scotch-Irish side. If ideology did cross the Atlantic to raise questions about the Irish caste system, it seems a far more genuine force in Ulster than in Dublin as far as a reading of the pamphlet can tell us.

8. One sometimes wonders whether certain 20th-century historians of American birth and Americanist preoccupation would not, in fact, offer such a pre-eminence to Bradstreet and Wigglesworth; if they do not complete the logical conclusions of their economia explicitly, at least the absence of reference to Milton and Marvell has an inferential weight. But one does not encounter this mentality in the Europe-conscious 18th century. As to Swift, there is no alternative to the study of his writings but Oliver Watkins Ferguson, **Jonathan Swift and Ireland** (Urbana, III, 1962) offers a starting point for investigation of his Irish interests. The critical decade for our purposes is the 1720s.

9. I have explored the American interest in Molyneux and Lucas in my "American Image of Ireland". It is possible that the lack of attention to Swift and Berkeley rested on their contemporary lack of favour - a situation which extended to Swift's writings generally (Michael Foot ascribes the rediscovery of Swift to Hazlitt's work in the initial instance) and to Berkeley's political reflections. Professor Bailyn has commented to me on the extraordinary absence of Swift from the mass of pamphlet citations and evident influence. Lucas's revival of Molyneux, Molyneux's obvious relevance for the American quarrel, and Molyneux's possible uses for Irish parliamentarians in search of economic improvement for their caste, no doubt combined to give rise to the number of editions of his **The Case of Ireland's being bound by Acts of Parliament in England, stated** which appeared in the 1770s: it was republished in London in 1770, Dublin in 1773 and Belfast in 1776. It was clearly the first of these which Franklin sent to America. There was much interest in Berkeley's philosophy among the American revolutionaries, but they make little of his polemics. His **The Querist, containing several queries proposed to the consideration of the public** was first published in Dublin in 1735 (dated 1725) and had several British republications in the next twenty years. It was occasionally bound with his later work **A Word to the Wise: or an exhortation to the Roman Catholic clergy of Ireland** whose fourth edition was published in Boston in 1750. I know of no 18th century American edition of **The Querist.**

10. Owen Dudley Edwards ed., **Benjamin Franklin's Ireland** (Dublin, 1976) may be useful in this connection. Franklin was the more ready to supply Irish analogies for the American dissidents when the Irish Parliament, during his visit thereto, greeted him as the representative of "some English **Parliament** in America" (Franklin to his son William, 30 Jan., 1772, quoted Cecil B. Currey, **Road to Revolution - Benjamin Franklin in England 1765-1775** (Garden City, N.Y., 1968), 270). Dr Currey shrewdly comments: "It was not accidental that he italicised the word 'Parliament'. Franklin's ego must have been thoroughly elated by such occurances". Thus Franklin, and to a lesser extent his American correspondents and sympathisers, found a further means by which the idea of their own identity was enlarged by the Irish parallel, provided, of course, that it was conceded to be a parallel.

11. Schuyler, **Parliament and the British Empire - Some Constitutional Controversies Concerning Imperial Legislative Jurisdiction** (New York, 1929), 42-55; the entire chapter, "Irish Patriotism and British Imperialism" is a classic exposition of the Irish arguments and the criticisms levelled at them, replying to Charles H. McIlwain, **The American Revolution: A Constitutional Interpretation** (New York, 1923).

12. I pass over the sinister parallel offered by Molyneux's adversary, William Atwood, who not only denied the sovereignty of the Irish Parliament but also held, in a later work, that Scotland was dependent on the Crown of England before and after the Union of Crowns and had been so from earliest times. This won him the honour of having the treatise in question burnt by the common hangman by order of the Scottish Parliament, a distinction the English Parliament had conferred on Molyneux's book. Atwood became Chief Justice of New York in 1701 (Schuyler, **Parliament and the British Empire,** 84-86 and 243, n. 121). John Adams was ready enough to make Scottish parallels of a kind more comforting to the American revolutionaries than those of Atwood: "the Massachusetts is a realm, New York is a realm, Pennsylvania another realm, to all intents and purposes, as much as Ireland is, or England or Scotland ever were. The King of Great Britain is the sovereign of all these realms". (**Novanglus**, no. VIII, Charles Francis Adams ed., **The Works of John Adams** (Boston, 1851, IV, 123): his references to Scotland were few - the case on which he chose to enlarge, other than that of Ireland, was Wales, apart from some remarks on the Channel Islands and the counties palatine of Chester and Durham. In passing, he slightly weakened his own argument by the ascription of sovereignty to the "King of Great Britain", whose title to Ireland rested on his being "King of Ireland". But this was clearly a slip arising from haste. Where Scotland was of more interest to Adams was in the failure of the Act of Union of 1707 to allude to America (Adams, **loc. cit.**).

13. Dudley Edwards, "American Image of Ireland", first section **passim.** Adams's argument found its logic in questioning the applicability to America of English answers to the case for Irish legislative independence, but he expressed grave doubts as to the existence of a contract "of the Irish nation, to be governed by the English parliament". He also pointed to the presence of a standing army in Ireland as evidence of Irish refusal to accept subordinate status. This was to glide agreeably over the fact that the Parliament in Ireland for which sovereignty was claimed was what required the standing army against the threat from the other Ireland (Adams, "Novanglus", 165, 158).

14. See in particular his **The Elizabethans and the Irish** (Ithaca, N.Y., 1966), especially chapter IX, "Ireland and America Intertwined". It is with much pleasure that I record how great was the debt of our Conference to the presence of David and Alison Quinn.

15. "Elegie xix, 'Going to Bed'", lines 25-50:
"Licence my roaving hands, and let them go,
Before, behind, between, above, below.
O my America! my new-found land,
My kingdome, safeliest when with one man mann'd,
My Myne of precious stones, My Emperie,
How blest am I in this discovering thee!"

16. "And sure it is a most beautiful and sweet country as any is under heaven, seamed throughout with many goodly rivers replenished with all sorts of fish most abundantly, sprinkled with very many sweet islands and goodly lakes like little inland seas, that will carry even ships upon their waters, adorned with goodly woods fit for building of houses and ships so commodiously, as that if some prices in the world had them, they would soon hope to be lords of all the seas and ere long of all the world, also full of very good ports and havens opening upon England and Scotland, as inviting us to come unto them, to see what excellent commodities that country can afford, besides the soil itself most fertile, fit to yield all kind of fruit that shall be committed thereinto: and, lastly, the heavens most mild and temperate, though somewhat more moist than the parts towards the west". (Spenser, **A View of the Present Sate of Ireland** ed. W. L. Renwick (Oxford, 1970),

125

18-19.

17. W. E. H. Lecky, **A History of Ireland in the Eighteenth Century** (New York, 1893, rev. edn.), I. 227, 241; Howard Mumford Jones, **O Strange New World** (New York, 1964), 167-73. This analogy in the minds of contemporaries requires much further research and analysis: in particular it is worth investigating the American folk memory of Amerindian massacres (of Whites) as compared with Protestant Irish folk memories of the insurrection, of 1641. As regards backwardness, James Wilson was ready enough to bracket contemporary Highland concepts of land ownership with those of "the Indians of Peru" (Robert Green McCloskey ed., **The Works of James Wilson** (Cambridge, Mass., 1967), II. 714-15).

18. **Henry V**, III. ii. 124-26. I took Macmorris or, more correctly, Mackmorice, for a Gael when I remarked on the lines in Owen Dudley Edwards et al., (**Celtic Nationalism** (London, 1968), I. section 2, and Professor Quinn sees it as a "well-defined characterisation of an Irish professional soldier, excitable, proud, extravagant in language" (**The Elizabethans and the Irish**, 161). But I think the question remains as to whether the original was as Gaelic in origin as Shakespeare thought. Of course Professor Marshall is right in saying, as he does in his essay in this volume, that the English distinguished in theory between the Protestant and Catholic Irish, although it is significant that, as he points out, both groups are seen as sufficiently malcontent to raise suspicions of possible rebellion. But in the crudities of verbal exchanges even those refinements would become blurred. Obviously, I owe the idea developed here to Professor Marshall's inspiration in the first instance.

19. Daniel J. Boorstin, **The Exploring Spirit - America and the World Experience** (London, 1976), 36-37.

20. This of course is all very crude. The ideological assumptions carried with them beliefs about economic self-interest, and at many points it would be impossible to judge whether economic or ideological motivation was in the ascendant in specific cases. Moreover the degree of altruism involved, insofar as patriotism can be altruism and not merely ego-enlargement, varies very much with persons and times. But however fuelled by prejudice, ignorance, self-interest and innumerable other factors, in the cases of the major ideologists one must justly speak of ideology at certain stages being in control.

21. The actual form of the poetry is of importance here. The early 18th century Galic poets were sufficiently conscious of the need for clear communication of contant to write their **Aislingí**, or patriotic dream-poems, with some degree of austerity, numerous though their pathetic fallacies and lyrical touches were. The later eighteenth century **Aislingí** are highly convoluted and sophisticated performances in which style, and not content, is evidently the poet's chief preoccupation.

22. Lecky, **Ireland in the Eighteenth Century**, I. 146.

23. "When the Declaration of Independence was under the consideration of Congress, there were two or three unlucky expressions in it which gave offence to some members. The words 'Scotch and other foreign auxiliaries' excited the ire of a gentleman or two of that country. . . . the offensive expressions were immediately yielded . . .". (Thomas Jefferson, "Anecdotes of Benjamin Franklin". c. 4 Dec. 1818, in Adrienne Koch and William Peden, eds. **The Life and Selected Writings of Thomas Jefferson**, 178). See also "Envoi" below on Franklin's allusions to and exchanges with Scots during the debate on the Articles of Confederation, as reported by Jefferson. Jefferson's comment is curiously reminiscent of the surprise of an upper-class gentleman in the late 19th or 20th century when a joke of his is stigmatised as racist: in Jefferson's case his innocence on the matter might be open to question, given the impetus to his cause anti-Scottish attitudes had been. But he was writing forty years after, when a selectivity respecting the past naturally induced itself, consciously or unconsciously. What really does look like innocence was his assumption that Wilson and Witherspoon would not object to the word "other". But the anti-Scottish paranoia, like other forms of racism, evidently coexisted with some of one's best friends being Scots. Franklin's flippant reaction to the incident is also highly suggestive (**ibid.**, 178-79).

24. Doulgas C. Riach, "Ireland and the Campaign Against American Slavery, 1830-1860" (unpublished Ph.D. dissertation, Edinburgh, 1976) is the authoritative study on that subject, and it is a great honour to have been its co-supervisor, with Professor Shepperson. Dr Riach's work is in a sense a companion study to Dr Duncan Rice's dissertation on the Scottish aspect of the American anti-slavery struggle, and I have learned much from the manner in which Dr Riach examined Dr Rice's conclusions for Scotland, in an Irish context. There is clearly much fruitful work to be done on the comparison and interaction of Scotland and Ireland in relation to many other topics of American history.

25. "To Thomas Hume, Esq., M.D. from the city of Washington", c. June 1804, in **The Poetical Works of Thomas Moore** (London, 1853), 122. Another poem of the same date, "To the Lord Viscount Forbes from the city of Washington" included the lines

    Those vaunted demagogues, who nobly rose
    From England's debtors to be England's foes,
    Who could their monarch in their purse forget,
    And break allegiance but to cancel debt.

In his subsequent editorial notes Moore hoped he would not "be suspected of a wish to justify those arbitrary steps of the English government which the colonies found it necessary to resist; my only object here is to expose the selfish motive of some of the leading American demagogues". (**Ibid.**, 121). In his prefaces to the collected edition of 1841-42 Moore recorded that his sentiments were partly induced by his acquaintance in America with British Navy officers and angry Federalists such that "it was the only period of my past life during which I have found myself at all sceptical as to the soundness of that Liberal creed in politics, in the profession and advocacy of which I may be almost literally said to have begun life, and shall most probably end it". (**Ibid.**, xxii). However anti-democratic the Federalists were at that point, the sincerity of Federalist opposition to slavery is in many instances not open to question, especially in Pennsylvania where Moore most notably moved in Federalist circles. This is not to say that Moore's anti-slavery sentiments made him pro-Black. He argued that Jeffersonian ravings about liberty must induce comparable sentiments among the slaves, with inevitable White emigration from the South and an increase in the proportion of Blacks "to a degree which must ultimately be ruinous". (**Ibid.**, 121).

26. Professor Murphy's essay on the American impact on Irish nationalism will be published in the proceedings of the Irish commemoration of the American bicentennial, to be edited by David N. Doyle. Dr Doyle's own study of the Irish-American connection during the revolution will appear shortly as a publication of the Cultural Relations Committee of the Department of Foreign Affairs, Ireland. Dr Cruise O'Brien's is printed above. I would reiterate the regret expressed in the editorial that family bereavement prevented Ms Maire Cruise O'Brien from preparing the text of her paper at the Scottish conference for publication here, but I, in common with her audience at the panel, found our understanding of the Gaelic world and its relationship, and to a great extent, non-relationship, with the American revolution immeasurably enhanced insofar as it had hitherto existed at all for us. Her work provided the cultural strength from which any analysis of Irish history at this time should properly derive.

THE ARCHIVAL SITUATION
A Report of the Panel

J M SMETHURST

Archives:
a note on the panel meeting. American Bicentennial Conference.

Chairman:
J. M. Smethurst, Librarian, University of Aberdeen.

Panellists:
Richard F. Dell, City of Glasgow Archives.
Dr John Imrie, Keeper, Scottish Record Office.
Dr Edward C. Papenfuse, Maryland State Archives.
Michael Moss, Archivist, University of Glasgow.

"He has called together legislative bodies at places unusual, uncomfortable and distant from the depository of their public records."
Declaration of Independence

That the Scottish Universities' American Bicentennial Conference found time in a crowded programme to include two sessions devoted to archives, at a place within walking distance of Register House, was most appropriate. When the idea of a conference was first discussed at a meeting in Dundee, the group of archivists and librarians assembled there suggested that a programme of listing and publishing sources of material related to the Scottish-American connection would be a most valuable way of permanently celebrating the Bicentenary. The discussions at the conference took this idea a stage further and, indeed, it now seems probable that a practical and comparatively inexpensive listing of American source material might be begun by a graduate programme at Old Dominion University. An equally exciting project which has also arisen from the earlier meeting is the establishment of the Denis Brogan Centre at Glasgow University, a joint venture of the Scottish Universities to form a centre of excellence for the study of the Scottish-American connection.

The conference discussed the work which had already been done in making available primary source materials and records. Dr John Imrie, the Keeper of the Scottish Record Office, gave a brief history and description of the Records Office and its work, and stressed the value of the Scottish Regional Surveys in locating and listing records in private ownership. One of the major problems faced by researchers working with manuscripts relating to America is the lack of an up-to-date general guide, and since there is such a wide range of material relating to America, there is also an urgent need for much of this to be collated and indexed. The revision of Crick and Alman's **Guide to manuscripts relating to America in Gt. Britain & Ireland**, British Association for American Studies, 1961, is continuing, but may not be completed until 1978. For the Scottish holdings of American documents, however, the **List of American Documents in the Scottish Record Office**, H.M.S.O., 1976, which Dr Imrie presented to the conference, is an invaluable aid. This list, which originated as part of the Scottish section in Crick and Alman's **Guide**, incorporates all known documents accessioned by the Record Office up to December 1975, and contains a useful appendix giving a selection of the American material which has been listed by the surveys of the National Register of Archives (Scotland). Though most of this material remains in private hands, some has passed to the National Library of Scotland, the University libraries and various local museums, libraries and record offices.

Dr Edward Papenfuse, State Archivist, Maryland Hall of Records, talked of the work of the Maryland Hall of Records Legislative History Project, which for two years has been compiling biographies of the 1,500 members of the Maryland General Assembly who served between 1635 and 1789. The sheer magnitude of this undertaking is in itself significant, and the project was only possible because of the excellent preservation of the legislature, judicial, religious and personal data of the period in the state archive. Dr Papenfuse described the methods used by the team of researchers to analyse the data and to reconstruct profiles of the members' careers, and touched upon the tentative conclusions which might be drawn from the project concerning political involvement at the time of the revolution, and the conflicts of interest and conscience among the Maryland delegates.

The second conference session provided an opportunity for panellists and conference delegates to consider in detail the many problems faced by researchers and archivists in locating, recording and exploiting records. The discussions were lively. Many examples were given illustrating the need for improved funding to support extended work in indexing and abstracting records, and to support the preservation of that material which will be of importance to research in the future. Since many of the documents relating to the Scottish interest in America are in American archives, there is a particular need to provide listings, and to hold microfilm copies of the more important papers in this country. In general, it is clear that, too often, the detailed calendaring of archival material has to take second place to the more urgent task of locating, listing and taking into care that material which may otherwise be lost. It is equally clear that most archives are critically short of staff, and when they stimulate use of the collections in their care by publicising them in any way, they are frequently embarrassed by the additional demands upon their time that this increased use brings. Concern was also expressed at the generally low level of precise information which was given by students undertaking searches, and it would appear that there is often a lack of understanding and knowledge of published sources of information.

The participants of these sessions agreed that the conference had provided a rare opportunity for scholars, archivists and librarians to meet together and publicly discuss important matters of common interest, and it was proposed that a Scottish Record Association might be formed to encourage a regular interchange of information and opinion. The chairman offered to hold a meeting in Aberdeen to assess reaction to the proposal. This was held in September and was well attended, with representation from various interested groups from throughout Scotland. The meeting agreed to appoint a steering committee to draw up a constitution for the proposed Association, and to hold a further general meeting to discuss these. (Further information on the proposed Association can be obtained from C. A. McLaren, Secretary to the Steering Committee, Aberdeen University Library; information concerning the Denis Brogan Centre can be obtained from Michael Moss, University Archivist, University of Glasgow.)

AMERICAN STUDIES IN SCOTLAND
Past, Present and Future

GEORGE SHEPPERSON

(A revised and shortened version of the opening address on 25 March 1975 at the University of Dundee to the conference of Scottish university teachers and administrators which discussed the academic commemoration of the Bicentennial of the U.S.A. and agreed to hold the Scottish Universities American Bicentennial Conference in 1976.)

Scottish concern with American studies is older than the United States of America as anyone can see by consulting the section entitled "Of the Advantages which Europe has derived from the Discovery of America" in Adam Smith's **The Wealth of Nations** where the sage of Kirkcaldy. Glasgow and Edinburgh subjects the British and the Americans on the eve of the War of Independence to an incisive analysis. The first edition of **The Wealth of Nations**, with its penetrating study of the mercantile system of which the British American colonies were a product, was published on the 9th March 1776. The Declaration of Independence of the United States of America was issued four months later on the 4th of July 1776.

It is of course, rather a resounding generalisation to say that "Scottish concern with American studies is older than the United States of America". For Scotland, as, indeed, for the whole of the British Isles, for Europe, and for many other parts of the world beyond America, American studies, however defined or organised, do not enter into the curricula of universities,

colleges, adult educational programmes and schools, on anything more than the very smallest of scales until after the Second World War. It is this post-1945 period that, arbitrarily because of shortage of time, I shall call "the present". The future, equally arbitrarily, may be referred to as the period after the bicentennial of the U.S.A. on the 4th of July 1976. It is to these two periods, the present and the future, that we must give most of our attention.

Nevertheless, the past, considered, again quite arbitrarily, as the pre-1945 period, deserves the attention of anyone seriously concerned with American studies in Scotland and with the Scottish contribution to the study of America which is almost, but not quite, the same thing. Scottish concern with American studies before 1945 has little of the institutional about it but it is "concern" — by individuals rather than by institutions, but "concern" none the less. In this sense, the claim that Scottish concern with American studies is older than the United States of America is not quite such a resounding generalisation as it may appear, at first hearing.

I would not want to take this pre-4th of July 1776 concern too far back. I think we may omit Sir William Alexander, later Earl of Stirling, and his **An Encouragement to Colonies** which was published in 1625, three years after his small band of colonists laid the shaky foundations of Scottish settlement in Nova Scotia. Seventeenth-century evidences of specifically Scottish interest in the study of America exist, indeed, as any student of the ill-fated Darien venture knows. They provided that too-often unacknowledged pioneer of American studies in Scotland, George Pratt Insh of Jordanhill, with the opportunity to write not only on the Darien scheme but also his important book, **Scottish Colonial Schemes, 1620-1686**, which Insh published in 1922 — a work which, in my opinion, is long overdue for republication. But, in the academic sense, Scottish interest in American studies, I feel, begins with three eighteenth-century books, work on which must have begun well before the year of American independence.

The first of these, Adam Smith's **The Wealth of Nations**, I have already mentioned. The second I consider to be William Julius Mickle of Langholm's translation of Luis de Camoens' sixteenth-century epic poem of Portuguese exploration and commerce, **The Lusiads**, which was published in 1776. And the third is, of course, Principal William Robertson of Edinburgh University's **History of America**, the first two volumes of which were published in 1777.

These three volumes, it seems to me, display some of the most significant characteristics of Scottish writing on America for the pre-1945 period; a broad, almost synoptic attitude to the colonisation of the New World; a comparative approach to history; and, in spite of this wide sweep, a proclivity to analysis. These characteristics are to be found in the introduction and the footnotes to Mickle's translation of **The Lusiads**, (1) of course, and not in the poem itself, although Camoens did not lack a comparative approach, being carried along on the great sweep of Vasco da Gama's voyages: what Adam Smith, in the section from his great book from which I have just quoted, called "the Advantages which Europe has derived from the Discovery . . . of a Passage to the East Indies by the Cape of Good Hope". William Robertson's approach to American history was intrinsically synoptic and comparative. He saw Spanish America as, in his words, "a proper introduction to the history of all the European establishments in America". (2) In this way, he anticipated the "wider horizons of American history" approach of the twentieth-century Californian historian, Herbert Eugene Bolton; and one can understand why the nineteenth-century American historian of Latin America, W. H. Prescott, was his enthusiastic follower.

William Robertson, to be sure, did not lack his American critics. No less a person than the great Thomas Jefferson, who was not enamoured of Robertson's somewhat sceptical attitude towards life in America, declared sourly that "Robertson was never in America, he relates nothing on his own knowledge". (3) However, contributions to American studies were made over a century ago by Scots who had been to America. One of these was Robertson's great contemporary, John Witherspoon, whose important presidency of the College of New Jersey (later to be called Princeton University), should remind us that perhaps the greatest of contributions by Scots to American studies have been made in educational fields. But Witherspoon also made minor contributions to American studies in the academic sense, of which, perhaps, the most interesting is his essay on the English language in America which appeared in 1781 and in which he coined the word "Americanism".

Another Scot who travelled to America and who wrote about it was that early nineteenth-century pioneer of "women's lib" from Dundee and Glasgow, Frances Wright, who published in 1821 her enthusiastic book, **Views of Society and Manners in America.** Fanny Wright was no De Tocqueville; but I think that her study should help us not to forget one important category of Scottish writing on the United States: the travel book.

The years from the mid-eighteenth century until the 1830s, the age of Jacksonian Democracy in the States, are what is called by some "the Golden Age of Scottish Culture" and by others, the "Scottish Enlightenment". What they mean for American studies, not only in the form of books and articles by Scottish writers but also by their methodological and educational influences in North America, has yet to be completely established by scholars. An important contribution to this fascinating subject has been made recently by Dr Andrew Hook of the Department of English at the University of Aberdeen in his book, **Scotland and America: A Study of Cultural Relations, 1750-1835**, which was published in 1975.

It was Dr Hook, furthermore, who, a dozen years ago, drew the attention of British Americanists to the first history of American literature by a British author. (4) This was **American Literature: An Historical Sketch,** 1620-1880, which was published in Edinburgh in 1882 by Professor John Nichol of the Chair of English Literature at Glasgow University. Nichol visited America in 1865 and met Longfellow, Emerson and Oliver Wendell Holmes. Nichol, however, had his limitations in his study of American literature, perhaps the most notable of which was his consignment of Herman Melville, as the author of **Typee and Omoo** only, to a list of minor writers. It was left to other Scots, Robert Buchanan and Hugh MacDiarmid, to aid in the rehabilitation of Melville's reputation; and one ought to note that, from 1926, when the first edition of MacDiarmid's remarkable poem, **A Drunk Man Looks at the Thistle**, was published, until at least 1955 when his last major work, **Homage to James Joyce**, appeared, MacDiarmid has made a number of references to Herman Melville which deserve to be collected and included in any anthology of Melville criticism.

MacDiarmid, indeed, as the references to American history, literature and language in his idiosyncratic but important autobiography, **Lucky Poet** (first published in 1943), indicate, stands for those Scots whose interest in America was fostered outwith the orthodox channels of education — in his case, the Langholm Library. They are a group we should never forget. Whether the proposals in the Alexander Report for continuing education in Scotland, if effected, would promote or subdue individuals of this sort is for the future to show. They often have an importance for American studies far beyond the range of their published work — and I think that it would be a sad day for Scotland if over-organisation of education in the future subdued mavericks of the MacDiarmid mode.

A Scottish maverick of the past, strangely like MacDiarmid, in my opinion, although their formal ideologies differed, was Thomas Carlyle. The fragments of his writing on the New World should not be overlooked when discussing American studies in Scotland, especially his anti-democratic essay of 1867, "Shooting Niagara: and After?", which stimulated Walt Whitman's violently pro-democratic essay of 1871, **Democratic Vistas.**

Carlyle's essay was influenced by what he considered to be the abuses of democracy in the American Civil War. Scots were greatly interested in this conflict; and it would be a happy moment for me if I could record that a contemporary Scot wrote with as much acumen, in a major work, on the American Civil War as Adam Smith did on the War of Independence. The major contemporary work by a writer from the British Isles on the Civil War, to be sure, was by a writer with a Scottish name: John E. Cairnes. But Cairnes' famous and influential work, **The Slave Power**, was first given as a series of lectures in 1861 in the University of Dublin. We have had to wait over a century for a major work on the American Civil War to come out of the Scottish universities. But come it has — in **The American Civil War** by Professor Peter Parish of the University of Dundee which was published in 1975. This single-volume, synoptic work is, in my opinion, in the Scottish tradition, as one would expect from Professor Parish, who spent many years at the University of Glasgow before he went to Dundee.

Similarly, it seems to me that James Bryce's **The American Commonwealth**, first published in 1888, is also in a Scottish tradition, not only of political and sociological writing in general but also of American studies in particular. Although he was born in Belfast, Bryce came of a distinguished Scottish intellectual family; was educated at Glasgow High School and Glasgow University where he knew John Nichol; was Member of Parliament for South Aberdeen from 1885 to 1907; and, at his death in 1922, was buried in the Grange Cemetery, Edinburgh . . . all of which, I think, qualifies him for more than honorary membership of an academic St Andrew's Society! I need hardly stress the importance of Bryce's **American Commonwealth** which, with De Tocqueville's **Democracy in America**, will always be required reading for any serious student of the United States, from whatever point of view he approaches this great country.

Students of American history, today, are not required very often to read F. S. Oliver's life of Alexander Hamilton which was first published in 1906. Yet Frederick Stanley Oliver of George Watson's Boys' School and Edinburgh University must be listed as one of the pioneers of Alexander Hamilton studies, and his book had an influence which went far beyond his own country.

Perhaps the same could be said about the last of the great Scottish writers on the United States of America: Denis Brogan (1900-1974) who, from the time of his first book, **The American Political System,** originally published in 1933, never ceased to instruct and to entertain — not always a characteristic of Socttish writing on America! As Professor Harry Allen pointed out in an obituary notice on Denis Brogan in the British Association for American Studies **Journal**, "He has only been surpassed as a British exponent of American history and institutions by his great predecessor, James Bryce".(5) What Professor Allan, however, did not mention is that they were both writing in a Scottish tradition of American studies: synoptic, comparative and analytical. (6)

This tradition, as I have tried to indicate, came partly from the Scottish universities, in the days when professorships and principalships were respected institutions and their incumbents could use them to get on with their great works in a single-minded manner; and partly from a continuing interest of individual Scots in North America, when the frontier, either of land or of opportunity, seemed wide open to lads and lasses o' pairts. It was a tradition of American studies which was rooted mainly in the humanities and their most closely allied social sciences: in history, politics, economics, a little literary criticism, and a good deal of education. We must ask ourselves if this tradition has survived the Second World War to any extent - or indeed if, in an age of increasing and often unavoidable specialism, it is desirable that it should.

Before one does this, however, it is worth pointing out that perhaps the most distinctive difference between American studies in Scotland before 1945 and after this date is the relative lack of formal instruction in matters concerning the United States at all levels before the Second World War. At the University level in the nineteenth century, a few enthusiastic individuals may have arranged brief courses of lectures. One such was Professor J. Kirkpatrick of the History Department at Edinburgh University, who started in 1889-90 a yearly course of 20 lectures on "The History and Constitution of the United States of America". In the twentieth century St Andrews took the lead by starting a regular course of lectures in American history in 1927 and by creating a lectureship in Colonial and American History in 1930. Other University teachers may have included American elements — a little knowledge of federalism can be spread large — in their courses. And so, indeed, may teachers in other parts of the educational system in Scotland: in colleges for teacher training; in schools; and in extra-mural courses, not forgetting the Workers' Educational Association in Scotland and the now defunct National Council of Labour Colleges at Tillicoultry. An enthusiast for American history, such as Thomas Henderson, secretary of the Educational Institute of Scotland, collected American books and made them available to his colleagues, as the existence of the Henderson Memorial Library in the E.I.S. and its published catalogue indicate. But, at the formal, educational level, I do not think that it amounted to much. Perhaps future historical research into curricula at all levels in the Scottish educational system will prove me wrong. But I would be more than prepared, at this very moment, to take a substantial bet on it. In the past, as I see it, the characteristic Scottish tradition of study of North America has been largely an individual, unorganised affair.

The Second World War, however, and the realities of the British-American alliance, in the peace to come as well as in the war itself, began to change this situation. It was a change, of course, which came only very slowly. In the immediate post-1945 period, furthermore, the new positions which were created in the then four Scottish universities were not usually lectureships exclusively in American subjects. In the field of history, for example, American history was often coupled with British Imperial history. Such linkages may have been for reasons of economy: they may also have been due to the traditional coupling of American studies with various aspects of the expansion of Europe.

In the period from 1945 to 1976 which I have arbitrarily called "the present", an important feature has been the slow move in the Scottish universities away from American studies taught by academics who are also responsible for other subjects towards instruction about the United States by specialised teachers who are not usually called upon to tackle other subjects. Of course, the situation is by no means uniform; and it is perhaps not desirable that it should be. And there are still far too few specialised posts in American history, geography, literature, politics, economics, etc., in the Scottish universities. Indeed, after nearly 28 years of residence in Scotland, I am now sufficiently Scotocentric to assert that it is my impression that, if a comparative study were made of the English and Scottish universities, it would be found that, in spite of Scotland's interesting tradition of American studies and its close ties of kith and kin with the United States, it has less specialised posts in American fields in its universities than England. And to be sure, Scotland has practically none at all, so far as I know, in its teacher-training colleges, its schools and its adult educational organisations. Nevertheless, the slowly increasing number of specialised posts in American subjects in the universities of Scotland — which, it must be remembered, have grown from four to eight in number in this period — has meant that no student is denied the opportunity of learning something about American history and institutions. This has had repercussions at other levels of the Scottish educational system, especially in the schools, where it is now possible to take a certain amount of American history, etc., especially in the Certificate of Sixth Year Studies.

In the 1945 to 1976 period, the approach to American studies in Scottish universities has been largely to fit them into undergraduate degrees which are not primarily concerned with area studies. You take your American history, literature, geography, politics, etc. either in one of the general degrees or in an honours degree specialising in history, geography, literature, politics, etc. There is some experiment with an integrated type of American studies curriculum:

but this is more marked at the postgraduate than at the undergraduate level. The Scottish student, therefore, who wishes to take an American studies type of degree may have to take the long, long trail a-winding to Keele or a kindred English institution.

American elements in the curricula of Scottish universities in the 1945 to 1976 period have been largely historical in their orientation. This parallels the experience of the British Isles as a whole, as is symbolised by the fact that all of the chairmen of the British Association for American Studies have, to date, been historians. Perhaps one should not lament too much that history has dominated American studies in Scotland: after all, American history is a many-splendoured thing which it is difficult to teach realistically without paying attention to geography, politics, literature, economic growth, elementary sociology, et al. Nevertheless, I think that one may legitimately regret that the study of the American experience in Scotland since 1945 has not ramified to any considerable extent into fields other than history. Geography, of course, has always kept its end up; and politics has always managed to creep into some form of American studies in Scottish universities. A fascinating manifestation of this was that that unacknowledged pioneer of American studies in Scotland, Professor Laurence J. Saunders, formerly of the University of Wisconsin, used to prescribe **The Federalist** for study in his course of Constitutional Law at the University of Edinburgh in the immediate post-war years. One result of this was that when Julius Nyerere was a student at Edinburgh between 1949 and 1952, he was obliged to study the experience of Hamilton, Madison and Jay in coping with the problems of the first new nation of the modern world: and when President Nyerere came to head his own new nation of Tanzania, I do not think that the lessons were lost upon him

The subject, however, which many will regret has not been studied more in the Scottish universities is American literature. Like Scottish literature, it has struggled against the academic monopoly of specifically English literature;and,it could be argued, that it needs a background of English literature for its fullest appreciation. Nevertheless, American literature is now very much a subject in its own right; and I believe that the relative lack of attention which has been paid to it in Scottish universities since the Second World War is the most serious weakness in American studies in Scotland today.

In the years following the Second World War, American studies in Scotland, as in other parts of the United Kingdom, have benefited from the help of external agencies such as the United States-United Kingdom Educational Commission, the Fulbright Commission as it is popularly called. The importance of American Fulbright teachers and scholars for the promotion of American studies in Scotland, indeed, must not be gainsaid. Not only did they teach; they also researched. And out of their researches have come some significant books, and articles, for Scotland as well as for the United States: I think here particularly of Professor W. Turrentine Jackson's **The Enterprising Scot**, a study of Scottish investments in the American West, which came out of his period at Glasgow; and of Professor Joseph F. Wall's examination of an even more enterprising Scot, his massive biography of Andrew Carnegie which won a Pulitzer Prize and some of which, as he has been the first to acknowledge, derived from his period as a Fulbright scholar in Edinburgh. It is a thousand pities, to put it mildly, that this supply of Fulbright scholars and teachers, which was never an absolute spate, has now dwindled to a trickle, certainly as far as Scotland is concerned. One of the most urgent inquiries of the future is into a scheme to replace the Fulbrighters in Scotland and to maintain a constructive flow of American teachers and scholars at all levels, into the educational system of Scotland.

However, the present momentum of American studies in Scotland, whilst acknowledging the help which it has received from good friends across the Atlantic and their representatives in this country, has developed largely through its own resources. Yet, in spite of the undoubted tradition of Scottish knowledge of and rapport with North America, this momentum has not been achieved without opposition. It has been — and is — an opposition claiming that teaching and research into American subjects in Scotland is a waste of time and money which could be better devoted to topics and tasks nearer to home. To this charge, I presume, the answer is, as Professor Gordon Donaldson pointed out right at the start of his book, **The Scots Overseas**, "The history of the Scottish nation has for many centuries now been something more than the history of the geographical bounds of a small, poor and remote country".(7) Anti-American prejudice also has had to be faced in the promotion of American studies in Scotland. I remember an amusing example of this from my first year north of the Tweed. This was in 1948, during Harry S. Truman's first presidency. I went in search of lodgings in the New Town of Edinburgh from a dear, genteel old lady, who, when I replied to her question about what was I teaching at Edinburgh University, expressed considerable surprise that it should be American history. They were not really a nice people, the Americans, she told me: look at that dreadful man, Truman, whom they had elected to their chief office of state. Of course, with fond memories of Dwight D. Eisenhower's connections with Scotland during and immediately after the war, she would make an exception for General Eisenhower. But, on the whole, they were really not a nice people. And then, with that pastoral interest which has often characterised Edinburgh landladies of all social grades , she drew my attention to a recently published book which essayed a psychological interpretation of the United States. "You should read Geoffrey Gorer's **The Americans**", this dear old lady said to me, "it explains them, you know".

One of the major tasks of American studies in Scotland since 1945 has not been so much to explain the Americans as to utilise their experience for easing our own way into the future.

How far this has been successful, it is difficult to judge. How much, for example, have the British Isles as a whole, let alone Scotland in particular, learned from the successes — and the mistakes — of the democratisation of education in the United States? Precious little, one is sometimes inclined to say, when we witness so many of our educational institutions, at all levels, going through the same apparent cycle of mistakes as most Americans would be the first to acknowledge they have endured in their schools, colleges and universities. And what have we in Scotland, at a time of intense concern with devolution, learned from the whole history of the United States' federal experiment? Again, precious little, many would be inclined to argue. Yet I am by no means convinced that three decades of American studies in Scotland since the end of the Second World War have had no lessons to teach its people.

In the future, to which I would now like to turn, the study of the American experience could be especially relevant to Scotland if it would allow it to be. Let me list just a few of the subjects which are of vital concern to us in the future and on which the American experience, surely, throws more than a little light; the balance of power between central and regional governments; the balance of power between public and private finance in a country's economic system; the balance of power between nationalism and internationalism; the problems of creating and maintaining a national literature and language; the problems of an increasing demand for and democratisation of education from the cradle to the grave; the threat of technology to the natural environment; the threat of many kinds of racial disharmonies to public peace and order; and the threat of many kinds of sectional pressure groups to the general welfare. All of these questions, and many more, are extensively examined in a flood of American scholarly and expert writing which, in the future, it could be claimed Scotland will neglect at its peril.

A beginning, but only a beginning, in the academic exploration of this many-sided American experience for Scotland was made when the British Association for American Studies held its first Conference in Scotland in 1963 at Edinburgh. The theme of this conference was "The City in American Life" and it was interpreted in a broad comparative manner, as befits the City of Patrick Geddes, by utilising the services of international experts,who have never hesitated to draw lessons from the American experience for their own countries, such as Professor Jean Gottman of the Sorbonne who spoke on "The American Megalopolis". I believe that the development of such conferences and seminars is an important task for all who are concerned with American studies in Scotland in the future.

But inflation makes attempts at planning for American studies extremely difficult. If it all gets completely out of hand, we may be forced to abandon any attempts at planning, and to let American studies in Scotland find their natural level, as they did in the past. If this has to happen, we have the assurance that we have managed before, and that from Adam Smith and William Robertson to James Bryce and Denis Brogan, we did not do so badly, at least on the individual level.

It ought not to be, however, the individual level that worries us so much as we look into the future — although obviously we should not want to diminish Scotland's capacity to produce outstanding individual chroniclers and interpreters of the American experience. It should be the possibility of diminishing drastically, if not of losing entirely the momentum of American studies that has built up in Scotland since 1945 that should worry us: a momentum which has reached out and is reaching out to wider and wider circles.

The threat to it comes not entirely from escalating inflation, although this is undoubtedly the major problem in the maintenance of a reasonable level of American studies in Scotland today. This threat comes also from competing allegiances in the academic world, influenced very often by political and social as well as by academic pressure groups. As greater devolution of internal government is promised for Scotland and achieved, and the prospect of independence can no longer be considered a chimera, the claim is made — and surely it is not an unreasonable one — that Scottish universities, colleges and schools should include more Scottish studies in their curricula. This must consume both time and money which might otherwise go to American studies — as, indeed, may be argued **vice versa**. If American studies is put in the position of competing with Scottish studies, I believe that both have much to lose. They must, in my opinion, search not simply for a **modus vivendi**. They must also realise that they both have much to offer each other. (An interesting example is what Scotland has learned about the collection of its folk lore from the American experience.) And it seems to me that American studies and Scottish studies will help each other to ride out the tempests of the future if they never cease to look for forms of co-operative activity.

Co-operative activity could be considered the key to the resolution of future conflicts between American studies and its other rivals in Scotland today: European studies; Canadian studies; Commonwealth studies; Latin American studies; Asian studies, particularly Chinese and Japanese studies; and Black studies — and these, with an increasing attention being paid in Scotland and elsewhere in the British Isles to race relations, must be considered as a distinct possibility for those universities and colleges which do not already have them in their curricula, whether in purely African, Afro-American or Caribbean forms, or in some form of combination of all three.

Of course, co-operative activity between American studies in Scotland and rival area studies comes more easily in some cases than in others. It is not particularly difficult with Canadian studies or with Commonwealth studies; indeed, it is highly desirable for both of them. It is obviously easier with Latin American studies than with Japanese studies, although the impact of the United States on Japan since the arrival of Commodore Matthew Perry and his American naval expedition in Tokyo Bay in 1853 supplies a link between the two fields. The same, to a very much lesser extent, applies to Chinese studies. But here, as with Japanese studies, the problem of language is a forbidding factor militating against too much co-operation. This might also be claimed about the relationship between American and European studies in our curricula today, although French, Spanish, German, Italian — even Portuguese, Russian, Serbo-Croat, etc. — are less of a problem to co-operation than the Asiatic languages. With Black studies, especially when Afro-American and Caribbean considerations play a leading role in them, the co-operation of American studies is not difficult and, again, is highly desirable.

But, to be sure, there are limits to co-operation between American and other forms of area studies if they are not to lose their individual, distinctive characteristics. An element of competition, therefore, between American and other area studies in Scotland must be considered inevitable in the future; although, as I have just tried to indicate, co-operative activities, where possible and desirable, should mollify and, one hopes, eliminate altogether their roles, actual and potential, as antagonists in internecine, academic warfare. In the element of competition, however, which must remain for American studies in Scotland, the assistance of financial sources from outside our educational system can be of considerable value — and, **in extremis**, might prevent them from being dragged down entirely.

But, must American studies be considered as just another form of area studies? The United States of America is not one but a collection of area studies. It is a world in itself, containing within its boundaries a greater range of national, religious, racial and ethnic groups than any other geographical and political entity on earth — even more so since, in 1959, its number of states increased from 48 to 50 by the entry into the Union of Alaska and Hawaii, two states which lay right outside its main territorial boundaries. The U.S.A., however, is something more than a collection of area studies: it is, taken in all its vast whole, an area study that transcends all other area studies. I believe that, in order to preserve the momentum of American studies that has been engendered in Scotland since 1945 and, whenever possible, to extend it, those of us who are seriously concerned with the study of the United States of America and who are convinced that it has important lessons to teach us about the past, present and future must be prepared to employ both arguments: that the United States is not just another form of area studies; it is both a collection of them and an area study that transcends all other area studies.

If we are prepared to do this, we should be able to meet most objections in the future to the continuation and extension of American studies in Scottish educational institutions at a time when the tide is flowing against too much money and time being spent on the study of areas that are still, even in these days of supersonic flight, relatively remote from our shores.

And I think we must also bring into operation the powerful argument that no modern man can consider himself really educated without some knowledge of American history, institutions, literature and culture. Looking much further into the future than we have done so far, it may be that American subjects, judiciously studied and taught in our universities, colleges and schools, could take the place that the classics, the study of Greece and Rome, once held in Scottish curricula in the days of what Dr George Davie has called "the democratic intellect" in the Scottish educational system in the eighteenth and nineteenth centuries. It would be highly undesirable — and indeed, hardly possible — that American studies should entirely supplant the classics. What would those wise old gentlemen, the American Founding Fathers, have said about such a suggestion, knowing, as they did so well, what the study of Greece and Rome meant for the foundation of their own Republic? One shudders to think! Indeed, it could be that, at a time when classical studies in our universities and other educational institutions are in a beleaguered position, they could gain strength by being studied, in parallel as well as in series, as it were, with the American experience from colonial times to the present day. In this respect, has anyone ever suggested a joint degree — a real joint degree not just, as is so often the case, a bogus juxtaposition and flimsy fusion of existing courses and part-courses — in classics and American studies? Such a joint approach would not be altogether outwith the Scottish tradition. In this respect, let us remember that Fanny Wright followed her **Views of Society and Manners in America**, which she published in 1821, with a book the year after entitled **A Few Days in Athens**, a study of Epicureanism that Walt Whitman later called his "daily food".

This is the one speculation about the future of American studies in Scotland that I will permit myself. Perhaps I have been too much concerned with continuity rather than with innovation.

Yet there is one question of continuity that I think we should not avoid. If there has been, as I am convinced there has been, a Scottish tradition in American studies which, whilst not avoiding analysis, has laid emphasis on the synoptic and comparative approach, can we, in the universities of Scotland, maintain this tradition; indeed, ought we to attempt to do so at a time when academic research moves more and more into highly specialised fields? We must ask ourselves what is to happen if the pull of minutiae in research forces the universities of Scotland to forsake this tradition. Will other parts of the Scottish educational system continue it?

This reference to other parts of our educational system provides me with the opportunity to raise the special problems of American studies and adult education, call it "continuing education" if you like, in Scotland in the future. What will the universities do about these? What, indeed, will the libraries, the museums and the archives of Scotland do about them? And they are surely equally involved with the universities in these matters. Of one thing I am very sure; and that is

that those of us who are concerned with American studies and whose primary base is the university have much to learn from participation in the many forms, present and to come, of adult education. I remember very well how much I learned about the American political system when I offered a one-day school on that subject many years ago for the W.E.A. in the Leith Dockers' Club. There was assembled in that group a collection of what Melville called affectionately in **Moby-Dick** "meanest mariners, renegades and castaways" who, in their various voyages and visits to the United States had acquired, often through personal participation in it, a knowledge of the American political system that several years of book-learning had not bestowed upon me. Indeed, we need an oral history project in Scotland, similar to the one which was launched at Columbia University some 30 years ago, to preserve and analyse the memories of Scots who have and have had close ties, in many forms, with North America. Perhaps out of participation between those interested in American and Scottish studies in our universities and the many interesting Scots with North American experience whom the varied channels of adult education can introduce to us such an oral history project could be launched. It would be possible to spend money on many far less productive forms of American studies in Scotland.

In my necessarily brief review of American studies in Scotland, past, present and future, I am only too conscious of having emphasised the humanities and the social sciences and of having neglected other aspects: scientific, technical, theological, philosophical, etc. I particularly regret not spending some time on the links between Scottish and American theologians. These are of long-standing; and, at the grassroots level, display themselves in the frequent interchanges of pulpits by Scottish and American Presbyterian ministers. One must remember also the service which the Gifford Lectureships in Natural Theology, which were instituted for the four older Scottish universities under the will of Adam Gifford, one of the Senators of the College of Justice, who died in 1887, have provided for the study of religion in America. To give but one example, William James' famous **The Varieties of Religious Experience** which was the subject of his Gifford Lectures for 1901. Yet, whilst such works count as Scottish contributions to American studies or, to be more exact, to studies by Americans, have Scots themselves made any substantial contribution to the study of religion in America? This could be a matter, I think, for a good deal of argument. To be sure, books like **The Scottish Philosophy** (first published in 1875) by another Scottish-born president of Princeton, James McCosh, have played a role in the development of religion as well as of philosophy in the United States. But of Scottish works which are direct studies of religion in America, I doubt if there is an outstanding specimen.

But the core of American studies, as that expression has been used in our universities since 1945, is and will remain with the humanities and the social sciences. Any attempt to go too far beyond these into other disciplines could have the effect of turning "American studies" into an amorphous concept for us. This, of course, is not to say that those of us who practise American studies in traditional disciplines cannot learn much from the freshness of approach to American phenomena which our technical and scientific colleagues (8) often display; nor is it to imply that they, like ourselves, cannot benefit from periodical visits to the United States of America. But they — and our colleagues in the social sciences, so called — have opportunities of acquiring funds for research which are too often not available to practitioners of American studies in the humanities. There is a Social Sciences Research Council in Great Britain; but there is not, as yet, a Humanities Research Council. When academic foundations and generous friends of American studies in Scotland and other parts of the United Kingdom are considering the division of necessarily limited funds in the future, this is an important point to be borne in mind. For example, any attempt to sponsor archival projects in American studies in Scotland might perhaps extract a little money from the Social Sciences Research Council but the greater part of it would have to come from other sources because they would be considered to lie largely in the field of the humanities.

The bicentenary of the Declaration of Independence of the United States of America offers those of us who are concerned with American studies in Scotland the opportunity of taking stock of our disciplinary and methodological origins, of the present trends and opportunities in our particular fields, and of the many complex and challenging problems which confront them in the future. Financial considerations will obviously affect much of what we can and want to do. And yet I hope that we shall not let ourselves become over-conscious of the cash nexus. Where there is no vision, no speculation, no indulgence perhaps in flights of fancy, in impossible "maybes" and "might-have-beens", American studies in our universities, like other academic ventures, can stick in the mud of mediocrity and, possibly, sink irretrievably into it. Utopia is as essential for academia as for other walks of life. Here, perhaps, the American experience has a built-in safety mechanism: those "backwoods utopias", to employ the expression of a good American friend of American studies in the United Kingdom, Arthur Bestor, which in one form or another have been a refreshing and rejuvenating feature of the American experience from its beginnings. We, too, at a time when financial, social and political pressures constantly threaten to enclose us within narrowing and introverting horizons, must keep alive the utopian spirit — or risk the possibility of going under entirely.

REFERENCES

1 E.g. William Julius Mickle, **The Lusiad** (Oxford, 1776), vii-viii; xlvi; 462, etc.
2 William Robertson, **History of America** (London, 1800), p. vi.
3 Julian P. Boyd, **The Papers of Thomas Jefferson** (Princeton, 1953), VIII, p. 185.
4 Andrew Hook, "John Nichol, American Literature and Scottish Liberalism", **Bulletin of the British Association for American Studies,** New Series, 6, June 1963, pp. 20-30.
5 "Sir Denis Brogan, 1900-1974", **Journal of American Studies,** VIII, 1, 1974, p. 63.
6 An important by-product of this Bicentennial year has been the establishment of the Denis Brogan Centre for research in North American History by the University of Glasgow. Its first project will be a survey of the bibliographical aids, printed sources, Government documents, and periodicals relating to American history and social science in Scottish libraries.
7 Gordon Donaldson, **The Scots Overseas** (London, 1966), p. 9.
8 Academics in the sciences in Scotland may like to be reminded that they have something of a Scottish-American tradition within which they can operate, if they wish. It is worth remembering here that, on the 28th April 1788, the pro-American Earl of Buchan sent to George Washington an engraving of John Napier of Merchiston, inventor of logarithms, which is now held at the American national shrine, Mount Vernon, Washington's estate.

ENVOI

The United States of America gained their independence seventy years after Scotland lost its. The two processes were not unconnected; and it is hoped that the papers in this volume have indicated some of the links between the two countries.

But there is still much to be learned about these links. For example, what was the effect on America of the changing constitutional relationship between England and Scotland from the union of the Crowns in 1603 to the union of the Parliaments in 1707? We know that, as early as Penn's plan for a union of the British American colonies in 1697, the Scottish example was drawn upon when Penn suggested that, in the annual meeting of the American colonies which he envisaged and which he suggested should take place in New York, "the governor of the colony may therefore also be the King's high commissioner during the session, after the manner of Scotland". (1) And, in the debate on the Articles of Confederation for an independent America in 1776, Benjamin Franklin and Scottish-born John Witherspoon interpreted the example of the Anglo-Scottish Parliamentary union of 1707 in different ways. To the view that the smaller American states would be swallowed up by the larger in a confederation, Franklin, as Thomas Jefferson noted, "brought the debate to a close with one of his little apologues" which, most probably, came from his periods of residence in the British Isles as Agent for Pennsylvania. Franklin observed that "at the time of the union of England and Scotland, the Duke of Argyle was

most violently opposed to that measure, and amongst other things predicted that, as the whale had swallowed Jonah, so Scotland would be swallowed by England. However," said the doctor, "when Lord Bute came into the government, he soon brought into its administration so many of his countrymen, that it was found in event that Jonah swallowed the whale." (2) Franklin, however, in the proposed American national assembly, wanted the vote to be according to the "number of taxables", not according to the number of States. Franklin, recorded Jefferson, "distinguished between an incorporating and a federal union". John Witherspoon, on the other hand, objected to this, and recorded Jefferson, "distinguished between an incorporating and a federal union". The union of Scotland with England, he said, "was an incorporating one; yet Scotland had suffered from that union; for its inhabitants were drawn from it by the hopes of places and employments: nor was it an instance of equality of representation". (3)

And what was the effect of America on Scotland from colonial times to the making of the United States Constitution? Little enough is known about this, although it has been clear for a long time that one of the factors in the creation of the Treaty of Union in 1707 was undoubtedly the desire of certain mercantile Scots to get their share of the emerging wealth of England's empire in the western hemisphere.

Scotland, once American independence was achieved, was ripe for the influence of the new land of liberty. Yet it is strange that the United States of America as the symbol of liberty for Scotland has received so little attention from scholars. There is an interesting study still to be written about Robert Burns and the American Revolution. Burns may only have been 17 years of age when the Declaration of Independence was issued by the American rebels but it did not pass unnoticed by him. Burns, in fact, grew to manhood during the era of the American Revolution. Such of his poems as "When Guildford Guid", a satire on Lord North and his cronies, "Ode for General Washington's Birthday", "Address of Beelzebub" and "The Tree of Liberty" which uses a symbol of American origin in a French Revolutionary context indicated the impression which the War of Independence made upon him. And when Burns wrote a letter to the **Edinburgh Evening Courant** on 9 February 1789, in which he linked the problem of the Stuarts in 1688, the year of the so-called "Glorious Revolution" in England, with the era of the American Revolution, he showed clearly that the American experience was never far away from him:

I dare say (wrote Burns) the American Congress, in 1776, will be allowed to have been as able and as enlightened and, a whole empire will say, as honest, as the English Convention in 1688, and that the fourth of July will be as sacred to their posterity as the fifth of November is to us. (4)

Indeed, the American War of Independence as a symbol of liberty has been used by Scottish writers and speakers from the days of Robert Burns to the days of Hugh MacDiarmid. MacDiarmid, for example, has written:

One of the great stories always in my mind is that of the bitter encampment at Valley Forge, where the flame of revolt was mysteriously kept alive — kept alive by the resolution of Washington and by the genius common soldiers seem to have for enduring almost anything — that patient fortitude which, as Lafayette said, "was a continual miracle that each moment renewed". (5)

The "genius of the common soldiers for enduring almost anything" evoked the spirit of '76 again in Hugh MacDiarmid when he wrote "To Those of My Old School who fell in the Second World War":

Symbol of human freedom forever,
You endured more
Than any other citizen army in history,
Even that which, in June 1778
Marched on the heels of the retreating
 British
With William Billings, "blind and slovenly"
But full of fire, setting the key for the
 song:
**"Let tyrants shake their iron rods
And slavery clank her galling chains;
We wear them not. . . ."** (6)

How many British poets today, apart from the polymathic MacDiarmid, have ever heard of William Billings, Boston tanner turned composer, who wrote patriotic songs during the American War of Independence and, in fine old Scottish manner, paraphrases of the Psalms, invoking God's grace exclusively for the American rebels?

The image of liberty, culled from the American Revolutionary experience, is one of the many aspects of the interaction of Scotland and the era of the War of Independence which remains for scholars to investigate. If this special issue of **The New Edinburgh Review** can draw such neglected subjects to their attention, it will more than have served its purpose.

REFERENCES

1. Henry Steele Commager, editor, **Documents of American History** (New York, 1949), p. 39.
2. Adrienne Koch and William Peden, editors, **The Life and Selected Writings of Thomas Jefferson** (New York, 1944), p. 177.
3. Ibid., pp. 33-35.
4. N. T. Phillipson and Rosalind Mitchison, editors, **Scotland in the Age of Improvement** (Edinburgh, 1970), pp. 120-121.
5. Hugh MacDiarmid, **Lucky Poet** (London, 1943), p. 10.
6. Hugh MacDiarmid, **A Clyack-Sheaf** (London, 1969), p. 32.